Using Apple Business Computers

Using Apple Business Computers

Kenniston W. Lord, Jr.

VNR

VAN NOSTRAND REINHOLD COMPANY

NEW YORK CINCINNATI TORONTO LONDON MELBOURNE

Library of Congress Catalog Card Number: 83-6654
ISBN: 0-442-26016-4
ISBN: 0-442-25933-6 pbk.

Manufactured in the United States of America

Published by Van Nostrand Reinhold Company Inc.
135 West 50th Street
New York, New York 10020

Van Nostrand Reinhold Company Limited
Molly Millars Lane
Wokingham, Berkshire RG11 2PY, England

Van Nostrand Reinhold
480 Latrobe Street
Melbourne, Victoria 3000, Australia

Macmillan of Canada
Division of Gage Publishing Limited
164 Commander Boulevard
Agincourt, Ontario M1S 3C7, Canada

15 14 13 12 11 10 9 8 7 6 5 4 3 2 1

Library of Congress Cataloging in Publication Data

Lord, Kenniston W.
Using Apple business computers.

Includes index.
1. Apple III (Computer) – Programming.
2. Business – Data processing. I. Title.
QA76.8.A663L67 1984 001.64'2 83-6654
ISBN 0-442-26016-4
ISBN 0-442-25933-6 (pbk.)

Preface

I encountered my first computer more than twenty years ago. It was a so-called first generation computer known as the UNIVAC File Computer. The room it occupied was as large as a moderately sized firehouse and it took many tons of air conditioning to keep its vacuum tubes from overheating. It was not uncommon to find a human physically located within the innards of the machine, working on a problem.

Those days are but two decades removed, and the concept of a personal computer has to boggle the mind of those of us who revelled in making 2K, 4K, 8K, and 16K machines "do their thing." In fact, we wondered how we would ever be able to use all the available memory. It wasn't long, however, before the integrated circuit was upon us and those computers – and in fact the second generation which followed it – became obsolete. With the birth of the microcomputer in 1975, the face of computing would change forever.

This book is about the *Apple III,* the second foray into the marketplace by one of the premier developers of microcomputers. This system has, as its intended market, the small business which has the potential for becoming larger. It would not add to this book to recount the history of the Apple Computer Corporation, but suffice it to say that they have had an active hand in the development of the microcomputer from the beginning. For those of you who have had some other exposure to the more advanced microcomputers, there might logically be a question as to why the Apple III comes with only one in-board disk drive. Because Apple has recognized that your business may grow beyond the capabilities of a very small microcomputer, the system has been designed around its Profile hard disk, with a single diskette drive as an integral part of the unit. A second diskette drive can be added, and, in fact, this book will deal with a second drive. The addition of hard disk, however, expands the capabilities of the system to support a wide range of businesses.

The Apple III wasn't my first microcomputer, and certainly not the first about which I have written. But it is a capable system and a worthy purchase. Apple, after suffering a short term mistake surrounding the III (which is really the ///), has rallied to produce a fine business product. They've gone one step further. Recognizing the plethora of software which has been developed for the Apple II, they have added emulation capability to the III which will permit operation of those Apple II programs.

The reference manuals which accompany the Apple III are well written and extensive, covering certainly far more than we will cover in this book. Apple, in its attempt to be all things to all people, however, has provided much more capability with the machine than the neophyte can easily assimilate. In this book, then, we're going to put together a single something that will work with the Apple III system, recognizing that if the reader can be walked through a few learning exercises, and then come up with a workable product of his efforts, he'll be a more knowledgeable and productive microcomputer user and can branch out from there.

This book will sample several of the common uses of the Apple III computer, including some applications which are nonbusiness applications. Most of the applications will be business-oriented, however, as the Apple III is a business machine. This is not a book of programs, per se, though there are included many useful programs. There will be plenty of books of programs on the market which will be adaptable to the machine. There will be many books of programs which you can copy. Primarily we will emphasize the development of applications which fit the reader, while at the same time exposing him to some more advanced concepts, such as the Sophisticated Operating System (SOS). The Apple III is a good machine, and we need to find a way to make it pay for itself quickly. We will teach you about putting programs together, about how to develop applications for your business, and how to use the machine. It'll probably not be all you'll ever need to know about the Apple III, but it'll be more than you knew yesterday.

My thanks to Apple Computer for loan of their system for use in preparing this book.

KENNISTON W. LORD, JR., CDP

Contents

Using Apple Business Computers

1
Is There A Computer In Your Future?

Forty years ago there was no such thing as an electronic computer, as we know them today. Forty years ago we were embroiled in World War II and electronics development was just coming of age. Although the *concept* of computers had been with us for at least 200 years, it was not until 1930 that an American scientist built the first general-purpose *analog* computer. The war spurred progress, however, and the first electronic *digital* computer was to have been a device capable to calculate artillery shell trajectories. The British produced an electronic device that successfully cracked Axis radio codes. But it would rest with a professor named Howard Aiken, in 1944, to develop the first *information processing* digital computer. The first commercial computer would not hit the market until 1951, founding an industry whose growth limits have yet to be discovered.

The possibility of the modern computer had existed since the eighteenth century, when scientist Joseph Jacquard designed the first automated loom to weave patterns. Another scientist who followed in the next century, Charles Babbage, invented a mechanical calculator that was not only a direct ancestor of today's computing machines, but exhibited all their basic concepts. These were the forerunners of the concepts of computer *hardware* – the physical parts of a computing machine, its nuts and bolts. All the while there were other pioneers who were developing techniques that would ultimately be implemented upon the computer, either in the form of applications *software* – the programs that enable the system to function – or of improvements to the working hardware.

For more than 30 years now we have been improving on both hardware and software at a rapid pace. With each technological change, new and interesting devices emerge. We have often developed devices before finding profitable and useful ways in which to use them. It can safely be said, however, that the computer has touched our lives in many ways. Often it may seem that we have been reduced to the status of a number for processing through a computer. Even though we may be unaware of it, the computer has made our lives a little easier. One thing is certain – like it or not, the computer is here to stay. And as of now, there are any number of computers you can purchase, the Apple III being but one of them. Whereas for years we could claim that we didn't understand them, it is now possible to understand not only how they work but how best to put them to use in support of a home, school, or business.

The first microcomputer offered to the public was the Altair 8800 in 1975. It was a kit and not very successful, but it did open up the market to the hobby computerist. Recognizing a trend in consumer electronics, two more manufacturers became involved, and in 1977 the TRS-80 Model I (Radio Shack) and the Apple II (Apple Computers, Inc.) were introduced. The former was a large company already in the comsumer electronics business. The latter was a couple of young men working from a garage. Both devices met with phenomenal results. Many manufacturers climbed on the bandwagon; some fell by the wayside, such as IMSAI; some have been marginally successful, such as Compucolor; and some have been successful on a grand scale, such as the IBM Personal Computer. The Apple III is targeted at a single segment of the market – the business segment, where it will function quite successfully.

The Apple III is a good microcomputer and represents Apple's serious foray into the business world. The Apple II has some business capabilities, but the Apple III has a future different from the older model.

A GLIMPSE AT THE FUTURE

Toward the end of the twentieth century, or early in the twenty-first, we will begin sending our correspondence by electronic mail. Some companies are already doing that with communications networks. The U.S. Postal Service has just begun, at this writing, a form of Electronic Mail Service (EMS), which will function similarly to the Mailgram service currently being offered. But even that will change as electronic exchange will ultimately replace paper exchange. You'll write a letter on your microcomputer, transmit it, and the letter itself will appear on the computer of the recipient at some distant point, having traveled through the telephone or satellite network. The response can appear on your computer within minutes. It is possible that the charge for such a service will be small in comparison to postal or long-distance telephone rates. One advantage among many might be guaranteed delivery at very competitive prices in comparison to other forms of guaranteed delivery. We are beginning to see some evidence of such message-handling procedures now with the appearance of computerized bulletin boards throughout the country. There are also a variety of services that will provide information directly to the computer – agricultural news and information, stock market news time sharing networks, and the like. A company near Boston now actively advertises that you can call their computer with your computer to determine what job opening exist.

People without microcomputers would be able to receive messages through a service similar to that of the current Mailgram. Junk mail could be screened out by blocking it with codes given to a computer program. Although advertisers might have a fit, this feature would allow individuals to exercise some control over incoming mail and manage their time more profitably. They might decide to have the computer produce a list of their correspondents to determine which mail to read first. In fact, it may become possible for a home or business to read all correspondence and present only the most important items for viewing. The next logical step would be to have the computer automatically reply to routine correspondence, based upon guidelines prepared by the individual.

Using a micro, you would be able to prepare a single invitation and have the computer distribute it to potential guests via their own home computers. They, in turn, would be able to reply in a matter of minutes. The same concept could be extended to business tele-conferencing. Such conveniences are for the future, of course, but it is a realistic view of the future. Even now, you can use a micro to remind you of birthdays and anniversaries. You can even use it to generate nearly similar letters. One day it will enable you to order that new outfit from Sears, a special tool from Black & Decker, your groceries, or whatever. Coupled to a standard television set, your computer will enable you to view these purchases before you buy them. Think of the possibilities the computer offers to those people who are housebound. In fact, strong evidence indicates that more and more work will be done at home with a micro interfaced to a larger computer. Trips to the office will then be the exception, not the rule. The same can be said for specialized education.

The electronic funds transfer system (EFTS), already in existence, will find its full implementation in the microcomputer. Using EFTS, you'll be able to complete both a purchase and all the financial work at the same time. The sequence of events will work like this: any purchase will result in the purchased product being sent to your home or business establishment, as applicable. The act of the purchase will cause funds to be transferred from the appropriate bank account directly to the bank account of the supplying firm. At that point, that firm's computer will take over, keeping its books, accounting for its inventory, etc. The microcomputer will allow you to have more control over the process, providing reports of purchases, alerting you to the availability of bargains, and so forth. In other words, the micro will be able to do the shopping.

These conveniences apply equally to the home and small business. The very same activities required of General Motors are also required by Acme Machine Repair; only the scale is different. GM must maintain a payroll. So must Acme. GM must purchase raw materials. So must Acme. GM has an assembly line to schedule. Acme, a large machine repair company, also requires some scheduling. GM must plan its cash flow. Acme has been planning its own with pencil and paper, but could well use a computer. GM must track its payables. Acme has bills to pay, as well. And so on and on. The point is that microcomputers can provide the capabilities of a very large business to the Mom and Pop store on the corner.

Whole libraries will be placed "on-line" to microcomputers. Your Johnny will be able to research his paper at the country's largest libraries. Lawyers will be able to subscribe to research facilities, such as Westlaw, saving them hundreds of hours of investigation. The ability to capture the best of what others have already accomplished will be at your fingertips.

For a number of years, computers have been the basis of word-processing systems, used until now exclusively in businesses, and large businesses at that. A microcomputer will put word processing at your own beck and call. You can do form letters, produce manuscripts like this one, maintain mailing lists. Students will love the ability to produce letter-perfect documents. We've advanced so far that there are even automated dictionaries that check each word entered for correctness of spelling and grammar.

What does the proprietor of a small machine shop have in common with Johnny's mother? Both are responsible for someone who needs to learn. For Johnny, a microcomputer can be a tireless tutor to train him in his multiplication tables or his deductive reasoning through scientific analysis. For the machine shop proprietor, a microcomputer can provide a tool for the job education of his employees. Using microcomputers as a teaching device is one of their best applications and we will live to see the time when it will be possible to check out a tutorial program from a library as easily as it is now possible to check out a book.

The computers will be an integral part of the design of the home of the future and will provide a variety of services for its management. It will be installed much as heating or plumbing systems are installed today. It will take over the kitchen functions of food storage, preparation, and cooking. It will provide security functions, from screening visitors to locking doors at predetermined times. It will be applied to energy conservation, selecting forms of energy to be used in terms of cost and comfort. Not least, it will become a handy tool for entertainment.

You probably would not want the computer used for entertainment in a small business environment (or at least to let your employees know it could be), but there will be plenty of work for it to do. This book discusses in detail some of the things the computer can accomplish at work. If you want to stay at work after hours to play chess against the computer, who would mind? But you should not purchase a microcomputer for home or office for the sole purpose of playing games. Less expensive devices are available for that. Just remember that there are quite a number of things the computer can do for you in a business environment which are equally applicable to the home.

MONEY MANAGEMENT

Logging Checks

Needless to say, every check you write will not automatically appear on your computer. You'll have to enter such information as it occurs. The computer will keep an accurate balance of your account, however. To be sure, you could do that with an inexpensive calculator, but consider how much time and expense you could save if, at the end of the year, your computer tells you precisely how much sales tax you have paid and how much you have spent for medical expenses, auto repairs, etc. These necessary details for itemizing expenditures on your tax report could result in savings that alone would justify the purchase of the computer. In a small business, your accountant will insist that such costs be itemized, because they are part of the cost of doing business.

Balancing the Checkbook

A computer can post returned checks and then compute the balance automatically. We have been moving for some years now toward what has been termed a "checkless society." In time, thanks to the microcomputer, the use of checks to effect transactions may disappear altogether. Although the checkless society will not be with us for some time, in the meantime it's nice to have a microcomputer to take over the balancing headaches we face every month. That's one chore a small businessman can do without. Even if he hires a bookkeeper, the latter's task can be greatly simplified by a microcomputer.

Investments

If you have an interest in stocks or bonds, the microcomputer will allow you to manage your own portfolio. Having your own device to compare investments, returns on investments, and potential areas of investment could not only save brokerage fees but allow you to plan your investment programs more thoroughly. If your investments are in the form of property – or if your small business is the purchase and operation of property – a microcomputer can provide the necessary procedures to tracking rents, scheduling repairs, planning escrow accounts, comparing interest rates on available money sources, etc. Computer programs already exist to assist you in such planning.

Cash Management

A computer can advise you when bill payments are due and also specify the optimum time for making those payments. Many first offer terms for early payment, such as a 2 percent discount if the invoice is paid within 10 days. Since money can be saved by keeping track of when those discounts are available, you can draw interest up until the final day when the invoice must be paid.

Other Business Uses

Anything that can be counted, scheduled, sequenced, or controlled is a likely candidate for the microcomputer. Business accounts receivable, customer files, salesman records, payroll, commissions, raw material planning, business forecasting, and general ledger accounting are just a few of the jobs a microcomputer may be applied to in a business setting. So you're not GM – perhaps you're only Acme – but you must still do these things, even if some of them only intuitively.

Other Personal Uses

You can use the microcomputer to keep track of your car's mileage, using the data to determine your operating costs, schedule necessary maintenance, and account for taxes. You can use the microcomputer to plan trips and give cost-effective alternatives. You can use it to shop for groceries, keep inventory of the pantry or the freezer, prepare the meals, schedule critical tasks (like the kids' chores), monitor heat costs, and so on. If you must supply heat to rental property, monitoring the gallon usage can be extremely important.

Education

Don't overlook the tremendous value of microcomputers for education, both at home and on the job. As educators become accustomed to their use, entire learning modules similar to those now used by schools will be developed in a variety of subject areas for home and business applications. The computer has tremendous capabilities for subject exploration and repetitive drill. Unlike human teachers, it never gets angry or tired. And even though many things cannot be computerized – one could never learn how to handle dynamite using the computer, or season a steak, or play a piano – a micro can certainly be used to tutor a child in geography, a young man in auto mechanics, a young lady in pattern-making, an adult in computer programing or systems analysis, and a retiree in tracing his genealogy. It can even help a part-time writer do his thing. I know.

The song is endless, and there will be enough variations on the theme for people to find the microcomputer up to the challenge for decades. Unquestionably, it will become ever more capable. What I can now hold in my hand, twenty years ago I would have had to walk into. Twenty years from now will hold many more miracles, and our children will find the computer to be as commonplace as television. Some reading this book will remember, as I do, a time when there was no television, when we wondered if our grandparents had had automobiles when they were kids. Read on.

2
How Computers Work

If you could look inside the Apple III, you might become convinced that if you can't understand what you see, it might be beyond you. Nothing could be further from the truth. We need not be experts on the internal combustion engine to use the family car; we need not be refrigeration experts to use a refrigerator or air conditioner. There are many devices we use daily whose inner workings are *technically* beyond our understanding but which we know we can use for our benefit. The same is true of the microcomputer.

What *is* important is that we understand how the computer *operates* and how we can cause it to perform functions for us. It's something like the control exercised by pressing on an accelerator, which causes a car to increase speed. Such action activates a lever, which in turn causes certain changes to take place in the car's engine. With a computer, control takes two forms: *external* controls, which cause certain things to happen inside the computer, and *internal* controls, which cause things to happen automatically.

The external controls take the form of switches and keys on the computer's keyboard. The internal controls are customarily embodied in a *program.* A program is a sequence of steps defined to the computer in advance in such a way that the computer can perform them automatically. Although there are many ways to program a computer, the programing is usually the function of a computer *language.* Many languages are available for the Apple III; among them are Pascal, a microcomputer scientific language; Assembler, which is the closest thing to native language for the machine; and BASIC (*B*eginner's *A*ll-purpose *S*ymbolic *I*nstruction *C*ode). Other languages are no doubt available, such as FORTH and COBOL (an English-like programming language).

In simple terms, every computer must have a means for accepting the entry of data – a process called *input.* The means available to the Apple III take several forms, the most common being a *keyboard.* With a keyboard you can develop programs, build data files, respond to program commands, and so on. The Apple III keyboard is part of the main unit. Another means of entering programs or data to an Apple III is the diskette drive. Other devices, including digitizers (graphics tablets) and "joy sticks" (game paddles) are available.

The Apple III is a business machine. Because of that, we'll concentrate strictly upon the business version. Included in this package is an *operating system* – the Sophisticated Operating System (SOS, pronounced "sauce"). The intricacies of SOS are beyond this book, but we'll show you enough about SOS for you to make the Apple III do its useful work, and in the process, we'll introduce you to the Owner's Manual, the Business BASIC Manual, and the Utilities Manual.

Every computeı has a place to store programs and information. This place is called *memory.* The memory of the Apple III is called a *chip* and is available in 128K to 256K memory sizes. "K" is equal to 1,024 positions of memory. Thus, a 128K system actually contains 131,072 positions, whereas the 256K system contains 262,144 positions. The memory is used to hold both programs and the SOS. Further, a portion of memory is given over to *variables,* special positions of memory designed to contain numeric or alphabetic data.

In addition to the memory, the circuitry contains the electronic hardware that controls the *logic,* that is, the sequence of events that takes place within the computer. The logic section is part of the arithmetic/logic unit (ALU), which also contains the electronics for the performance of calculations.

Finally, every computer has some form of *output.* Output from the Apple III can take the form of a variety of hardware devices – a selection of printers, communications interfaces, etc. The SOS software must be configured for the operating equipment which you'll be using – more on that as we dig deeper into the machine.

Memory positions are technically called *bytes.* Each byte can be used to store a single alphabetic character (letters A to z), a single *special character* (punctuation marks and symbols), or a numeric value in the range of zero to 255. Many of these bytes will be used to contain the program you develop or purchase and are *running.*

Some will be used to contain the data upon which the program will operate. These data are called *variables,* of which there is a variety of types. For simplicity, we'll refer only to *numeric variables* and to *alphabetic variables* (often called *string variables*). Numeric variables are named with alphabetic names beginning with A and ending with Z, and may be up to 64 characters in length. String variables are named similarly, except that each name must end with a dollar sign ($). There are many other types and configurations of variables, but these two account for the majority of types you will encounter until you begin to use your Apple III more extensively.

NUMERIC VARIABLES

Let's concentrate first upon the numeric variable. Suppose, for instance, the numeric variables A to Z represent addresses of houses on a street, addresses that correspond to persons whose last names begin with one of those letters. Your name is Jones and you live in house J. Mrs. Smith customarily lives at house S, but is currently in the hospital. You have decided to collect money from your neighbors for a get-well present for Mrs. Smith. Other people who live on the street are: Mr. Brown, who lives at house B; Mrs. Greene, who lives at house G; Mrs. Martin, who lives at house M; and Mrs. Rogers, who lives at house R. Get the picture? We have labeled each house with a letter that serves as a symbol for its occupant and its address, and we'll treat each address as a repository of funds. For purposes of this example, your house and the total dollars you collect will *both* be given the name of the numeric variable J. You decide to kick the fund off with a contribution of $8. At this moment,

```
J = B
```

In the computer, we would place the number 8 – meaning 8 dollars – in the numeric variable J.

Mr. Brown chips in 10 lovely crisp dollar bills. Up to this point, those 10 dollars were located at B; that is, B = 10. But now, since Mr. Brown has given them over to you, B = 0. (While a zero is often slashed on a microcomputer, we'll avoid doing so here.)

Up to this point, all that was located at J was B, but because Mr. Brown was generous, there are now $18 at your house. In other words,

```
J = J + 10
```

That equation might seem a little confusing. How can J be equal to itself plus 10? Well, the *first* letter J is known as the *result* or *sum.* Taking the original value of J, 8, and adding to it the 10 that represents Mr. Brown's contribution, provides a *new* J, or result, of 18. If we knew for sure that all the money Mr. Brown had was $10, then the equation could have been expressed as J = J + B. But we do not know that for certain. In our example, we will continue to compound the dollars at the single address J.

Technically, your original fund contained nothing – 0. Thus, initially,

```
J = 0
```

To that you added $8, as follows:

```
J = J + 8
```

And then, Mr. Brown's $10:

```
J = J + 10
```

J now holds the number 18, which is the representation of the $18 you have acquired for the fund for Mrs. Smith. Next, Mrs. White appears and she offers to double the amount you have already collected – two time $18, or $36. How would that be expressed on the computer? Like this:

```
J = J * 2
```

In the computer language BASIC, the asterisk (*) signifies multiplication. In this case, we took the value of J, 18, multiplied it by 2, and stored it again at J. J now has a new value of 36, representing $36 for the Smith Fund. The use of the asterisk is required by computer convention to distinguish it from the "X" we use when calculating by hand. Don't forget that X is one of the numeric variables.

Mrs. Smith calls from the hospital to say she's just heard about the fund. Although appreciative of your efforts, she tells you that she's quite comfortable and doesn't really need the money. She asks you instead to distribute the money to her three favorite charities: the Heart Fund, the Cancer Fund, and the Home for Little Wanderers. Furthermore, she advises that Mrs. Greene (house G), Mrs. Martin (house M), and Mrs. Rogers (house R) are collecting, respectively, for those funds. How do we indicate that on the computer? Well, we know that Mrs. Greene is going to get one-third of the Smith Fund for the Heart Fund and that she lives at house G. We therefore divide our pile of dollars by three, as follows:

```
G = J / 3
```

In this instance, we took the values of the dollars at J, divided it by 3 (the slash, /, is the computer's division symbol), and stored 12 at G. In other words, we said that G is equal to one-third of J, but just because we said so does not mean that we have taken the 12 away from J to give it to G. We must now tell the computer that the fund (J) is minus $12. That's done like this:

```
J = J - G
```

Why didn't we just say that J was equal to J minus 12? We could have done so in *this* instance, because we *know* the value of J. Suppose, however, that there had been other contributors. We needed to take merely a third of the Smith Fund and that third is presently located at G. Thus, if the dollars at G are removed from the dollars at J, our totals will remain accurate.

Now there are $24 left at J, half of which is to go to Mrs. Martin for the Cancer Fund and half to Mrs. Rogers for the Home For Little Wanderers. The following instructions will place the funds in the proper place:

```
M = J / 2
R = J / 2
```

Of course, since nothing is left in your fund now, once again:

J = 0

There are, of course, many ways to obtain the desired result. We could have repeated the steps taken above and subtracted from the variable J (J = J –M) and (J = J – R), but the result would have been the same.

On first examination, you'll note that we have created a series of very simple formulas. Programing the Apple III need be no more complicated than this for any problem.

If you have bought this book *after* acquiring your Apple III, you may already be familiar with the instructions Apple has provided, and no doubt the place where you purchased the computer has shown you how to hook it up and get it started. We'll be concentrating largely on problem solving – but one of the problems to be solved immediately is getting started on the machine, and that means SOS and disk. That comes next.

GETTING STARTED

The Apple III, as you receive it, is comprised of a keyboard/base unit and a monitor. You may have purchased other hardware, such as the Profile hard disk or another floppy diskette drive. For our purposes, we'll assume one inboard disk drive and one outboard disk drive. Figure 2.1 is a picture of the equipment for which this book has been configured.

The keyboard provides the essential means of communication with the computer. The computer's system unit houses one disk drive (5¼"), all the electronics, and the keyboard. Also, a monitor is a part of the package. Shown is the Monitor III, containing a screen that is 24 lines of 80 characters, in green phosphor.

There are two switches that are required to turn the unit on and make it workable. The first is on the lower right of the face of the monitor and the second is at the left rear of the system unit. Ensure that the monitor is turned on first – you'll see the red light. When the system unit has been turned on, you'll see the word "ON" illuminated in the space beside the "open Apple."

Figure 2.1. Apple III with outboard disk drive.

Find the diskette in your package called "Demonstration Diskette." Place it into the inboard drive, label facing upwards, and close the door. Now, with your left hand, reach around the left of the system unit, find the switch at the left rear of the unit, and turn on the system unit. Immediately, the inboard disk unit will come to life, and you'll be off and running with the automated demonstration. There are also some demonstrations you control there, so give them a try.

Familiarize yourself with the Apple III's keyboard. The typewriter portion (known as the QWERTY keyboard) is standard. There are some additional keys. On the left find the ESCape key, the Control key, the shift lock key, and a couple keys with pictures of Apples on them – one solid and one hollow (or "open"). These "Apple keys" are technically *function keys,* and will have specific uses as you go along. For the time being, observe that the open Apple and the question mark can bring up a HELP screen for you. There is an alphabetic shift, which is not the same as a capital shift on the typewriter – it works for alphabetic characters only. Press it and type. Press it again, and type. Note the differences.

```
*********************************************
*                                           *
*   D - Device handling commands            *
*   F - File handling commands              *
*   S - Systems Configuration Program (SCP) *
*   Q - Quit                                *
*                                           *
*********************************************
```

Figure 2.2. Utilities opening menu.

On the right is a RETURN key, which you may also know as an ENTER key or a Carriage Return. Also, there are arrow keys – these are used to move the cursor, which is the blinking indication of the position where you are working on the screen. There are shift keys on both sides, which will give you opposite characters and upper level characters on the number and punctuation keys. At the extreme right is a standard numeric keypad with another ENTER key (ENTER and RETURN are the same function).

The Sophisticated Operating System (SOS) is distributed among your program diskettes – the utilities diskette, the demonstration diskette, the device driver programs (if you have them) and the Business BASIC. Thus, to use Business BASIC, you need only to load it into the inboard drive (known as .D1) and "boot" it (booting is done either by turning the machine on or by holding down the CONTROL and RESET keys simultaneously. The RESET key is at the rear of the keyboard on the right side.).

Since we must use diskette storage to save any programs we might develop, it will be necessary to prepare one or more diskettes to receive them. Therefore, with a blank diskette in the outboard drive (.D2), find the system utilities diskette, place it in .D1, and boot it. Figure 2.2 will show on the display.

```
************************************
*                                  *
*  C - Copy one volume onto another *
*  R - Rename a volume              *
*                                  *
*  F - Format a volume              *
*  V - Verify a volume              *
*                                  *
*  L - List devices configured      *
*  T - Set time and date            *
*                                  *
************************************
```

Figure 2.3. Device handling commands.

At this stage, we're interested in the device handling commands, so press D. Figure 2.3 will come up. We're interested at this time, in formating the diskette, so press F. The above display will disappear and at the lower left of the screen will appear this message:

Format for the medium of the volume:

There will be a pair of brackets. If the designator .D2 is there, simply press RETURN. If not, enter .D2 and then press it. Next will come the message:

with the new volume name:

Type (between the brackets) whatever you would like the diskette to be called (e.g., APPLE3.BOOK). That will be its name until you change it. The formating will commence and you will be told, when it's done, whether all went well. You can verify using the V command of the utilities menu. Enter 280 as the number of blocks.

Before leaving the utility programs, it would be useful to show you how to determine what files and/or programs are on a diskette. Back to the Utilities Menu, as shown in Figure 2.2. Press F for the File handling commands. That will bring up the menu shown in Figure 2.4.

At this point it would be wise to back up your software. Look back at Figure 2.3 and select the Copy Volume instruction. You will then be asked to designate first the drive which contains the *source* volume. Let's make a habit of copying *from* drive .D1 and *to* drive .D2.

```
********************************************
*                                          *
*   L - List files                         *
*                                          *
*   C - Copy files                         *
*   D - Delete files                       *
*   R - Rename files                       *
*                                          *
*   M - Make new subdirectory              *
*                                          *
*   W - set Write protection (lock/unlock) *
*   P - set Prefix                         *
*                                          *
********************************************
```

Figure 2.4. File handling commands.

There will be exceptions, of course. In any event, the copy of the entire volume will format the new diskette ahead of the copy. You'll be asked if the name is the same, and it should be so long as you're simply making backup copies. Copy the Utilities diskette first, as it's already in place, make a couple of copies of each. Place the originals in an environmentally safe place.

Now, remove the utilities diskette from .D1, if it's still there, find the Business BASIC diskette, place it into the diskette drive, and boot it. Several messages in motion will be shown on the screen, followed by a display of the directory and the realization that there isn't room enough left on that diskette to place anything. It will have to go onto a blank diskette in .D2. Make certain you have one ready – or several.

Your are encouraged to read, in detail, the Operating System instructions in the Owner's Guide. Quickly, we'll cover some of the concepts which you must have to continue.

Character Devices

The keyboard and the screen are character devices. Information is entered to the former and displayed upon the latter a character at a time. Other character devices are the serial interface and the printer. Apple III is configured for a serial printer, but we will be using the parallel printer card (known as the UPIC – Universal Printer Interface Card) along with a common parallel printer, the Epson MX-80, in our discussions.

Block Devices

Generally, block devices are diskette or hard disk. Blocks are stored and moved in increments of 512 characters (bytes). Files can only be stored on block devices.

Device Names

The disk drive designators we have been using (.D1 and .D2) are the logical names for the inboard and outboard diskette drives, respectively.

The name .PRINTER is used to specify the printer driver in use. The name .SERIAL is used to specify the serial interface driver. The device name may be up to 15 characters in length. A block device (.BLOCKDEVICE is a legal name) is accessible by its *volume name.* Recall that we identified the diskette with the volume name APPLE3.BOOK. There are rules for proper specification of names and if you violate those rules, you can be in trouble. In general, stick with 15 or fewer characters and limit the internal punctuation to periods and you've got it.

Files

A file is a collection of information. It may be a file of data or a file which is a program. Many such files can be stored on a diskette and filed under a hierarchy of directories known as directory/subdirectory/pathname. Up to this point, we have this means of finding the file: /.D2/APPLE3.BOOK. Suppose we chose to assign a portion of this diskette to this chapter. Now we would have: /.D2/APPLE3.BOOK/CHAPTER.2. And then, given the possibility that we would like to designate a program number within it: /.D2/APPLE3.BOOK/CHAPTER.2/PROGRAM.1. That's the *complete* address, but if APPLE3.BOOK is mounted in .D2, then we have only to ask for /.D2/CHAPTER.2/PROGRAM.1. In this instance, CHAPTER.2 would show in the directory for .D2, while PROGRAM.1 would only show in a subdirectory listing for CHAPTER.2. Got that? The designation of subdirectories becomes necessary only when the number of programs is large and logically split. In practice, you'll not need to use them very much. As you gain experience with the system, you'll find that it's possible to find files with suffixes only – abbreviated names, if you will. For purposes of this book, however, stick to the full name.

System Configuration

The Apple III can support more hardware, and different hardware than you may purchase with it. It can support many printers, for instance. But to do so, each printer must have a unique software package known as a *driver.* Every input/output device associated with the system, in fact, has a driver. Some of the more standard drivers are a part of the SOS that has been placed on the Business BASIC diskette and the utilities diskette. Others are a part of the utilities diskette itself. The standard device driver include drivers for the console (keyboard and display unit), the printer driver (serial), the audio driver (for tone generator), the RS232 driver (for communications), and the Silentype driver (for the Silentype printer the "normal" printer purchase). The driver for the parallel printer which will be used in this text accompanies the UPIC card which was installed in the computer. The boot record on each bootable diskette also contains certain system parameters, including the number of diskettes, the keyboard layout, the character set in use, etc. The Systems Configuration Program (SCP) which is part of the utilities, you will recall, will be used to set up any driver that you may need. The Owner's Manual gives step by step instructions for the SCP. Our only interest at this time is to tell the system that we have two diskette units. This the System Configuration Program Menu is shown in Figure 2.5.

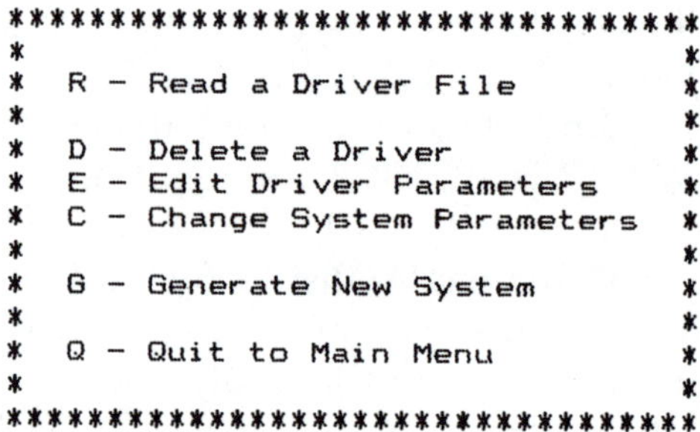
```
*********************************
*                               *
*  R - Read a Driver File       *
*                               *
*  D - Delete a Driver          *
*  E - Edit Driver Parameters   *
*  C - Change System Parameters *
*                               *
*  G - Generate New System      *
*                               *
*  Q - Quit to Main Menu        *
*                               *
*********************************
```

Figure 2.5. System configuration program menu.

Now you can't edit the driver parameters (at this moment we only wish to display them) until that driver file has been read, so press R. On the author's system, Figure 2-6 was displayed.

On the author's system, the .SILENTYPE driver was dropped in favor of the UPIC, which required .PRINTER. The next step is to determine what the system parameters are, and if necessary, change them. Editing them will bring them up for display. So will changing them and ESCape from that can be effected if no change is necessary.

```
**********************
*  1     .FMTD1      *
*  2  +  .FMTD2      *
*  3  +  .FMTD3      *
*  4  +  .FMTD4      *
*  5     .SILENTYPE* *
*  6     .SERIAL     *
*  7     .CONSOLE    *
*  8     .PRINTER    *
**********************
```

Figure 2.6. Current driver configuration; * = inactive.

The screen shown in Figure 2.7 comes up.

```
*************************************************************
*                                                           *
*   CURRENT SYSTEM PARAMETERS:                              *
*                                                           *
*        1 - Number of Disk III Drives.......     2         *
*                                                           *
*        2 - Peripheral Slot Assignments                    *
*                                                           *
*        3 - Standard Character Set..........     STANDARD  *
*                                                           *
*        4 - Keyboard Layout.................     SHOLES    *
*                                                           *
*        5 - Invert Standard Character Set                  *
*                                                           *
*        6 - Change All System Parameters                   *
*                                                           *
*************************************************************
```

Figure 2.7. Current system parameters.

In general, there are two character sets – STANDARD and the nonstandard set you will define. And there are two keyboard layouts – SHOLES (what was previously called QWERTY) and DVORAK. Don't ask. I've no doubt that other, non-English, character sets can be defined, as well. In any event, if you do not have two drives defined, do so by making the change. Recall that the assumption of this book is two drives. If you've but one drive, then you may have to change the approach you take to the programs contained in this book. If you've more than two drives, indicate those drives you have.

FILE OPERATIONS

It is not the intent to here duplicate Apple's excellent manuals. The File Operations section of the utilities manual is superb, and you are encouraged to read it. It details these capabilities of the File Operations Utility:

- List files – lists the files by name on the screen.
- Copy files – copies a file from one device to another.
- Delete files – removes the file from a media.
- Rename files – assigns an entirely new name to a file.
- Make a subdirectory – do so only if you need it.
- Set Write protection – a means to keep from overwriting.
- Set Prefix – allows the path to be assigned to a file.

AND NOW, A LITTLE BASIC

We've concluded most of what you must know about SOS in order to survive this book. There will be a few more things along the way, and we'll concentrate on disk applications in a later chapter. But for the balance of the book, we'll be working largely with BASIC. Before you leave SOS entirely, format several blank diskettes.

We never really leave SOS. Each software diskette is provided with those "kernels" of the SOS which are necessary to perform the function of the software. From this point on, we'll be working with the Business BASIC diskette. Find it, place it in .D1, and boot it.

Note that the directory of the BASIC diskette indicates that there are many programs on that diskette. We'll use one or more of them as we go on. Note also that there is very little space left. Therefore, those programs which you may wish to keep will have to be kept on diskette.

At the very bottom of the screen, at the left side, is the BASIC prompt –) . It is simply a right parenthesis. Each time you see it, you'll know that you are in BASIC and the BASIC interpreter is waiting for you to tell it something to do.

KEYBOARD FINAL

Two other things of immediate concern about the keyboard, before we progress: First, the alpha key shifts the lower case letters to upper case letters *only*. It *does not* shift the upper case letters to lower case, as some other computers do. It is not, therefore, a "toggle."

Second, the ESCape/arrow combination. In BASIC, enter a few instructions and you'll probably find that you've made an error. Most of us do. You can retype the command, replacing it. Or you can edit it. To edit it, you must press the ESCape key (which will place a + in the middle of the block cursor) and then you can move the cursor around at will. Once on the screen line, you can add characters, delete characters, etc. The RETURN key cancels the EDIT mode and writes the corrected instruction back to memory – BUT BE CAREFUL. If you press the RETURN anywhere in the middle of the line, you truncate the balance of the line. Move to the end of the line by pressing the right arrow, and then press the RETURN key. Also, you may cancel an entire line by pressing the CONTROL key and the X key simultaneously. This is called a CONTROL-X.

SMITH FUND ACCOUNTING

Now that we have all that SOS knowledge and have put the machine into BASIC mode, we can again walk through, from the perspective of the BASIC programer, just what we tried to accomplish before. Type the following into the Apple III; end all lines with a RETURN.

```
J = 8
```

What happened? What you typed is visible on the screen, often called the CRT (Cathode Ray Tube), but otherwise nothing much seems to have happened. So try this next:

```
PRINT J
```

Well, this is different. In addition to the things you've typed, there now appears the number 8. What happened was that with J = 8 you set the variable J equal to 8, and with PRINT J you instructed the computer to display the value of variable J on the screen, which it did. Now type this:

```
J = J + 10
```

Other than what you just typed, nothing else seems to have happened. So type this:

```
PRINT J
```

The number 18 comes back. So far the program seems to be working just like the example. Type this:

```
J = J * 2
PRINT J
```

If you did everything correctly, the answer 36 should now be displayed. To proceed, type this:

```
G = J / 3
PRINT G, J
```

Here we've done something slightly different. We've set G equal to a third of the value of J and then displayed the values of both G and J. As you can see, G certainly equals 12, but J still contains 36. In other words, J is unchanged. That's why you should type the next instructions:

```
J = J - G
PRINT G, J
```

The variables should now be shown at their proper values. When you PRINT more than one variable, separated by a comma, the values of the variables will be "printed" (displayed) in different *zones.* There are several zones on the screen. If such use is important to you, then you would be wise to limit your displays to the zones alone. To print the variables closer together, substitute a semicolon (;) for the comma, like this:

```
PRINT G; J
```

See the difference? Now it's time to divide up the remainder of the fund between Mrs. Martin and Mrs. Rogers with the following instructions:

```
M = J / 2
R = J / 2
PRINT G, J, M, R
```

If you did this correctly, the screen should show, left to right, the numbers 12, 24, 12, and 12, one to each zone. Now, to "empty" J, type:

```
J = 0
PRINT G, J, R, R
```

The screen should now show 12, 0, 12, and 12. Does it?

Now, let's dress this display up a bit by identifying who gets what, as follows:

```
PRINT "Mrs. Greene", G
```

What happened? Did Mrs. Greene's name and the value 12 appear on the screen? They should have, because any time you PRINT something that is enclosed in quotation marks, it should appear on the screen. Be very careful about where you type the quote in relation to the comma. "Mrs. Greene," will produce an error because a comma before a quote is used to separate the *operands* of a PRINT instruction. If you used the comma correctly, Mrs. Greene's name will appear in Zone 1 and the amount (variable G) in Zone 2.

Up to this point, we've operated in direct mode, often known as immediate, external, or calculator mode. That is, we have used the Apple III in much the same manner as we might use an inexpensive hand-held calculator. In the direct mode, things happen more or less immediately. However, the strength of the computer is its *indirect mode,* which causes things to happen *automatically.* A program can therefore be developed to handle specific data, even though that data is unknown until the program is operated. That subject will be expanded further.

Before we leave the direct mode, however, let's try something else, using this pair of instructions:

```
J = ((G * 2) + M) / R
PRINT J
```

If you typed that into the computer and pressed RETURN, the computer will tell you how many people contributed to the fund.

As you can see, the formula is different from the earlier one, but, in fact, you have done nothing different from what you've been doing all along. The inserted parentheses group the actions to be taken in a specified sequence. In the computer's order of things, you have to multiply G by 2 *before* you can add M to it, and you have to add M *before* dividing the total by R. The parentheses, in other words, specify the *order of operation* of parts of an instruction within the computer. The inside parentheses must always be "cleared" first, followed by the next set.

Try the operation this way:

```
PRINT ((G * 2) + M) / R
```

It works just the same. To illustrate the importance of the parentheses, try the same formula without them, as follows:

```
PRINT G * 2 + M / R
```

In the first instance, you came up with 3. In the second, you came up with 25. Do you know why? Here's how to find out. Type:

```
G * 2
```

and you should get back 24. Type:

```
PRINT M / R
```

and you should get back 1. The sum of them, of course, is 25.

ENOUGH, ALREADY – LET'S PROGRAM

You could continue to operate in the calculator mode and cause the computer to produce answers for you. Suppose, however, that you want to display all the answers at once, rather than singly as they occur. Furthermore, suppose that you want a method whereby *any* contributor could contribute to *any* fund, which would then be redistributed to *any* charity of his or her choosing. In other words, the very concept of a program is that it can be operated automatically so long as you provide data for it, presenting the information you choose. Moreover, you want *one* computer to provide all those services.

A program is to a computer what a road map is to a traveler. It is a way to get from here to there, making the necessary stops along the way and making the necessary alterations en route occasioned by changes that can only be determined en route. To the computer, a program is the prespecification (thinking through) of a process you wish it to undertake. Like a note left for a friend, you detail the steps you'd like him to accomplish, advising him of alternatives, and instructing him in methods. And just like you do in the note, you number the steps. In BASIC, the short program that plots the route for the Smith Fund is shown in Figure 2.8.

```
10 J = 0
20 J = J + 10
30 J = J * 2
40 G = J / 3
50 J = J - G
60 M = J / 2
70 R = J / 2
80 J = 0
```

Figure 2.8.

When you have completed the entry of these instructions, LIST them. To do so, simply type LIST, and they will appear on the screen. If you wish to have a hardcopy list (on paper), then it will be necessary to place the instruction you can read the accompanying documentation from the file RENUMBER.DOC by this means – in BASIC:

```
NEW
LOAD "RENUMBER.DOC"
RUN
```

This is a BASIC program which explains the renumbering utility. We will continue to extract that information for inclusion here.

Once an invokable module has been loaded, as above, it is executed by the PERFORM command. The important thing to remember is that (1) you are in BASIC and (2) these commands are assembler commands which work from inside BASIC.

The renumber invokable module offers three services:

- Cross-reference listings by line references
- Appending/Merging of two programs
- Renumber/Resequencing of a program

Line References

There are two similar procedures for locating program lines referenced by other lines in a program – XLIST, which produces a list of all line numbers and references to those line numbers; and XREF, which produces a list of only those line numbers to which references have been made.

You may obtain these services, respectively, by using the following PERFORM commands, *after* the invokable module has been loaded:

```
PERFORM XLIST (@IN$, @OUT$)
PERFORM XREF (@IN$, @OUT$)
```

where IN$ is a string containing the name of the BASIC program to be analyzed and OUT$ is a string containing the name of the file where the output is to be sent (i.e., a filename or character device).

Append/Merge

First, the difference. To append one program to another means simply to add it on at the end. To do so requires that the line numbers be entirely different and that the line numbers of the file which is to be appended are greater than those of the file to which the appending is to be accomplished. A merge, on the other hand, involves the combination of two programs on the basis of their line numbers, irrespective of whether or not the line numbers of the second program are larger than the line numbers of the first. If line numbers are intermeshed, they will be placed together in numerical order, and may produce programs which are a little strange if not used carefully.

The APPEND procedure combines two BASIC programs and puts them into a single output file. One of the programs must have all its line numbers higher or lower than the other, and the effect will be as if one program was appended to the other. If there are number conflicts, then one of the programs should be renumbered to keep the line numbers different. The command format is:

```
PERFORM APPEND (@FIRST$, @SECOND$, @OUT$)
```

where FIRST$ and SECOND$ are strings containing the names of the two BASIC programs to be appended. Once appended, the file is sent to the filename designated by the string OUT$.

The MERGE procedure also combines two BASIC programs and puts them into a single output file. If the programs have line numbers that overlap in range, the programs will be merged in numerical order. The command format is:

```
PERFORM MERGE (@FIRST$, @SECOND$, @OUT$)
```

where FIRST$ and SECOND$ are strings containing the names of the two BASIC programs to be merged. Once combined, the file is sent to the filename designated by the string OUT$. If both programs have a line with the same line number, a RANGE ERROR will occur.

Renumber/Resequence

The RENUMBER procedure allows you to renumber all or part of any BASIC program and output the renumbered version to a designated file name. The procedure will require you to provide the old starting line number, the old ending line number, the new starting line number, and the new line increment. If renumbering a line or group of lines will move those lines to another place in the program, you will be told that a RANGE ERROR exists. The RESEQNCE procedure is identical to the RENUMBER procedure, except that the RESEQNCE procedure will allow the renumbering of a line or group of lines to move those lines to another place in the program. The command formats are:

```
PERFORM RENUM (@IN$, @OUT$, %BEGIN, %END, %START, %INC)
PERFORM RESEQNCE (@IN$, @OUT$, %BEGIN, %END, %START, %INC)
```

where IN$ is a string containing the name of the BASIC program to be renumbered or resequenced, OUT$ is a string containing the name of the file where the output is to be directed, %BEGIN and %END are the beginning and ending line numbers within the original program, %START is the value of the first renumbered line, and %INC is the numbering increment. In both procedures, every line number that references another line number has the reference changed to the new number.

SAVING YOUR PROGRAM

Before very long, you'll find that it's desirable to place your program into a disk file, from which you will be able, using the COPY utility to COPY the file to the .PRINTER. For the time being, let's concentrate upon simply saving the program to disk. Using a disk which you have *already formated,* type:

```
SAVE .D2/FIG2.8
```

The light on the outboard disk drive will illuminate, there will be the sound of motion in the disk drive, and then you'll see the BASIC prompt once again –) . Now, type NEW, followed by LIST. Nothing should be there. NEW clears memory and LIST places any program on the screen. You may return the program to memory by loading it back from the diskette, like this:

```
LOAD .D2/FIG2.8
```

Wasn't that easy? Let's talk about BREAK and LIST. BREAK is the means to interrupt the processing of a program. If your program continues as if it's never going to stop and you would like to stop it – don't turn the computer off. Simply press the CONTROL key in combination with the letter C. You'll find that the CONTROL-C combination works as a BREAK key on a number of microcomputer systems – a custom, if not a standard.

The program you've just written, SAVEd, and reLOADed, can be shown on the screen with the LIST command. This particular program isn't very long, so it will show on the screen in its entirety. However, sooner or later you will develop a program which is much longer. Then, when you LIST it, the screen will continue to fill from the bottom while the program slips away at the top. This is known as *scrolling*. You can arrest the scroll simply by using the CONTROL key in association with the number 7 on the keypad. But LIST has other capabilities:

LIST	list all statements.
LIST -100	list all statements through 100.
LIST 100-200	lists all statements from 100 through 200.
LIST 100-	lists all statements from 100.

OK, make sure the program is in memory and type RUN. This causes the program to commence execution. What happened? It looks as if nothing has happened, but many things have happened *inside* the Apple III. All the answers determined by the program now reside in the computer, but the computer hasn't told anyone about it. You didn't tell it to.

As you typed the instructions into the Apple III, you may have wondered why you didn't number the steps 1, 2, 3, etc. You did; only you did it in multiples of 10. You could have used any number, so long as the next number was larger than its predecessor, but spacing of 10 units between instructions is normal because it allows you to insert instructions later between the ones you've already written. For example, type the instructions shown in Figure 2.9.

```
15 PRINT J
25 PRINT J
35 PRINT J
45 PRINT G,J
55 PRINT G,J
65 PRINT M,J
75 PRINT R,J
85 PRINT J
```

Figure 2.9.

When you have completed the entry of these instructions, LIST them, as we've discussed. If you wish to have a hardcopy listing, SAVE the program to the diskette in .D2 and then use the COPY utility to produce your paper listing.

Now RUN the program again. This display should look like Figure 2.10.

```
 8
18
36
12        36
12        24
12        24
12        24
 0
```

Figure 2.10.

Well, you have your answers, but there are other items of information on the screen, and you don't really know, from looking at them, what those numbers really represent. To get rid of the extra information on the screen, insert the following instruction:

5 HOME

A microcomputer uses a character set known as the *A*merican *S*tandard *C*ode for *I*nformation *I*nterchange (ASCII). The ASCII value 7, for instance, produces a tone when it is "printed," like this:

90 PRINT CHR$(7)

Add it to your program, for the effect.

RUN the program again. Doesn't that look better? Did you hear the beep? Sounds a little squeaky, doesn't it? OK, we're going to change those instructions we added up in Figure 2.9: look at Figure 2.11.

```
15 PRINT " MRS. SMITH'S FUND: "; J
25 PRINT " MRS. SMITH'S FUND: "; J
35 PRINT " MRS. SMITH'S FUND: "; J
45 PRINT "MRS. GREENE'S FUND: "; G,"MRS. SMITH'S FUND: "; J
55 PRINT "MRS. GREENE'S FUND: "; G,"MRS. SMITH'S FUND: "; J
65 PRINT "MRS. MARTIN'S FUND: "; M,"MRS. SMITH'S FUND: "; J
75 PRINT " MRS. ROGERS' FUND: "; R,"MRS. SMITH'S FUND: "; J
85 PRINT " MRS. SMITH'S FUND: "; J
```

Figure 2.11.

These numbers have been used before. When you retype them, they replace the old statements. The ability to do so is useful so long as the instructions are improved, as they are in this case, but be careful not to rewrite an instruction you don't intend to rewrite. (Note that there is a space after the colon in each of the statements; this space keeps the number contained in the variable separated from the message.

RUN the revised program. Doesn't it look better?

What you've done is to trace the progress of the Smith Fund, the Cancer Fund, the Heart Fund, and the Fund for the Home For Little Wanderers. Generally speaking, we're interested only in the final results and not in the process and contents as we go along. The exception is when we must use the intermediate results to *debug* (check for errors) the program. So, let's get out the eraser. Since you can delete a line simply by typing its line number (followed by RETURN), type 5, 15, 25, 35, 45, 55, 65, 75, and 85. Was all that effort wasted? Not really, because you did get to see what was happening, and now you know some of the steps you must take to debug the program.

With that done, add the instructions shown in Figure 2.12.

```
90 PRINT " MRS. SMITH'S FUND: "; J
100 PRINT "MRS. GREENE'S FUND: "; G
110 PRINT "MRS. MARTIN'S FUND: "; M
120 PRINT " MRS. ROGERS' FUND: "; R
```

Figure 2.12.

RUN the program again. There should now be four lines in the upper left-hand corner of the screen, containing the name and amount of each fund. Add the following termination instruction (merely a branch to itself to freeze the display), and run the program again:

```
130 GOTO 130
```

You have now written and successfully run a computer program. The GOTO of the last statement is called an *unconditional branch* because it offers a means to change sequence without having to meet conditions. In this instance, the GOTO references the instruction that contains it. It keeps the computer operative, but in a "locked" mode.

Let's recap what we've done so far. We have talked about the *immediate* or *calculator* (direct) *mode* and seen what it can do. We have talked about the *command* (indirect) *mode.* Recall that the calculator mode functions precisely as a hand held electronic calculator. The command mode includes all those actions at the keyboard that provide, among other things, the means to list a program on the screen.

By now you've discovered that your Apple III can handle upper and lower case letters. We've learned that we can use letters to represent numbers or, more specifically, the *value* of numbers. The letters used (J, G, M, and R) are called *numeric variables.* Actually, the setting of the numeric variable to a value is an abbreviated form of another BASIC instruction called LET. Statement 10 could have been written like this:

```
10 LET J = 8
```

The designers, in their wisdom, however, decided to let us express the instruction without having to type LET every time.

We've also learned that information can be displayed on the screen by using the PRINT instruction and that anything enclosed in quotation marks appears on the screen just as it has been typed. We've learned, moreover, that semicolons in the PRINT instruction cause numbers to be displayed in positions adjacent to other displayed information and that commas present information in zones.

And finally, we've learned that if we want to "short circuit" the instruction sequence, we have only to instruct the computer to GOTO some statement number. In the preceding example, we had the BASIC instruction 130 GOTO go to itself, thereby causing the computer to seem to stop. In reality, it continues to operate, but the operation is not obvious because it takes place inside the machine and is not apparent on the display.

REMarkable PROGRAM

Look at the list you produce on the display and at the hardcopy list if you prepared one. At this moment, you are fully aware of what you have accomplished. But in six months, after a few hundred more programs, you might have difficulty capturing what you originally tried to accomplish. It would be useful to be able to put comments in the program, right? Right. Comments are entered with REMark statements, such as the following:

```
1 REM * MY FIRST PROGRAM *
```

The REM statement allows you to enter up to 250 characters of descriptive information (in fact, any instruction line cannot exceed 250 characters). REM statements may not include executable code. Good practice indicates that you should keep your REM statements confined to one line and use several lines, if necessary. Further, remember, that while REMarks are both useful and necessary, they do occupy space and take time to print. Therefore, use them wisely. When memory space gets tight, the REMark statements are usually the first to be removed.

STOP, END, CONTinue

When we wrote statement 130, we wrote it as a GOTO itself, causing the computer to continue to operate and to "hang." If you really do want the computer to come to a halt, replace statement 130 with either the command work END or the command word STOP. END, when used, will simply bring up the BASIC prompt –) . STOP will produce a message: ?BREAK IN 130. STOP will also close any executing file, return BASIC to immediate execution, and redisplay the prompt. In either case – END or STOP – or when the CONTROL-C (BREAK) combination has been hit, execution of the program may be resumed using the CONT command. The CONT command won't reopen any files and can be used to restart after an error. However, if there is no program in memory or the program cannot be restarted, you will be told by the message ?CAN'T CONTINUE ERROR.

ADAPT, ADAPT

Given the fund raising problem and the values we have been using, the resulting answers will be precisely the same each time the program is run. Suppose, however, that we don't know the initial value of J and want to adapt the program to allow *any* value. Here's what to do:

```
10 INPUT J
```

That's all. Now, instead of giving J an initial value of 8, the computer will ask you what you'd like J to be. It will give a prompt, followed by a question mark, followed by the cursor (the position indicator on the screen). You must then enter the value that you'd like J to be. Note that the INPUT statement caused the computer to stop temporarily to await an answer. If you change statement 130 to GOTO 5, the computer will stop at statement 10 every time. Try doing so, entering different values for J. Note that as long as you enter a number, you will get an answer in return. Now try the same thing again, entering an alphabetic letter. You'll see that the computer will not permit you to do so and will indicate an error.

The INPUT instruction is like PRINT because it allows a message to be displayed on the screen. Retype statement 10 as follows:

```
10 INPUT "ENTER AMOUNT CONTRIBUTED TO THE SMITH FUND: ";J
```

and run the program again. You'll see that it takes the value you give it – J in this case – and returns the correct answer.

DETERMINING THE SIZE OF MEMORY

Sometimes it's important to know how much memory is available. Each character on the screen that you have entered occupies one memory position, *except* for the line number. The line number is stored in *binary* and occupies two bytes only. Two bytes seems like little. However, when things are tight, instructions can be combined by placing colon separators (:) on the statement line, releasing one byte for each combination. The mandatory space after the line number accounts for a third byte, and that byte is also released when instructions are combined. Unfortunately, all the memory you purchased is not available to you. There are overheads which must be paid. To determine the precise amount of available memory (e.g., for a 128K machine), do this:

```
PRINT (128 * 1024) - FRE(0)
```

ERROR CONDITIONS

The Apple III has several error conditions. There are error conditions for SOS and for Business BASIC – as well as any error messages which may be contained in your program. You'll find SOS and BASIC error messages, and their potential remedies, documented in the books pertinent to each.

MATH OPERATORS

In our little fund raising program we use some *math operators,* the symbols =, +, –, *, and /. Respectively, they indicate equation, addition, subtraction, multiplication, and division. The computer is, of course, a number machine, but it is decimally, not fractionally, oriented. When you begin to use or obtain very large or very small numbers, therefore, some strange things happen. The Apple III uses *standard scientific notation* (also called *exponential notation,* or more simply *E notation*) in the presentation of very large or very small numbers. To illustrate, let's examine the number 8 in our decimal system. In the decimal system, the number is really 8. (eight, followed by a decimal point, or 8.0). What would 8 million look like? It would look like 8000000. (Commas are not used to punctuate numerical data within a computer). That's eight, followed by six zeroes and a decimal point. In mathematical paralance, 8 million is:

$$8 * 10 * 10 * 10 * 10 * 10 * 10 \quad \text{or} \quad 8 * 10^{+6}$$

The Apple III, like many computers, would express this number in E notation. Eight million would then look like 8E+06. If the number gets too large, the Apple III indicates overflow. Thus 8, followed by 37 zeroes, would become 8E+37. Add one more zero, and overflow occurs. It's not likely that you'll encounter many numbers like this, but it's helpful to know what you're looking at. The important thing to remember is that counting begins at the decimal point.

RELATIONAL OPERATORS

The computer is also a *logic* machine. It has a mechanical ability, or more specifically, an electronic ability, to reason. By *reason,* we mean the ability to make very simple decisions of the IF ... THEN variety. In reasoning, the computer also uses its numbering abilities to compare numbers of characters to other numbers or characters. It can do so because each number or character has a numerical value or weight. The number 2 is "heavier" – that is, larger – than the number 1. The letter B is "heavier" than the letter A. In the APPLE III, each letter is represented by a number. The number for the capital letter A is 65; for capital Z, 90; for small letter a, 97; for small letter z, 122. Thus, when sorted, small letters sort out after large letters. As was explained before, the character set of the APPLE III is known as ASCII.

Suppose that we have two numeric variables, A and B. Both contain a number, but these numbers are not known. The numbers may be alike, or they may be dissimilar. Variable A may be greater than variable B (correspondingly, variable B is less than variable A). A may not be equal to B. B may be equal to or greater than A (which is, by definition, less than or equal to B). Get the picture? On the Apple III, we express it by using the *relational operators* shown in Figure 2.13.

OPERATOR	RELATION TESTED	EXAMPLE
=	EQUALITY	A = B
<> OR ><	INEQUALITY	A <> B ; A >< B
<	LESS THAN	A < B
>	GREATER THAN	A > B
<= OR =<	LESS THAN OR EQUAL TO	A <= B ; A =< B
>= OR =>	GREATER THAN OR EQUAL TO	A >= B ; A => B

Figure 2.13.

These relational operators are customarily placed into an IF, as shown in Figure 2.14.

```
10 B = 8
20 IF B >= 6 THEN 50
```

Figure 2.14.

In this instance, B contains the value 8, which is definitely greater than or equal to 6. The program sequence will then proceed to statement 50.

The use of the relational operators in an IF ... THEN statement constitutes a *conditional branching* situation. The first variable (or number) following the IF is compared to the second variable (or number), and a branch is taken to the THEN address if the condition is met. The statement could have been written as in Figure 2.15 with the same results.

```
20 IF 6 <= B THEN 50
```

Figure 2.15.

It is important to remember that the branching takes place conditionally upon the relationship of the first variable to the second variable, or, more specifically, the contents of those variables. If the branching to the THEN statement address is not taken, the computer assumes that the condition has not been met, and the program proceeds with the statement that follows statement 20.

In our funds program at statement 130, we told the computer to GOTO. GOTO is an example of an *unconditional* branch, that is, one that requires no conditional operators. The GOTO is customarily used to return to an instruction at the beginning of a process called *looping.* It's also used for changing direction within a program. Let's try some of these abilities in a program. Refer to Figure 2.16.

```
5 HOME
10 A = 0
20 B = 5
30 C = 10
40 IF A > B THEN 90
50 PRINT "A not greater than B"
60 IF A <> B THEN 120
70 PRINT "A is equal to B"
80 GOTO 140
90 IF A = C THEN 160
100 PRINT "A is greater than B but less than C"
110 GOTO 140
120 IF A > B THEN 90
130 PRINT "A is less than B"
140 A = A + 1
150 GOTO 40
160 PRINT "A is equal to C"
170 END
```

Figure 2.16.

```
A not greater than B
A is less than B
A not greater than B
A is less than B
A not greater than B
A is less than B
A not greater than B
A is less than B
A not greater than B
A is less than B
A not greater than B
A is equal to B
A is greater than B but less than C
A is greater than B but less than C
A is greater than B but less than C
A is greater than B but less than C
A is equal to C
```

Figure 2.17.

This little program exercises all but the greater than/equal combinations and thus gives an indication of how conditional branching systems work. Enter the program above into your Apple III and run it. Your display should look like Figure 2.17.

Now, just so you may see what has happened, the program will be modified slightly to present the variables as they are treated. Changes have been made in statements 50, 70, 100, and 160. Additions have been made in 55, 75, 105, 135, and 165, as shown in Figure 2.18.

```
5 HOME
10 A = 0
20 B = 5
30 C = 10
40 IF A > B THEN 90
50 PRINT "A not greater than B";
55 PRINT,,A;"      ";B;"      ";C
60 IF A <> B THEN 120
70 PRINT "A is equal to B";
75 PRINT,,,A;"      ";B;"      ";C
80 GOTO 140
90 IF A = C THEN 160
100 PRINT "A is greater than B but less than
105 PRINT,A;"      ";B;"      ";C
110 GOTO 140
120 IF A > B THEN 90
130 PRINT "A is less than B";
135 PRINT,,A;"      ";B;"      ";C
140 A = A + 1
150 GOTO 40
160 PRINT "A is equal to C";
165 PRINT,,,A;"      ";B;"      ";C
170 END
```

Figure 2.18.

Run the modified program, and Figure 2.19 will result. Do not be concerned about the alignment of numbers in the final line. Examine the modified and additional statements and you'll note that the first variable was printed on a zone boundary.

```
A not greater than B                              0     5     10
A is less than B                                  0     5     10
A not greater than B                              1     5     10
A is less than B                                  1     5     10
A not greater than B                              2     5     10
A is less than B                                  2     5     10
A not greater than B                              3     5     10
A is less than B                                  3     5     10
A not greater than B                              4     5     10
A is less than B                                  4     5     10
A not greater than B                              5     5     10
A is equal to B                                   5     5     10
A is greater than B but less than C               6     5     10
A is greater than B but less than C               7     5     10
A is greater than B but less than C               8     5     10
A is greater than B but less than C               9     5     10
A is equal to C                                   10     5     10
```

Figure 2.19.

IF YOU HAVE TROUBLE

Since expertise in the saving, loading, renumbering, etc., of programs comes with practice, you'll be an expert once you have practiced twice. But sooner or later, you'll have trouble. Dust or other contamination will have done you in. It's good business to make backup copies of every diskette you produce. The best defense is a good offense. Make duplicates.

If you do run into difficulty, reformat the diskette and try again. Keep those diskettes away from dust, sunlight, electric motors (even battery-operated pencil sharpeners, I'm sad to say), or anything that could alter the magnetic characterstics of the diskette.

You will see articles in magazines suggesting that you can punch a second pilot hole and record on the back side of a diskette (creating a so-called "flippy diskette"). Yes, it will work – but you're asking for trouble if you do it. If your interest is to keep an extra copy of SPACE TREKKIES, that's OK. Don't even think of keeping your company's records in that manner.

LOOP CONTROL

When a sequence of instructions is repeated, the process is called *looping.* Occasionally it is necessary to control the number of times we go through the loop. This process is called *iteration.* The instruction t be used is the FOR instruction, which works in conjunction with the NEXT instruction. The pair of instructions surrounds the loop.

Consider the instruction sequence shown in Figure 2.20. The FOR instruction involves the use of a numeric variable (in this case S) and a range through which the count is to be made (in this case 0 to 59). It is possible to add a STEP value to the FOR instruction to change the method of calculation. At the moment, the FOR instruction is *technically* FOR S = 0 TO 59 STEP 1.

```
10 HOME
20 FOR S = 0 TO 59
30       PRINT S;
40       NEXT S
50 GOTO 10
```

Figure 2.20.

Run the program. What happened? Oops! That's *movin'!* In fact, it's moving off the screen, clearing the screen, and continuing to move. It would continue forever unless you interrupt it with a CONTROL-C or the power fails. How could that possibly be useful? Who wants to count from 0 to 59 anyway? Anyone who wants to build a clock. Look over the above and you'll see that what we've set up is a nifty way to count seconds. Unfortunately, it's moving too fast to be accurate, and so we change the program to look like Figure 2.21.

```
10 HOME
20 FOR S = 0 TO 59
30       PRINT S;
35       FOR N = 1 TO 500:NEXT N
40       NEXT S
50 GOTO 10
```

Figure 2.21.

Run the program again. What happened? It slowed down, didn't it? Break the program sequence with a CONTROL-C and run the program again, this time with a sweep-second wristwatch in hand. Time the computer against the wristwatch. A new number should appear on the screen every second. If the hand on the watch runs faster than the computer, decrease the count at statement 35. If the hand on the watch runs slower than the computer, increase the count at statement 35. Note that the extra spacing in statements 30 and 35 are for readibility. The Apple III indents differently than you enter the program. You'll see that if you type the indentations under the FOR ... NEXT loops as they have been presented. You can merely indent them a couple extra spaces, and they will align properly when you LIST. Alternatively, you can change the indentation scheme by using the reserved variable INDENT. All you need to do is to include in your program an instruction to that effect (e.g., 10 INDENT = 5).

How does the program work? The first thing we did was to set up a controlled loop that begins at 0, increments by 1 until variable S reaches 59, and then starts over again. That controlled loop looks like Figure 2.22.

```
20 FOR S = 0 TO 59
        . . .
        . . .
40      NEXT S
```

Figure 2.22.

In other words, those instructions that fall between statement 20 and statement 40 will be done a total of 60 times (0 to 59). Embedded within the FOR ... NEXT loop just mentioned is another FOR ... NEXT loop that counts from 1 to 500. The Apple III can perform approximately 500 single-step FOR ... NEXT loops in one second. Thus, for every time through the "S" loop, the printing of the variable S will be done at a rate of approximately one per second.

Thus, the "N" loop has been made subordinate to the "S" loop. This procedure is called *nesting.* Loop "S" has a nested loop "N." Can that same principle be extended to the hour and minute hands? Certainly, but we'll have to start over. By the way, the addition of the semicolon to statement 30 merely allows continuous printing on the line. Delete it, run the program again, and watch it work without it. You can delete any instruction merely by typing the statement number and pressing the RETURN key. Or, you can delete a statement with the DEL command (DEL 10). The DEL command gives you the ability to remove several instructions (DEL 10 – 40). You can delete an entire program merely by typing NEW.

Now type the program shown in Figure 2.23. It is suggested that you observe the indentation (plus 2 spaces, as described above), as it will make the program much more easily readable and traceable. Note that the FOR ... NEXT loops are paired.

```
10 HOME
20 FOR H = 0 TO 23
30      FOR M = 0 TO 59
40           FOR S = 0 TO 59
50                HOME
60                PRINT H; ":";M; ":";S
70                FOR N = 1 TO 500:NEXT N
80                NEXT S
90           NEXT M
100      NEXT H
110 GOTO 110
```

Figure 2.23.

The Apple III does have the ability to pinpoint a position on the screen, and we will deal with that later when we address ourselves specifically to the display screen use.

This setup is all very nice, but unless you plan to wait until midnight to run it, it won't keep accurate time, no matter how accurately you adjust the timing loop. If you take out the timing loop, you'll be able to see the whole thing function under test. How should the "clock" be set? Enter the lines shown in Figure 2.24.

```
12 INPUT "ENTER HOUR"; A
14 INPUT "ENTER MINUTE";B
16 INPUT "ENTER SECOND";C
```

Figure 2.24.

Now replace statements 20, 30, and 40, substituting "A," "B," and "C" for the zero in each case, respectively. Also, calibrate the "clock" by changing statement 70, as previously discussed. Run the program and let it go for 5 minutes or so.

At the end of some significant time, look at your watch. Does the time indicated on the screen match your watch? If you made the entry at the beginning of the hour, it's probably pretty close. But if you made your entry at 10 minutes to the hour or 10 seconds to the minute, you'll note that something is not quite right. Let the computer run another 10 or 15 minutes. When you come back, you'll note that things have gone from bad to worse. Why? Probably the hour indicator is still OK, because you haven't been gone that long. But no doubt the minutes indicator is 15 or so more than it should be, and the seconds indicator is liable to be anywhere.

The reason why this has happened is that a FOR ... NEXT loop increments from the initial value you give it – which in this case was the hour (A), minute (B), and second (C) – continues through until it finds the higher value – and then *resets to the initial value that you gave it.* If you had made your entry at 10 minutes before the hour (50), you'll "burn up" an hour every time you count to 10. Obviously, that's not right. We want that 59 at the second and minute indicators to revert to 0 even though we have entered something else at first. Figure 2.25 shows what you should do to make this happen.

```
85 C = 0
95 B = 0
105 A = 0
```

Figure 2.25.

Adjust the horizontal spaces on these instructions to make the symmetry correct, if you care to. Now run the program again, entering the correct time to begin with, and then check the time again in 5 minutes or so. It should be pretty close. To calibrate the "clock" more closely, all you'll have to do is modify the count in statement 70.

Want to have a little fun? Try the changes shown in Figure 2.26. Make the entries and run the program to see what it does, but first note the changes in the FOR statements. The controlled loop can be incremented (+) or decremented (–) by adding the STEP modifier discussed previously.

```
20 FOR H = 23 TO A STEP -1
30        FOR 59 TO B STEP -1
40                 FOR S = 59 TO C STEP -1
85                 C = 59
95        B = 59
105 A = 23
```

Figure 2.26.

PRINTing TO THE DISPLAY SCREEN

PRINTing is really another way to say that a computer must have a means to produce output. There are several forms of output available to the Apple III – hardcopy printout, diskette, and even communications lines. The form we must study, however, is the display on the output screen. The terms "display screen" and "monitor" are interchangeable.

The BASIC command PRINT sends output to the display screen. But before the PRINT command is issued, there are a few other things which are provided and/or required by the Apple III:

- LIST – lists the BASIC program on the screen, as previously discussed. LIST, by itself, will display the entire program. LIST, when used with one or more line numbers, can display selected portions of the program. LIST is not used to display a program's output on the screen.
- INDENT – specifies the number of positions an indented program statement will be offset from the left margin (statement number). Two is standard. INDENT is not used to tabulate an output report.
- OUTREC – The display has 80 columns to the row and will "wrap" (go on to the next line) if overflowed. Since the PRINT statement is used, in conjunction with other commands, to communicate output to the hardcopy printer, OUTREC must be used if the linewrap is not available on the printer. Hardcopy printout techniques will be discussed later in the book.
- WINDOW – The screen for the Apple III is 80 columns wide, 24 rows long. It is possible, however, to redefine that screen to be smaller, using the WINDOW command. The command WINDOW 1,1 TO 80,10 would create a portal of 10 lines of 80 characters across the top of the screen. In this portal only would the Apple III present its messages.
- TEXT – This statement sets the display screen to the full screen mode. It also resets the screen after graphics use, which we'll discuss further on into the book.
- VPOS – Vertical Position. You can position the cursor on any line using the VPOS command (e.g., VPOS = 10). Important point: The VPOS command works within the WINDOW in use.

If the WINDOW is restricted, the VPOS will work within that restriction. Remember that if WINDOW begins at line 10, then the VPOS = 1 is line 10.

- HPOS – Horizontal Position. You can position the cursor on any column of the line (either next or specified) using the HPOS command (e.g., HPOS = 10). Important point: The HPOS command works within the WINDOW in use. If the WINDOW is restricted, the HPOS will work within that restriction. An HPOS which is outside the specification will be ignored.
- HOME – we've used this one before. It clears the current window (we've used it to clear the screen) and positions the cursor in the upper left-hand corner of the window.
- INVERSE – sets all subsequent display to black letters on green (or white) background. Continues until changed by NORMAL, next.
- NORMAL – sets all subsequent display to green (white) letters on black background. Continues until changed by INVERSE, above.
- TAB – moves to a specific place on the PRINT line. Movement is only rightward. Example: PRINT TAB(5);"Message"
- SPC – moves a predetermined number of spaces to the right on the PRINT line. Maximum size for SPC is 255. Several SPC commands may be combined to exceed that limitation.

The responsibility for positioning of printing is yours. Perhaps the simplest way to develop a screen is to develop an array which will be subsequently printed on the screen. You will not understand everything which is shown here, but Figure 2.27 gives one means to develop a screen.

```
10 HOME
20 DIM SCREEN$(24)
30 FOR N = 1 TO 24
40      SCREEN$(N) = STR$(N)
50      NEXT N
60 FOR N = 1 TO 23
70      PRINT SCREEN$(N)
80      NEXT N
90 PRINT SCREEN$(24);
100 GOTO 100
```

Figure 2.27.

Statement 20 DIMensions an array called SCREEN$ and designates it to have 24 elements. It's up to you to ensure that each element never exceeds 80 characters (really 78).

Statements 30 to 50 simply load the array with the *string value* of the number from the FOR ... NEXT loop. We'll talk about STR$ later in the book, but let's simply say that the array had been defined as string variable (the $), and N is a numeric variable. The STR$ converts the numeric value to a string value.

In that there are but 24 lines on the screen, a linefeed (which occurs on a normal PRINT statement) will shift the line upward. The 24th line would shift upward, leaving a blank line. Thus, 23 of the lines are printed as a function of the FOR ... NEXT loop, while the 24th is printed separately, ended with a semicolon, which is the way the linefeed is suppressed.

Statement 100 freezes the display, else the BASIC prompt would be displayed, shifting the entire screen display upward. Enter the program and try it.

It is important to distinguish between the *physical line* on the screen and the *logical line* that is to be displayed. In simple terms, a physical line is a fixed area of space on the face of the screen. There are 24 physical lines on the monitor of the Apple III. Also, there are 80 physical columns per line. These are available to VPOS and HPOS instructions, so the numbering scheme is real.

Therefore, for a message to appear properly on the screen, its presentation must be planned. For the most part, you will wish messages to be fewer than 81 characters if the PRINT instruction is terminated by a semicolon and fewer than 80 if it is not, owing to the carriage return and linefeed that are added to the line.

If the semicolon is used, the cursor will be placed at the next position immediately following the printed message. This, then, makes spacing considerations important when you wish to combine messages. Examine, please, the two instructions in Figure 2.28. Enter them, run them, and then add a semicolon to the end of statement 10 and run them again.

```
10 PRINT "This statement contains";"an error."
20 PRINT "This statement contains";" no errors."
```

Figure 2.28.

As can be seen, the instruction in statement 10 will create an erroneous message (which will nevertheless be displayed). The means to correct the message is to embed a space before the second part of the message, as in statement 20. The displayed output from these instructions will look like Figure 2.29.

```
This statement containsan error.
This statement contains no errors.
```

Figure 2.29.

The spacing of mixed lines is extremely important. Look back at the PRINT line used in the clock example. It was carefully constructed as PRINT H;":";M;":";S. If you took a good look at the screen while that example was working, you may have noted that there were spaces surrounding the numeric variables. This space is customarily reserved for a sign, and positive signs (+) are not displayed. In this instance, the colon is enclosed within the quotation marks, meaning that it is a part of the data to be displayed. If it were between two instructions on the same line, it would function as an *instruction separator.* Insofar as BASIC instructions are concerned, there must be spaces surrounding numbers; spaces surrounding operands are not always mandatory, but are acceptable for readibility.

The completion of a PRINT instruction forces a carriage return (linefeed). Ordinarily, any PRINT instruction following a PRINT instruction with carriage return will display on the next available line. However, if the PRINT instruction is terminated by a semicolon, the carriage return will be suppressed. For example, the instructions shown in Figure 2.30 produce output that looks like Figure 2.31 on the screen.

```
10 PRINT "Printing this way ";
20 PRINT "allows you to ";
30 PRINT "break up the ";
40 PRINT "instruction without ";
50 PRINT "breaking up ";
60 PRINT "the line."
```

Figure 2.30.

```
inting this way allows you to break up the instruction without breaking up
e line.
```

Figure 2.31.

Now a word of caution. The appending of a printed line to a previously printed line is strictly contingent upon the ability, spacewise, to fit *the entire next message on the same display line.* Observe statements 50 and 60 in Figure 2.3 and then observe the printed output or display upon the screen. The addition of the two words in statement 60 was too much for a defined screenwidth. Although you can enter an instruction with as many as three lines of characters, and the line will "wrap" as needed, the same is not true of printed output. It looks that way, of course, but move the word *the* from statement 60 to statement 50 and you will see the output shown in Figure 2.32.

```
Printing this way allows you to break up the instruction without
breaking up the line.
```

Figure 2.32.

If you type PRINT with nothing following, you'll get only a linefeed, giving you a blank line. There is a shorthand notation for the PRINT instruction. Type a ? (question mark) under a numbered statement. LIST it and you'll observe that it has been translated to PRINT. This is because the ASCII token for the PRINT instruction is the question mark. What's a token? Each of the instructions in BASIC is reduced to a single character by the interpreter. That single character is known as a token.

If you follow the PRINT statement with a variable expression (A, B, C, etc.), the values of those variables will be displayed – contiguously if separated by a semicolon or in one of the zones if separated by a comma. If you wish to use a string expression, you may use either a string variable (A$, B$, C$, etc.) or enclose the string with the PRINT instruction inself, between quotation marks. If spacing for several messages is required and you find that the previously described methods don't work, there are still a couple of ways to accomplish it – embedded spaces (SPC, discussed above) or tabulation (TAB, discussed above).

TABULATION

One interesting variation of the PRINT command is the ability to structure the screen into columns very easily. It could be structured into zones, of course, but this approach limits you in presenting information on the screen. That problem is solved by the TAB subsection of the PRINT command. Consider the instructions shown in Figure 2.33.

```
10 PRINT TAB(10);"CHECK";TAB(20);"PERSON";
20 PRINT TAB(30);"AMOUNT";TAB(40);"DATE OF"
30 PRINT TAB(9);"NUMBER";TAB(21);"PAID";
40 PRINT TAB(31);"PAID";TAB(41);"CHECK"
```

Figure 2.33.

```
 CHECK      PERSON     AMOUNT     DATE OF
NUMBER       PAID       PAID       CHECK
```

Figure 2.34.

If you enter these statements and then run them, you'll see headings line up as in Figure 2.34. Then, in successive lines, you can align the data to be presented in the same manner. There are two important things to remember about TAB:

1. It is a separate operation in the PRINT command and *must* be both preceded and followed by a semicolon, unless specified first after the PRINT statement.
2. It is descriptive of a position in the physical line itself, with a range of 1 to 80.

THIS BLINKING DISPLAY

While there are color capabilities for the monitor, to be discussed below, and even for the monochrome (green) screen, there are other ways to draw someone's attention to a display. One method is the INVERSE/NORMAL method described before. Yet another can be accomplished simply by repeating overlay of the message with interchanging "blank" messages with "word" messages in a pattern which appears to make the system flash. Try the instructions given in Figure 2.35.

```
10 A$ = "THIS MESSAGE WILL BLINK ON AND OFF"
20 B$ = "                                  "
30 HOME
40 FOR N = 1 TO 10
50     PRINT
60     NEXT N
70 PRINT TAB(10);C$
80 FOR Z = 1 TO 200:NEXT Z
90 IF S = 0 THEN S = 1:C$ = B$:GOTO 30
100 IF S = 1 THEN S = 0:C$ = A$:GOTO 30
```

Figure 2.35.

In this example, the screen is cleared and 10 blank lines are "printed." A simple switching mechanism is incorporated in statements 90 and 100 (S = 0, S = 1) and the space on the screen is turned on and off. In the "on" position, the string variable C$ is loaded with a message (from A$). In the "off" position, the string variable is loaded with blanks (from B$). There are more efficient ways to do this, but this will demonstrate the point.

CHR$

The Apple III is designed to operate in ASCII (*A*merican *S*tandard *C*ode for *I*nformation *I*nterchange). Let's examine the character set that can be displayed on the screen. Enter and run the program given in Figure 2.36.

```
10 HOME
20 FOR N = 32 TO 255
30     PRINT N;CHR$(N);
40     FOR Z = 1 TO 500:NEXT Z
50     NEXT N
```

Figure 2.36.

This routine shows you the character set beginning with ASCII code 32, as it is implemented on the Apple III itself. Those codes which lie between 0 and 31 are known as screen control codes.

Many of these codes have a different meaning to a printer. ASCII 12, for instance, causes the paper to eject. If the printer has an audible alarm or "horn" (as does the author's MX-80), you'll hear it at 7 and again at 147. Some of the characters are printable graphics characters, and the MX-80, which has graphics capabilities, rises to the occasion.

Even if you do not have an MX-80, but if you do have a printer, try the instructions in Figure 2.37. You should get Figure 2.38 back.

```
10 HOME
20 OPEN #1,".PRINTER"
30 OUTPUT #1
40 FOR X = 1 TO 16
50     PRINT X+159;"   ";CHR$(X+159);
60     PRINT TAB(10);X+159+16;CHR$(X+159+16);
70     PRINT TAB(20);X+159+32;CHR$(X+159+32);
80     PRINT TAB(30);X+159+48;CHR$(X+159+48);
90     PRINT " "
100    NEXT X
110 CLOSE #1
120 END
```

Figure 2.37.

```
160        176        192        208
161        177        193        209
162        178        194        210
163        179        195        211
164        180        196        212
165        181        197        213
166        182        198        214
167        183        199        215
168        184        200        216
169        185        201        217
170        186        202        218
171        187        203        219
172        188        204        220
173        189        205        221
174        190        206        222
175        191        207        223
```

Figure 2.38.

BACK TO THE PRINTER

With the Epson MX-80 printer there are a few differences that can be made to your printed output through the use of specialized ASCII characters and CHR$ codes. The same is no doubt true with other types of printers. Refer to the ASCII charts in the Apple literature and with any printer you may have. These are the codes which work with the MX-80:

CHR$(7)	Will sound a horn at the printer when used in a PRINT # or OUTPUT # statement where the devicename has been established to be ".PRINTER".
CHR$(14)	will set the print to double size (and therefore take up double the horizontal space on the paper). Note that the vertical spacing does not change.
CHR$(15)	will set the print size to smaller than normal size with a compression that allows 132 characters to be printed within the width normally used by 80 characters.
CHR$(18)	turns off the compressed mode.
CHR$(20)	turns off the double size mode.
	These two mode changes must be used when returning from the selected size to the normal size of print, which is 10 characters to the inch.
CHR$(27)	is the code for ESCape. This code must be used preceding those CHR$ codes that follow in this list, as the ESCape code clears the buffer. (A buffer is a temporary location for data or programs between memory and the diskette drive or between memory and the printer. The Apple III is fully buffered.)

CHR$(69) turns on an emphasized mode of print. Since ASCII 69 is also the letter "E," that letter may be used when preceded by CHR$(27).

CHR$(70) turns off the emphasized mode. Since ASCII 70 is also the letter "F," that letter may be used when preceded by CHR$(27).

CHR$(71) turns on the double strike mode of print. ASCII 71 is also the letter "G," enabling that letter to be used when preceded by CHR$(27).

CHR$(72) turns off the double strike mode. Since ASCII 72 is also the letter "H," that letter may be used when preceded by CHR$(27).

Now enter the program shown in Figure 2.39. Run it and you will achieve the output shown in Figure 2.40.

```
10 HOME
20 OPEN #1,".PRINTER"
30 OUTPUT #1
10 PRINT CHR$(14);"      TITLE LINE"
20 PRINT
30 PRINT "Normal Line"
40 PRINT
50 PRINT CHR$(15);"This line is in condensed print"
60 PRINT
70 PRINT CHR$(18);"Normal again"
80 PRINT
90 PRINT CHR$(27);"E";"This line is emphasized print"
100 PRINT
110 PRINT CHR$(27);"F";"Back to normal again"
120 PRINT
130 PRINT CHR$(27);"G";"This is double strike print"
140 PRINT
150 PRINT CHR$(27);"H";"Back to normal again"
160 CLOSE #1
170 END
```

Figure 2.39.

```
TITLE LINE

Normal Line

This line is in condensed print

Normal again

This line is emphasized print

Back to normal again

This is double strike print

Back to normal again
```

Figure 2.40.

WHO WAS THAT MASKED CHARACTER?

Recall the program which printed the test results of the Smith Fund? In it, the last set of numbers were two-digit numbers and did not align on the one-digit numbers when they were printed on a zone. The reason was that the numbers had to begin on a zone boundary. What would be required to have them line up correctly? Glad you asked! We now introduce PRINT USING.

We shall also introduce what is commonly called the *print mask.* The print mask is a filter through which *editing* of a numeric or alphabetic string can be accomplished. Concentrating first upon numeric strings, by editing we mean the insertion of things like decimal points, commas, dollar signs, algebraic signs, floating asterisks, etc. Consider the program given in Figure 2.41.

```
10 HOME
20 INPUT "ENTER A NUMBER: ";A
30 PRINT "THE NUMBER YOU ENTERED WAS: ";
40 PRINT USING "$6&.2#";A
50 PRINT
60 INPUT "ENTER TWO NUMBERS, SEPARATED BY A COMMA: ",A,B
70 PRINT "THE NUMBERS YOU ENTERED WERE: ";
80 PRINT USING "$6&.2#";A,B
90 PRINT:PRINT
100 END
```

Figure 2.41.

Review the above, paying particular attention to statements 40 and 80. Statement 40's editing picture ($6&.2#) seems different from that of statement 80 ($##.##), and yet they perform similar functions. The key is the fact that the pound sign (#) and the ampersand (&) are both characters which may be replaced with data. The difference is that the # provides direct replacement, whereas the & punctuates with a comma every three positions away from the decimal point. The particular configuration (6&) merely means repeat the & six times. It could just as easily have been written as &&&&&&. The $ is fixed, in this example, and does not slide. Now consider the two output sets from this program shown in Figure 2.42.

```
ENTER A NUMBER: 1234.56
THE NUMBER YOU ENTERED WAS: $1,234.56

ENTER TWO NUMBERS, SEPARATED BY A COMMA: 12.34,56
THE NUMBERS YOU ENTERED WERE: $12.34$56.00

ENTER A NUMBER: .23678
THE NUMBER YOU ENTERED WAS: $     0.24

ENTER TWO NUMBERS, SEPARATED BY A COMMA: .14,1234.56
THE NUMBERS YOU ENTERED WERE: $ 0.14 !!!!!!
```

Figure 2.42.

In set 1, you'll note that the comma was indeed inserted. The same editing mask may be used for more than one value, but you can achieve no spacing between – at least without an IMAGE statement, discussed later. Note, however, that the second parameter of the second question has been entered as a whole number. When edited, it appears with two zeroes to the right of the decimal point.

In set 2, in the first question, a decimal value which is longer than the two positions allowed in the edit mask is entered. Note that the entered figure is rounded upward (rule of 5) and that the presented amount reflects that rounding. In the second question, first parameter, note the zero to the left of the decimal point when a decimal value is entered. The difference between that figure and the rounded figure just discussed is the ampersand (&). On the second parameter of the second question, a value which is much too large for the whole number portion of the edit mask is entered, with the result being changed to exclamation points.

WE MUST WATCH OUR IMAGE

The illustration given above was nice, but who really likes to have the numbers run together? There are many ways to combine the editing mask with the PRINT USING statement, as shown. More often than not, however, there are some editing masks which are common. These editing masks can contain a string variable which has been given the mask value (e.g., A$ = "$6&.##") and can be used in the PRINT USING statement (e.g., PRINT USING A$;A). Or, instead, an IMAGE statement can be established, and used as necessary to produce the editing required. Consider changing the second question in Figure 2.41 to look like this:

```
75 IMAGE ##.##,10X,##.##
80 PRINT USING 75;A,B
```

It won't overcome the problem when the number entered is too large, but it *will* insert ten blanks between the numbers. The IMAGE statement, then, becomes a more or less universal editing mask. In that regard it will allow editing of not only dollar fields, but data strings (known as stringspec), literals (known as literalspec), and numeric (known as numericspec). The dollar fields are one form of numericspec, the fixed-point specification (fixspec). There are two other forms of numericspec – the scientific notation specification (scispec) and the engineering notation specification (engrspec).

Since the majority of uses in this book are for the numeric fixspec, we'll concentrate upon its use, but will summarize the elements of each. More detail may be obtained from the sections covering these sections in the Apple Business BASIC manual.

StringSpec	Defines the field format and witdth for a string value, defining whether the string will be left-justified (A), centered (C), or right-justified (R). Can be repeated by insertion of a number (i.e., 6A is the same as AAAAAA). The number of characters to be accepted dictates the IMAGE mask. An example of this concept given in the Apple Business BASIC book follows:

```
10  IMAGE 15A, 15C, 15R
15  PRINT
100 PRINT USING 10; "COMPOSER",
    "TITLE", "KEY"
```

As you will see in the manual, the first string in this example happens also to be a literal (defined as a word in quotations) is left-justified, the second is centered, and the third is right-justified. These could have just as easily been string variables names (e.g., A$).

LiteralSpec

There are three main purposes of the LiteralSpec: to insert a fixed number of spaces, a fixed number of returns, or a fixed string into the output, X prints a space. 4X would print four of them. The character / prints a return (carriage return), and 2/ would do it twice. A pair of quotations around one character will repeat that character as many times as the repeating function requires. Thus, 6"*" will give you ******. These can be combined: 4 spaces, 6 asterisks, and two returns would be placed in the IMAGE statement in this manner: 4X,6"*",2/. It is important to note that this is but a part of the IMAGE statement, and there is no reason not to mix specifications, as we did in the revision of Figure 2.41.

FixSpec

The FixSpec will be the one most used for dollar amounts. These are the rules for the IMAGE statement:

+ Reserves a character position for a sign.

-	Reserves a character position for a minus sign which is used only if the number is negative.
$	Reserves a position for the dollar sign.
**	Prints asterisks instead of leading spaces – known as "asterisk fill."
++	Reserves rightmost positions for signs and dollar sign.
--	Same as ++ but used only if number is negative.
$$	This is the sliding dollar sign.
#	Replacement character.
&	Replacement character with comma punctuation to the left of the decimal.
Z	Print leading zeroes.

SciSpec, EngrSpec, and SCALE

Nothing much complicated about these. SciSpec has the character E which permits the editing to be done in E-notation. EngrSpec is similar except that it forces an exponent value which is a multiple of three, and a maximum of three digits to the left of the decimal scaling (powers of 10) to occur. If you have need for these, please refer to the manual. They are not germane to this book.

SO GO, ALREADY

It often happens that you must change direction within a program. You may wish to change direction unconditionally; that's done with GOTO. You may wish to change direction with anticipation of returning; that's done with GOSUB. Or you may wish to do either on the basis of a selection of values; that's done with the instructions ON ... GOTO and ON ... GOSUB.

The GOTO is straightforward. You've completed a loop (look back at several of the program examples we've discussed) and you wish to repeat it. The GOTO statement will *unconditionally branch* to the statement you want.

Often it happens that you might want to develop an amount of instruction coding that can be used over and over again but you don't want to code it each time it is needed. At such times you can resort to a *subroutine.* A subroutine is any routine that is terminated with a RETURN command, as shown in Figure 2.43. Although this routine simply exchanges messages on the screen, it clearly demonstrates the use of the subroutine. To get into a subroutine, you need a GOSUB. To get back to the next suquential instruction, there must be a RETURN at the end of the subroutine.

```
10 HOME
20 VPOS=13:HPOS=32
30 PRINT "PERFORM A SUBROUTINE"
40 FOR N = 1 TO 500:NEXT N
50 GOSUB 1000
60 GOTO 10
1000 '*****************************************
1010 '*                                       *
1020 '*          THIS IS A SUBROUTINE         *
1030 '*                                       *
1040 '*****************************************
1050 HOME
1060 VPOS=13:HPOS=34
1070 PRINT "DISPLAY A MESSAGE"
1080 FOR N = 1 TO 500:NEXT N
1090 RETURN
```

Figure 2.43.

When your responses are in a defined order, it's possible to place a multiple branch within the same statement. For instance, suppose that you had begun your program with a *menu.* A menu is, as the word denotes, a selection of options. Enter the program in Figure 2.44 and run it.

As you can see, if you select one of the offered options (follow your entry with the RETURN), that option will be displayed. Try one that is not offered, and you'll see that the selected option is rejected. This is called *error trapping.*

```
10 HOME
20 VPOS=10:HPOS=30
30 PRINT "1.     MENU OPTION ONE"
40 VPOS=12:HPOS=30
50 PRINT "2.     MENU OPTION TWO"
60 VPOS=14:HPOS=30
70 PRINT "3.     MENU OPTION THREE"
80 VPOS=16:HPOS=30
90 PRINT "4.     MENU OPTION FOUR"
100 PRINT:PRINT
110 INPUT "SELECT: ",A
120 ON A GOTO 140,160,180,200
130 GOTO 10
140 PRINT:PRINT "YOU SELECTED MENU OPTION ONE"
150 END
160 PRINT:PRINT "YOU SELECTED MENU OPTION TWO"
170 END
180 PRINT:PRINT "YOU SELECTED MENU OPTION THREE"
190 END
200 PRINT:PRINT "YOU SELECTED MENU OPTION FOUR"
210 END
```

Figure 2.44.

```
10 HOME
20 VPOS=10:HPOS=30
30 PRINT "1.     MENU OPTION ONE"
40 VPOS=12:HPOS=30
50 PRINT "2.     MENU OPTION TWO"
60 VPOS=14:HPOS=30
70 PRINT "3.     MENU OPTION THREE"
80 VPOS=16:HPOS=30
90 PRINT "4.     MENU OPTION FOUR"
100 PRINT:PRINT
110 INPUT "SELECT: ",A
120 ON A GOSUB 140,170,200,230
130 GOTO 10
140 PRINT:PRINT "YOU SELECTED MENU OPTION ONE"
150 GOSUB 260
160 RETURN
170 PRINT:PRINT "YOU SELECTED MENU OPTION TWO"
180 GOSUB 260
190 RETURN
200 PRINT:PRINT "YOU SELECTED MENU OPTION THREE"
210 GOSUB 260
220 RETURN
230 PRINT:PRINT "YOU SELECTED MENU OPTION FOUR"
240 GOSUB 260
250 RETURN
260 FOR N = 1 TO 1000:NEXT N:RETURN
```

Figure 2.45.

The same result can be achieved with GOSUB. Modify the preceding program as shown in Figure 2.45. One minor twist occurs here. Note that within each separate subroutine, a common subroutine is executed – a subroutine within a subroutine. The latter is known as a *nested subroutine.*

POP GOES THE SUBROUTINE

One must exercise considerable care with nested subroutines. Occasionally you find yourself in the midst of the nested subroutine and find that you do not wish to simply return to the next sequential instruction in the originating subroutine. You wish, instead, to return to the statement following the very first reference to a subroutine.

What to do? The POP command will take you out of the nested subroutine, removing the need to resolve the RETURN. This will take some study in the manual and some experimentation before use – but it is infinitely better than merely plunking a GOTO somewhere in the middle of a nested subroutine.

KEYBOARD ENTRY

Up to this point, when we needed to obtain input from the keyboard, we used the INPUT instruction. There are at least two other means to obtain input from the keyboard – the KBD statement and the GET statement.

The KBD statement functions as a means to divert program control at any time a key has been pressed. Generally at the head of the program will be a statement which centralizes the treatment of the keyboard: ON KBD GOTO XXX. XXX, of course, is the address where the ASCII value of the keyboard entry is interpreted.

By and large, the KBD functions as what is commonly called an *interrupt,* in that the address to which control is to go is established early on, and the subroutine which contains the coding to interpret that coding remains unused until either the ON KBD GOTO function is exercised or cancelled. The important thing to remember is that the program will continue to function as if the ON KBD GOTO function did not exist. When, however, a key has been pressed, off you go to the subroutine. This, then, is the means to incorporate in your program the interpretation of CONTROL keys, the ESCape key, and other specialized keys. It should not be used where the direction of your program depends upon the input, unless you are well into the level of knowledge required to assemble a keyed input on a character by character basis – and even at that, it's easier with the GET statement.

The GET statement accepts a single character, in string format, and waits for the input. You may then either use that input as entered

```
10 HOME
20 VPOS=10:HPOS=30
30 PRINT "1.     MENU OPTION ONE"
40 VPOS=12:HPOS=30
50 PRINT "2.     MENU OPTION TWO"
60 VPOS=14:HPOS=30
70 PRINT "3.     MENU OPTION THREE"
80 VPOS=16:HPOS=30
90 PRINT "4.     MENU OPTION FOUR"
100 PRINT
110 PRINT
120 PRINT "SELECT: ";
130 GET Z$
140 IF Z$ = "1" THEN A = 1:GOTO 200
150 IF Z$ = "2" THEN A = 2:GOTO 200
160 IF Z$ = "3" THEN A = 3:GOTO 200
170 IF Z$ = "4" THEN A = 4:GOTO 200
180 GOSUB 350
190 GOTO 20
200 PRINT A
210 ON A GOSUB 230,260,290,320
220 GOTO 10
230 PRINT:PRINT "YOU SELECTED MENU OPTION ONE"
240 GOSUB 420
250 RETURN
260 PRINT:PRINT "YOU SELECTED MENU OPTION TWO"
270 GOSUB 420
280 RETURN
290 PRINT:PRINT "YOU SELECTED MENU OPTION THREE"
300 GOSUB 420
310 RETURN
320 PRINT:PRINT "YOU SELECTED MENU OPTION FOUR"
330 GOSUB 420
340 RETURN
350 PRINT
360 VPOS=22:HPOS=1
370 PRINT "INVALID SELECTION -- RE-ENTER"
380 GOSUB 420
390 VPOS=22:HPOS=1
400 PRINT "                                        "
410 RETURN
420 FOR N = 1 TO 1000:NEXT N:RETURN
```

Figure 2.46.

(in the case of alphabetic data) or convert it (in the case of numeric data). The GET statement, while it obtains but a single character at a time, can be placed in a FOR ... NEXT loop for fixed input. The loop must be constructed to permit *concatenation* of variables. If the GET statement accepts one value at Z$, then the statement A$ = A$ + Z$ will concatenate the second value to the first. Repetition of the loop will develop a progressively larger value at A$. One need only include the routine to interpret the receipt of the RETURN key (IF Z$ = CHR$(13)) and the input may be terminated in that manner. More importantly, GET waits for the input, and it is the GET which is used in the routine shown in Figure 2.46.

Most of this program should be straightforward. The GET merely waits for the response and then the response is tested for four acceptable values. There is a more sophisticated way to do this. Study Figure 2.47.

```
10 HOME
20 VPOS=10:HPOS=30
30 PRINT "1.     MENU OPTION ONE"
40 VPOS=12:HPOS=30
50 PRINT "2.     MENU OPTION TWO"
60 VPOS=14:HPOS=30
70 PRINT "3.     MENU OPTION THREE"
80 VPOS=16:HPOS=30
90 PRINT "4.     MENU OPTION FOUR"
100 VPOS=20:HPOS=1:PRINT "SELECT: ";
110 GET Z$
120 IF VAL(Z$) < 1 OR VAL(Z$) > 4 THEN 140
130 GOTO 170
140 PRINT "INVALID SELECTION"
150 GOSUB 320
160 GOTO 10
170 PRINT VAL(Z$)
180 ON VAL(Z$) GOSUB 200,230,260,290
190 GOTO 10
200 PRINT:PRINT "YOU SELECTED MENU OPTION ONE"
210 GOSUB 320
220 RETURN
230 PRINT:PRINT "YOU SELECTED MENU OPTION TWO"
240 GOSUB 320
250 RETURN
260 PRINT:PRINT "YOU SELECTED MENU OPTION THREE"
270 GOSUB 320
280 RETURN
290 PRINT:PRINT "YOU SELECTED MENU OPTION FOUR"
300 GOSUB 320
310 RETURN
320 FOR N = 1 TO 1000:NEXT N:RETURN
```

Figure 2.47.

Here we have taken the VALue of the string variable Z$ and used it in an ON ... GOSUB. For either of the conditional branching instructions (ON ... GOTO and ON ... GOSUB) to work, values in the range of 1, 2, 3, etc., must be developed. A value of 1 will cause the first address to be taken; 2 the second, and so on. That's what occurs in the ON ... GOSUB in Figure 2.47.

SUMMARY

As this chapter closes, let's take stock of how far we have come. We'll do so by reviewing the commands, statements, and functions we have already learned to use. You may then be assured that you are acquainted with all the pertinent ones to which reference has been made, with the added advantage that the explanations are concentrated for easy reference.

AND — Used as a conjunction between two parts of an IF ... THEN statement where you wish to ascertain that both values are present. Consider the following example:

```
100 IF (A=5) AND (B=10) THEN 300
```

CHR$ — Used for special codes which are not represented on the keyboard and to represent the alphabetic values using the ASCII code. For example, the letter A:

```
100 A$ = CHR$(65)
```

CLOSE — Makes a file or character device no longer available for input or output. CLOSE, when issued with a buffer number (e.g., CLOSE #1) will close only that buffer. The CLOSE statement, when issued alone, closes all buffers.

CONT — Resumes program execution at the occurrence of a STOP command or END statement.

DEL — Used to remove instructions from a BASIC program. Single instructions may be removed merely by typing the line number. Multiple instructions may be removed by providing the inclusive statement numbers, like this:

```
DEL 1000-1500
```

This statement may also be included within a program to delete portions of the program when they will no longer be required.

END — Terminates the program statements and returns control to the BASIC interpreter. It need not be the very last physical line of the program; there may be more than one of them; or you can leave it out all together. However, END returns the system to BASIC control.

FOR — The first part of a FOR ... NEXT loop. Used to establish the number of iterations (repetitions) for the loop, giving an initialization value, a termination value, and – if used – a STEP value.

```
100 FOR S = 60 TO 1 STEP -1
```

FRE — Used to determine how much memory is still FREe – that is, unused by program or string storage. It performs a "garbage collector" function in that FRE, when used, releases string storage which is no longer being used.

```
100 PRINT FRE
```

GET — One character input from the keyboard. The program waits for the input.

```
100 GET Z$
```

GOSUB — Provides subroutine linkage. A RETURN statement is required in the subroutine to return control to the statement following the statement which contained the GOSUB. May be conditional when combined with ON.

```
100 GOSUB 1000
200 ON A GOSUB 1000,2000,3000
```

GOTO — The unconditional branch; a redirection of sequence. No tests are made and no control is exhibited. It may be conditional, when combined with ON.

```
100 GOTO 200
200 ON A GOTO 300,400,500
```

HOME — Clears the screen and returns to the HOME position. This is the same as PRINT CHR$(18).

```
100 HOME
```

HPOS — The Horizontal POSition, in the range of 1–80, on the monitor. Used to set up displays in specific screen locations. Customarily used in conjunction with VPOS.

```
100 HPOS=10
```

IF — Used to set up a logical comparison test. The first portion of the IF ... THEN relationship. A part of a conditional branching situation based on the relationship of two values.

```
100 IF A > 10 THEN 500
```

IMAGE — Used to establish editing patterns for alphabetic, numeric, scientific, and engineering data. Punctuates dollar values when functioning with a PRINT USING command. IMAGE must precede the PRINT USING command and occupy a statement by itself.

```
100 IMAGE $6&.2#,5X,$6&.2#
200 PRINT USING 100;A,B
```

INPUT — Used to accept either alphabetic or numeric data. May include a message. If the variable which is to receive the data is preceeded by a semicolon, a question mark will appear. Change the semicolon to a comma and the question mark is suppressed. Multiple inputs may be obtained by separating the operands with commas.

```
100 INPUT "ENTER VALUE: ";A
200 INPUT "ENTER NAME: ",A$
300 INPUT "TWO VALUES: ",A,B
```

INVERSE — Used to highlight the display by black on green, rather than the NORMAL green on black. Causes extremes of colors on color monitors.

INVOKE — Used to load machine language programs from BASIC. Example given in the book was that of the renumbering/resequencing program. Reuires a PERFORM to begin execution.

KBD — The constant keyboard strobe – requiring a routine to handle the interruptions.

```
ON KBD GOTO 500
```

LET — This is the traditional equality. J = 8 is the same as LET J = 8, and the LET specification is therefore not required.

LIST — LISTs the BASIC program on the screen (unless an OUTPUT statement is included). LIST by itself will list everything, scrolling the screen. LIST with a statement number or range of statement numbers will display only what is shown. This is a keyboard, not a program, function.

```
LIST
LIST 100
LIST 100-300
```

LOAD — Used to retrieve programs from diskette. LOADs programs which have been stores via SAVE.

```
LOAD .D2/PROGRAM
```

NEW — Clears a prior program from memory.

NEXT — The last part of the FOR ... NEXT loop. Redirects control to the head of the loop.

```
200 NEXT N
```

NORMAL — Resets the screen color to green on black. The opposite of INVERSE.

```
100 NORMAL
```

OPEN — Opens a file or a character device for input or output, and assigns that to a buffer.

```
100 OPEN #1,FILENAME$
```

OR — Used in a compound conditional statement where a choice of two values is acceptable.

```
100 IF (A=5) OR (B=10) THEN 200
```

OUTPUT — Used to direct screen-displayed presentation to a character device other than the monitor. It is in this manner that printing on the ".PRINTER" is accomplished.

```
100 OUTPUT #1
```

PERFORM — Initiates execution on the machine language program which was loaded by an INVOKE statement. Again, we used this when using the resequencing program.

POP — Breaks the RETURN of a nested subroutine.

PRINT — Displays information on the screen. Can be located with VPOS and HPOS instructions, through repeated PRINT statements which occupy blank lines, or with TAB functions for spacing. Printing may be contiguous, zoned, or linefeed suppressed.

```
100 PRINT LITERALS$;DATA$,NUMERICS;
```

RETURN — Returns control from a subroutine reached by a GOSUB, ON ... GOSUB, or ON KBD.

```
100 RETURN
```

RUN — begins execution of the BASIC program with the first (lowest numbered) statement. May specify a specific place to start.

```
RUN 100
```

SAVE — Stored the program on disk for later retrieval.

```
SAVE .D2/PROGRAM
```

STEP — Changes the increment of a FOR ... NEXT loop.

```
100 FOR N = 1 TO 100 STEP 5
```

STOP — STOPs execution. Program may be restarted with CONT.

TAB — TABulates across a print (or printer) line. Range of 1–80 on the screen; a function of printer configuration. Part of the PRINT instruction.

```
100 PRINT TAB(5);A
```

TEXT — Places the screen in TEXT mode. Resets the TEXT WINDOW to full size and cancels graphics mode – to be discussed later.

```
100 TEXT
```

THEN — The result of a comparison – IF ... THEN.

```
100 IF A = 5 THEN 500
```

TO — Specifies the target of a FOR ... NEXT loop.

```
100 FOR N = 1 TO 100
```

USING — Aligns an edit mask or IMAGE statement for display with the PRINT command.

```
100 PRINT USING 10;A
```

VPOS	Vertical POSitioning. In other words, the screen line, in the range of 1-24. 100 VPOS=10
WINDOW	Specifies the WINDOW coordinates for full or partial size screen. Defaulted to full screen. Smaller size may be specified. 100 WINDOW 37,9 TO 44,16

3 Developing and Manipulating Data

Already having a solid idea of how the Apple III functions, we can now turn our attention to the development of programs, routines, and methods of handling data. Data, of course, is the raison d'etre for possessing a computer. Even if you devote your Apple III to playing Space Invaders, which you probably will not, the program within the computer must work upon data that is (1) either already contained within the computer, (2) entered from outside the computer, or (3) developed as a result of previous manipulations on either or both (1) and (2).

Before progressing, let's pick up a couple of threads – things which are useful information, but which don't require a special treatment to use the machine. The first is a reserved variable called INDENT. If you have been trying to indent your instructions as shown in, for example, a FOR ... NEXT loop, you're aware that they do not come out looking like the example. You do get an automatic indentation of two characters, but you can change it to any value. Simply type INDENT= and give it a value (e.g., INDENT=5).

Next, the statements NEW and CLEAR. NEW was mentioned before, as clearing memory. It differs, however, from CLEAR, in that CLEAR sets all numeric variables to zero, all string variables to null (the lowest ASCII value), clears any BASIC pointers, and closes all open disk files other than a file in execution.

Up to now we have referred to files with a device name (.D2) and a file name (PROGRAM) in the format .D2/PROGRAM. That has been necessary, as we have SAVEd and LOADed programs from the keyboard. The same can be done internally, of course, but if you want *all* your references to be a single drive within the program itself, it is necessary to use the reserved variable PREFIX$ (PREFIX$ = ".D2"). Thereafter, all file references can be to the file name (DATAFILE). Bit by bit we'll cover all the reserved variables. You'll find a list of reserved words in the manual.

When you have developed your program and it is doing strange things, then it becomes necessary to *debug* it. One of the ways to do that is to execute a TRACE. TRACE will display the line numbers of instructions through which you pass, and will continue until a NOTRACE command is found. You may invoke the TRACE from the keyboard, but if you do, you will have to CONTROL-C to BREAK. Or, you can invoke the TRACE from inside the program, where you feel the problem may be located. NOTRACE can be invoked either from the keyboard or the program.

You may add comments to your program by using a REMarks statement. Either on its own line, or appended to another line, REM isolates the line or the balance of the line to be a comment. REMarks are not executable code, although if you GOTO a line which is a REMark statement, it will pass through.

VARIABLES, VARIABLES

Thus far, we have used certain types of data – namely numeric variables and alphabetic variables – the latter being signified by the terminating dollar sign on the name (label) of the data. A variable may be thought of as a specific place in which to store things, a place where there are size and type limitations. In the majority of microcomputers on the market, data variables can be identified by one, two, or three characters. Some can have longer names, but only the first three characters are relevant. The Apple III also has a limitation – 64 characters, that is, the first 64 characters are the significant characters. Anything beyond that limit is not treated as relevant. You should certainly have no trouble being sufficiently descriptive within 64 characters. To be more precise, a variable name must *begin* with a letter, and thereafter any of the available letters, digits, or periods may be used.

There are limitations on variable names, of course, in that the reserved words cannot be used. There are actually two uses for variables. One use is for the storage of transient data – information which comes and goes. The other is for constant data, data which is assigned to the variable and then is not changed. In the case of constant data, the instruction which sets the variable equal to the constant must be executed once, and then the constant data is available until the variable is, for some reason, changed.

There are four variable types within the Apple III:

Variable Type	*Variable Name*
Real	DISTANCE
Integer	INTEREST%
Long Integer	NATIONAL.DEBT&
String	THREAD$

The *real* variable is what we have been calling a numeric variable. By and large, reals are what you will commonly use for handling numeric values. There are exceptions to this, dealing with storage space on files and the representation of very large numbers for scientific and engineering calculations, but you will find that mostly you will use reals. Reals are used where numbers may have a fractional part – as when expressing dollars and cents.

An integer is, by definition, the whole number part of a number. In the real 33.3, the integer portion is the 33. If the variable which was to hold 33.3 were defined as an integer, only the 33 portion would remain. Integers are useful when fractional parts are not needed. They can speed up calculations where a large amount of computation is to be done.

Long integers are integers which are up to 19 digits in length. Other computers call this double precision. The idea is to be able to express very large or very small numbers. When calculations must be done with micrometer precision, the long integer will be required. To figure your accounts receivable, you probably will not need it.

String variables are used to encase alphabetic data or – and this is an important distinction – a numeric value wherein the numbers are to be represented in individual bytes. Each character of a string variable takes one byte, or position of memory. Thus there is a difference between the numeric variable 111 and the string variable "111." If you try to calculate with the latter, you'll be told how erroneous your assumption is. You can get at the value, however, by using the VALue instruction. If A$ = "111" then you can create a numeric value by stating the following: A = VAL(A$). Because string variables are surrounded by quotation marks, you cannot therefore set a string variable equal to quotation marks. This will not work: A$ = """". However, code A$ = CHR$(34) + "KEN" + CHR$(34), and when you PRINT A$, the name will be surrounded by the quotes.

The only real restriction to the use of variable names is confined to the use of reserved words. END, by itself, is not allowed as a variable name; END.ROUTINE, however, would be perfectly permissible.

The following are the reserved words which cannot be used alone as variable names:

ABS(	DIV	INT(	PDL(
AND	ELSE	INVERSE	PERFORM
AS	END	INVOKE	POP
ASC(	EOF	KBD	PREFIX$
ATN(	ERR	LEFT$	PRINT
BUTTON(	ERRLIN	LEN(	READ
CAT	EXFN	LET	REC(
CATALOG	EXFN%	LIST	REM
CHAIN	EXP(	LOAD	RENAME
CHR$(	EXTENSION	LOCK	RESTORE
CLEAR	FN	LOG(	RESUME
CLOSE	FOR	MID$(	RETURN
CONT	FRE	MOD	RIGHT$
CONV(	GET	NEW	RND(
CONV$(	GOSUB	NEXT	RUN
CONV%(	GOTO	NORMAL	SAVE
CONV&(	HEX$(	NOT	SCALE(
COS(	HOME	NOTRACE	SGN(
DATA	HPOS	OFF	SIN(
DEF	IF	ON	SPC(
DEL	IMAGE	OPEN	SQR(
DELETE	INPUT	OR	STEP
DIM	INSTR(	OUTPUT	STOP

STR$	TEN(	TRACE	VAL(
SUB$	TEXT	TYP(	VPOS
SWAP	THEN	UNLOCK	WINDOW
TAB(	TO	USING	WRITE
TAN(			

Avoid using these, or use them in combination with other words, and there should be no difficulty.

A PLACE FOR EVERYTHING

A variable is a place to *put something,* to store alphabetic or numeric data. It may be a *constant* (A$ = "STRING CONSTANT"). It may be a *literal* (PRINT "HELLO"). It may be a value used by an instruction (FOR N = 1 TO 10). The point is that variables are places to store data. The names you assigned to variables must, of necessity, occupy space. If you make a habit of using 64-character labels, the available memory will be quickly consumed. Thereafter, each time you define or develop variables, they will utilize the size defined. At some point you will have memory restriction, irrespective of the amount of memory purchased. It's called *Parkinson's Law,* and it will eventually force you to condense your variables.

Apple Business BASIC reserves part of memory for use by strings. How much memory is available for string storage will depend on the number of other variables and arrays (yet to be discussed) in the program. One way to keep the allocation of memory to a minimum is to reuse defined variables. In any event, that space which is not used must wait for the "garbage man" for release. You can accelerate this release with the FRE command. However, when you have run out of memory, you have run out of memory. A CLEAR statement will find more memory for you by clearing out all variables currently in use. It's important to recognize that there are overheads in your memory allocation. Just because you have purchased 256K of memory doesn't mean that it's all available. Load BASIC (which, you will recall, also loads some of SOS) and then PRINT FRE, and you will find that very nearly 70,000 positions of memory are not available to your BASIC program. String storage is taken from that yet.

Up to this point we have dealt exclusively with storage space taken by numeric and alphabetic constants. Other places data may reside are as follows:

1. They may reside as a DATA statement (stored within the program itself), which is accessed by a READ instruction. The DATA statement is a *permanent constant* that can store both alphabetic and numeric data. Once set, these are not modifiable by the BASIC program using them. As with every rule, there is an exception. BASIC DATA statements can be modified by a machine-language knowledgeable person.
2. They may reside as an element of an array. Arrays will be discussed later on. They are used as the place to store data arriving from input media or to develop data targeted for output media.
3. They may reside on diskette. Data can be read from diskette (or other attachable media) or written to it and are moved into variables or, more usually, into an array when staged.

IT'S CALLED CONCATENATION

It's possible to add to alphabetic fields together; at least it seems that way. In one method, it's called *appending.* In another, it's called *concatenation.* Note the definitions of the variables A$ and B$ in statements 10 and 20 in Figure 3.1. Statement 30 *appends* the two variables to itself into a permanent variable, C$. That combination is displayed in statement 50. In statement 40, however, the two variables are joined temporarily *(concatenated)* for purposes of the display. Both ways work, but concatenation occupies less memory.

```
10 A$ = "BELL"
20 B$ = "WEATHER"
30 C$ = A$ + B$
40 PRINT A$ + B$
50 PRINT C$
```

Figure 3.1.

THE DATA STATEMENT

Consider Figure 3.2.

```
1000 DATA 42377,KEN,LORD,007328933,9,3,36
1010 DATA 27365,NANCY,LORD,024372122,10,19,36
1020 DATA 34582,KAREN,LORD,073327344,12,12,59
1030 DATA 57263,TIMOTHY,LORD,008328814,9,11,61
1040 DATA 23649,SCOFIELD,SANDRA,012663429,12,4,65
```

Figure 3.2.

Here is structured data about five people, data that will be used by a program to perform some function – perhaps for display in a report. From left to right, each DATA statement contains a number (perhaps an employee number), a first name, a last name, a social security number, and the month, day, and year of birth. Note that each line is structured in precisely the same manner. Note also that the first item is numeric, the next two are alphabetic, and the remaining four are numeric. Thus, in sequence, they can be described as:

EMPLOYEE.NUMBER
FIRST.NAME$
LAST.NAME$
SOCIAL.SECURITY.NUMBER$
MONTH.OF.BIRTH
DAY.OF.BIRTH.
YEAR.OF.BIRTH

Figure 3.3 is a routine to READ the DATA lines and to present them on the screen. Each is presented twice for comparison of the treatment of the birthdate as numeric or alphabetic. The social security number has been defined as a string variable to preclude suppression of leading zeroes and the presentation of the numbers in mathematical notation. The output looks like Figure 3.4.

As you examine this program, some questions are certain to arise. What's a RESTORE? Why are the PRINT statements broken down? Isn't this the kind of data that would normally reside on some sort of media?

```
10 HOME
20 PRINT "Date Of Birth (Numeric)":PRINT
30 FOR N = 1 TO 5
40      READ EMPLOYEE.NUMBER,FIRST.NAME$,LAST.NAME$
50      READ SOCIAL.SECURITY.NUMBER$
60      READ MONTH.OF.BIRTH,DAY.OF.BIRTH,YEAR.OF.BIRTH
70      PRINT EMPLOYEE.NUMBER,FIRST.NAME$,LAST.NAME$,;
80      PRINT SOCIAL.SECURITY.NUMBER$,;
90      PRINT MONTH.OF.BIRTH;"/";DAY.OF.BIRTH;"/";YEAR.OF.BIRTH
100     NEXT N
110 PRINT:PRINT
120 RESTORE
130 PRINT "Date Of Birth (Alphabetic)":PRINT
140 FOR N = 1 TO 5
150      READ EMPLOYEE.NUMBER,FIRST.NAME$,LAST.NAME$
160      READ SOCIAL.SECURITY.NUMBER$
170      READ MONTH.OF.BIRTH$,DAY.OF.BIRTH$,YEAR.OF.BIRTH$
180      PRINT EMPLOYEE.NUMBER,FIRST.NAME$,LAST.NAME$,;
190      PRINT SOCIAL.SECURITY.NUMBER$,;
200      PRINT MONTH.OF.BIRTH$;"/";DAY.OF.BIRTH$;"/";YEAR.OF.BIRTH$
210      NEXT N
220 END
1000 DATA 42377,KEN,LORD,007328933,9,3,36
1010 DATA 27365,NANCY,LORD,024372122,10,19,36
1020 DATA 34582,KAREN,LORD,073327344,12,12,59
1030 DATA 57263,TIMOTHY,LORD,008328814,9,11,61
1040 DATA 23649,SANDRA,SCOFIELD,012663429,12,4,65
```

Figure 3.3.

```
Date Of Birth (Numeric)

  42377        KEN          LORD         007328933      9 / 3 / 36
  27365        NANCY        LORD         024372122      10 / 19 / 36
  34582        KAREN        LORD         073327344      12 / 12 / 59
  57263        TIMOTHY      LORD         008328814      9 / 11 / 61
  23649        SANDRA       SCOFIELD     012663429      12 / 4 / 65

Date Of Birth (Alphabetic)

  42377        KEN          LORD         007328933     9/3/36
  27365        NANCY        LORD         024372122     10/19/36
  34582        KAREN        LORD         073327344     12/12/59
  57263        TIMOTHY      LORD         008328814     9/11/61
  23649        SANDRA       SCOFIELD     012663429     12/4/65
```

Figure 3.4.

The pattern of the READ instruction is that DATA line elements are read one at a time in the sequence in which they are called. However, you'd better be very certain that you call for what you need. READs can be single or multiple-variable types, with no punctuation specifications. The PRINT statements are broken down simply because the limited page size of this book doesn't permit full-width instructions *or* data. Recall that so long as linefeeds are suppressed (by the semicolon), the printing will be contiguous.

Finally, of course, this sort of data customarily resides on magnetic media. What is ordinarily kept in DATA lines is the sort of information that is basically unchanging, such as rate tables.

ALL RIGHT, POST A SENTINEL

We know that precisely five DATA lines were required to do the preceding program. And we will know (because we program it) what the count will be at any time. Suppose, however, that the table is constantly changing and that we must make additions to and deletions from the table. Every change in the table will require a corresponding change in the count of the FOR ... NEXT loop used to control the READ instructions. That's too much like work.

To get around that hassle, we can add a sentinel line as the *last* DATA line in the given sequence. (DATA lines can be located *anywhere* within a program and are treated as if they were contiguous.) RESTORE resets the pointer to the first DATA record. As a matter of convenience, however, DATA lines are customarily located en masse at the end of the program. This sentinel line is something

```
10 HOME
20 FOR N = 1 TO 1000
30     READ EMPLOYEE.NUMBER,FIRST.NAME$,LAST.NAME$
40     READ SOCIAL.SECURITY.NUMBER$
50     READ MONTH.OF.BIRTH$,DAY.OF.BIRTH$,YEAR.OF.BIRTH$
60     IF EMPLOYEE.NUMBER = 99999 THEN 120
70     PRINT EMPLOYEE.NUMBER,FIRST.NAME$,LAST.NAME$,;
80     PRINT SOCIAL.SECURITY.NUMBER$,;
90     PRINT MONTH.OF.BIRTH$;"/";DAY.OF.BIRTH$;"/";YEAR.OF.BIRTH$
100 NEXT N
110 END
120   PRINT:PRINT "SENTINEL LOCATED"
130 END
1000 DATA 42377,KEN,LORD,007328933,9,3,36
1010 DATA 27365,NANCY,LORD,024372122,10,19,36
1020 DATA 34582,KAREN,LORD,073327344,12,12,59
1030 DATA 57263,TIMOTHY,LORD,008328814,9,11,61
1040 DATA 23649,SANDRA,SCOFIELD,012663429,12,4,65
5000 DATA 99999,ZZZZZ,ZZZZZ,ZZZZZ,ZZZZZ,ZZZZZ,ZZZZZ
```

Figure 3.5.

uniquely distinguishable and unlikely to occur of natural causes. The most commonly used sentinels are 9's for numeric fields and Z's for alphabetic fields. As a result, the loop (FOR ... NEXT) must be structured toward an impossible-to-reach number, and a test for the sentinel must be contained within the FOR ... NEXT loop, as shown in Figure 3.5. Figure 3.6 will show that the sentinel was indeed located.

```
42377          KEN            LORD           007328933      9/3/36
27365          NANCY          LORD           024372122      10/19/36
34582          KAREN          LORD           073327344      12/12/59
57263          TIMOTHY        LORD           008328814      9/11/61
23649          SANDRA         SCOFIELD       012663429      12/4/65

SENTINEL LOCATED
```

Figure 3.6.

ARRAY (OF SUNSHINE?)

Although the DATA statement is a good way to provide temporary input to a program, it is by no means the only way to introduce data to the system. Another is the use of an array. As previously stated, it is into the array that data retrieved from a diskette is placed.

An array can be thought of as a series of mailboxes or pigeon holes into which items of data can be sorted. There are essentially two types of arrays: unidimensional and multidimensional.

The unidimensional array is merely a sequential list, just as if we had used separate variables. Figure 3.7 shows an example of a six-element array (ARRAY.A$) with locations (mailboxes) 0 through 5 (yes, 0 is a number).

```
.........................
.      ARRAY.A$(0)      .
.........................
.      ARRAY.A$(1)      .
.........................
.      ARRAY.A$(2)      .
.........................
.      ARRAY.A$(3)      .
.........................
.      ARRAY.A$(4)      .
.........................
.      ARRAY.A$(5)      .
.........................
```

Figure 3.7.

The multidimensional array is comprised of rows and columns. There are boxes across the horizontal span, and there are boxes along the vertical span. Figure 3.8 is an example of an array consisting of four rows of four elements (mailboxes).

```
                        Columns
          ...................................
          . B(0,0) . B(0,1) . B(0,2) . B(0,3) .
          ...................................
          . B(1,0) . B(1,1) . B(1,2) . B(1,3) .
Rows      ...................................
          . B(2,0) . B(2,1) . B(2,2) . B(2,3) .
          ...................................
          . B(3,0) . B(3,1) . B(3,2) . B(3,3) .
          ...................................
```

Figure 3.8.

TAKING A DIM VIEW

In order to use an array, it is necessary to specify its characteristics to BASIC. The process is called DIMensioning. It requires an instruction within the program *after* any CLEAR statement. The DIM statements for the previously illustrated arrays look like this:

```
10 DIM ARRAY.A$(5)
20 DIM B(2,3)
```

If you're sharp, something doesn't look quite right. The illustration of ARRAY.A$ had *six* elements, not five. The illustration of Array B had 12 little mailboxes, not the six it would seem that you asked for. There is, however, a common thread to the quandary. Of the six boxes, one of them had a zero reference. Of the 12 boxes, six of them had a zero reference. Therefore, what the DIMension statement does for you is to identify the *top* position relative to zero. You can use the zero referenced places. What will happen in practice is that you'll use them for work space.

Go back to the multidimensional array and darken the outline of boxes B(1,1), B(1,2), B(1,3), B(2,1), and B(2,3). For all intents and purposes, these are the working elements of the array. The first position to be referenced, therefore, is B(0,0) plus one. The "plus one" is commonly callced a *subscript.* To illustrate it, consider Figure 3.9.

```
10 DIM ARRAY.A$(5)
20 HOME
30 FOR N = 1 TO 5
40      ARRAY.A$(N) = "ELEMENT " + STR$(N)
50      NEXT N
60 FOR N = 1 TO 5
70      PRINT ARRAY.A$(N)
80      NEXT N
90 END
```

Figure 3.9.

In this program, we have dimensioned the single-dimensioned array and have loaded a value into it. The program loads into the array the word "ELEMENT" followed by a number. There is a new instruction in statement 40 – STR$. Because of it, statement 40 concatenates and stores two values in the array. Since it is impossible to concatenate an alphabetic value and a numeric value and since the FOR ... NEXT loop is controlled by the numeric variable, it is necessary to convert the numeric value to an alphabetic value. STR$ is the precise opposite of the VAL function discussed before.

Figure 3.10 shows a similar program to load a multidimensioned array. Enter and run the program and you'll see that the several elements of the array have indeed been filled – with an incremental constant. In case you're wondering about the spacing of the printed output (between the parentheses, as shown in Figure 3.11), recall that all numbers are signed and the positive sign (+) does not print. To avoid the spacing you would have to complicate the PRINT instruction to insert a backspace, ASCII 008.

```
10 DIM B(2,3)
20 CONSTANT = 111
30 HOME
40 FOR N = 1 TO 2
50      FOR X = 1 TO 3
60          B(N,X) = CONSTANT
70          CONSTANT = CONSTANT + 111
80          NEXT X
90      NEXT N
100 FOR N = 1 TO 2
110     FOR X = 1 TO 3
120         PRINT "ELEMENT B(";N;",";X;") = " B(N,X)
130         NEXT X
140     NEXT N
150 END
```

Figure 3.10.

```
ELEMENT B( 1 , 1 ) =  111
ELEMENT B( 1 , 2 ) =  222
ELEMENT B( 1 , 3 ) =  333
ELEMENT B( 2 , 1 ) =  444
ELEMENT B( 2 , 2 ) =  555
ELEMENT B( 2 , 3 ) =  666
```

Figure 3.11.

ARRAYS AND FILES

There are, of course, similarities between the loading of arrays from DATA lines and the loading of arrays from magnetic diskette files. To this point we've concentrated on the mechanics of loading arrays, with no concept of what the array represented. Let us now use the PERSONNEL.FILE$ illustration we first presented in Figure 3.3.

Examine the DATA lines and you will see there are six rows of seven elements. It follows, therefore, that the DIMension must be 6 by 7. Let's call the array by its name – PERSONNEL.FILE$. It is an attribute of an array that it must be either numeric or alphabetic, but never both or mixed. Since we have a mixture of data types, let's treat them all as alphabetic, because we know that with the STR$ and VAL functions we can change them at will. Just so we are clear as to what goes where, the following will define the first record in detail:

```
PERSONNEL.FILE$(1,1) = 42377
PERSONNEL.FILE$(1,2) = KEN
PERSONNEL.FILE$(1,3) = LORD
PERSONNEL.FILE$(1,4) = 007328933
PERSONNEL.FILE$(1,5) = 9
PERSONNEL.FILE$(1,6) = 3
PERSONNEL.FILE$(1,7) = 36
```

Nancy's record would then begin at 2,1; Karen's at 3,1; and so forth.

Before we proceed, let's merely load the DATA lines into the array and print them off to ensure that we understand what is where. Refer to Figure 3.12. Note as you examine this program that it was not necessary to identify as target the original names assigned and then transfer them to the array. It was necessary only to identify the array parts. We used variable X to scan the columns and variable N to scan the rows, producing the output shown in Figure 3.13.

```
10 HOME
20 FOR N = 1 TO 1000
30      PRINT "READING RECORD: ";N
40      FOR X = 1 TO 7
50           READ PERSONNEL.FILE$(N,X)
60           PRINT "    ";PERSONNEL.FILE$(N,X);
70           IF PERSONNEL.FILE$(N,X) = "99999" THEN 120
80           NEXT X
90      PRINT
100     NEXT N
110 END
120 PRINT:PRINT "SENTINEL LOCATED"
130 END
1000 DATA 42377,KEN,LORD,007328933,9,3,36
1010 DATA 27365,NANCY,LORD,024372122,10,19,36
1020 DATA 34582,KAREN,LORD,073327344,12,12,59
1030 DATA 57263,TIMOTHY,LORD,008328814,9,11,61
1040 DATA 23649,SANDRA,SCOFIELD,012663429,12,4,65
1050 DATA 99999,ZZZZZ,ZZZZZ,ZZZZZ,ZZZZZ,ZZZZZ,ZZZZZ
```

Figure 3.12.

```
READING RECORD:  1
  42377  KEN  LORD  007328933  9  3  36
READING RECORD:  2
  27365  NANCY  LORD  024372122  10  19  36
READING RECORD:  3
  34582  KAREN  LORD  073327344  12  12  59
READING RECORD:  4
  57263  TIMOTHY  LORD  008328814  9  11  61
READING RECORD:  5
  23649  SANDRA  SCOFIELD  012663429  12  4  65
READING RECORD:  6
  99999
SENTINEL LOCATED
```

Figure 3.13.

OK, the array is loaded, you've used the data, and now you need the storage. What next? Simple: When you've finished with an array and find that you need the space that had been occupied by the array, you can issue the CLEAR. But be careful – CLEAR clears *all* variables, so if you do that, make certain that you reload all variables you need.

Look carefully at the previous program. Note that it does not contain a DIMension statement. Why? The reason is that BASIC will automatically define a minimum 10 by 10 matrix for you without this statement. For any larger matrix, however, BASIC will give you an error message requiring one.

STRINGS AND THINGS

In business applications you will find yourself manipulating more nonnumeric data than you will numeric data. The specification of "nonnumeric" should not be arbitrarily assumed to be alphabetic,

```
10 HOME
20 TEST.STRING$ = "ABCDEFGHI"
30 VPOS=8:HPOS=20
40 PRINT "TEST STRING POSITION:   123456789"
50 VPOS=10:HPOS=20
60 PRINT "TEST STRING CHARACTER: ";TEST.STRING$
70 VPOS=14:HPOS=1
80 PRINT "LEFT THREE CHARACTERS:"
90 VPOS=14:HPOS=30
100 PRINT LEFT$(TEST.STRING$,3)
110 VPOS=16:HPOS=1
120 PRINT "CENTER THREE CHARACTERS:"
130 VPOS=16:HPOS=30
140 PRINT MID$(TEST.STRING$,4,3)
150 VPOS=18:HPOS=1
160 PRINT "RIGHT THREE CHARACTERS:"
170 VPOS=18:HPOS=30
180 PRINT RIGHT$(TEST.STRING$,3)
190 FOR X = 11 TO 14
200     VPOS=X:HPOS=44
210     PRINT "¦"
220     NEXT X
230 FOR Y = 35 TO 43
240     VPOS=X-1:HPOS=Y
250     PRINT "."
260     NEXT Y
270 FOR X = 11 TO 16
280     VPOS=X:HPOS=47
290     PRINT "¦"
300     NEXT X
310 FOR Y = 35 TO 46
320     VPOS=X-1:HPOS=Y
330     PRINT "."
340     NEXT Y
350 FOR X = 11 TO 18
360     VPOS=X:HPOS=50
370     PRINT "¦"
380     NEXT X
390 FOR Y = 35 TO 49
400     VPOS=X-1:HPOS=Y
410     PRINT "."
420     NEXT Y
430 VPOS=14:HPOS=55
440 PRINT "LEFT$(TEST.STRING$,3)"
450 VPOS=16:HPOS=55
460 PRINT "MID$(TEST.STRING$,4,3)"
470 VPOS=18:HPOS=55
480 PRINT "RIGHT$(TEST.STRING$,3)"
490 PRINT
```

Figure 3.14.

for as we have seen, it's possible to treat numeric data (from DATA lines or from diskette) as if it were alphabetic (nonnumeric) data. It would therefore behoove us to become acquainted with how the Apple III handles string data. The first three instructions required are those that can be used to "break down" an alphabetic string. They are LEFT$, MID$, and RIGHT$. With LEFT$ and RIGHT$, you can specify the number of characters you wish to extract (copy) from the left or right side of the string. With MID$ you can extract from the center (or anywhere along the entire length) of the string; the only difference here is that you must specify the beginning position of the extraction. In the following example, LEFT$, RIGHT$, and MID$ are the *source* of data. As the *target* of data, only MID$ is workable.

Enter the program shown in Figure 3.14. You will achieve the results shown in the output in Figure 3.15 (modified for readability).

```
                         TEST STRING POSITION:   123456789

                         TEST STRING CHARACTER: ABCDEFGHI
                                                  !  !  !
                                                  !  !  !
                                                  !  !  !
LEFT THREE CHARACTERS:        ABC    .........!  !  !    LEFT$(TEST.STRING$,3)
                                                     !  !
CENTER THREE CHARACTERS:      DEF    ............!  !    MID$(TEST.STRING$,4,3)
                                                        !
RIGHT THREE CHARACTERS:       GHI    ...............!    RIGHT$(TEST.STRING$,3)
```

Figure 3.15.

All this is well and good, and we have extracted from a string whose size is known to be a specified number of characters. Suppose, however, that we were searching through data for a specified combination of characters, such as could be used, for example, in a keyword. What then? The INSTR function will tell where in the string the specific sequence of characters is located. For instance, if from our brief alphabetic sequence we wished to locate the substring EFG, we would assume that the computer would tell us that they are located in the fifth position. Once known, the data can be accessed. Enter and try the program shown in Figure 3.16.

Occasionally it's important to know the length of a given string of data. Let's say, perhaps, that you can print only the first 10

```
10 HOME
20 TEST.STRING$ = "ABCDEFGHI"
30 INPUT "ENTER THE STRING YOU SEEK: ",A$
40 X = INSTR(TEST.STRING$,A$)
50 IF X > 0 THEN PRINT "THE LOCATION OF ";A$;" IS";X:GOTO 70
60 PRINT A$;" IS NOT LOCATED IN THE TARGET STRING"
70 PRINT
80 GOTO 20
```

Figure 3.16.

characters of a field on a page of printed output. To determine the length, the LENgth function is used. Once the length is known, you can determine the size of the data to be presented. For instance, consider Figure 3.17.

```
10 HOME
20 TEN$ = "         1         2         3         4"
30 UNIT$ = "1234567890123456789012345678901234567890"
40 VPOS=6:HPOS=1
50 PRINT "SCALE:"
60 VPOS=5:HPOS=20
70 PRINT TEN$
80 VPOS=6:HPOS=20
90 PRINT UNIT$
100 VPOS=8:HPOS=1
110 PRINT "ENTER STRING:"
120 VPOS=8:HPOS=20
130 INPUT "",A$
140 VPOS=10:HPOS=1
150 PRINT "SIZE OF OUTPUT:"
160 VPOS=10:HPOS=20
170 INPUT "",SIZE
180 VPOS=12:HPOS=1
190 PRINT "RESULTING STRING:"
200 VPOS=12:HPOS=20
210 IF LEN(A$) < SIZE THEN PRINT "IMPOSSIBLE!":GOTO 230
220 PRINT LEFT$(A$,SIZE)
230 VPOS=14:HPOS=1
240 PRINT "PRESS ANY KEY TO CONTINUE"
250 GET Z$
260 IF Z$ = "" THEN 250 ELSE 10
```

Figure 3.17.

Here we see a variable length-field entered and are presented with an opportunity to specify the output length. This approach would work as surely as if we were to trim all variables down to a common size. Observe the ELSE command in statement 260. The ELSE is a default which functions as if it were a GOTO in the following statement.

In this particular example, the coding advises you if it is impossible to specify a length for a field to be entered. In actuality, you would accept any length up to and including the length specified. The output should look as shown in Figure 3.18.

```
                                 1         2         3         4
SCALE:               1234567890123456789012345678901234567890

ENTER STRING:        ABCDEFGHIJKLMNOPQRSTUVWXYZ

SIZE OF OUTPUT:      15

RESULTING STRING:    ABCDEFGHIJKLMNO

PRESS ANY KEY TO CONTINUE
```

Figure 3.18.

YOU TAKE THE HIGH ROAD. . . .

One of the better techniques in common use in computer applications is the binary search. "Binary" means "two" and the principle of the binary search assumes the following:

1. That whatever you're searching for is in some predetermined sequence, usually ascending.
2. That the field of search can be narrowed merely by using the "rule of halves," that is, by dividing the object of the search into equal parts, determining the relationship of the item for which you're searching to the midpoint, selecting the proper half, dividing *it* into two equal parts, and then continuing in the same fashion until the required item is found. In other words, a computerized twenty-questions-type game.

That's how it works, but what is it? Suppose that there is a very long list, such as a list of names, perhaps of a thousand names. If the list were compiled in just any random sequence, it would be very difficult to find the name of any one person, say John Smith. What is needed is a list arranged in alphabetical sequence, beginning with A and ascending through the alphabet to Z. Now, when you wish to search the list for Smith, your eyes fall to the S's, you look at them one by one until you find the Smiths, and then, you look for John. The computer works in the same way, except it cannot "see" the S's. What happens is that after the list has been put into alphabetic sequence, it must be divided right down the middle, between M and N. The name Smith (S) is checked against N and found to be larger since it is known that S falls somewhere between N and Z. The "bottom half" of the alphabet (A to M) is therefore not searched. The next step is to split the upper half of the alphabet so that the midpoint is now T. Since S is smaller than T, the upper quarter of the top half of the alphabet is no longer searched. It is known then that S falls somewhere between N and T, and so on.

Although the development of games is a topic for later consideration, there is one game we can now develop to illustrate this search. Known by the general title of "guess the number," it can be programed as follows.

```
10 HOME
20 A%=0:C%=0
30 PRINT "PICK A NUMBER FROM 1 TO 100":PRINT
40 PRINT "PRESS ANY KEY WHEN YOU HAVE DECIDED ON THE NUMBER."
50 GET Z$
60 IF Z$ = "" THEN 50
```

Figure 3.19.

The program begins as in Figure 3.19. The purpose of these instructions is merely to give you time to select a number in the range of 1 to 100. You do not need to tell that number to the computer. Simply write it down or keep it in mind. The integer definitions of statement 20 will ensure our dealing with whole numbers. Numeric variable A is used as part of an ON ... GOTO statement, C is used to keep track of your guesses. Statements 50 and 60 form a tight loop that waits for the keyboard entry.

The computer doesn't know the number you have in mind, of course, but it does know the range it has offered you and the extremes and midpoint of that range because of the additional statements given in Figure 3.20. These statements define the midpoint, clear the screen, and establish the linkage to a subroutine. In the subroutine, three alternatives will be displayed (see Figure 3.21).

```
70 RANGE.MIDPOINT% = 50:RANGE.TOP% = 100:RANGE.BOTTOM% = 0
80 HOME
90 GOSUB 210
```

Figure 3.20.

```
210 REM ***********************************
220 REM *        DISPLAY SUBROUTINE        *
230 REM ***********************************
240 PRINT TAB(30);"1.   GREATER THAN ";RANGE.MIDPOINT%
250 PRINT
260 PRINT "IS IT:";TAB(30);"2.   EQUAL TO ";RANGE.MIDPOINT%
270 PRINT
280 PRINT TAB(30);"3.   LESS THAN ";RANGE.MIDPOINT%
290 PRINT
300 PRINT "WHICH";
310 GET Z$
320 IF Z$ = "" THEN 310
330 IF VAL(Z$) > 3 OR VAL(Z$) < 1 THEN 310
340 A% = VAL(Z$)
350 C% = C% + 1
360 RETURN
```

Figure 3.21.

Here we have a simple menu arrangement with three options. Presentation of the menu is straightforward enough, right down to statement 330. What happens there? Recall that GET accepts an *alphabetic* input. Because we wish to use numeric variable A for an ON ... GOTO, the input value must be changed to a numeric type. Simultaneously, the validity of the entry is error-trapped, and if you enter a value greater than 3 it will be rejected. The same is true if you try a value less than 1 (0, –1, etc.). Try it. The integer variable A is established in statement 340, the "guess" counter in incremented in 350, and the computer leaves the subroutine at 360.

In the subroutine, you are asked to compare the number in your head to the current midpoint. "Greater than" is option No. 1; "equal to" is option No. 2; and "less than" is option No. 3. These values correspond to the ON ... GOTO in statement 100, shown with four new statements in Figure 3.22. In this program, only the "equal to" has been coded, recognizing that at some point you must (if you're honest) respond to this condition.

```
100 ON A% GOTO ___, 120, ___
110 GOTO 70
120 PRINT:PRINT:PRINT "HA! HA!  I GUESSED YOUR NUMBER IN ONLY ";
130 PRINT C%;" TRIES"
140 END
```

Figure 3.22.

Back to statement 100, amplified as shown in Figure 3.23, along with three new statements.

```
100 ON A% GOTO 150, 120, ___

150 RANGE.BOTTOM% = RANGE.MIDPOINT%
160 GOSUB 370
170 GOTO 80
```

Figure 3.23.

Now we can concentrate upon the "greater than" side of the option. In the "greater than" situation, the range is 50 to 100. The first thing to do, therefore, is to establish that range. Recall that the program is being developed to make the routines useful no matter what the numbers may be. What is now known, however, is that there is a new midpoint (RANGE.MIDPOINT). Before the old midpoint value is destroyed, however, the variable used for the bottom of the range (RANGE.BOTTOM) must be established with the *current* value of variable RANGE.MIDPOINT. That occurs in statement 150. Now a new midpoint must be established (the subroutine at 370), although the upper limit (RANGE.TOP) does not need adjustment. That subroutine is given in Figure 3.24. This sends us back again to statement 100 and an additional set of statements shown in Figure 3.25.

```
370 REM ***********************************
380 REM *       UPPER HALF SUBROUTINE     *
390 REM ***********************************
400 RANGE.MIDPOINT% = (RANGE.MIDPOINT% + RANGE.TOP%)/2
410 RETURN
```

Figure 3.24.

```
100 ON A% GOTO 150, 120, 180

180 RANGE.TOP% = RANGE.MIDPOINT%
190 GOSUB 420
200 GOTO 80

420 REM ***********************************
430 REM *       LOWER HALF SUBROUTINE     *
440 REM ***********************************
450 RANGE.MIDPOINT% = (RANGE.MIDPOINT% + RANGE.BOTTOM%)/2
460 RETURN
```

Figure 3.25.

On the "less than" side, the range is now 0 to 50, although those values cannot be used directly. The upper limit must be adjusted, and that is done in statement 180. The lower limit remains as it is.

It is now necessary to find a new midpoint, a job done by the subroutine at 420.

The complete program is given in Figure 3.26.

If the variables had not been defined as integers, there would have been one minor problem. When the ranges are such that the midpoint

```
10 HOME
20 A%=0:C%=0
30 PRINT "PICK A NUMBER FROM 1 TO 100":PRINT
40 PRINT "PRESS ANY KEY WHEN YOU HAVE DECIDED ON THE NUMBER."
50 GET Z$
60 IF Z$ = "" THEN 50
70 RANGE.MIDPOINT% = 50:RANGE.TOP% = 100:RANGE.BOTTOM% = 0
80 HOME
90 GOSUB 210
100 ON A% GOTO 150, 120, 180
110 GOTO 70
120 PRINT:PRINT:PRINT "HA! HA!  I GUESSED YOUR NUMBER IN ONLY ";
130 PRINT C%;" TRIES"
140 END
150 RANGE.BOTTOM% = RANGE.MIDPOINT%
160 GOSUB 370
170 GOTO 80
180 RANGE.TOP% = RANGE.MIDPOINT%
190 GOSUB 420
200 GOTO 80
210 REM ************************************
220 REM *       DISPLAY SUBROUTINE         *
230 REM ************************************
240 PRINT TAB(30);"1.  GREATER THAN ";RANGE.MIDPOINT%
250 PRINT
260 PRINT "IS IT:";TAB(30);"2.  EQUAL TO ";RANGE.MIDPOINT%
270 PRINT
280 PRINT TAB(30);"3.  LESS THAN ";RANGE.MIDPOINT%
290 PRINT
300 PRINT "WHICH";
310 GET Z$
320 IF Z$ = "" THEN 310
330 IF VAL(Z$) > 3 OR VAL(Z$) < 1 THEN 310
340 A% = VAL(Z$)
350 C% = C% + 1
360 RETURN
370 REM ************************************
380 REM *      UPPER HALF SUBROUTINE       *
390 REM ************************************
400 RANGE.MIDPOINT% = (RANGE.MIDPOINT% + RANGE.TOP%)/2
410 RETURN
420 REM ************************************
430 REM *      LOWER HALF SUBROUTINE       *
440 REM ************************************
450 RANGE.MIDPOINT% = (RANGE.MIDPOINT% + RANGE.BOTTOM%)/2
460 RETURN
```

Figure 3.26.

develops a decimal (for example, half of 25 is 12.5), a specific position cannot be determined, and therefore a number cannot be selected from the list. To ensure that that does not happen (if the variable has not been defined as an integer), a new instruction is required – the INTeger instruction. The INTeger instruction selects only the whole number portion of a number, disregarding the decimal fraction. It may not be absolutely precise, but it suits the problem. The general format of the instruction is A = INT(B). In this particular program, you will become aware of the problem if you continue to answer the menu on the high side. After it reaches 99, it will go to 100 and stay there. The same is true on the low side, where it rests at zero.

Spend some time tracing the program through using data of your own choice. You'll find that it works not only for the upper half and the lower half, but also for the upper quarter of the lower half and the lower quarter of the upper half. Isn't that great? Terrific! Once that is accomplished, finding the number that you "dreamed up" is not difficult; in fact, you should find it within 18 tries. There are more sophisticated routines for "guessing the number," but this example illustrates the binary search principle. *You* might have been able to figure from 1 to 100, but suppose the range had been from 10,000 to 10,000,000. Things might have been a little more difficult.

HANDS ON THE TABLE

Taking the process a step further, this technique might be applied to searching a table for the presence of a number. Up to this point, an absolute match has been the goal. To search a number table, we must remember that the number may *or may not* be in the table and that it is our responsibility to determine the matter.

The first step, naturally, is to build a table. It is possible to take one from a data file (diskette or DATA lines), but even that would have to be built first. To illustrate the principle, we'll do a little simple construction. We'll *generate* our own table. Assume that the table consists of three elements – a stock number (in the range of 1 to 10,000), a description (which will be generated merely for illustrative purposes), and a quantity-on-hand (in the range of 1 to 10,000). Enter and run the little program of Figure 3.27.

```
10 HOME
20 FOR X = 1 TO 100
30      PRINT INT(RND(X) * 10000),;
40      NEXT X
50 END
```

Figure 3.27

In this example, the program generates 100 random numbers. The RND instruction generates a decimal value less than one; it is thus multiplied by a large value to place it into the integer (greater than 0) range. What is actually generated is the *integer* of a random number (RND(X)). The 10,000 multiplier places the number into the 1 to 10,000 range. The list of random numbers shown in Figure 3.28 was generated. Yours could be different.

```
1884     6005     5221     5323     5046
5947     725      6032     1268     3269
5197     6805     5343     6057     6459
6908     3585     6586     8489     8543
5898     2457     1929     2890     5520
6010     2912     5732     5103     9696
2547     2994     4552     143      8948
746      9710     7575     918      1503
6614     3590     8609     3178     1893
8981     229      5216     7874     8933
3683     298      9400     866      3981
1057     710      8567     4014     8788
8629     1091     5057     3049     4641
5340     5684     7162     9260     4568
6160     7099     4338     5343     3414
9349     798      5536     7134     5745
9541     5154     7492     4557     7172
6522     6816     423      8600     2690
6694     8688     6037     4918     8610
1562     7010     1407     7529     3430
```

Figure 3.28.

You'll note that since the random numbers do not appear in any specific sequence, it will be difficult to do a binary search. To be usable, they will have to be arranged in an ascending sequence. Before we do that, however, we need to develop an array (DIM INVENTORY.TABLE$(100,3)) into which we can store the item number, the description, and the quantity on hand. Because no calculation is done on these figures, the table is a string variable table, which means that the number generated by the table program must be changed somewhat. The program in Figure 3.29 is sufficient to generate and display the array and for us to build upon.

```
10 HOME
20 DIM INVENTORY.TABLE$(100,3)
30 '**********************************************
40 '*      THIS ROUTINE GENERATES THE TABLE      *
50 '**********************************************
60 FOR X = 1 TO 10
70      STOCK.NUMBER = INT(RND(X) * 10000)
80      INVENTORY.TABLE$(X,1) = STR$(STOCK.NUMBER)
90      INVENTORY.TABLE$(X.2) = "ITEM DESCRIPTION"
100     QUANTITY.ON.HAND = INT(RND(X) * 10000)
110     INVENTORY.TABLE$(X,3) = STR$(QUANTITY.ON.HAND
120 NEXT X
130 '**********************************************
140 '* THIS ROUTINE DISPLAYS THE GENERATED TABLE  *
150 '**********************************************
160 FOR X = 1 TO 10
170      PRINT INVENTORY.TABLE$(X,1);TAB(20);
180      PRINT INVENTORY.TABLE$(X,2);TAB(50);
190      PRINT INVENTORY.TABLE$(X,3)
200 NEXT X
```

Figure 3.29.

At this point, the really interesting things begin to happen. Recall that the premise of a binary search is that a table may or may not contain a stock number. As the table is presently constructed, such a search is impossible, since the table must be in *ascending order* on the *key field.* The key field is that field on which sequence is to be accomplished. In this case, it's the first of the three array elements: item number. Consequently, the table must be sorted.

Of the many ways to perform a sort, the easiest to construct and explain is called the *exchange sort.* The exchange sort is useful for small amounts of data, but should not be used for extensive files. Another type of sort, more useful to that purpose, is the *Shell-Metzner* Sort. The Shell-Metzner Sort will be explained later in the book.

The exchange sort examines array elements in pairs, changing the positions of each pair within the table such that the largest constituent of the pair is in the higher position within the array. In this manner, array element 1 (corresponding to array elements 1, 2, and 3, which contain the complete record) is compared with array element 4 (corresponding to array elements 4, 5, and 6 – the next record). In a multidimensioned array, we're really talking about (1,Y) being compared to (2,Y), and so on. If the second record is larger than the first record (a higher inventory number), or if it is equal, then nothing changes except that you are now able to compare the second and third pairs, and the process continues. In this instance, we'll not worry about eliminating duplicate table entries. If, on the other hand, the first record is larger than the second, the first record must be removed from the table and placed in a temporary work area, the second record must take over the space formerly occupied by the first record, and the first record must then be removed from the temporary work area and take over the space formerly occupied by the second record. Got that? The process can be simplified somewhat by the SWAP instruction, but we're not ready for that.

Just one more thing, and then we'll take the plunge. When you're sorting *and an exchange is made,* it is necessary to identify that it has, in fact, occurred. It is possible to exchange two numbers that are not only out of sequence *between themselves* but also out of sequence *within the entire set of numbers.* Thus we set an internal switch (often called a *flag*). The switch is set to "ON" or 1 when an exchange has been made. The program can then be told to continue through the list of data until the flag has not been set (no exchange

```
210 REM ***************************************************
220 REM * TERMINATE THE ARRAY WITH A SENTINEL; SET FLAG *
230 REM ***************************************************
240 FOR Y = 1 TO 3
250      INVENTORY.TABLE$(X,Y) = "ZZZZZ"
260      NEXT Y
270 FLAG$ = "OFF"
280 REM ***************************************************
290 REM *          EXCHANGE SORT THE ARRAY ROUTINE        *
300 REM ***************************************************
310 FOR X = 1 TO 100
320      IF INVENTORY.TABLE$(X,1) = "ZZZZZ" THEN 450
330      IF INVENTORY.TABLE$(X + 1,1) > = INVENTORY.TABLE$(X,1) THEN 440
340      TEMP.ITEM$ = INVENTORY.TABLE$(X,1)
350      TEMP.DESCRIPTION$ = INVENTORY.TABLE$(X,2)
360      TEMP.QUANTITY$ = INVENTORY.TABLE$(X,3)
370      INVENTORY.TABLE$(X,1) = INVENTORY.TABLE$(X + 1,1)
380      INVENTORY.TABLE$(X,2) = INVENTORY.TABLE$(X + 1,2)
390      INVENTORY.TABLE$(X,3) = INVENTORY.TABLE$(X + 1,3)
400      INVENTORY.TABLE$(X + 1,1) = TEMP.ITEM$
410      INVENTORY.TABLE$(X + 1,2) = TEMP.DESCRIPTION$
420      INVENTORY.TABLE$(X + 1,3) = TEMP.QUANTITY$
430      FLAG$ = "ON"
440      NEXT X
450 IF FLAG$ = "OFF" THEN 510
460 FLAG$ = "OFF"
470 GOTO 310
```

Figure 3.30.

has been made). When the program goes entirely through a table without making an exchange, then the table is in sequence. These procedures require additional program statements, as shown in Figure 3.30.

The flag is now set, the table is sealed with sentinels, and the sorting process begins as previously described. We now add the routine shown in Figure 3.31. Run it and you'll note something peculiar. There may be a stock number that is smaller than 1000 but nevertheless is left-justified in the number field. That's because we have treated this field as an alphabetic field, and alphabetic fields align to the *high order* (left-justified), whereas numeric fields align to the *low order* (right-justified). There are several ways to solve this problem, but since this is a demonstration program only, change statement 70 to look like Figure 3.32.

```
480 REM ***************************************************
490 REM *      THIS ROUTINE DISPLAYS THE SORTED TABLE      *
500 REM ***************************************************
510 PRINT
520 FOR X = 1 TO 10
530      PRINT INVENTORY.TABLE$(X,1);TAB(20);
540      PRINT INVENTORY.TABLE$(X,2);TAB(50);
550      PRINT INVENTORY.TABLE$(X,3)
560      NEXT X
570 END
```

Figure 3.31.

```
70      STOCK.NUMBER = INT(RND(X) * 10000):IF STOCK.NUMBER <1000 THEN 70
```

Figure 3.32.

Figure 3.33 shows the program in its entirety.

The exchange sort is not the fastest sort, as stated, but it is very effective and easily implemented. This particular example has been structured on the basis of 100 numbers. If the amount to be sorted is sufficiently large, it would be wise to add instructions to display the items sorted as they are being sorted, just so you are assured that something is happening. Again, the exchange sort should not be used for large files.

```
10 HOME
20 DIM INVENTORY.TABLE$(100,3)
30 REM **********************************************
40 REM *      THIS ROUTINE GENERATES THE TABLE       *
50 REM **********************************************
60 FOR X = 1 TO 10
70     STOCK.NUMBER = INT(RND(X) * 10000):IF STOCK.NUMBER <1000 THEN 70
80     INVENTORY.TABLE$(X,1) = STR$(STOCK.NUMBER)
90     INVENTORY.TABLE$(X.2) = "ITEM DESCRIPTION"
100    QUANTITY.ON.HAND = INT(RND(X) * 10000)
110    INVENTORY.TABLE$(X,3) = STR$(QUANTITY.ON.HAND
120    NEXT X
130 REM **********************************************
140 REM * THIS ROUTINE DISPLAYS THE GENERATED TABLE  *
150 REM **********************************************
160 FOR X = 1 TO 10
170     PRINT INVENTORY.TABLE$(X,1);TAB(20);
180     PRINT INVENTORY.TABLE$(X,2);TAB(50);
190     PRINT INVENTORY.TABLE$(X,3)
200     NEXT X
210 REM *************************************************
220 REM * TERMINATE THE ARRAY WITH A SENTINEL; SET FLAG *
230 REM *************************************************
240 FOR Y = 1 TO 3
250     INVENTORY.TABLE$(X,Y) = "ZZZZZ"
260     NEXT Y
270 FLAG$ = "OFF"
280 REM *************************************************
290 REM *        EXCHANGE SORT THE ARRAY ROUTINE        *
300 REM *************************************************
310 FOR X = 1 TO 100
320     IF INVENTORY.TABLE$(X,1) = "ZZZZZ" THEN 450
330     IF INVENTORY.TABLE$(X + 1,1) > = INVENTORY.TABLE$(X,1) THEN 440
340     TEMP.ITEM$ = INVENTORY.TABLE$(X,1)
350     TEMP.DESCRIPTION$ = INVENTORY.TABLE$(X,2)
360     TEMP.QUANTITY$ = INVENTORY.TABLE$(X,3)
370     INVENTORY.TABLE$(X,1) = INVENTORY.TABLE$(X + 1,1)
380     INVENTORY.TABLE$(X,2) = INVENTORY.TABLE$(X + 1,2)
390     INVENTORY.TABLE$(X,3) = INVENTORY.TABLE$(X + 1,3)
400     INVENTORY.TABLE$(X + 1,1) = TEMP.ITEM$
410     INVENTORY.TABLE$(X + 1,2) = TEMP.DESCRIPTION$
420     INVENTORY.TABLE$(X + 1,3) = TEMP.QUANTITY$
430     FLAG$ = "ON"
440     NEXT X
450 IF FLAG$ = "OFF" THEN 510
460 FLAG$ = "OFF"
470 GOTO 310
480 REM **************************************************
490 REM *     THIS ROUTINE DISPLAYS THE SORTED TABLE     *
500 REM **************************************************
510 PRINT
520 FOR X = 1 TO 10
530     PRINT INVENTORY.TABLE$(X,1);TAB(20);
540     PRINT INVENTORY.TABLE$(X,2);TAB(50);
550     PRINT INVENTORY.TABLE$(X,3)
560 NEXT X
570 END
```

Figure 3.33.

TABLE MAINTENANCE

The actual input/output with diskette is not complicated. We've generated data for a table and have sorted it. At this stage, the ability to write a table on diskette or to the printer in the form of a report is simply an interface step.

We will now concentrate, therefore, upon building a table directly from input entered at the keyboard and upon the routines needed to add to the table, delete from the table, change a table entry, sort it upon any data elements (using the exchange method), and report from it. Let's make a decision up front: Our inventory table will never exceed 100 items.

While we're at it, let's consider *all* the features that are necessary to table handling:

1. We must be able to add to the table, and do so in any sequence.
2. We must be able to change an entry already made to the table.
3. We must also be able to delete a table entry.
4. Simple inquiry facilities are needed. We might not want to make a second entry under the same control element.
5. A facility is needed to display and (upon selection of the option) to produce a hardcopy output of the table.
6. A facility is needed to sort the table in preparation for its storage on magnetic media.
7. Interfaces are needed to load the table *from* magnetic media and dump it *to* magnetic media.

As you might surmise, these requirements will produce a program of considerable size. The program now to be discussed has been developed in *modules.* If memory is a limiting factor to you, these modules must be selected and combined as necessity demands. The minimum Apple III memory size should be more than sufficient, however.

Figure 3.34 is a block diagram which identifies the elements of the Inventory Data Entry Program. The opening menu looks like Figure 3.35. The table is a 100 X 3 element array, organized as follows:

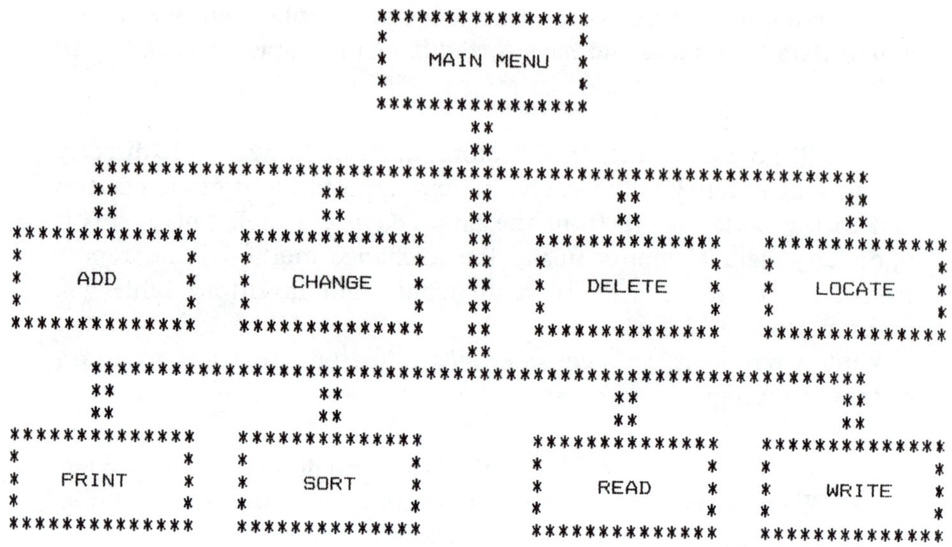

Figure 3.34.

```
I N V E N T O R Y   D A T A   E N T R Y

      A.  ADD DATA TO THE TABLE

      C.  CHANGE DATA ON THE TABLE

      D.  DELETE DATA FROM THE TABLE

      L.  LOCATE DATA (ITEM NUMBER)

      P.  PRINT (DISPLAY OR PAPER)

      S.  SORT THE TABLE

      R.  READ THE TABLE FROM MEDIA

      W.  WRITE THE TABLE TO MEDIA

      X.  TERMINATE THE PROGRAM
SELECT:
```

Figure 3.35.

Element 1 *4-position item code, alphanumeric:* If the number is to be numeric, it should be converted and tested before storage. This feature is not included in the program. Since the program provides acceptance features and modification capabilities, it was not necessary to do so.

Element 2 *35-position description, alphanumeric.*

Element 3 *4-position quantity-on-hand, alphanumeric:* Since this is strictly a data entry module and no calculation is to be made on this field, alphanumeric is used to simplify storage in the same array. Any enhancements that require calculations on this field will necessitate conversion to numeric.

Sentinel Five z's are loaded into each element at the end of the table. As the size of the table increases, the sentinels are moved forward. Displays of the table include the first sentinel.

PROGRAM DESCRIPTION

This is a data entry program only. It permits loading of a data array from the keyboard. Correction of data is offered both at entry and after the array has been loaded. Data may be deleted from the array. The program includes printing and sorting facilities as well as interfaces to read and write any media modules that may be added later.

Add Option

The program permits the addition of as many 3-element entries as necessary. On request, the program returns to the main menu to permit sorting or printing and correction or deletion before resuming acceptance of additional entries. No rejection is made of duplicate item numbers.

Change Option

The program permits display of a single array entry by key (item number). The operator is asked if the code is known. If the code is not known and the operator responds accordingly, the program returns to the main menu where the operator can obtain a display or list of the entire array. Once the key is known, the entry can be called out again and corrected.

Delete Option

As with the change option, and by the same procedure, once the key is known, an entry can be called out and deleted. The operator must confirm the deletion. Deletions are not actually removed from the array; they are merely changed to "/////" for removal in the sort module.

Locate Option

This is the inquiry module. The operator enters the key (item number), and the item is displayed if it is in the table. If it is not in the table, the program says so and returns to the main menu.

Print Option

This is simple output of data on the screen (by screen option) on hardcopy that is not formatted. It is accomplished 10 units at a time with a "go forward" mechanism.

Sort Option

This sort is an exchange sort on item number. Deleted entries are dropped since the array is copied to a work array without them. Sort completion invoices the main menu.

Read/Write Options

At this stage only the interfaces have been installed. The modules, to be completed, must be based upon similar illustrations from those chapters which deal with diskette operations.

Discussion

As the program is discussed, bear in mind that the statement numbers correspond to the location of the instruction in the completed program. The parts will be presented, not in sequence, but in terms of their logical relationship to the whole. We will first discuss the overheads.

OVERHEADS

The function of statements 10 to 170 is to make room for a large number of alphanumeric items and to establish the set-aside memory for screen display. These statements are given in Figure 3.36.

```
10 HOME
20 CLEAR
40 DIM SCREEN.LOCATOR(30,3)
50 FOR N = 1 TO 30
60      READ SCREEN.LOCATOR(N,1)
70      READ SCREEN.LOCATOR(N,2)
80      READ SCREEN.LOCATOR(N,3)
90      NEXT N
100 RESTORE
110 DIM INVENTORY.TABLE$(101,3)
120 FOR N = 1 TO 3                                :REM LOAD SENTINEL
130      INVENTORY.TABLE$(1,N) = "ZZZZZ"          :REM AT HEAD OF TABLE
140      NEXT N
150 DIM WORK.TABLE$(101,3)
160 ITEMS.LOADED = 1
170 GOSUB 610            :REM SCREEN FRAMING SUBROUTINE
```

Figure 3.36.

Because of the way memory is allocated, this program will use up the available string storage quite fast, depending upon the number of data entries made. There is a way around that memory usage, and when we get to the SWAP instruction, it will be evident. In the meantime, simply remember that the string storage is allocated every time something is moved, which in the sort module will be quite a bit. And after the move is made, BASIC releases the unused space. You can accelerate that with the FRE command.

Statements 50–90 collect the screen coordinates from the DATA statements, presented further into the text. Those screen coordinates will be used in other coding.

Statements 120 to 140 are the loading for the first three elements of the data array with the sentinel "ZZZZZ." Once we have begun to add data, this sentinel will be "slid along" to the second set of three, the third, and so on.

Because this program has a delete feature which merely changes the data being deleted to "/////," there must be some means to eradicate the deleted records. One way is to compress the table by scanning it and moving records up, overwriting the deleted records. It's a little easier to comprehend, however, when the data array (INVENTORY.TABLE$) is simply copied to a work array (WORK.TABLE$) *without* the deleted records. This is done in the SORT module.

And finally, since one item, the sentinel, had been located, we keep count of the ITEMS.LOADED, beginning in statement 160.

Because it *isn't* so very easy to mix graphics and text on the screen – and we'll get to graphics presently – we'll defer the use of graphics at this time. We will add graphics of a sort by simply placing borders and lines of asterisks, as shown in Figure 3.37.

Actually, this coding includes titles, headings, and border. Now for discussion, beginning with the screen frame subroutine.

- In statements 610 to 680, the asterisk graphics are placed on the screen in a tabular form.
- Thereafter, headings are placed with traditional positioning instructions.
- Statements 800–910 represent one way to clear screen lines. In this particular instance, a specific clearing routine is established, the clearing routine which will overlay the screen display with blanks. (This is one of two methods for clearing portions of a display screen. The other is presented in Figure 3.38.)
- Statements 920 to 1050 simply place a heading.

In addition, it is necessary to establish some overhead routines to clear entire screen lines and to generate full-length character lines. Those are shown in Figure 3.38. The CHR$(223) simply draws a line.

The third of the three routines opens the printer, prints the line, and then closes the printer. Remember that the printer functions as any other character device. Once the printer has been opened, any PRINT statement's output is destined to go to the hardcopy printer. Thus, it is necessary to open and close it with each usage.

```
610 REM ***********************************************
620 REM *           SCREEN FRAME SUBROUTINE           *
630 REM ***********************************************
640 FOR Y = 1 TO 24
650     VPOS=Y:HPOS=1
660     PRINT "*";TAB(20);"*";
670     PRINT TAB(60);"*";TAB(79);"*"
680     NEXT Y
690 VPOS=1
700 LINE.LENGTH = 79:GOSUB 5730
710 VPOS=2:HPOS=20
720 PRINT "I N V E N T O R Y   D A T A   E N T R Y          "
730 VPOS=3:HPOS=20
740 PRINT "                                                 "
750 VPOS=4
760 LINE.LENGTH = 79:GOSUB 5730
770 VPOS=24
780 LINE.LENGTH = 79:GOSUB 5730
790 RETURN
800 REM ***********************************************
810 REM *        CLEAR SCREEN FRAME SUBROUTINE        *
820 REM ***********************************************
830 FOR SCREEN.LINE = 6 TO 22
840     VPOS=SCREEN.LINE:HPOS=2
850     PRINT "      ";
860     VPOS=SCREEN.LINE:HPOS=22
870     PRINT "                                    ";
880     VPOS=SCREEN.LINE:HPOS=62
890     PRINT "        ";
900     NEXT SCREEN.LINE
910 RETURN
920 REM ***********************************************
930 REM *         SCREEN HEADING SUBROUTINE           *
940 REM ***********************************************
950 VPOS=6
960 LINE.LENGTH = 79:GOSUB 5730
970 VPOS=7:HPOS=5
980 PRINT "ITEM NUMBER"
990 VPOS=7:HPOS=35
1000 PRINT "DESCRIPTION"
1010 VPOS=7:HPOS=68
1020 PRINT "QUANTITY"
1030 VPOS=8
1040 LINE.LENGTH = 79:GOSUB 5730
1050 RETURN
```

Figure 3.37.

MENU MODULE

The menu selection module actually has begun above, with the screen clearing and framing. The concept of a menu display is to make the program as "user friendly" as possible. There are many facets of user friendliness, but one of them is always knowing what the options are.

```
5650 REM **************************
5660 REM * CLEAR THE LINE ROUTINE *
5670 REM **************************
5680 FOR Z = 1 TO 79
5690      HPOS = Z
5700      PRINT " ";
5710      NEXT Z
5720 RETURN
5730 REM *****************
5740 REM * GENERATE LINE *
5750 REM *****************
5760 FOR Z = 1 TO LINE.LENGTH
5760      HPOS = Z
5770      PRINT CHR$(223);
5780      NEXT HPOS
5790 RETURN
5800 REM ********************
5810 REM * HARDCOPY OPTION *
5820 REM ********************
5830 OPEN #1,".PRINTER"
5835 OUTPUT #1
5840 PRINT INVENTORY.TABLE$(X,Y)
5850 PRINT
5860 CLOSE #1
5870 RETURN
```

Figure 3.38.

This module displays the program's options: adding data to the table; changing data on the table; deleting data from the table; inquiring on table contents; printing on display or paper; and sorting the table. There is also an option to terminate the program. The menu portion of the program is given in Figure 3.39.

The whole concept of a menu is that you should select something from it. That something is given to the machine via the GET of instruction 450. There is a conversion of the entered code to a number in the instructions through 560, permitting a range check of permissible options in 570 and an ON ... GOSUB in 590. In actuality, the entire program is a series of subroutines, beginning with the Add module, next.

ADD MODULE

The add module is a fairly large module, relative to the size of the program itself. Its function is strictly to accept data, without editing, and add it to the array in the next available position. No attempt is made to rule out duplicates. It simply asks for an item number, a description, and a quantity. If it is acceptable, then it's filed away. If not, you're asked to provide the entry again.

```
180 REM **********************************************
190 REM *               OPTION SELECTION MENU        *
200 REM **********************************************
210 ERROR.MESSAGE$ = ""
220 GOSUB 5070           :REM ERROR MESSAGE SUBROUTINE
230 ERROR.MESSAGE$ = "PRESS 'X' TO TERMINATE THE PROGRAM"
240 GOSUB 5070           :REM ERROR MESSAGE SUBROUTINE
250 SCREEN.LINE = 6
260 SCREEN.COLUMN = 25
270 VPOS=SCREEN.LINE:HPOS=SCREEN.COLUMN
280 PRINT "A.  ADD DATA TO THE TABLE"
290 VPOS=SCREEN.LINE + 2:HPOS=SCREEN.COLUMN
300 PRINT "C.  CHANGE DATA ON THE TABLE"
310 VPOS=SCREEN.LINE + 4:HPOS=SCREEN.COLUMN
320 PRINT "D.  DELETE DATA FROM THE TABLE"
330 VPOS=SCREEN.LINE + 6:HPOS=SCREEN.COLUMN
340 PRINT "L.  LOCATE DATA (ITEM NUMBER)"
350 VPOS=SCREEN.LINE + 8:HPOS=SCREEN.COLUMN
360 PRINT "P.  PRINT (DISPLAY OR PAPER)"
370 VPOS=SCREEN.LINE + 10:HPOS=SCREEN.COLUMN
380 PRINT "S.  SORT THE TABLE"
390 VPOS=SCREEN.LINE + 12:HPOS=SCREEN.COLUMN
400 PRINT "R.  READ THE TABLE FROM MEDIA"
410 VPOS=SCREEN.LINE + 14:HPOS=SCREEN.COLUMN
420 PRINT "W.  WRITE THE TABLE TO MEDIA"
430 VPOS=SCREEN.LINE + 16:HPOS=SCREEN.COLUMN
440 PRINT "SELECT: ";
450 GET Z$
460 IF Z$ = "" THEN 450
470 IF Z$ = " " THEN 450
480 IF Z$ = "X" THEN PRINT Z$:END
490 IF Z$ = "A" THEN MENU.SELECTION = 1
500 IF Z$ = "C" THEN MENU.SELECTION = 2
510 IF Z$ = "D" THEN MENU.SELECTION = 3
520 IF Z$ = "L" THEN MENU.SELECTION = 4
530 IF Z$ = "P" THEN MENU.SELECTION = 5
540 IF Z$ = "S" THEN MENU.SELECTION = 6
550 IF Z$ = "R" THEN MENU.SELECTION = 7
560 IF Z$ = "W" THEN MENU.SELECTION = 8
570 IF (MENU.SELECTION < 1) OR (MENU.SELECTION > 8) THEN 450
580 PRINT Z$
590 ON MENU.SELECTION GOSUB 1060,1920,2890,3510,4070,4510,5530,5590
600 GOTO 170
```

Figure 3.39.

The module begins by formatting the screen and determining (statements 1100 to 1120) the size of the table (untouched or up to 101 positions). Refer to Figure 3.40.

The screen heading is prepared and then the data gathering begins (thirty elements – 10 lines of 3 elements each). In rapid succession you are asked for information, and then that information is presented, along with a verification question. If it is not verified, then the process is repeated. If it is verified, the array is loaded with the data and

```
1060 REM ************************************************
1070 REM *         TABLE ADDITION SUBROUTINE             *
1080 REM ************************************************
1090 IF INVENTORY.TABLE$(1,1) = "ZZZZZ" THEN 1150
1100 FOR X = 1 TO 101
1110      IF INVENTORY.TABLE$(X,1) = "ZZZZZ" THEN 1140
1120      NEXT X
1130 GOTO 1150
1140 ITEMS.LOADED = X
1150 GOSUB 800          :REM CLEAR OUT INSIDE OF FRAME
1160 GOSUB 920          :REM ADDITION HEADING
1170 VPOS=5:HPOS=20
1180 PRINT "TYPE 'STOP' UNDER ITEM TO TERMINATE ENTRY             "
1190 ERROR.MESSAGE$ = "TABLE ADDITION"
1200 GOSUB 5070         :REM ERROR MESSAGE SUBROUTINE
1210 GOSUB 5290         :REM CLEAR AND NUMBER LINES
1220 FIELDS.RECEIVED = 0
1230 FOR N = 1 TO 30
1240      LINE.NUMBER = SCREEN.LOCATOR(N,1)
1250      COLUMN.NUMBER = SCREEN.LOCATOR(N,2)
1260      DATA.LENGTH = SCREEN.LOCATOR(N,3)
1270      HOLD.LINE.NUMBER = LINE.NUMBER
1280      HOLD.COLUMN.NUMBER = COLUMN.NUMBER
1290      VPOS=LINE.NUMBER:HPOS=COLUMN.NUMBER
1300      A$ = ""
1310      GET Z$
1320      IF Z$ = "" THEN 1310
1330      HOLD.COLUMN.NUMBER = COLUMN.NUMBER
1340      PRINT Z$;
1350      A$ = A$ + Z$
1360      IF A$ = "STOP" THEN 1850
1370      IF LEN(A$) = DATA.LENGTH THEN 1400
1380      IF (Z$ = CHR$(13)) AND (LEN(A$) = 1) THEN GOSUB 1860:GOTO 1310
1390      IF (Z$ = CHR$(13)) AND (LEN(A$) > 1) THEN 1400 ELSE 1310
1400      FIELDS.RECEIVED = FIELDS.RECEIVED + 1
1410      IF FIELDS.RECEIVED = 1 THEN INVENTORY.TABLE$(ITEMS.LOADED,1) = A$
1420      IF FIELDS.RECEIVED = 2 THEN INVENTORY.TABLE$(ITEMS.LOADED,2) = A$
1430      IF FIELDS.RECEIVED = 3 THEN INVENTORY.TABLE$(ITEMS.LOADED,3) = A$
1440      INVENTORY.TABLE$(ITEMS.LOADED + 1,1) = "ZZZZZ"
1450      INVENTORY.TABLE$(ITEMS.LOADED + 1,2) = "ZZZZZ"
1460      INVENTORY.TABLE$(ITEMS.LOADED + 1,3) = "ZZZZZ"
1470      IF FIELDS.RECEIVED <> 3 THEN 1840
1480      FIELDS.RECEIVED = 0
1490      ERROR.MESSAGE$ = "ACCEPTABLE (Y/N)?"
1500      GOSUB 5070      :REM ERROR MESSAGE SUBROUTINE
1510      GET Z$:IF Z$ = "" THEN 1510
1520      IF Z$ = "N" THEN 1580
1530      IF Z$ < > "Y" THEN 1510
1540      ITEMS.LOADED = ITEMS.LOADED + 1
1550      ERROR.MESSAGE$ = ""
1560      GOSUB 5070      :REM ERROR MESSAGE SUBROUTINE
1570      GOTO 1840
1580      ERROR.MESSAGE$ = "ENTRY REJECTED"
1590      GOSUB 5070      :REM ERROR MESSAGE SUBROUTINE
1600      N = N - 2
1610      A1 = SCREEN.LOCATOR(N,1)
1620      A2 = SCREEN.LOCATOR(N,2)
1630      A3 = SCREEN.LOCATOR(N,3)
1640      B1 = SCREEN.LOCATOR(N + 1,1)
1650      B2 = SCREEN.LOCATOR(N + 1,2)
1660      B3 = SCREEN.LOCATOR(N + 1,3)
1670      C1 = SCREEN.LOCATOR(N + 2,1)
1680      C2 = SCREEN.LOCATOR(N + 2,2)
1690      C3 = SCREEN.LOCATOR(N + 2,3)
1700      VPOS=A1:HPOS=A2
```

Figure 3.40.

```
1710      FOR Z = 1 TO A3
1720          PRINT CHR$(223);
1730          NEXT Z
1740      VPOS=B1:HPOS=B2
1750      FOR Z = 1 TO B3
1760          PRINT CHR$(223);
1770          NEXT Z
1780      VPOS=C1:HPOS=C2
1790      FOR Z = 1 TO C3
1800          PRINT CHR$(223);
1810          NEXT Z
1820      FIELDS.RECEIVED = 0
1830      N = N - 1
1840      NEXT N
1850 RETURN
1860 ERROR.MESSAGE$ = "MANDATORY ENTRY"
1870 GOSUB 5070          :REM ERROR MESSAGE SUBROUTINE
1880 COLUMN.NUMBER = HOLD.COLUMN.NUMBER
1890 VPOS=LINE.NUMBER:HPOS=COLUMN.NUMBER
1900 A$ = ""
1910 RETURN
```

Figure 3.40. (continued)

the sentinels are pushed down the line one notch. The count is updated and you are asked if you wish to terminate the input. If you do, then you go back to the main menu. If you do not, then the module is repeated.

Note in the routine how information is concatenated using the variables A$ and Z$. The concatenation takes place one character entry at a time. When a CHR$(13) is received, the entry is complete, as CHR$(13) is the enter key.

CHANGE MODULE

The change routine, like the add routine, is lengthy. Much of that length is taken up by internal messages, the reason being that you are asked for the key (item number) and if you do not know it, you are directed back to the main menu so that you can review the entire contents of the array. If you know the key, the array is searched for it. If the key is not located within the array, you are so notified. The table change subroutine is given in Figure 3.41.

The idea of the change routine is not to have to retype a valid entry. Thus, you are told simply to press the RETURN key if an item is not to be changed. Therefore, each of the HOLD variables is reduced to null, and printing will be bypassed with the presence of a null.

```
1920 REM ************************************************
1930 REM *            TABLE CHANGE SUBROUTINE            *
1940 REM ************************************************
1950 A$ = "":B$ = "":C$ = ""
1960 IF ITEMS.LOADED > 1 THEN 2000
1970 ERROR.MESSAGE$ = "NO TABLE TO CHANGE"
1980 GOSUB 5070          :REM ERROR MESSAGE SUBROUTINE
1990 RETURN
2000 GOSUB 800           :REM CLEAR OUT INSIDE OF FRAME
2010 GOSUB 920           :REM HEADING SUBROUTINE
2020 ERROR.MESSAGE$ = "TABLE CHANGE"
2030 GOSUB 5070          :REM ERROR MESSAGE SUBROUTINE
2040 FOR Z = 1 TO 500:NEXT Z
2050 VPOS=10:HPOS=23
2060 PRINT "CHANGE WORKS ON ONE ELEMENT ONLY.";
2070 VPOS=12:HPOS=23
2080 PRINT "IF YOU KNOW THE ITEM NUMBER, THEN";
2090 VPOS=13:HPOS=23
2100 PRINT "ANSWER YES TO THE QUESTION.  IF";
2110 VPOS=14:HPOS=23
2120 PRINT "YOU DO NOT KNOW IT, ENTER PRINT";
2130 VPOS=15:HPOS=23
2140 PRINT "AT THE MAIN MENU, VPOS=THE ITEM";
2150 VPOS=16:HPOS=23
2160 PRINT "NUMBER AND COME BACK TO HERE."
2170 ERROR.MESSAGE$ = "DO YOU KNOW THE ITEM NUMBER (Y/N)?"
2180 GOSUB 5070          :REM ERROR MESSAGE SUBROUTINE
2190 GET Z$:IF Z$ = "" THEN 2190
2200 IF Z$ < > "Y" THEN RETURN
2210 ERROR.MESSAGE$ = "ENTER THE ITEM NUMBER: "
2220 GOSUB 5070          :REM ERROR MESSAGE SUBROUTINE
2230 GET Z$:IF Z$ = "" THEN 2230
2240 IF Z$ = CHR$(13) THEN 2290
2250 A$ = A$ + Z$
2260 ERROR.MESSAGE$ = "ITEM NUMBER: " + A$
2270 GOSUB 5070          :REM ERROR MESSAGE SUBROUTINE
2280 GOTO 2230
2290 FOR X = 1 TO 101
2300     IF INVENTORY.TABLE$(X,1) = A$ THEN 2360
2310     IF INVENTORY.TABLE$(X,1) = "ZZZZZ" THEN 2330
2320     NEXT X
2330 ERROR.MESSAGE$ = "ITEM NOT ON TABLE"
2340 GOSUB 5070          :REM ERROR MESSAGE SUBROUTINE
2350 RETURN
2360 GOSUB 800           :REM CLEAR INSIDE OF FRAME
2370 GOSUB 920           :REM HEADING SUBROUTINE
2380 VPOS=10:HPOS=8
2390 PRINT INVENTORY.TABLE$(X,1);
2400 VPOS=10:HPOS=23
2410 PRINT INVENTORY.TABLE$(X,2);
2420 VPOS=10:HPOS=65
2430 PRINT INVENTORY.TABLE$(X,3);
2440 ERROR.MESSAGE$ = "CORRECT RECORD (Y/N)?"
2450 GOSUB 5070
2460 GET Z$:IF Z$ = "" THEN 2460
2470 IF Z$ < > "Y" THEN RETURN
```

Figure 3.41.

```
2480 VPOS=12:HPOS=8
2490 PRINT "____";
2500 VPOS=12:HPOS=23
2510 PRINT "___________________________________";
2520 VPOS=12:HPOS=65
2530 PRINT "____";
2540 A$ = "":B$ = "":C$ = ""
2550 ERROR.MESSAGE$ = "ENTER THE CORRECTED ITEM - ALL ELEMENTS"
2560 GOSUB 5070            :REM ERROR MESSAGE SUBROUTINE
2570 VPOS=12:HPOS=8
2580 GET Z$:IF Z$ = "" THEN 2580
2590 IF Z$ = CHR$(13) THEN 2640
2600 PRINT Z$;
2610 A$ = A$ + Z$
2620 IF LEN(A$) = 4 THEN 2640
2630 GOTO 2580
2640 VPOS=12:HPOS=23
2650 GET Z$:IF Z$ = "" THEN 2650
2660 PRINT Z$;
2670 IF Z$ = CHR$(13) THEN 2710
2680 B$ = B$ + Z$
2690 IF LEN(B$) = 35 THEN 2710
2700 GOTO 2650
2710 VPOS=12:HPOS=65
2720 GET Z$:IF Z$ = "" THEN 2720
2730 IF Z$ = CHR$(13) THEN 2780
2740 PRINT Z$;
2750 C$ = C$ + Z$
2760 IF LEN(C$) = 4 THEN 2780
2770 GOTO 2720
2780 ERROR.MESSAGE$ = "IS THE CORRECTION CORRECT (Y/N)?"
2790 GOSUB 5070            :REM ERROR MESSAGE SUBROUTINE
2800 GET Z$:IF Z$ = "" THEN 2800
2810 IF Z$ = "N" THEN 2480
2820 IF Z$ < > "Y" THEN 2800
2830 INVENTORY.TABLE$(X,1) = A$
2840 INVENTORY.TABLE$(X,2) = B$
2850 INVENTORY.TABLE$(X,3) = C$
2860 ERROR.MESSAGE$ = "CORRECTED RECORD RE-FILED INTO THE ARRAY"
2870 GOSUB 5070            :REM ERROR MESSAGE SUBROUTINE
2880 RETURN
```

Figure 3.41. (continued)

The data is presented in specific locations on the screen and made available under program control for modification. Once verified, the data is represented for acceptance. Note again how concatenation is used.

DELETION MODULE

There are two schools of thought about designing a deletion module. The first involves total removal of the record and compression of the

```
2890 REM ****************************************************
2900 REM *           TABLE DELETION SUBROUTINE               *
2910 REM ****************************************************
2920 A$ = ""
2930 IF ITEMS.LOADED > 1 THEN 2970
2940 ERROR.MESSAGE$ = "NO TABLE TO DELETE"
2950 GOSUB 5070          :REM ERROR MESSAGE SUBROUTINE
2960 RETURN
2970 GOSUB 800            :REM CLEAR OUT INSIDE OF FRAME
2980 GOSUB 920            :REM HEADING SUBROUTINE
2990 ERROR.MESSAGE$ = "TABLE DELETE"
3000 GOSUB 5070           :REM ERROR MESSAGE SUBROUTINE
3010 FOR Z = 1 TO 500:     NEXT Z
3020 VPOS=10:HPOS=23
3030 PRINT "DELETE WORKS ON ONE ELEMENT ONLY.";
3040 VPOS=12:HPOS=23
3050 PRINT "IF YOU KNOW THE ITEM NUMBER, THEN";
3060 VPOS=13:HPOS=23
3070 PRINT "ANSWER YES TO THE QUESTION.  IF";
3080 VPOS=14:HPOS=23
3090 PRINT "YOU DO NOT KNOW IT, ENTER PRINT";
3100 VPOS=15:HPOS=23
3110 PRINT "AT THE MAIN MENU, VPOS=THE ITEM";
3120 VPOS=16:HPOS=23
3130 PRINT "NUMBER AND COME BACK TO HERE."
3140 ERROR.MESSAGE$ = "DO YOU KNOW THE ITEM NUMBER (Y/N)?"
3150 GOSUB 5070           :REM ERROR MESSAGE SUBROUTINE
3160 GET Z$:IF Z$ = "" THEN 3160
3170 IF Z$ < > "Y" THEN RETURN
3180 ERROR.MESSAGE$ = "ENTER THE ITEM NUMBER: "
3190 GOSUB 5070           :REM ERROR MESSAGE SUBROUTINE
3200 GET Z$:IF Z$ = "" THEN 3200
3210 IF Z$ = CHR$(13) THEN 3260
3220 A$ = A$ + Z$
3230 ERROR.MESSAGE$ = "ITEM NUMBER: " + A$
3240 GOSUB 5070           :REM ERROR MESSAGE SUBROUTINE
3250 GOTO 3200
3260 FOR X = 1 TO 1001
3270     IF INVENTORY.TABLE$(X,1) = A$ THEN 3330
3280     IF INVENTORY.TABLE$(X,1) = "ZZZZZ" THEN 3300
3290     NEXT X
3300 ERROR.MESSAGE$ = "ITEM NOT ON TABLE"
3310 GOSUB 5070           :REM ERROR MESSAGE SUBROUTINE
3320 RETURN
3330 GOSUB 800            :REM CLEAR INSIDE OF FRAME
3340 GOSUB 920            :REM HEADING SUBROUTINE
3350 VPOS=10:HPOS=8
3360 PRINT INVENTORY.TABLE$(X,1);
3370 VPOS=10:HPOS=23
3380 PRINT INVENTORY.TABLE$(X,2);
3390 VPOS=10:HPOS=65
3400 PRINT INVENTORY.TABLE$(X,3);
3410 ERROR.MESSAGE$ = "CORRECT RECORD (Y/N)?"
3420 GOSUB 5070           :REM ERROR MESSAGE SUBROUTINE
3430 GET Z$:IF Z$ = "" THEN 3430
3440 IF Z$ < > "Y" THEN 2970
3450 INVENTORY.TABLE$(X,1) = "/////"
3460 INVENTORY.TABLE$(X,2) = "/////"
3470 INVENTORY.TABLE$(X,3) = "/////"
3480 ERROR.MESSAGE$ = "RECORD DELETED FROM THE ARRAY"
3490 GOSUB 5070           :REM ERROR MESSAGE SUBROUTINE
3500 RETURN
```

Figure 3.42.

table at the same time the record is removed. The second involves "flagging" that record for removal at some more convenient time. The latter alternative has been chosen for this example.

Within that choice lie two schools of thought, as well. Either the record can be flagged in a special flagging position, leaving it identifiable, or the record can be totally destroyed by the flagging. Again, the second approach has been selected. We're trying to acquaint you with the process and how the machine works – *not* make super-sophisticated programers of you.

As in the change routine, the operator is asked if the key of the record is known. If the key is not known, the program returns to the main menu so that you can choose whether to display or print the table. If the item number is known, the record is presented for confirmation of the deletion. If the confirmation is not forthcoming, the process is repeated. If the deletion is confirmed, each element of the record is overlaid with five slashes (/////), and the operator is alerted that the record has been deleted. The actual removal of the deleted record does not take place until the sort module.

The deletion module is shown in Figure 3.42.

INQUIRY MODULE

The inquiry module – or table location module as it's called in the program – is a simple sequential key search. The operator is asked for the key, as before, and the table is searched on the assumption that the operator is merely trying to determine whether the key is located in the table so that he can enter it. If the key is already in the table, there is a duplicate key situation, and you do not wish to have two records on file with the same identifying information.

If the key is on the file, the entry is displayed. If the key is not on file, the operator is notified of that fact, as well. If the record is displayed, the program is set up to freeze the display until the operator releases it.

The inquiry module is given in Figure 3.43.

PRINTING MODULE

The printing module *always* displays the array contents and will also, at your option, produce a hardcopy printout of the array. Because

```
3510 REM ***********************************************
3520 REM *        TABLE LOCATION SUBROUTINE            *
3530 REM ***********************************************
3540 A$ = ""
3550 IF ITEMS.LOADED > 1 THEN 3590
3560 ERROR.MESSAGE$ = "NO TABLE TO QUERY"
3570 GOSUB 5070          :REM ERROR MESSAGE SUBROUTINE
3580 RETURN
3590 GOSUB 800            :REM CLEAR OUT INSIDE OF FRAME
3600 GOSUB 920            :REM HEADING SUBROUTINE
3610 ERROR.MESSAGE$ = "TABLE INQUIRY"
3620 GOSUB 5070           :REM ERROR MESSAGE SUBROUTINE
3630 FOR Z = 1 TO 500:NEXT Z
3640 VPOS=10:HPOS=23
3650 PRINT "LOCATE WORKS ON ONE ELEMENT ONLY.";
3660 VPOS=12:HPOS=23
3670 PRINT "IF YOU KNOW THE ITEM NUMBER, THEN";
3680 VPOS=13:HPOS=23
3690 PRINT "ANSWER YES TO THE QUESTION.  IF";
3700 VPOS=14:HPOS=23
3710 PRINT "YOU DO NOT KNOW IT, ENTER PRINT";
3720 VPOS=15:HPOS=23
3730 PRINT "AT THE MAIN MENU, LOCATE THE ITEM";
3740 VPOS=16:HPOS=23
3750 PRINT "NUMBER AND COME BACK TO HERE."
3760 ERROR.MESSAGE$ = "DO YOU KNOW THE ITEM NUMBER(Y/N)?"
3770 GOSUB 5070           :REM ERROR MESSAGE SUBROUTINE
3780 GET Z$:IF Z$ = "" THEN 3780
3790 IF Z$ < > "Y" THEN RETURN
3800 ERROR.MESSAGE$ =  "ENTER THE ITEM NUMBER: "
3810 GOSUB 5070           :REM ERROR MESSAGE SUBROUTINE
3820 GET Z$:IF Z$ = "" THEN 3820
3830 IF Z$ = CHR$(13) THEN 3880
3840 A$ = A$ + Z$
3850 ERROR.MESSAGE$ = "ITEM NUMBER: " + A$
3860 GOSUB 5070           :REM ERROR MESSAGE SUBROUTINE
3870 GOTO 3820
3880 FOR X = 1 TO 1001
3890     IF INVENTORY.TABLE$(X,1) = A$ THEN 3950
3900     IF INVENTORY.TABLE$(X,1) = "ZZZZZ" THEN 3920
3910     NEXT X
3920 ERROR.MESSAGE$ = "ITEM NOT ON TABLE"
3930 GOSUB 5070           :REM ERROR MESSAGE SUBROUTINE
3940 RETURN
3950 GOSUB 800            :REM CLEAR INSIDE OF FRAME
3960 GOSUB 920            :REM HEADING SUBROUTINE
3970 VPOS=10:HPOS=8
3980 PRINT INVENTORY.TABLE$(X,1);
3990 VPOS=10:HPOS=23
4000 PRINT INVENTORY.TABLE$(X,2);
4010 VPOS=10:HPOS=65
4020 PRINT INVENTORY.TABLE$(X,3);
4030 ERROR.MESSAGE$ = "PRESS ANY KEY TO CONTINUE"
4040 GOSUB 5070           :REM ERROR MESSAGE SUBROUTINE
4050 GET Z$:IF Z$ = "" THEN 4050
4060 RETURN
```

Figure 3.43.

of the means whereby the screen must be formatted, ten elements are formatted at a time.

If the hardcopy option has been selected, each of those ten prints before the display is made. This was the selection of a choice of options which would have required a second pass through the same data had it not been chosen to print as the display was being formatted. Further, the requirements of the APPLE III for printer output place the need to open and close the printer file with each line to be printed. Separation of those functions could have removed that restraint.

For the moment, simply continue paging through until the sentinel is located. Assuming that you completely fill the array, which you may not, that's but 10 taps on the space bar (or any key).

The printing module is shown in Figure 3.44.

```
4070 REM ************************************************
4080 REM *          TABLE PRINT SUBROUTINE              *
4090 REM ************************************************
4100 LINECOUNT = 0
4110 IF ITEMS.LOADED > 1 THEN 4150
4120 ERROR.MESSAGE$ = "NO TABLE TO PRINT"
4130 GOSUB 5070          :REM ERROR MESSAGE SUBROUTINE
4140 GOTO 4440
4150 GOSUB 800           :REM CLEAR OUT INSIDE OF FRAME
4160 GOSUB 920           :REM HEADING SUBROUTINE
4170 ERROR.MESSAGE$ = "TABLE PRINT - HARDCOPY (Y/N)?"
4180 GOSUB 5070          :REM ERROR MESSAGE SUBROUTINE
4190 GET Z$:IF Z$ = "" THEN 4190
4200 IF Z$ = "Y" THEN HARDCOPY = 1:GOTO 4220
4210 IF Z$ = "N" THEN HARDCOPY = 0:GOTO 4230
4220 ERROR.MESSAGE$ = "HARDCOPY REQUESTED":GOTO 4240
4230 ERROR.MESSAGE$ = "HARDCOPY NOT REQUESTED"
4240 GOSUB 5070          :REM ERROR MESSAGE SUBROUTINE
4250 GOSUB 5290          :REM LOAD NUMBERS AND LINES
4260 N = 1
4270 FOR X = 1 TO 101
4280      Y = 1
4290      LINE.NUMBER = SCREEN.LOCATOR(N,1)
4300      COLUMN.NUMBER = SCREEN.LOCATOR(N,2)
4310      VPOS=LINE.NUMBER:HPOS=COLUMN.NUMBER
4320      PRINT INVENTORY.TABLE$(X,Y);
4330      IF HARDCOPY = 1 THEN GOSUB 5800
4340      IF INVENTORY.TABLE$(X,Y) = "ZZZZZ" THEN GOTO 4450
4350      LINECOUNT = LINECOUNT + 1
4360      IF LINECOUNT = 30 THEN LINECOUNT = 0:GOTO 4450
4370      N = N + 1
4380      IF N = 31 THEN N = 1
4390      IF Y = 3 THEN Y = 0:GOTO 4430
4400      Y = Y + 1
```

Figure 3.44.

```
4410      GOTO 4290
4430      NEXT X
4440 RETURN
4450 ERROR.MESSAGE$ = "PRESS ANY KEY TO CONTINUE - PRESS 'X' TO ABORT"
4460 GOSUB 5070          :REM ERROR MESSAGE SUBROUTINE
4470 IF Z$ = "X" THEN 4440
4480 GET Z$:IF Z$ = "" THEN 4480
4490 IF INVENTORY.TABLE$(X,Y) = "ZZZZZ" THEN 4440
4500 GOTO 4370
```

Figure 3.44. (continued)

SORT MODULE

The final module to be discussed is the sort module, which employs the exchange method of sorting previously discussed.

In the sort module, deleted records are dropped by copying INVENTORY.TABLE$ (which contains the deleted records) to a temporary array (WORK.TABLE$) and bypassing the slashed (deleted) records in the process. The purged array is then copied back to the original array, and the sorting process continues. You are advised by messages of Phase I (Compression), Phase II (Recopy), and Phase III (Sorting). You are also apprised when an exchange has been made. The idea is to keep you aware that something is happening. The longer the table is; the more out of sequence it is, the longer the sort time. That time could seem lengthy if you weren't certain that the sort was working properly.

If an exchange is made, a flag (switch) is turned on. After each pass through the array, the flag is checked. If it is on, an exchange has been made, it is turned off, and another pass must be taken. After a pass has been taken, if the flag remains off, the table is in sequence.

The sort module is shown in Figure 3.45.

```
4510 REM **********************************************
4520 REM *            TABLE SORT SUBROUTINE            *
4530 REM **********************************************
4540 IF ITEMS.LOADED > 1 THEN 4590
4550 A$ = ""
4560 ERROR.MESSAGE$ = "NO TABLE TO SORT"
4570 GOSUB 5070          :REM ERROR MESSAGE SUBROUTINE
4580 RETURN
4590 GOSUB 800           :REM CLEAR OUT INSIDE OF FRAME
4600 GOSUB 920           :REM HEADING SUBROUTINE
```

Figure 3.45.

```
4610 ERROR.MESSAGE$ = "TABLE SORT"
4620 GOSUB 5070           :REM ERROR MESSAGE SUBROUTINE
4630 BUMP = 1
4640 FOR X = 1 TO 101
4650      IF INVENTORY.TABLE$(X,1) = "/////" THEN 4730
4660      WORK.TABLE$(BUMP,1) = INVENTORY.TABLE$(X,1)
4670      WORK.TABLE$(BUMP,2) = INVENTORY.TABLE$(X,2)
4680      WORK.TABLE$(BUMP,3) = INVENTORY.TABLE$(X,3)
4690      IF INVENTORY.TABLE$(X,1) = "ZZZZZ" THEN 4740
4700      BUMP = BUMP + 1
4710      VPOS=10:HPOS=23
4720      PRINT "COMPRESSING THE TABLE";
4730      NEXT X
4740 FOR X = 1 TO 101
4750      INVENTORY.TABLE$(X,1) = WORK.TABLE$(X,1)
4760      INVENTORY.TABLE$(X,2) = WORK.TABLE$(X,2)
4770      INVENTORY.TABLE$(X,3) = WORK.TABLE$(X,3)
4780      IF WORK.TABLE$(X,1) = "ZZZZZ" THEN 4820
4790      VPOS=10:HPOS=23
4800      PRINT "COPYING THE TABLE";"            ";
4810      NEXT X
4820 FOR X = 1 TO 101
4830      VPOS=10:HPOS=23
4840      PRINT "SORTING: ";INVENTORY.TABLE$(X,1);"             ";
4850      IF INVENTORY.TABLE$(X,1) = "ZZZZZ" THEN 5000
4860      IF INVENTORY.TABLE$(X + 1,1) > = INVENTORY.TABLE$(X,1) THEN 4990
4870      TEMP.ITEM$ = INVENTORY.TABLE$(X,1)
4880      TEMP.DESCRIPTION$ = INVENTORY.TABLE$(X,2)
4890      TEMP.QUANTITY$ = INVENTORY.TABLE$(X,3)
4900      INVENTORY.TABLE$(X,1) = INVENTORY.TABLE$(X + 1,1)
4910      INVENTORY.TABLE$(X,2) = INVENTORY.TABLE$(X + 1,2)
4920      INVENTORY.TABLE$(X,3) = INVENTORY.TABLE$(X + 1,3)
4930      INVENTORY.TABLE$(X + 1,1) = TEMP.ITEM$
4940      INVENTORY.TABLE$(X + 1,2) = TEMP.DESCRIPTION$
4950      INVENTORY.TABLE$(X + 1,3) = TEMP.QUANTITY$
4960      FLAG$ = "ON"
4970      VPOS=10:HPOS=23
4980      PRINT "          ";
4990      NEXT X
5000 IF FLAG$ = "OFF" THEN 5030
5010 FLAG$ = "OFF"
5020 GOTO 4820
5030 ERROR.MESSAGE$ = "SORT COMPLETE"
5040 GOSUB 5070           :REM ERROR MESSAGE SUBROUTINE
5050 GOSUB 4240           :REM JUMP INTO MIDDLE OF PRINT ROUTINE
```

Figure 3.45. (continued)

MORE OVERHEADS

Figure 3.46 shows those other overheads which are required to make the program work – the error message subroutine, the screen line numbers, and the screen coordinates.

MEDIA MODULES

As mentioned before, we will delay discussion of the media options until we have had the opportunity to discuss diskette usage at length.

```
5070 REM ***********************************************
5080 REM *              ERROR MESSAGE SUBROUTINE       *
5090 REM ***********************************************
5100 PRINT CHR$(7)
5110 VPOS=25:GOSUB 5650
5120 HPOS=1
5130 PRINT ERROR.MESSAGE$;
5140 RETURN
5150 REM ***********************************************
5160 REM *    SCREEN COORDINATES FOR LOAD AND CHANGE   *
5170 REM ***********************************************
5180 DATA 10,8,4,10,23,35,10,65,4
5190 DATA 11,8,4,11,23,35,11,65,4
5200 DATA 12,8,4,12,23,35,12,65,4
5210 DATA 13,8,4,13,23,35,13,65,4
5220 DATA 14,8,4,14,23,35,14,65,4
5230 DATA 15,8,4,15,23,35,15,65,4
5240 DATA 16,8,4,16,23,35,16,65,4
5250 DATA 17,8,4,17,23,35,17,65,4
5260 DATA 18,8,4,18,23,35,18,65,4
5270 DATA 19,8,4,19,23,35,19,65,4
5280 DATA 99999,99999,99999
5290 REM ***********************************************
5300 REM *     SCREEN LINE NUMBERS AND BLANK LINES     *
5310 REM ***********************************************
5320 VPOS=10:HPOS=4:PRINT " 1.";
5330 VPOS=11:PRINT " 2.";
5340 VPOS=12:PRINT " 3.";
5350 VPOS=13:PRINT " 4.";
5360 VPOS=14:PRINT " 5.";
5370 VPOS=15:PRINT " 6.";
5380 VPOS=16:PRINT " 7.";
5390 VPOS=17:PRINT " 8.";
5400 VPOS=18:PRINT " 9.";
5410 VPOS=19:PRINT "10.";
5420 RESTORE
5430 FOR N = 1 TO 30
5440     READ LINE.NUMBER,COLUMN.NUMBER,SHADE.LENGTH
5450     VPOS=LINE.NUMBER:HPOS=COLUMN.NUMBER
5460     FOR Z = 1 TO SHADE.LENGTH
5470         PRINT CHR$(223);
5480         NEXT Z
5490     NEXT N
5500 PRINT CHR$(7)
5510 RESTORE
5520 RETURN
```

Figure 3.46.

That discussion would be a bit much at this stage. The media interfaces are included, as given in Figure 3.47, but since they merely advise the operator that the module is not installed at this time, they are of little value other than for documentation.

```
5530 REM ************************************************
5540 REM *          READ FROM MEDIA SUBROUTINE          *
5550 REM ************************************************
5560 ERROR.MESSAGE$ = "MODULE NOT INSTALLED AT THIS TIME"
5570 GOSUB 5070          'ERROR MESSAGE SUBROUTINE
5580 RETURN
5590 REM ************************************************
5600 REM *          WRITE TO MEDIA SUBROUTINE           *
5610 REM ************************************************
5620 ERROR.MESSAGE$ = "MODULE NOT INSTALLED AT THIS TIME"
5630 GOSUB 5070          'ERROR MESSAGE SUBROUTINE
5640 RETURN
```

Figure 3.47.

THE COMPLETE PROGRAM

The program in its entirety is given in Figure 3.48.

```
10 HOME
20 CLEAR
40 DIM SCREEN.LOCATOR(30,3)
50 FOR N = 1 TO 30
60     READ SCREEN.LOCATOR(N,1)
70     READ SCREEN.LOCATOR(N,2)
80     READ SCREEN.LOCATOR(N,3)
90     NEXT N
100 RESTORE
110 DIM INVENTORY.TABLE$(101,3)
120 FOR N = 1 TO 3                              :REM LOAD SENTINEL
130     INVENTORY.TABLE$(1,N) = "ZZZZZ"         :REM AT HEAD OF TABLE
140     NEXT N
150 DIM WORK.TABLE$(101,3)
160 ITEMS.LOADED = 1
170 GOSUB 610            :REM SCREEN FRAMING SUBROUTINE
180 REM ************************************************
190 REM *          OPTION SELECTION MENU               *
200 REM ************************************************
210 ERROR.MESSAGE$ = ""
220 GOSUB 5070           :REM ERROR MESSAGE SUBROUTINE
230 ERROR.MESSAGE$ = "PRESS 'X' TO TERMINATE THE PROGRAM"
240 GOSUB 5070           :REM ERROR MESSAGE SUBROUTINE
250 SCREEN.LINE = 6
260 SCREEN.COLUMN = 25
270 VPOS=SCREEN.LINE:HPOS=SCREEN.COLUMN
280 PRINT "A.  ADD DATA TO THE TABLE"
290 VPOS=SCREEN.LINE + 2:HPOS=SCREEN.COLUMN
300 PRINT "C.  CHANGE DATA ON THE TABLE"
310 VPOS=SCREEN.LINE + 4:HPOS=SCREEN.COLUMN
320 PRINT "D.  DELETE DATA FROM THE TABLE"
330 VPOS=SCREEN.LINE + 6:HPOS=SCREEN.COLUMN
340 PRINT "L.  LOCATE DATA (ITEM NUMBER)"
350 VPOS=SCREEN.LINE + 8:HPOS=SCREEN.COLUMN
360 PRINT "P.  PRINT (DISPLAY OR PAPER)"
370 VPOS=SCREEN.LINE + 10:HPOS=SCREEN.COLUMN
380 PRINT "S.  SORT THE TABLE"
390 VPOS=SCREEN.LINE + 12:HPOS=SCREEN.COLUMN
400 PRINT "R.  READ THE TABLE FROM MEDIA"
410 VPOS=SCREEN.LINE + 14:HPOS=SCREEN.COLUMN
```

Figure 3.48.

```
420 PRINT "W.  WRITE THE TABLE TO MEDIA"
430 VPOS=SCREEN.LINE + 16:HPOS=SCREEN.COLUMN
440 PRINT "SELECT: ";
450 GET Z$
460 IF Z$ = "" THEN 450
470 IF Z$ = " " THEN 450
480 IF Z$ = "X" THEN PRINT Z$:END
490 IF Z$ = "A" THEN MENU.SELECTION = 1
500 IF Z$ = "C" THEN MENU.SELECTION = 2
510 IF Z$ = "D" THEN MENU.SELECTION = 3
520 IF Z$ = "L" THEN MENU.SELECTION = 4
530 IF Z$ = "P" THEN MENU.SELECTION = 5
540 IF Z$ = "S" THEN MENU.SELECTION = 6
550 IF Z$ = "R" THEN MENU.SELECTION = 7
560 IF Z$ = "W" THEN MENU.SELECTION = 8
570 IF (MENU.SELECTION < 1) OR (MENU.SELECTION > 8) THEN 450
580 PRINT Z$
590 ON MENU.SELECTION GOSUB 1060,1920,2890,3510,4070,4510,5530,5590
600 GOTO 170
610 REM ***********************************************
620 REM *           SCREEN FRAME SUBROUTINE           *
630 REM ***********************************************
640 FOR Y = 1 TO 24
650     VPOS=Y:HPOS=1
660     PRINT "*";TAB(20);"*";
670     PRINT TAB(60);"*";TAB(79);"*"
680     NEXT Y
690 VPOS=1
700 LINE.LENGTH = 79:GOSUB 5730
710 VPOS=2:HPOS=20
720 PRINT "I N V E N T O R Y   D A T A   E N T R Y
730 VPOS=3:HPOS=20
740 PRINT "
750 VPOS=4
760 LINE.LENGTH = 79:GOSUB 5730
770 VPOS=24
780 LINE.LENGTH = 79:GOSUB 5730
790 RETURN
800 REM ***********************************************
810 REM *       CLEAR SCREEN FRAME SUBROUTINE         *
820 REM ***********************************************
830 FOR SCREEN.LINE = 6 TO 22
840     VPOS=SCREEN.LINE:HPOS=2
850     PRINT "      ";
860     VPOS=SCREEN.LINE:HPOS=22
870     PRINT "
880     VPOS=SCREEN.LINE:HPOS=62
890     PRINT "       ";
900     NEXT SCREEN.LINE
910 RETURN
920 REM ***********************************************
930 REM *         SCREEN HEADING SUBROUTINE           *
940 REM ***********************************************
950 VPOS=6
960 LINE.LENGTH = 79:GOSUB 5730
970 VPOS=7:HPOS=5
980 PRINT "ITEM NUMBER"
990 VPOS=7:HPOS=35
1000 PRINT "DESCRIPTION"
1010 VPOS=7:HPOS=68
1020 PRINT "QUANTITY"
1030 VPOS=8
1040 LINE.LENGTH = 79:GOSUB 5730
1050 RETURN
```

Figure 3.48. (continued)

```
1060 REM **********************************************
1070 REM *          TABLE ADDITION SUBROUTINE         *
1080 REM **********************************************
1090 IF INVENTORY.TABLE$(1,1) = "ZZZZZ" THEN 1150
1100 FOR X = 1 TO 101
1110      IF INVENTORY.TABLE$(X,1) = "ZZZZZ" THEN 1140
1120      NEXT X
1130 GOTO 1150
1140 ITEMS.LOADED = X
1150 GOSUB 800             :REM CLEAR OUT INSIDE OF FRAME
1160 GOSUB 920             :REM ADDITION HEADING
1170 VPOS=5:HPOS=20
1180 PRINT "TYPE 'STOP' UNDER ITEM TO TERMINATE ENTRY
1190 ERROR.MESSAGE$ = "TABLE ADDITION"
1200 GOSUB 5070            :REM ERROR MESSAGE SUBROUTINE
1210 GOSUB 5290            :REM CLEAR AND NUMBER LINES
1220 FIELDS.RECEIVED = 0
1230 FOR N = 1 TO 30
1240      LINE.NUMBER = SCREEN.LOCATOR(N,1)
1250      COLUMN.NUMBER = SCREEN.LOCATOR(N,2)
1260      DATA.LENGTH = SCREEN.LOCATOR(N,3)
1270      HOLD.LINE.NUMBER = LINE.NUMBER
1280      HOLD.COLUMN.NUMBER = COLUMN.NUMBER
1290      VPOS=LINE.NUMBER:HPOS=COLUMN.NUMBER
1300      A$ = ""
1310      GET Z$
1320      IF Z$ = "" THEN 1310
1330      HOLD.COLUMN.NUMBER = COLUMN.NUMBER
1340      PRINT Z$;
1350      A$ = A$ + Z$
1360      IF A$ = "STOP" THEN 1850
1370      IF LEN(A$) = DATA.LENGTH THEN 1400
1380      IF (Z$ = CHR$(13)) AND (LEN(A$) = 1) THEN GOSUB 1860:GOTO 1310
1390      IF (Z$ = CHR$(13)) AND (LEN(A$) > 1) THEN 1400 ELSE 1310
1400      FIELDS.RECEIVED = FIELDS.RECEIVED + 1
1410      IF FIELDS.RECEIVED = 1 THEN INVENTORY.TABLE$(ITEMS.LOADED,1) = A$
1420      IF FIELDS.RECEIVED = 2 THEN INVENTORY.TABLE$(ITEMS.LOADED,2) = A$
1430      IF FIELDS.RECEIVED = 3 THEN INVENTORY.TABLE$(ITEMS.LOADED,3) = A$
1440      INVENTORY.TABLE$(ITEMS.LOADED + 1,1) = "ZZZZZ"
1450      INVENTORY.TABLE$(ITEMS.LOADED + 1,2) = "ZZZZZ"
1460      INVENTORY.TABLE$(ITEMS.LOADED + 1,3) = "ZZZZZ"
1470      IF FIELDS.RECEIVED <> 3 THEN 1840
1480      FIELDS.RECEIVED = 0
1490      ERROR.MESSAGE$ = "ACCEPTABLE (Y/N)?"
1500      GOSUB 5070      :REM ERROR MESSAGE SUBROUTINE
1510      GET Z$:IF Z$ = "" THEN 1510
1520      IF Z$ = "N" THEN 1580
1530      IF Z$ < > "Y" THEN 1510
1540      ITEMS.LOADED = ITEMS.LOADED + 1
1550      ERROR.MESSAGE$ = ""
1560      GOSUB 5070      :REM ERROR MESSAGE SUBROUTINE
1570      GOTO 1840
1580      ERROR.MESSAGE$ = "ENTRY REJECTED"
1590      GOSUB 5070      :REM ERROR MESSAGE SUBROUTINE
1600      N = N - 2
1610      A1 = SCREEN.LOCATOR(N,1)
1620      A2 = SCREEN.LOCATOR(N,2)
1630      A3 = SCREEN.LOCATOR(N,3)
1640      B1 = SCREEN.LOCATOR(N + 1,1)
1650      B2 = SCREEN.LOCATOR(N + 1,2)
1660      B3 = SCREEN.LOCATOR(N + 1,3)
1670      C1 = SCREEN.LOCATOR(N + 2,1)
1680      C2 = SCREEN.LOCATOR(N + 2,2)
1690      C3 = SCREEN.LOCATOR(N + 2,3)
```

Figure 3.48. (continued)

```
1700      VPOS=A1:HPOS=A2
1710      FOR Z = 1 TO A3
1720          PRINT CHR$(223);
1730          NEXT Z
1740      VPOS=B1:HPOS=B2
1750      FOR Z = 1 TO B3
1760          PRINT CHR$(223);
1770          NEXT Z
1780      VPOS=C1:HPOS=C2
1790      FOR Z = 1 TO C3
1800          PRINT CHR$(223);
1810          NEXT Z
1820      FIELDS.RECEIVED = 0
1830      N = N - 1
1840      NEXT N
1850 RETURN
1860 ERROR.MESSAGE$ = "MANDATORY ENTRY"
1870 GOSUB 5070          :REM ERROR MESSAGE SUBROUTINE
1880 COLUMN.NUMBER = HOLD.COLUMN.NUMBER
1890 VPOS=LINE.NUMBER:HPOS=COLUMN.NUMBER
1900 A$ = ""
1910 RETURN
1920 REM **********************************************
1930 REM *          TABLE CHANGE SUBROUTINE           *
1940 REM **********************************************
1950 A$ = "":B$ = "":C$ = ""
1960 IF ITEMS.LOADED > 1 THEN 2000
1970 ERROR.MESSAGE$ = "NO TABLE TO CHANGE"
1980 GOSUB 5070          :REM ERROR MESSAGE SUBROUTINE
1990 RETURN
2000 GOSUB 800           :REM CLEAR OUT INSIDE OF FRAME
2010 GOSUB 920           :REM HEADING SUBROUTINE
2020 ERROR.MESSAGE$ = "TABLE CHANGE"
2030 GOSUB 5070          :REM ERROR MESSAGE SUBROUTINE
2040 FOR Z = 1 TO 500:NEXT Z
2050 VPOS=10:HPOS=23
2060 PRINT "CHANGE WORKS ON ONE ELEMENT ONLY.";
2070 VPOS=12:HPOS=23
2080 PRINT "IF YOU KNOW THE ITEM NUMBER, THEN";
2090 VPOS=13:HPOS=23
2100 PRINT "ANSWER YES TO THE QUESTION.  IF";
2110 VPOS=14:HPOS=23
2120 PRINT "YOU DO NOT KNOW IT, ENTER PRINT";
2130 VPOS=15:HPOS=23
2140 PRINT "AT THE MAIN MENU, VPOS=THE ITEM";
2150 VPOS=16:HPOS=23
2160 PRINT "NUMBER AND COME BACK TO HERE."
2170 ERROR.MESSAGE$ = "DO YOU KNOW THE ITEM NUMBER (Y/N)?"
2180 GOSUB 5070          :REM ERROR MESSAGE SUBROUTINE
2190 GET Z$:IF Z$ = "" THEN 2190
2200 IF Z$ < > "Y" THEN RETURN
2210 ERROR.MESSAGE$ = "ENTER THE ITEM NUMBER: "
2220 GOSUB 5070          :REM ERROR MESSAGE SUBROUTINE
2230 GET Z$:IF Z$ = "" THEN 2230
2240 IF Z$ = CHR$(13) THEN 2290
2250 A$ = A$ + Z$
2260 ERROR.MESSAGE$ = "ITEM NUMBER: " + A$
2270 GOSUB 5070          :REM ERROR MESSAGE SUBROUTINE
2280 GOTO 2230
2290 FOR X = 1 TO 101
2300      IF INVENTORY.TABLE$(X,1) = A$ THEN 2360
2310      IF INVENTORY.TABLE$(X,1) = "ZZZZZ" THEN 2330
2320      NEXT X
2330 ERROR.MESSAGE$ = "ITEM NOT ON TABLE"
```

Figure 3.48. (continued)

```
2340 GOSUB 5070          :REM ERROR MESSAGE SUBROUTINE
2350 RETURN
2360 GOSUB 800           :REM CLEAR INSIDE OF FRAME
2370 GOSUB 920           :REM HEADING SUBROUTINE
2380 VPOS=10:HPOS=8
2390 PRINT INVENTORY.TABLE$(X,1);
2400 VPOS=10:HPOS=23
2410 PRINT INVENTORY.TABLE$(X,2);
2420 VPOS=10:HPOS=65
2430 PRINT INVENTORY.TABLE$(X,3);
2440 ERROR.MESSAGE$ = "CORRECT RECORD (Y/N)?"
2450 GOSUB 5070
2460 GET Z$:IF Z$ = "" THEN 2460
2470 IF Z$ < > "Y" THEN RETURN
2480 VPOS=12:HPOS=8
2490 PRINT "____";
2500 VPOS=12:HPOS=23
2510 PRINT "___________________________________";
2520 VPOS=12:HPOS=65
2530 PRINT "____";
2540 A$ = "":B$ = "":C$ = ""
2550 ERROR.MESSAGE$ = "ENTER THE CORRECTED ITEM - ALL ELEMENTS"
2560 GOSUB 5070          :REM ERROR MESSAGE SUBROUTINE
2570 VPOS=12:HPOS=8
2580 GET Z$:IF Z$ = "" THEN 2580
2590 IF Z$ = CHR$(13) THEN 2640
2600 PRINT Z$;
2610 A$ = A$ + Z$
2620 IF LEN(A$) = 4 THEN 2640
2630 GOTO 2580
2640 VPOS=12:HPOS=23
2650 GET Z$:IF Z$ = "" THEN 2650
2660 PRINT Z$;
2670 IF Z$ = CHR$(13) THEN 2710
2680 B$ = B$ + Z$
2690 IF LEN(B$) = 35 THEN 2710
2700 GOTO 2650
2710 VPOS=12:HPOS=65
2720 GET Z$:IF Z$ = "" THEN 2720
2730 IF Z$ = CHR$(13) THEN 2780
2740 PRINT Z$;
2750 C$ = C$ + Z$
2760 IF LEN(C$) = 4 THEN 2780
2770 GOTO 2720
2780 ERROR.MESSAGE$ = "IS THE CORRECTION CORRECT (Y/N)?"
2790 GOSUB 5070          :REM ERROR MESSAGE SUBROUTINE
2800 GET Z$:IF Z$ = "" THEN 2800
2810 IF Z$ = "N" THEN 2480
2820 IF Z$ < > "Y" THEN 2800
2830 INVENTORY.TABLE$(X,1) = A$
2840 INVENTORY.TABLE$(X,2) = B$
2850 INVENTORY.TABLE$(X,3) = C$
2860 ERROR.MESSAGE$ = "CORRECTED RECORD RE-FILED INTO THE ARRAY"
2870 GOSUB 5070          :REM ERROR MESSAGE SUBROUTINE
2880 RETURN
2890 REM ******************************************************
2900 REM *           TABLE DELETION SUBROUTINE               *
2910 REM ******************************************************
2920 A$ = ""
2930 IF ITEMS.LOADED > 1 THEN 2970
2940 ERROR.MESSAGE$ = "NO TABLE TO DELETE"
2950 GOSUB 5070          :REM ERROR MESSAGE SUBROUTINE
2960 RETURN
2970 GOSUB 800           :REM CLEAR OUT INSIDE OF FRAME
```

Figure 3.48. (continued)

```
2980 GOSUB 920             :REM HEADING SUBROUTINE
2990 ERROR.MESSAGE$ = "TABLE DELETE"
3000 GOSUB 5070            :REM ERROR MESSAGE SUBROUTINE
3010 FOR Z = 1 TO 500:NEXT Z
3020 VPOS=10:HPOS=23
3030 PRINT "DELETE WORKS ON ONE ELEMENT ONLY.";
3040 VPOS=12:HPOS=23
3050 PRINT "IF YOU KNOW THE ITEM NUMBER, THEN";
3060 VPOS=13:HPOS=23
3070 PRINT "ANSWER YES TO THE QUESTION.  IF";
3080 VPOS=14:HPOS=23
3090 PRINT "YOU DO NOT KNOW IT, ENTER PRINT";
3100 VPOS=15:HPOS=23
3110 PRINT "AT THE MAIN MENU, VPOS=THE ITEM";
3120 VPOS=16:HPOS=23
3130 PRINT "NUMBER AND COME BACK TO HERE."
3140 ERROR.MESSAGE$ = "DO YOU KNOW THE ITEM NUMBER (Y/N)?"
3150 GOSUB 5070            :REM ERROR MESSAGE SUBROUTINE
3160 GET Z$:IF Z$ = "" THEN 3160
3170 IF Z$ < > "Y" THEN RETURN
3180 ERROR.MESSAGE$ = "ENTER THE ITEM NUMBER: "
3190 GOSUB 5070            :REM ERROR MESSAGE SUBROUTINE
3200 GET Z$:IF Z$ = "" THEN 3200
3210 IF Z$ = CHR$(13) THEN 3260
3220 A$ = A$ + Z$
3230 ERROR.MESSAGE$ = "ITEM NUMBER: " + A$
3240 GOSUB 5070            :REM ERROR MESSAGE SUBROUTINE
3250 GOTO 3200
3260 FOR X = 1 TO 1001
3270      IF INVENTORY.TABLE$(X,1) = A$ THEN 3330
3280      IF INVENTORY.TABLE$(X,1) = "ZZZZZ" THEN 3300
3290      NEXT X
3300 ERROR.MESSAGE$ = "ITEM NOT ON TABLE"
3310 GOSUB 5070            :REM ERROR MESSAGE SUBROUTINE
3320 RETURN
3330 GOSUB 800             :REM CLEAR INSIDE OF FRAME
3340 GOSUB 920             :REM HEADING SUBROUTINE
3350 VPOS=10:HPOS=8
3360 PRINT INVENTORY.TABLE$(X,1);
3370 VPOS=10:HPOS=23
3380 PRINT INVENTORY.TABLE$(X,2);
3390 VPOS=10:HPOS=65
3400 PRINT INVENTORY.TABLE$(X,3);
3410 ERROR.MESSAGE$ = "CORRECT RECORD (Y/N)?"
3420 GOSUB 5070            :REM ERROR MESSAGE SUBROUTINE
3430 GET Z$:IF Z$ = "" THEN 3430
3440 IF Z$ < > "Y" THEN 2970
3450 INVENTORY.TABLE$(X,1) = "/////"
3460 INVENTORY.TABLE$(X,2) = "/////"
3470 INVENTORY.TABLE$(X,3) = "/////"
3480 ERROR.MESSAGE$ = "RECORD DELETED FROM THE ARRAY"
3490 GOSUB 5070            :REM ERROR MESSAGE SUBROUTINE
3500 RETURN
3510 REM ***********************************************
3520 REM *         TABLE LOCATION SUBROUTINE           *
3530 REM ***********************************************
3540 A$ = ""
3550 IF ITEMS.LOADED > 1 THEN 3590
3560 ERROR.MESSAGE$ = "NO TABLE TO QUERY"
3570 GOSUB 5070            :REM ERROR MESSAGE SUBROUTINE
3580 RETURN
3590 GOSUB 800             :REM CLEAR OUT INSIDE OF FRAME
3600 GOSUB 920             :REM HEADING SUBROUTINE
3610 ERROR.MESSAGE$ = "TABLE INQUIRY"
```

Figure 3.48. (continued)

```
3620 GOSUB 5070          :REM ERROR MESSAGE SUBROUTINE
3630 FOR Z = 1 TO 500:NEXT Z
3640 VPOS=10:HPOS=23
3650 PRINT "LOCATE WORKS ON ONE ELEMENT ONLY.";
3660 VPOS=12:HPOS=23
3670 PRINT "IF YOU KNOW THE ITEM NUMBER, THEN";
3680 VPOS=13:HPOS=23
3690 PRINT "ANSWER YES TO THE QUESTION.  IF";
3700 VPOS=14:HPOS=23
3710 PRINT "YOU DO NOT KNOW IT, ENTER PRINT";
3720 VPOS=15:HPOS=23
3730 PRINT "AT THE MAIN MENU, LOCATE THE ITEM";
3740 VPOS=16:HPOS=23
3750 PRINT "NUMBER AND COME BACK TO HERE."
3760 ERROR.MESSAGE$ = "DO YOU KNOW THE ITEM NUMBER(Y/N)?"
3770 GOSUB 5070          :REM ERROR MESSAGE SUBROUTINE
3780 GET Z$:IF Z$ = "" THEN 3780
3790 IF Z$ < > "Y" THEN RETURN
3800 ERROR.MESSAGE$ =  "ENTER THE ITEM NUMBER: "
3810 GOSUB 5070          :REM ERROR MESSAGE SUBROUTINE
3820 GET Z$:IF Z$ = "" THEN 3820
3830 IF Z$ = CHR$(13) THEN 3880
3840 A$ = A$ + Z$
3850 ERROR.MESSAGE$ = "ITEM NUMBER: " + A$
3860 GOSUB 5070          :REM ERROR MESSAGE SUBROUTINE
3870 GOTO 3820
3880 FOR X = 1 TO 1001
3890      IF INVENTORY.TABLE$(X,1) = A$ THEN 3950
3900      IF INVENTORY.TABLE$(X,1) = "ZZZZZ" THEN 3920
3910      NEXT X
3920 ERROR.MESSAGE$ = "ITEM NOT ON TABLE"
3930 GOSUB 5070          :REM ERROR MESSAGE SUBROUTINE
3940 RETURN
3950 GOSUB 800           :REM CLEAR INSIDE OF FRAME
3960 GOSUB 920           :REM HEADING SUBROUTINE
3970 VPOS=10:HPOS=8
3980 PRINT INVENTORY.TABLE$(X,1);
3990 VPOS=10:HPOS=23
4000 PRINT INVENTORY.TABLE$(X,2);
4010 VPOS=10:HPOS=65
4020 PRINT INVENTORY.TABLE$(X,3);
4030 ERROR.MESSAGE$ = "PRESS ANY KEY TO CONTINUE"
4040 GOSUB 5070          :REM ERROR MESSAGE SUBROUTINE
4050 GET Z$:IF Z$ = "" THEN 4050
4060 RETURN
4070 REM ***********************************************
4080 REM *           TABLE PRINT SUBROUTINE            *
4090 REM ***********************************************
4100 LINECOUNT = 0
4110 IF ITEMS.LOADED > 1 THEN 4150
4120 ERROR.MESSAGE$ = "NO TABLE TO PRINT"
4130 GOSUB 5070          :REM ERROR MESSAGE SUBROUTINE
4140 GOTO 4440
4150 GOSUB 800           :REM CLEAR OUT INSIDE OF FRAME
4160 GOSUB 920           :REM HEADING SUBROUTINE
4170 ERROR.MESSAGE$ = "TABLE PRINT - HARDCOPY (Y/N)?"
4180 GOSUB 5070          :REM ERROR MESSAGE SUBROUTINE
4190 GET Z$:IF Z$ = "" THEN 4190
4200 IF Z$ = "Y" THEN HARDCOPY = 1:GOTO 4220
4210 IF Z$ = "N" THEN HARDCOPY = 0:GOTO 4230
4220 ERROR.MESSAGE$ = "HARDCOPY REQUESTED":GOTO 4240
4230 ERROR.MESSAGE$ = "HARDCOPY NOT REQUESTED"
4240 GOSUB 5070          :REM ERROR MESSAGE SUBROUTINE
4250 GOSUB 5290          :REM LOAD NUMBERS AND LINES
```

Figure 3.48. (continued)

```
4260 N = 1
4270 FOR X = 1 TO 101
4280     Y = 1
4290     LINE.NUMBER = SCREEN.LOCATOR(N,1)
4300     COLUMN.NUMBER = SCREEN.LOCATOR(N,2)
4310     VPOS=LINE.NUMBER:HPOS=COLUMN.NUMBER
4320     PRINT INVENTORY.TABLE$(X,Y);
4330     IF HARDCOPY = 1 THEN GOSUB 5800
4340     IF INVENTORY.TABLE$(X,Y) = "ZZZZZ" THEN GOTO 4450
4350     LINECOUNT = LINECOUNT + 1
4360     IF LINECOUNT = 30 THEN LINECOUNT = 0:GOTO 4450
4370     N = N + 1
4380     IF N = 31 THEN N = 1
4390     IF Y = 3 THEN Y = 0:GOTO 4430
4400     Y = Y + 1
4410     GOTO 4290
4430     NEXT X
4440 RETURN
4450 ERROR.MESSAGE$ = "PRESS ANY KEY TO CONTINUE - PRESS 'X' TO ABORT"
4460 GOSUB 5070          :REM ERROR MESSAGE SUBROUTINE
4470 IF Z$ = "X" THEN 4440
4480 GET Z$:IF Z$ = "" THEN 4480
4490 IF INVENTORY.TABLE$(X,Y) = "ZZZZZ" THEN 4440
4500 GOTO 4370
4510 REM ***********************************************
4520 REM *             TABLE SORT SUBROUTINE           *
4530 REM ***********************************************
4540 IF ITEMS.LOADED > 1 THEN 4590
4550 A$ = ""
4560 ERROR.MESSAGE$ = "NO TABLE TO SORT"
4570 GOSUB 5070          :REM ERROR MESSAGE SUBROUTINE
4580 RETURN
4590 GOSUB 800           :REM CLEAR OUT INSIDE OF FRAME
4600 GOSUB 920           :REM HEADING SUBROUTINE
4610 ERROR.MESSAGE$ = "TABLE SORT"
4620 GOSUB 5070          :REM ERROR MESSAGE SUBROUTINE
4630 BUMP = 1
4640 FOR X = 1 TO 101
4650     IF INVENTORY.TABLE$(X,1) = "/////" THEN 4730
4660     WORK.TABLE$(BUMP,1) = INVENTORY.TABLE$(X,1)
4670     WORK.TABLE$(BUMP,2) = INVENTORY.TABLE$(X,2)
4680     WORK.TABLE$(BUMP,3) = INVENTORY.TABLE$(X,3)
4690     IF INVENTORY.TABLE$(X,1) = "ZZZZZ" THEN 4740
4700     BUMP = BUMP + 1
4710     VPOS=10:HPOS=23
4720     PRINT "COMPRESSING THE TABLE";
4730     NEXT X
4740 FOR X = 1 TO 101
4750     INVENTORY.TABLE$(X,1) = WORK.TABLE$(X,1)
4760     INVENTORY.TABLE$(X,2) = WORK.TABLE$(X,2)
4770     INVENTORY.TABLE$(X,3) = WORK.TABLE$(X,3)
4780     IF WORK.TABLE$(X,1) = "ZZZZZ" THEN 4820
4790     VPOS=10:HPOS=23
4800     PRINT "COPYING THE TABLE";"            ";
4810     NEXT X
4820 FOR X = 1 TO 101
4830     VPOS=10:HPOS=23
4840     PRINT "SORTING: ";INVENTORY.TABLE$(X,1);"            ";
4850     IF INVENTORY.TABLE$(X,1) = "ZZZZZ" THEN 5000
4860     IF INVENTORY.TABLE$(X + 1,1) > = INVENTORY.TABLE$(X,1) THEN 49
4870     TEMP.ITEM$ = INVENTORY.TABLE$(X,1)
4880     TEMP.DESCRIPTION$ = INVENTORY.TABLE$(X,2)
4890     TEMP.QUANTITY$ = INVENTORY.TABLE$(X,3)
4900     INVENTORY.TABLE$(X,1) = INVENTORY.TABLE$(X + 1,1)
```

Figure 3.48. (continued)

```
4910      INVENTORY.TABLE$(X,2) = INVENTORY.TABLE$(X + 1,2)
4920      INVENTORY.TABLE$(X,3) = INVENTORY.TABLE$(X + 1,3)
4930      INVENTORY.TABLE$(X + 1,1) = TEMP.ITEM$
4940      INVENTORY.TABLE$(X + 1,2) = TEMP.DESCRIPTION$
4950      INVENTORY.TABLE$(X + 1,3) = TEMP.QUANTITY$
4960      FLAG$ = "ON"
4970      VPOS=10:HPOS=23
4980      PRINT "           ";
4990      NEXT X
5000 IF FLAG$ = "OFF" THEN 5030
5010 FLAG$ = "OFF"
5020 GOTO 4820
5030 ERROR.MESSAGE$ = "SORT COMPLETE"
5040 GOSUB 5070          :REM ERROR MESSAGE SUBROUTINE
5050 GOSUB 4240          :REM JUMP INTO MIDDLE OF PRINT ROUTINE
5060 RETURN
5070 REM ********************************************
5080 REM *            ERROR MESSAGE SUBROUTINE             *
5090 REM ********************************************
5100 PRINT CHR$(7)
5110 VPOS=25:GOSUB 5650
5120 HPOS=1
5130 PRINT ERROR.MESSAGE$;
5140 RETURN
5150 REM ********************************************
5160 REM *     SCREEN COORDINATES FOR LOAD AND CHANGE      *
5170 REM ********************************************
5180 DATA 10,8,4,10,23,35,10,65,4
5190 DATA 11,8,4,11,23,35,11,65,4
5200 DATA 12,8,4,12,23,35,12,65,4
5210 DATA 13,8,4,13,23,35,13,65,4
5220 DATA 14,8,4,14,23,35,14,65,4
5230 DATA 15,8,4,15,23,35,15,65,4
5240 DATA 16,8,4,16,23,35,16,65,4
5250 DATA 17,8,4,17,23,35,17,65,4
5260 DATA 18,8,4,18,23,35,18,65,4
5270 DATA 19,8,4,19,23,35,19,65,4
5280 DATA 99999,99999,99999
5290 REM ********************************************
5300 REM *      SCREEN LINE NUMBERS AND BLANK LINES       *
5310 REM ********************************************
5320 VPOS=10:HPOS=4:PRINT " 1.";
5330 VPOS=11:PRINT " 2.";
5340 VPOS=12:PRINT " 3.";
5350 VPOS=13:PRINT " 4.";
5360 VPOS=14:PRINT " 5.";
5370 VPOS=15:PRINT " 6.";
5380 VPOS=16:PRINT " 7.";
5390 VPOS=17:PRINT " 8.";
5400 VPOS=18:PRINT " 9.";
5410 VPOS=19:PRINT "10.";
5420 RESTORE
5430 FOR N = 1 TO 30
5440      READ LINE.NUMBER,COLUMN.NUMBER,SHADE.LENGTH
5450      VPOS=LINE.NUMBER:HPOS=COLUMN.NUMBER
5460      FOR Z = 1 TO SHADE.LENGTH
5470          PRINT CHR$(223);
5480          NEXT Z
5490      NEXT N
5500 PRINT CHR$(7)
5510 RESTORE
5520 RETURN
5530 REM ********************************************
5540 REM *           READ FROM MEDIA SUBROUTINE             *
```

Figure 3.48. (continued)

```
5550 REM ************************************************
5560 ERROR.MESSAGE$ = "MODULE NOT INSTALLED AT THIS TIME"
5570 GOSUB 5070          :REM ERROR MESSAGE SUBROUTINE
5580 RETURN
5590 REM ************************************************
5600 REM *         WRITE TO MEDIA SUBROUTINE            *
5610 REM ************************************************
5620 ERROR.MESSAGE$ = "MODULE NOT INSTALLED AT THIS TIME"
5630 GOSUB 5070          :REM ERROR MESSAGE SUBROUTINE
5640 RETURN
5650 REM **************************
5660 REM * CLEAR THE LINE ROUTINE *
5670 REM **************************
5680 FOR Z = 1 TO 79
5690     HPOS = Z
5700     PRINT " ";
5710     NEXT Z
5720 RETURN
5730 REM *****************
5740 REM * GENERATE LINE *
5750 REM *****************
5760 FOR Z = 1 TO LINE.LENGTH
5760     HPOS = Z
5770     PRINT CHR$(223);
5780     NEXT HPOS
5790 RETURN
5800 REM *******************
5810 REM * HARDCOPY OPTION *
5820 REM *******************
5830 OPEN #1,".PRINTER"
5835 OUTPUT #1
5840 PRINT INVENTORY.TABLE$(X,Y)
5850 PRINT
5860 CLOSE #1
5870 RETURN
```

Figure 3.48. (continued)

And that concludes the chapter. Next step: drivers – specifically, those used for graphics and music. Time to have a little fun.

SUMMARY

Before we do, however, let's pick up on those commands introduced in this chapter, plus a couple which don't fit anywhere specific:

AS	A portion of the OPEN statement.
CATALOG	Used to display the contents of a diskette. May be abbreviated to CAT. Example: CAT .D2.
CLEAR	Clears the contents of all variables and arrays.

DATA	Used for internal storage of constants which will not occupy string space. Alphabetic and numeric data may be mixed at will.
DIM	DIMensions an array and reserves variable storage. Provides the basis for subscripting or moving through the array by individual position.
ELSE	Used to detail a second branch address in an IF ... THEN statement. If A = 5 THEN 100 ELSE 200.
INDENT	Controls the depth of indentation of FOR ... NEXT loops from the left margin of the program listing.
INSTR(	Used to search a string for a given combination of string characters.
INT(	Returns the INTeger portion of a number, that portion which is to the left of the decimal point.
LEFT$	Used to address the left n characters of a string variable.
LEN(	Used to determine the length of a string variable.
LOCK	Used to prevent accidental deletion of a file on diskette. May be used directly or as part of a program. LOCK .D2/PROGRAM.
MID$(	Used to address the middle of a string variable (can also be used to address both the left and right sides. Uses a beginning position and a length attribute. Only MID$(can be the target of a move, whereas LEFT$(and RIGHT$(may not.
NOTRACE	Opposite of TRACE. Commands the microcomputer to no longer present statement numbers on the display screen.

ON	Establishes a conditional branching situation wherein there is either an error or a selection of options: ON A GOTO 100,200.
PREFIX$	Allows default disk drive assignment.
READ	Addresses the DATA statements in sequence and extracts values located there into variables which are part of the READ instruction. READ operates in a forward direction only, and is set at the top of the list of DATA instructions by a RESTORE.
RESTORE	Resets the READ pointer to the first DATA statement.
RIGHT$(	Used to address the right n characters of a string variable.
RND(	Returns a random number whose value is smaller than one. Number returned is a four-digit decimal number.
STR$	Returns the string representation of a numeric value, allowing the number to have alphabetic characteristics.
TRACE	Used for debugging the program. The TRACE will present the BASIC statement numbers on the display screen as the instructions are being executed. Must be turned off via NOTRACE.
VAL(	Returns the numeric value of a number stored in alphabetic or string form. Will not convert actual alphabetic values.

4
Drivers: Console, Graphics, and Audio

As was mentioned before, virtually every form of input or output within the Apple III system happens as a function of driver software. In general, a driver is a bit of programing code which captures the features of the device and interfaces them to the SOS, and thereby, to the program. With a knowledge of the driver's capabilities and responsibilities, you can often cause to happen things which cannot be directly handled in BASIC.

In this chapter we will concentrate once again on the console driver (we had dealt somewhat with it in a previous chapter), upon the graphics driver, and upon the audio driver. We'll not cover every facet of each, but enough so you get the general idea and can research the Standard Drivers Manual should you wish to do something differently.

CONSOLE

You will recall that we have talked about aspects of the display relative to screen (window) size. The screen is but one part of the console. The other is the keyboard. There are a number of things which you may affect with either. Let us concentrate first upon the display.

There are essentially three text modes of screen usage: (1) 24 X 40, black and white; (2) 24 X 40, color; and (3) 24 X 80, black and white. First off, it's important to note that 40 *is not* the left half of the screen. It merely means that anything done in a 40 column mode is done over the 80 character distance with characters which are twice the size. How we get them to be twice the size, and how we restore the system to mode 3 makes a pretty interesting story all by itself.

Consider Figure 4.1. Examine statement 30. The CHR$(16) is the mechanism whereby one of the three text modes is determined. CHR$(16) functions as a switch, telling the computer that a mode change is to be made. Next, note the CHR$(Z) which follows. Because of the value developed in the FOR ... NEXT loop (statements 20 and 80), the variable Z is exercised with three values (0 through 2), corresponding to the three modes indicated above.

```
10 HOME
20 FOR Z = 0 TO 2
30        PRINT CHR$(16);CHR$(Z)
40        FOR N = 1 TO 15
50             PRINT CHR$(19);CHR$(N);N
60             NEXT N
70        GET Z$
80        NEXT Z
90 PRINT CHR$(1):HOME
100 LIST
```

Figure 4.1.

Now examine statement 50. The CHR$(19) is the command to set foreground color. It will only function when the display mode is set to color text mode. In this program, that only happens when Z has the value 1. Enter the program and run it. The GET Z$ causes the program to stop with each display of 15 numbers. The middle group, when Z has the value 1, begins at a very faint color and becomes progressively stronger as the number climbs to 15. And while this is being presented on a green screen display, the difference is apparent, and you can see how the shaded graphics which appear with the demonstration program are produced.

The color codes for both foreground and background are as follows:

Black	0	Brown	8
Magenta	1	Orange	9
Dark blue	2	Gray	10
Lavender	3	Pink	11
Dark green	4	Green	12
Gray	5	Yellow	13
Medium blue	6	Aqua	14
Light blue	7	White	15

When the 40 character display is set, the viewport is automatically changed to accommodate it. Thus, were you simply to code the instruction HOME for statement 90, only the left half of the screen would be cleared, while garbage would appear on the right side of the screen. We get around that by using CHR$(1), which resets the viewport. Try it both ways, so you know what you're looking at.

Now let's add some instructions. (See Figure 4.2.) Observe statement 45 and those statements which have been added to the program (110–130). Enter and run the expanded program.

```
10 HOME
20 FOR Z = 0 TO 2
30      PRINT CHR$(16);CHR$(Z)
40      FOR N = 1 TO 15
45           PRINT CHR$(18);
50           PRINT CHR$(19);CHR$(N);N
60           NEXT N
70      GET Z$
80      NEXT Z
90 PRINT CHR$(1):HOME
100 LIST
110 PRINT CHR$(17);
120 HOME
130 LIST
```

Figure 4.2.

Statement 45 is what we had previously discussed as INVERSE. Statement 110 is what we had previously discussed as NORMAL. Insert INVERSE and NORMAL in their appropriate places, and note that it makes no difference. The purpose of the LIST commands is to simply place something on the screen for you to see that the change has indeed been made.

In this example, we have made the changes to incorporate INVERSE and NORMAL. We've also changed our consideration of the foreground (CHR$(19)) to consider the background (CHR$(20)). Enter the changes as in Figure 4.3, and run the program, noting how the letter density of the foreground melts into the background color.

Quite a difference, don't you think?

Now let's concentrate a bit on what happens to the cursor. By and large there are but four distinct categories of cursor actions which you may enable or disable. They are: (1) scroll, (2) wrap, (3) new line, and (4) advance. *Scroll,* you will recall, is that feature whereby lines move from bottom to top of the screen. *Wrap* is that

```
10 HOME
20 FOR Z = 0 TO 2
30       PRINT CHR$(16);CHR$(Z)
40       FOR N = 1 TO 15
45            INVERSE
50            PRINT CHR$(20);CHR$(N);N
60            NEXT N
70       GET Z$
80       NEXT Z
90 PRINT CHR$(1):HOME
100 LIST
110 NORMAL
120 HOME
130 LIST
```

Figure 4.3.

feature where text is continued off the right side of the screen onto the next line. *New line* is just what it says (think of PRINT statements which are terminated by a semicolon). And *advance* is what happens when you type a character and the cursor moves one position to the right. This is the character table:

Value	Char	Scroll	Wrap	New Line	Advance
0	0	no	no	no	no
1	1	no	no	no	yes
2	2	no	no	yes	no
3	3	no	no	yes	yes
4	4	no	yes	no	no
5	5	no	yes	no	yes
6	6	no	yes	yes	no
7	7	no	yes	yes	yes
8	8	yes	no	no	no
9	9	yes	no	no	yes
10	:	yes	no	yes	no
11	;	yes	no	yes	yes
12	<	yes	yes	no	no
13	=	yes	yes	no	yes
14	>	yes	yes	yes	no
15	?	yes	yes	yes	yes

This is the table, and CHR$(21) sets the stage to receive the code. The first example of this principle is Figure 4.4. It contains the first row from the above table (CHR$(0)). Note that once executed, everything functions in one position. Scroll and advance are inhibited.

```
10 PRINT CHR$(21);CHR$(0)
20 FOR N = 1 TO 15
30      PRINT N
40      NEXT N
50 END
```

Figure 4.4.

The next thing is to learn what happens when the entire remaining fifteen codes are executed. Enter and run the program of Figure 4.5. When the program comes to rest, your output should look like Figure 4.6.

```
10 FOR N = 1 TO 15
20      PRINT CHR$(21);CHR$(N);N
30      NEXT N
40 END
```

Figure 4.5.

```
8
9
0

11

2
13
4

15
```

Figure 4.6.

What in the world happened? First off, wherever scroll was inhibited, the number was simply overlaid. Thus, everything which preceded 8 was simply overwritten. Run it again and watch it closely. Next, those codes where advance was inhibited overwrote the first digit with the second. Such is the case with 12 and 14, for instance.

So what's the point? Simply this: you have total power over the cursor, whether you wish to accept a secret word without divulging it or whether you wish to position the cursor at a specific place on the line.

And while we're on the subject of specific places on the screen, the three examples of coding in Figure 4.7 produce precisely the same result. Pay your money and take your choice.

```
                    Illustration #1

10 HOME
20 VPOS=10:HPOS=10
30 PRINT "KEN"
40 VPOS=12:HPOS=10
50 PRINT "NANCY"

                    Illustration #2

10 HOME
20 PRINT CHR$(24);CHR$(10);CHR$(25);CHR$(10);"KEN"
30 PRINT CHR$(24);CHR$(12);CHR$(25);CHR$(10);"NANCY"

                    Illustration #3

10 HOME
20 PRINT CHR$(26);CHR$(10);CHR$(10);"KEN"
30 PRINT CHR$(26);CHR$(10);CHR$(12);"NANCY"
```

Figure 4.7.

GRAPHICS

Graphics on the Apple III are quite capable. They are also quite complex. Realistically, a full explanation of the graphic capabilities, and specifically of the color graphic capabilities, should be the subject of an entirely different volume. There simply is so much to learn about the subject. For that reason, and because it really is our purpose to introduce you to the business aspects of this mahcine, our use of graphics will be restricted to the representation of business data. In the process, we'll explain only a part of the mystery. It will then be up to you to investigate the graphics capabilities of the machine using this information as a launching position.

There are two ways for the BASIC programer to cause things to happen graphically on the Apple III. The first is to interact directly with the graphics driver, .GRAFIX. The second is to use what's known as the BGRAF invokable to interact with .GRAFIX for you. Even that is fairly complex, but workable. You will find full details on how to use the BGRAF invokable in your Business BASIC reference manual.

The graphics driver must be opened, as if it were a file being written. Observe statement 70 in Figure 4.8. Likewise, it must be closed. See statement 250. Between those two commands, everything which will happen graphically within the machine occurs.

Once that occurs, the BGRAF module is invoked. See statement 80. The balance of the graphics activities are done with PERFORM statements which are really calls to portions of the Assembly Language graphics module BGRAF.

In statements 40 through 60, the two graphics colors to be used are detailed. Note the statements which include the names COLORFILL and COLORPEN. These are not BASIC reserved words. I made them up. The values given them, however, are meaningful to the graphics section. All graphics are done as a function of a pen upon a background. Thus the value 0 given to each of them (on the basis of a question) stands for the absence of color (black), whereas 15 stands

```
10 REM GRAPH1
20 HOME
30 RESTORE
40 PRINT "BLACK ON WHITE (Y/N)? ":GET Z$
50 IF Z$ = "Y" THEN COLORFILL=15:COLORPEN=0:GOTO 70
60 COLORFILL=0:COLORPEN=15
70 OPEN#1,".GRAFIX"
80 INVOKE "BGRAF.INV"
90 PERFORM INITGRAFIX
100 MODE=2:BUFFER=1
110 PERFORM GRAFIXMODE(%MODE,%BUFFER)
120 PERFORM FILLCOLOR(%COLORFILL)
130 PERFORM FILLPORT
140 PERFORM GRAFIXON
150 FOR Z = 1 TO 23
160      READ A
170      FOR N = A TO A+6
180           B=175:C=100
190           PERFORM MOVETO(%N,%B)
200           PERFORM PENCOLOR(%COLORPEN)
210           PERFORM LINETO(%N,%C)
220           NEXT N
230      NEXT Z
240 GET Z$
250 CLOSE #1
260 TEXT
270 LIST
280 END
290 DATA 1,26,51,76,101,126,151,176,201,226,251,276
300 DATA 301,326,351,376,401,426,451,476,501,526,551,576
```

Figure 4.8.

for the presence of full color (white, or in the case of the green monitor, green). In this case, the question asked in statement 40 is used to determine if we want a fully white (green) foreground upon a fully black background. On the green monitor it is possible to obtain shades of green, in lieu of color shades, but the resolution is meaningless to anything we will attempt to do. Therefore we have concentrated upon the use of white on black and black on white for illustration. Note that COLORFILL and COLORPEN are used as function arguments in statements 120 and 200, respectively.

Statement 90 performs an initialization of the graphics driver. The initialization that it does lies at the heart of the graphics concept as implemented on the Apple III. First, the viewport is set at full screen size. By viewport, we merely mean that portion of the screen upon which graphics will be displayed. For all but the last illustration to follow, the viewport is left at full screen size. The use of the viewport to isolate graphics from text may be important in those applications where the picture is under constant revision. Second, the cursor position is set at 0,0 – which on the Apple III graphics presentation is at the *lower left corner of the viewport.* So long as the viewport is the entire screen, the cursor would be set at the first position at the lower left of the screen. Two other options are reset – color table and transfer option. Both have to do with color and/or sophisticated graphics techniques not herein presented.

Statements 100 and 110 function as a pair. Note that the mode has been set to 2, while the buffer has been set to 1. Each is used (in integer form) in the GRAFIXMODE instruction. There are four modes and two buffers which can be selected. The idea behind the two buffers is that you have the option to display using one buffer while you are preparing a slightly different display on the second buffer. This is how animation is accomplished. For our illustration, we'll stick with a single buffer, buffer 1.

As stated, there are four modes. Modes 0 and 2 are black and white modes, while modes 1 and 3 are color modes. Mode 0 defines the full screen as being 280 dots wide (range of 0 to 279) by 192 dots high (range of 0 to 191). Each of these dots, or *pixels,* as they are commonly called, may be illuminated. This is the low resolution display, in that the dots are larger, and there are fewer of them. The height of 192 dots, by the way, is true of all modes. Mode 2, which is the one we will use throughout this discussion, offers double the *horizontal* resolution (560 dots, keeping the vertical resolution at the same value), providing a range of 0 to 559. Mode 1 is double resolution color, whereas mode 3 is single resolution color. Neither will be discussed here.

Statement 120 identifies the FILLCOLOR, which will be the color of the background, while statement 130 actually performs the filling of the background with the color itself (FILLPORT). The actual number of the color could be substituted in the parentheses of statement 120 (range of 0 to 15), preceded by the percent sign. The colors have been detailed previously, so that listing will not be repeated here. For our purposes, we used 0 (black) and 15 (white). The reason the variable name is used is that, you will recall, we are interchanging colors.

Statement 140, GRAFIXON, turns the graphics on. It simply displays the buffer which you had previously identified. Had you been creating interchangeable buffers, you would have set another buffer on and turned it on with GRAFIXON.

Let's skip now to instructions 190–210. First, the PENCOLOR did not have to be established within the FOR ... NEXT loop, as illustrated. It could have been placed preceding the loop. It is placed in the center here to show where it would have to be were the pen color to be changed during the execution of the loop. The MOVETO and LINETO commands do the actual graphics drawing. MOVETO is how the graphics driver is directed to the starting point. Note that in the example the MOVETO is given integer X and Y coordinates. In essence, the driver is told to pick up the pen and drop it on those coordinates. Note that the coordinates are specified as integer variables. They could be actual numbers within the range as dictated by the MODE. The same concept is in force with LINETO, except that these are the *target* coordinates. Once you have determined the initial position of the cursor, the LINETO will complete the drawing of the line. In our illustrations the lines are all perpendicular. They could be diagonal in either direction. The precision of the line depends upon the resolution motif you have selected.

In statements 150 to 230 there is a FOR ... NEXT loop which controls the execution of 23 somethings. Those somethings are the drawing of lines which are 20 graphics units wide, as depicted in the FOR

... NEXT loop contained in statements 170 through 220. The specific screen loading positions for those 23 lines ("bars," if you will), are detailed from the DATA lines, read by the READ instruction at 160. The length of the bars is determined in instruction 180, graphics points 100 to 175.

Statement 260 returns the screen to text mode and the program is then listed, not so much to allow you to see the program, but to demonstrate the difference in the screen condition.

Figure 4.9 is the same program, modified to include text-oriented printing mixed into the graphics screen. In this instance, we have "lit the matches" using a caret. However, observe the statements from 250 to 300. The locator mechanism for the flame demonstrates a

```
10 REM GRAPH2
20 HOME
30 RESTORE
40 PRINT "BLACK ON WHITE (Y/N)? ":GET Z$
50 IF Z$ = "Y" THEN COLORFILL=15:COLORPEN=0:GOTO 70
60 COLORFILL=0:COLORPEN=15
70 OPEN#1,".GRAFIX"
80 INVOKE "BGRAF.INV"
90 PERFORM INITGRAFIX
100 MODE=2:BUFFER=1
110 PERFORM GRAFIXMODE(%MODE,%BUFFER)
120 PERFORM FILLCOLOR(%COLORFILL)
130 PERFORM FILLPORT
140 PERFORM GRAFIXON
150 A = -24
160 FOR Z = 1 TO 23
170      A=A+25
180      FOR N = A TO A+6
190           B=175:C=100
200           PERFORM MOVETO(%N,%B)
210           PERFORM PENCOLOR(%COLORPEN)
220           PERFORM LINETO(%N,%C)
230           NEXT N
240      NEXT Z
250 FLAME = 1
260 FOR N = 1 TO 23
270      PERFORM MOVETO(%FLAME,%180)
280      PRINT #1,"^"
290      FLAME=FLAME+25
300      NEXT N
310 GET Z$
320 CLOSE #1
330 TEXT
340 LIST
350 END
```

Figure 4.9.

second method (as compared to the instructions at 150 and following), but essentially the only difference was the mixture of text and graphics. The "^" could just as easily have been words. Note that since the graphics driver (.GRAFIX) has been opened to buffer 1, the only way to display something on the screen is with the PRINT# instruction. This changes with statement 330, the TEXT instruction.

While the line numbers may change (because they have been resequenced), much of these programs has been the same, with something new added to each illustration. Figure 4.10 takes ten values (contained in a DATA statement) and plots those values in the form of a histogram. No effort was made to draw any scale lines or to intersperse wording in this illustration, as you have enough tools at this point to do that. It is important to recognize that these factors in the DATA line are specific points on the graphics grid, and not values which are sales figures for a corporation, for example. Whereas this

```
10 REM GRAPH3
20 HOME
30 RESTORE
40 PRINT "BLACK ON WHITE (Y/N)? ":GET Z$
50 IF Z$ = "Y" THEN COLORFILL=15:COLORPEN=0:GOTO 70
60 COLORFILL=0:COLORPEN=15
70 OPEN#1,".GRAFIX"
80 INVOKE "BGRAF.INV"
90 PERFORM INITGRAFIX
100 MODE=2:BUFFER=1
110 PERFORM GRAFIXMODE(%MODE,%BUFFER)
120 PERFORM FILLCOLOR(%COLORFILL)
130 PERFORM FILLPORT
140 PERFORM GRAFIXON
150 A = 0
160 FOR Z = 1 TO 10
170      A=A+50
180      READ B
190      FOR N = A TO A+19
200           C=50
210           PERFORM MOVETO(%N,%B)
220           PERFORM PENCOLOR(%COLORPEN)
230           PERFORM LINETO(%N,%C)
240           NEXT N
250      NEXT Z
260 GET Z$
270 CLOSE #1
280 TEXT
290 LIST
300 END
310 DATA 175,105,123,156,111,117,132,137,169,170
```

Figure 4.10.

data has been given to the program via DATA lines, you could just as easily be working from actual data which had been loaded into an array. Note that the bottom has been established (statement 200) at 50 (in the range of 0 to 191). Thus, there is a spread of 140 points on which to plot, in this instance. You have only to convert dollars to percentage of that spread, and you have the basis to plot sales, income, or any other feature on the histogram. Then, if you wish to overlay this histogram with another, as is done in the Apple III demonstration program, you merely need to change the PENCOLOR of the graphics pen, and you can overwrite that portion which is necessary to represent something else.

Figure 4.11 introduces a new instruction: DOTAT. Pronounce that "dot at." The function of the DOTAT is to place a dot at a specific set of coordinates. In this example, a line of dots is drawn, so you may see the effect. In the first instance, the Y coordinate is given a value, while the X coordinate is exercised through a FOR ... NEXT loop. The opposite is true in the second instance, where the

```
10 REM GRAPH4
20 HOME
30 RESTORE
40 PRINT "BLACK ON WHITE (Y/N)? ":GET Z$
50 IF Z$ = "Y" THEN COLORFILL=15:COLORPEN=0:GOTO 70
60 COLORFILL=0:COLORPEN=15
70 OPEN#1,".GRAFIX"
80 INVOKE "BGRAF.INV"
90 PERFORM INITGRAFIX
100 MODE=2:BUFFER=1
110 PERFORM GRAFIXMODE(%MODE,%BUFFER)
120 PERFORM FILLCOLOR(%COLORFILL)
130 PERFORM FILLPORT
140 PERFORM GRAFIXON
150 Y = 90
160 PERFORM PENCOLOR(%COLORPEN)
170 FOR X = 1 TO 558 STEP 5
180      PERFORM DOTAT(%X,%Y)
190      NEXT X
200 X = 281
210 FOR Y = 0 TO 190 STEP 3
220      PERFORM DOTAT(%X,%Y)
230      NEXT Y
240 GET Z$
250 CLOSE #1
260 TEXT
270 LIST
280 END
```

Figure 4.11.

X value is established and the Y value is exercised. When you run this program, you will see what looks like the crosshairs of a telescopic sight.

The final figure in this series (Figure 4.12) does two things. First, it draws what is known as a "relative line," a line in relation to the first line. That is done on both axes, and is done with a DOTREL command. Read that "dot relative." In the DOTREL command it is first important to define the *offset relative* for the line. If it is specified as a positive quantity, then it moves to the right on the X axis and upward on the Y axis. If defined as a negative quantity, it's left on the X axis, and down on the Y axis. Reference points outside the viewport will wrap. Secondly, it establishes a viewport in which those lines are shown. It is important to note that the actual drawing of the line begins outside the viewport area, but that only the portion which is plotted inside the viewport is actually displayed on the screen.

```
10 REM GRAPH5
20 HOME
30 RESTORE
40 PRINT "BLACK ON WHITE (Y/N)? ":GET Z$
50 IF Z$ = "Y" THEN COLORFILL=15:COLORPEN=0:GOTO 70
60 COLORFILL=0:COLORPEN=15
70 OPEN#1,".GRAFIX"
80 INVOKE "BGRAF.INV"
90 PERFORM INITGRAFIX
100 MODE=2:BUFFER=1
110 PERFORM GRAFIXMODE(%MODE,%BUFFER)
120 PERFORM FILLCOLOR(%COLORFILL)
130 PERFORM FILLPORT
140 PERFORM GRAFIXON
150 Y = 90
160 PERFORM PENCOLOR(%COLORPEN)
170 LEFT=130:RIGHT=420:BOTTOM=30:TOP=160
180 PERFORM VIEWPORT(%LEFT,%RIGHT,%BOTTOM,%TOP)
190 FOR X = 1 TO 558 STEP 5
200       PERFORM DOTAT(%X,%Y)
210       MINUSX=0:MINUSY=20
220       PERFORM DOTREL(%MINUSX,%MINUSY)
230       NEXT X
240 X = 266
250 FOR Y = 0 TO 190 STEP 3
260       PERFORM DOTAT(%X,%Y)
270       PLUSX=40:PLUSY=0
280       PERFORM DOTREL(%PLUSX,%PLUSY)
290       NEXT Y
300 GET Z$
310 CLOSE #1
320 TEXT
330 LIST
340 END
```

Figure 4.12.

We know that the MOVETO graphics command allows us to move the cursor to a specific location. There is a similar command called MOVEREL. MOVEREL moves the cursor from its present position to a relative location which must first be specified with X and Y coordinates, as follows:

```
)DX = 35:DY = -74
)PERFORM MOVEREL (%DX,%DY)
```

In this example, which is copied straight from the reference manual, we have, in immediate or direct mode, directed the machine to move the cursor 35 positions to the right (X axis) and 74 points down (Y axis). It is important to remember that this instruction works *from wherever the cursor is at the time of its execution.* That makes knowing where your cursor is pretty important. That only moves the cursor. LINEREL works similarly, and draws a line from where the cursor was to where you tell it to be. Again, quoting from the reference manual:

```
)DX = 8:DY = 58
)LINEREL(%DX,%DY)
```

If you happen to have a color monitor, set up a table of screen colors, a table of random points to begin lines, and a table of random points as the target of the lines. The resulting multicolored line display should give you some solid idea how such is used in animation.

Up to this point we have concentrated upon getting drawings, color, and information *to* the screen. Suppose it were necessary to determine where on the screen you were and what color was at that location. The graphics driver has three external functions (known as EXFN%): XLOC (location of the X coordinate), YLOC (location of the Y coordinate), and XYCOLOR (determine the color at that location, or at any other specified location).

Briefly, they work this way:

```
)X% = EXFN.XLOC:Y% = EXFN.YLOC
```

will return the X and Y coordinates to the appropriate variables.

```
)COLOR% = EXFN%.XYCOLOR
```

will return the color in use there, in the form of an integer variable in the range of 0 to 15.

```
)X = 23:Y = 7
)PERFORM MOVETO(%X,%Y)
)COLOR% = EXFN%.XYCOLOR
```

is the way you'll look at a specific point, known beforehand.

There are other graphics features which will be useful to know a little something about:

NEWFONT — Allows you to change the style of printing. When you configure the Apple III, you have your choice of three character types. This is then known as the system font. You can change from the system font to one of your own design (and which you must develop in an array), using the NEWFONT graphics instruction. The width of this font is 12 dots wide by 7 dots high and must previously be stored in an integer array such as might be FONT%(0,0).

SYSFONT — This directs the graphics driver to restore the systems font to use.

DRAWIMAGE — This command draws a predefined shape on the screen. In order to do so, the image must be defined as bits. DRAWIMAGE is beyond the scope of this book.

GSAVE — This command will allow you to save the graphics display currently in use (saved from the buffer). You have only to give it a name. The command may be executed within the program or from the console, like this: PERFORM GSAVE "GRAF.PIC".

GLOAD	Similarly, you may load a picture: PERFORM GLOAD "GRAF.PIC".
RELEASE	For use when you have completed your graphics work. This releases the buffers which have been allocated for graphics use.

There's more, of course. But you now have enough to experiment with it for use with your business programs.

AUDIO

The audio driver exists for one purpose only – to make noise; or more specifically, to make music. While the Apple III doesn't pretend to provide orchestral tones, it is possible to beat out a melody to a specific rhythm using the audio driver.

Following are two programs which are designed solely to demonstrate two relatively different methods to make music. There are others, and we have not attempted to give you the tools to compose a song and to store that song on disk for retrieval. However, you will find reference to such in the periodicals. One such article is "Piano Plinkin'" in the January, 1983, issue of *inCider.*

In these illustrations you will be shown *how* to make music, but unfortunately not *why* the instructions work. The book shows the means, but is not very explicit as to why they work as they do. Unfortunately, the Apple people with whom I've talked about the instruction have not been able to shed any further light upon the question, either. After calls to my local office and to the parent company failed to bear fruit on this issue, I resigned myself to the perspective that perhaps it's sufficient to know how.

In the first audio program (Figure 4.13) there are three program lines, two input statements, and a list of 13 DATA line entries which make the entire thing work. Note the variables T (time) and V (volume) which are entered at statements 30 and 50, respectively. Simply note that both values are entered from the keyboard. We'll use them in other statements.

Now, move down to statement 100. In statement 100, the first of six special CHR$ values are given. The audio driver has been OPENed (statement 60), will be CLOSEd (statement 140) has been declared as OUTPUT (statement 70), and the PRINT statements (100 through 120) function to the audio driver. The first part of statement 100 is CHR$(128). Printing CHR$(128) apparently signals the audio driver that changes are coming. A word of caution about the semicolons at the end of statements 100 and 110 – they must be there. In essence, six continuous codes must be passed to the audio driver, commencing with CHR$(128). The second parameter in statement 100 is the volume setting. The volume setting may range from 0 (inaudible) to 63 (several db below the threshold of pain – as loud as it gets). In our example, it is set at 60. The volume control uses integers only and rejects anything that doesn't fall within the range of 1 to 63. Give it another number, and you have the sound of silence.

Jump now to the DATA lines. Note that there are 13 numbers. Those numbers correspond to the octave beginning at middle C, the 4th octave in the Apple III's range of capability, as detailed in the sections on the audio driver in the Standard Device Drivers Manual. There is no intent to duplicate that table here, except to detail those used in the program in Figure 4.13:

C	1946	F	1457	A	1157
C#	1836	F#	1376	A#	1092
D	1733	G	1298	B	1031
D#	1636	G#	1226	C	973
E	1544				

The numbers are known as *count values,* and the count value is given to the audio driver in the form of two bytes. Now we must be careful here. In order to generate a tone in the range of 31 Hz to 5000 Hz, it is necessary to establish a count range in the range of 16383 (low) to 100 (high). This is technically the "wavelength," or pitch of the tone, analogous to a violin string which makes a higher tone when it is shorter.

In any event, 16383 is more than can be represented in one byte (which has a maximum value of 255 – a total of 256 values). It does, in fact, take two full bytes. Now, how to pass the two full bytes to the audio driver such that the total value (binarily) represents the desired value? Look at statement 110. Note that from the value given to it, 256 is subtracted. The difference is the byte count which will be represented in the leftmost byte of the two-byte pair, after first being multiplied by the integer of the quotient derived when the count number is divided by the amount of the full byte. I'm not certain why, except that that same value is given to the rightmost byte.

The same thing happens to the time parameter, the next two parameters given to the audio driver. The time parameter is divided into sixtieths of a second, with a range of 0 to 300. A value of 0 produces silence, while a value of 300 gives a 5 second tone. In this problem, and in the one to follow, the time parameters are somewhat more narrow.

Figure 4.13 simply plays the scale, derived from the DATA lines, allowing you to change the volume setting and the time. You may wish to change this program to simply play the tone you wish, by direct entry of the variable N, and the removal of the DATA statements and the READ N in statement 90.

```
10 HOME
20 RESTORE
30 INPUT "ENTER TIMING: ",T
40 PRINT
50 INPUT "ENTER VOLUME: ",V
60 OPEN #1,".AUDIO"
70 OUTPUT #1
80 FOR X = 1 TO 13
90      READ N
100     PRINT CHR$(128);CHR$(V);
110     PRINT CHR$(N-256*INT(N/256));CHR$(INT(N/256));
120     PRINT CHR$(T-256*INT(T/256));CHR$(INT(T/256));
130      NEXT X
140 CLOSE #1
150 LIST
160 GET Z$
170 GOTO 10
180 DATA 1946,1836,1733,1636,1544,1457,1376
190 DATA 1298,1226,1157,1092,1031,973
```

Figure 4.13.

Time for a song. In Figure 4.14, which is merely a revamping of the previous program, the volume is set at a constant 60 and the count and timing are stored in DATA lines. They are then read as a pair (statement 60) and are exercised through the routine which will play them. In this example, the number of note/time pairs is placed in the FOR ... NEXT loop precisely, which only means that the notes were counted. You wouldn't have to do that if you used our old friend, the sentinel. The last DATA line would simply have to be a pair of lengthy 9s, which would be tested immediately after the read. Modify the previous program as shown in Figure 4.14 and run it. You'll enjoy the music.

```
10 HOME
20 RESTORE
30 OPEN #1,".AUDIO"
40 OUTPUT #1
50 FOR X = 1 TO 72
60     READ N,T
70     PRINT CHR$(128);CHR$(60);
80     PRINT CHR$(N-256*INT(N/256));CHR$(INT(N/256));
90     PRINT CHR$(T-256*INT(T/256));CHR$(INT(T/256));
100    NEXT X
110 CLOSE #1
120 LIST
130 GET Z$
140 GOTO 10
150 DATA 1946,5,1946,5,1544,5,1298,5,1298,10,649,5,649,10,772,5,772,10
160 DATA 1946,5,1946,5,1544,5,1298,5,1298,10,649,5,649,10,729,5,729,10
170 DATA 2061,5,2061,5,1733,5,1157,5,1157,10,578,5,578,10,729,5,729,10
180 DATA 2061,5,2061,5,1733,5,1157,5,1157,10,578,5,578,10,772,5,772,10
190 DATA 1946,5,1946,5,1544,5,1298,5,973,10,486,5,486,10,649,5,649,10
200 DATA 1946,5,1946,5,1544,5,1298,5,973,10,486,5,486,10,578,5,578,10
210 DATA 1733,5,1733,5,1457,5,1157,5,1157,20,1376,5,1298,5,772,30
220 DATA 973,5,1544,5,1544,10,1733,5,1157,10,1298,5
230 DATA 1946,10,1946,5,1946,3,1946,10
```

Figure 4.14.

Now, what is involved to develop your own songs? First, it would be nice if you knew something about music – knowledge of the piano keyboard would be most helpful. Next, experiment with timings. With what length will you be comfortable for a sixteenth note, an eighth note, a quarter note, half, whole, etc.? Once you have determined that, DIMension a pair of arrays (one for the note, one for the timing) large enough to hold your song and more, and use the first phase of your program to enter and correct the notes. You could include a subroutine for playing your song as far as it goes. A good technique is to load the first position of the arrays with the sentinel, and reposition the sentinel with each new value added to the array.

When the song is as you would like it, then you have only to write the array to a disk file, again using a FOR ... NEXT loop with a large value and looking for the sentinel as a means to terminate the writing to disk. A similar routine can load the song to the array from the disk file, and you will already have the playing mechanism in place, using those instructions contained in the program above.

Add a little sophistication for determining what to call the file you are writing and loading, and before you know it, you'll have a veritable juke box of tunes with which you can astound your friends.

We'll cover disk file writing and reading techniques in the next chapter, so it is a little premature to do so now. But this will give you something with which to experiment. And if you find out exactly *why* it works, let the world know.

SUMMARY

The console and audio drivers are generally a function of set up and use of CHR$ codes. It would therefore serve no purpose merely to restate those tables of values here. What we will summarize, therefore, are the elements of the BGRAF invokable, used with the graphics driver .GRAFIX.

DOTAT	Plots a single dot at a given position on the screen. The precise location will be a function of the mode in which the screen has been set.
DOTREL	Plots a dot relative to the current position of the cursor. Recall that it is relative to the last cursor position, so parallel lines must be done in tandem.
DRAWIMAGE	Draws a rectangular bit-map image at the current position. It is necessary to establish this bit-mapped image beforehand.
EXFN./EXFN%.	Calls a function external to the graphics driver.
FILLCOLOR	This sets the background color, but does not paint the screen with it.

FILLPORT	This fills the current viewport with the color you had determined with FILLCOLOR.
GLOAD	Loads and displays a graphics picture which had been stored to disk. The file on the disk is known as a FOTO file.
GRAFIXMODE	Establishes one of four modes and one of two buffers as those to be used by the following coding.
GRAFIXON	Turns the graphics on; switches display to the current graphics mode and buffer.
GSAVE	Used to save the current graphics display to a FOTO file on disk.
INITGRAFIX	Initializes the graphics driver, setting a full-screen viewport and places the cursor at the lower left-hand corner. Also sets some color variables.
LINEREL	Draws a line relative to the current position of the cursor. This is used for developing parallel lines, as the parameters denote offsets.
LINETO	Draws a line from the current cursor location to an absolute position on the screen.
MOVEREL	Used to locate the cursor relative to the current position of the cursor.
MOVETO	Used to locate the cursor at a specific position on the screen.
NEWFONT	Used to specify to the graphics driver that a new character font is to be used.

PENCOLOR	Sets the foreground color of the pen, plot, and draw.
RELEASE	Frees the highest graphics buffer memory for use by the BASIC program.
SETCTAB	Sets a color table entry – not treated in this book.
SYSFONT	Used to return to the normal system character after having used a different font via NEWFONT.
VIEWPORT	Establishes a window, generally smaller than the entire screen, upon which graphics may be drawn. The viewport may be full screen size.
XFEROPTION	Defines the placement of dots on the screen on the basis of logical operations. The subject is not dealt with in this book.
XLOC	Returns the X axis coordinate.
XYCOLOR	Returns the color of the dot on the screen at the current position of the X and Y axis coordinates.
YLOC	Returns the Y axis coordinate.

5
Disk Applications

The Apple III comes with one diskette unit, located inboard to the system unit. The diskette unit may be single or double density. To this single diskette unit may be added a second diskette unit, outboard, or the firm's hard disk option, Profile.

Technically, the media placed in the diskette drive is called a *diskette.* A diskette is a 5.25 inch sheet of mylar, punched in the shape of a doughnut (or a 45 rpm record), and mounted inside a sleeve. There are larger (8 inch) diskettes, and there are smaller (3.25 inch) diskettes. And their large counterparts, otherwise known as *hard disk drives* are becoming plentiful in a variety of sizes beginning at 5Mb (that's *megabyte*). The Profile unit begins at 5Mb. Removable cartridge hard disks are just being introduced, as of this writing. Disk units are highly accessible and can be "read" or "written" at moderate speed. The problem is, and will continue to be for some time, the lack of a backup capability. In any event, the general term applied to them all is *disk.*

Take a program – any program – and seal it in a small envelope. Mark that program Business BASIC. Take that envelope and seal it in a larger envelope marked Sophisticated Operating System (SOS). Do all this figuratively, at least. If you can conceptualize that this program solves a problem in a language called BASIC and functions through an operating system called SOS, then you pretty much have the idea. In technical terms, the operating system *executes* the BASIC program. It does so as shown in Figure 5.1.

PLAN FOR THE CHAPTER

In the balance of this chapter we'll deal first with the use of disk for the storage and retrieval of programs. In doing so we will talk about

```
*********************************************************************
*  SOPHISTICATED OPERATING SYSTEM (SOS)                             *
* *************************************************************** *
* *  BUSINESS BASIC                                              * *
* * *********************************************************** * *
* * *  FRAME (.D2/APPLE-5-1)                                   * * *
* * * ******************************************************* * * *
* * * * (.D2/APPLE-5-2)          *  (.D2/APPLE-5-5)          * * * *
* * * *                          *     GRADE SCHOOL MATH     * * * *
* * * *    BREAKEVEN ANALYSIS    *  ************************ * * * *
* * * *                          *  *     ROOT PROGRAM       * * * *
* * * ****************************  *                        * * * *
* * * * (.D2/APPLE-5-3)          *  ************************ * * * *
* * * *                          *  *          *             * * * *
* * * *  ENGLISH TO METRIC CONV. *  *    ADD   *     SUB     * * * *
* * * *                          *  *          *             * * * *
* * * ****************************  ************************ * * * *
* * * * (.D2/APPLE-5-4)          *  *          *             * * * *
* * * *                          *  *    MUL   *     DIV     * * * *
* * * *   TWENTY-THREE MATCHES   *  *          *             * * * *
* * * ****************************  ************************ * * * *
* * *********************************************************** * *
* *************************************************************** *
*********************************************************************
```

Figure 5.1.

Combining segments of programs into one program and about transferring control and data from one program to another. In the process we'll learn about disk techniques and the handling of data. The latter part of the chapter will begin an introduction of the use of disk for storage, retention, and retrieval of data. The chapter will present seven programs, as follows:

1. APPLE-5-1, which is a frame program for the next four programs, APPLE-5-2 through APPLE-5-5.
2. APPLE-5-2 – Breakeven Point Calculator.
3. APPLE-5-3 – English-to-Metric Conversion.
4. APPLE-5-4 – Twenty-three Matches.
5. APPLE-5-5 – Grade School Math, consisting of a root segment with four routines that must be called at run time.
6. The LAZY DAZE GOLF COURSE tee-off schedule.
7. The CAMP SLEAZY QUARTERMASTER (inventory program).

The names of the programs are critical for the first five, as the programs intercommunicate and those names are used within the programs themselves. The remaining two do not have that requirement.

A frame program operates within BASIC which operates within SOS – the envelope concept previously discussed. The purpose of a frame program is to simply provide the mechanism to call other programs. This is accomplished by the use of the frame as a menu – a means of offering the options. The screen from the frame program APPLE-5-1 is shown in Figure 5.2; the entire frame program is given in Figure 5.3.

```
THIS IS A FRAME PROGRAM.  YOU MAY SELECT ONE OF THESE PROGRAMS:

              1.   BREAKEVEN ANALYSIS

              2.   ENGLISH TO METRIC CONVERSION

              3.   TWENTY-THREE MATCHES

              4.   GRADE SCHOOL MATH


SELECT:
```

Figure 5.2.

From this short program several things may be learned. First, we must recognize that it is a feature of Business BASIC that once variables have values, those values will remain intact even though other programs have been called, and are only removed with a CLEAR statement. In this example, this program will be calling several other programs, which, as we will see, will call this program once again. Thus, the CLEAR of statement 20.

Control passes from this program to one of the other programs as a function of the CHAIN commands, statements 230 to 260. In this instance, control is passed to one of four programs residing on disk drive .D2. The CHAIN command will call in the requested program and commence execution at the first statement, as if you had previously loaded the program and typed RUN. Despite the fact that the called programs have not yet been written, you can execute this program. You will, however, obtain an error message. It *is* possible to intercept error situations. That's done with an ON ERR statement-number command. Using the ON ERR command, you can divert to determine where the error occurred, which will give you some idea of the nature of the error. When you no longer need to check for errors, then you can toggle it the other way with OFF ERR. Figure 5.4

```
10 HOME
20 CLEAR
30 INPUT "ENTER YOUR NAME: ",USER.NAME$
40 VPOS=10:HPOS=10
50 PRINT "THIS IS A FRAME PROGRAM.  YOU MAY SELECT ";
60 PRINT "ONE OF THESE PROGRAMS:";
70 VPOS=12:HPOS=20
80 PRINT "1.  BREAKEVEN ANALYSIS";
90 VPOS=14:HPOS=20
100 PRINT "2.  ENGLISH TO METRIC CONVERSION";
110 VPOS=16:HPOS=20
120 PRINT "3.  TWENTY-THREE MATCHES";
130 VPOS=18:HPOS=20
140 PRINT "4.  GRADE-SCHOOL MATH";
150 VPOS=24:HPOS=10
160 PRINT "SELECT: ";
170 GET Z$:IF Z$ = " " THEN 170
180 PROGRAM = VAL(Z$)
190 IF (PROGRAM < 1) OR (PROGRAM > 4) THEN 280
200 PRINT PROGRAM;
210 ON PROGRAM GOTO 230,240,250,260
220 GOTO 280
230 CHAIN .D2/APPLE-5-2
240 CHAIN .D2/APPLE-5-3
250 CHAIN .D2/APPLE-5-4
260 CHAIN .D2/APPLE-5-5
270 GOTO 10
280 PRINT CHR$(7)
290 VPOS=24:HPOS=1
300 FOR N = 1 TO 79
310      PRINT " ";
320      NEXT N
330 GOTO 150
```

Figure 5.3.

```
15  ON ERR GOSUB 500
    - - - -
500 IF ERRLIN = 230 THEN PRINT "BREAKEVEN UNAVAILABLE"
510 IF ERRLIN = 240 THEN PRINT "CONVERSION UNAVAILABLE"
520 IF ERRLIN = 250 THEN PRINT "MATCHES UNAVAILABLE"
530 IF ERRLIN = 260 THEN PRINT "MATH UNAVAILABLE
540 RESUME
```

Figure 5.4.

shows an example of how an error routine could be incorporated to advise that the programs to which you had CHAINed are not available. The RESUME does what it says – and is the return mechanism from the ON ERR error processing subroutine.

Now on to the second program: APPLE-5-3; refer to Figure 5.5.

This program has been sequenced differently from the others to illustrate that it really doesn't matter what the sequence numbers are.

```
1000 HOME
1010 PRINT "HELLO, ";USER.NAME$
1020 VPOS=3:HPOS=10
1030 PRINT "B R E A K E V E N   P O I N T   C A L C U L A T O R"
1040 VPOS=6:HPOS=31
1050 A$ = ""
1060 PRINT "ENTER FIXED COSTS: ";
1070 GET Z$
1080 IF Z$ = CHR$(13) THEN 1120
1090 PRINT Z$;
1100 A$ = A$ + Z$
1110 GOTO 1070
1120 VPOS=6:HPOS=31
1130 FIXED.COSTS = VAL(A$)
1140 PRINT "ENTER FIXED COSTS: ";FIXED.COSTS
1150 IF FIXED.COSTS < 0 THEN PRINT CHR$(7):GOTO 1040
1160 A$ = ""
1170 VPOS=9:HPOS=20
1180 PRINT "ENTER VARIABLE COST PER UNIT: ";
1190 GET Z$
1200 IF Z$ = CHR$(13) THEN 1240
1210 PRINT Z$;
1220 A$ = A$ + Z$
1230 GOTO 1190
1240 VPOS=9:HPOS=20
1250 VARIABLE.COST.PER.UNIT = VAL(A$)
1260 PRINT "ENTER VARIABLE COST PER UNIT: ";VARIABLE.COST.PER.UNIT
1270 IF VARIABLE.COST.PER.UNIT < 0 THEN PRINT CHR$(7):GOTO 1170
1280 A$ = ""
1290 VPOS=12:HPOS=29
1300 PRINT "ENTER THE UNIT PRICE: ";
1310 GET Z$
1320 IF Z$ = CHR$(13) THEN 1360
1330 PRINT Z$;
1340 A$ = A$ + Z$
1350 GOTO 1310
1360 VPOS=12:HPOS=29
1370 UNIT.PRICE = VAL(A$)
1380 PRINT "ENTER THE UNIT PRICE: ";UNIT.PRICE
1390 IF UNIT.PRICE <0 THEN PRINT CHR$(7):GOTO 1290
1400 QUANTITY = (FIXED.COSTS/(UNIT.PRICE - VARIABLE.COST.PER.UNIT))
1410 IF QUANTITY < 0 THEN QUANTITY = 1:QUANTITY.FLAG$ = "*":FLAG$ = "*"
1420 TOTAL.VARIABLE.COSTS = VARIABLE.COST.PER.UNIT * QUANTITY
1430 SALES.AT.BREAKEVEN = UNIT.PRICE * QUANTITY
1440 TOTAL.COSTS = FIXED.COSTS + (VARIABLE.COST.PER.UNIT * QUANTITY)
1450 UNIT.COST = TOTAL.COSTS/QUANTITY
1460 IF UNIT.COST < 0 THEN UNIT.COST = 1:UNIT.COST.FLAG$ = "*":FLAG$ = "*"
1470 HOME
1480 VPOS=8:HPOS=1
1490 FOR N = 1 TO 79:PRINT CHR$(223);:NEXT N
1500 VPOS=10:HPOS=20
1510 PRINT "B R E A K E V E N   A N A L Y S I S"
1520 VPOS=12:HPOS=20
1530 PRINT "BREAKEVEN QUANTITY: ";TAB(43);
1540 PRINT USING "5&";QUANTITY;
1550 PRINT TAB(52);QUANTITY.FLAG$;
1560 VPOS=13:HPOS=20
1570 PRINT "BREAKEVEN SALES: ";TAB(40);
1580 PRINT USING "$5&.2&";SALES.AT.BREAKEVEN;
1590 VPOS=16:HPOS=20
1600 PRINT "FIXED COSTS: ";TAB(40);
1610 PRINT USING "$5&.2&";FIXED.COSTS;
1620 VPOS=17:HPOS=20
1630 PRINT "VARIABLE COSTS: ";TAB(40);
1640 PRINT USING "5&.##";TOTAL.VARIABLE.COSTS;
```

Figure 5.5.

```
1650 VPOS=18:HPOS=20
1660 PRINT "";TAB(40);"__________";
1670 VPOS=19:HPOS=20
1680 PRINT "TOTAL COSTS: ";TAB(40);
1690 PRINT USING "$5&.2&";TOTAL.COSTS;
1700 VPOS=21:HPOS=20
1710 PRINT "UNIT COST: ";TAB(40);
1720 PRINT USING "$5&.2&";UNIT.COST;
1730 PRINT TAB(52);UNIT.COST.FLAG$;
1740 VPOS=22:HPOS=1
1750 FOR N = 1 TO 79:PRINT CHR$(223);:NEXT N
1760 VPOS=23:HPOS=20
1770 IF FLAG$ = "*" THEN PRINT "* INDICATES THAT THE FIELD WAS < 0";
1780 VPOS=25:HPOS=1
1790 PRINT "DO YOU WISH TO DO ANOTHER CALCULATION (Y/N)? ";
1800 GET Z$
1810 IF Z$ = "Y" THEN 1000
1820 CHAIN .D2/APPLE-5-1
```

Figure 5.5. (continued)

They can be the same as the frame program or they can be different – *provided that they are CHAINed.*

This is a straightforward little program for determining financial breakeven points. Note that the variable passed from the frame program – USER.NAME$ – is printed at 1010, along with a word of greeting. No attempt has been made to do any sophisticated programing to intercept a bogus value; thus if you use bonafide numbers, you will get bonafide answers. The single exception to this rule occurs when a figure is derived that is smaller than 1; such a figure is forced to be 1 and is flagged.

Recall that we discussed the fact that a numeric value, when printed, occupies one space for the sign and that only negative signs are printed. Perhaps you also noticed that decimal point alignment was difficult, as well. Statements 1540, 1580, 1610, 1640, 1690, and 1720 all contain what are called *edit masks.* The numeric variable specified *second* is filtered through the edit mask, specified *first* (following the USING clause). Again, this has been set to work with a specified field size. Larger fields will give exclamation points (!) in return, you will recall.

When you are asked if you require another calculation and you do, the program is repeated. If you do not, the program CHAINs back to the frame program in Statement 1820.

Except for its numbering sequence, there is nothing significantly different about the English-to-Metric Conversion program. Refer to Figure 5.6. In this program, the exit from the program is established as the value of zero on the option screen. It may not be immediately obvious, but there is a menu presented by statements 80 and 90. In programing, it makes little difference whether the internal branching is a function of an alphabetic menu or a numeric menu, except that the alphabetic menu is ordinarily used whenever the alphabetics have meaning. Such is the case, as we shall see, in the program called Grade School Math, APPLE-5-5.

```
1000 HOME
1010 PRINT "HELLO, ";USER.NAME$
1020 DIM A(17)
1030 PRINT "ENGLISH TO METRIC CONVERSION":PRINT
1040 PRINT " 0 .";TAB(10);"END THE PROGRAM"
1050 FOR N = 1 TO 17:READ A(N),A$,B$
1060      PRINT N;".";TAB(10);A$;" TO ";B$
1070      NEXT N
1080 RESTORE
1090 PRINT
1100 INPUT "WHICH CONVERSION DO YOU NEED";N
1110 IF N = 0 THEN CHAIN .D2/APPLE-5-1
1120 IF N > 17 THEN 1100
1130 FOR Z = 1 TO N:READ A(N),A$,B$:NEXT Z
1140 RESTORE
1150 INPUT "VALUE TO BE CONVERTED: ",I
1160 R = I*A(N):IF N = 17 THEN R =(I-32) * 5/9
1170 PRINT
1180 PRINT I;" ";A$;" ="R;" ";B$
1190 INPUT "PRESS ENTER TO GO AGAIN",B$:GOTO 1000
1200 DATA 2.54,INCHES,CENTIMETERS
1210 DATA 30.48,FEET,CENTIMETERS
1220 DATA .3048,FEET,METERS
1230 DATA .9144,YARDS,METERS
1240 DATA 1.609,MILES,KILOMETERS
1250 DATA 4.929,TSP.,CUBIC CM.
1260 DATA 14.788,TBSP,CUBIC CM.
1270 DATA .2366,CUPS,LITERS
1280 DATA .4732,PINTS,LITERS
1290 DATA .9463,QUARTS,LITERS
1300 DATA 3.785,GALLONS,LITERS
1310 DATA 35.24,BUSHELS,LITERS
1320 DATA 8.809,PECKS,LITERS
1330 DATA 28.3495,OUNCES,GRAMS
1340 DATA .4536,POUNDS,KILOGRAMS
1350 DATA 907.2,TONS,KILOGRAMS
1360 DATA .6214,DEGREES F.,DEGREES C.
```

Figure 5.6.

Some planning must be given to the numbering sequences of the programs, as mentioned. In the instance where a program is CHAINed, the numbers are meaningful only to the new program, and the former program has disappeared. If there is a possibility that some of the programs might be combined with other programs, you must be careful, for the incoming statement numbers would conflict with those already used. Again, we'll explore this with Grade School Math.

Since we didn't want this book to be completely about business, we've included a game (Twenty-Three Matches) and an educational program (the Grade School Math), both of which should be fun for any children in your life. The game program is given in Figure 5.7.

```
1000 HOME
1010 PRINT "HELLO, ";USER.NAME$
1020 ROW = 1
1030 VPOS=ROW + 1:HPOS=30
1040 PRINT "THIS IS THE GAME OF 23 MATCHES"
1050 VPOS=ROW + 3:HPOS=10
1060 PRINT "I WILL PLACE 23 MATCHES ON THE SCREEN.  ";
1070 PRINT "WE WILL TAKE TURNS REMOVING";
1080 VPOS=ROW + 4:HPOS=10
1090 PRINT "ONE, TWO, OR THREE MATCHES.  ";
1100 PRINT "IF YOU MUST REMOVE THE LAST MATCH, YOU";
1110 VPOS=ROW + 5:HPOS=10
1120 PRINT "WILL BE THE LOSER...";
1130 FOR Z = 1 TO 1000:NEXT Z
1140 MATCHES = 23
1150 MOVE = 1
1160 GOSUB 1260            :REM DRAW THE MATCHES
1170 PLAYER$ = "X":COMPUTER$ = ""
1180 GOSUB 1570            :REM DRAW THE SCOREBOARD
1190 GOSUB 1710            :REM MAKE THE PLAYER'S MOVE
1200 GOSUB 1260            :REM DRAW THE MATCHES
1210 PLAYER$ = "":COMPUTER$ = "X"
1220 GOSUB 1570            :REM DRAW THE SCOREBOARD
1230 GOSUB 1960            :REM MAKE THE COMPUTER'S MOVE
1240 GOSUB 1260            :REM DRAW THE MATCHES
1250 GOTO 1170
1260 REM *******************************
1270 REM * DRAW THE MATCHES AND FLAMES *
1280 REM *******************************
1290 HOME
1300 RESTORE
1310 COLORFILL=0:COLORPEN=15
1320 OPEN#1,".GRAFIX"
1330 INVOKE "BGRAF.INV"
1340 PERFORM INITGRAFIX
1350 MODE=2:BUFFER=1
1360 PERFORM GRAFIXMODE(%MODE,%BUFFER)
1370 PERFORM FILLCOLOR(%COLORFILL)
1380 PERFORM FILLPORT
1390 PERFORM GRAFIXON
1400 A = 1
```

Figure 5.7.

```
1410 FOR Z = 1 TO MATCHES
1420     FOR N = A TO A+6
1430         B=175:C=100
1440         PERFORM MOVETO(%N,%B)
1450         PERFORM PENCOLOR(%COLORPEN)
1460         PERFORM LINETO(%N,%C)
1470         A = A + 25
1480         NEXT N
1490     NEXT Z
1500 FLAME = 1
1510 FOR N = 1 TO MATCHES
1520     PERFORM MOVETO(%FLAME,%180)
1530     PRINT #1,"^"
1540     FLAME=FLAME+25
1550     NEXT N
1560 RETURN
1570 REM *************************
1580 REM * POSITION THE SCOREBOARD *
1590 REM *************************
1600 VPOS=18:HPOS=15
1610 PRINT "MOVE     MATCHES REMAINING     YOUR MOVE    MY MOVE"
1620 VPOS=20:HPOS=15
1630 PRINT MOVE
1640 VPOS=20:HPOS=30
1650 PRINT MATCHES
1660 VPOS=20:HPOS=50
1670 PRINT PLAYER$
1680 VPOS=20:HPOS=62
1690 PRINT COMPUTER$
1700 RETURN
1710 REM ************************************
1720 REM * ROUTINE TO GAIN THE PLAYER'S MOVE *
1730 REM ************************************
1740 MOVE = MOVE + 1
1750 VPOS=22:HPOS=10
1760 PRINT "HOW MANY MATCHES DO YOU WISH TO REMOVE (1, 2, OR 3)? ";
1770 GET Z$
1780 PRINT Z$
1790 FOR Z = 1 TO 1500:NEXT Z
1800 A = VAL(Z$)
1810 IF (A > 0) AND (A < 4) THEN 1910
1820 VPOS=25:HPOS=10
1830 PRINT "INVALID - RETRY";
1840 PRINT CHR$(7)
1850 FOR Z = 1 TO 1500:NEXT Z
1860 VPOS=22:HPOS=1
1870 PRINT SPACE$(79);
1880 VPOS=25:HPOS=1
1890 PRINT SPACE$(79);
1900 GOTO 1750
1910 MATCHES = MATCHES - A
1920 IF MATCHES = 3 THEN MATCHES = 4
1930 GOSUB 2150
1940 RETURN
1950 IF A > MATCHES THEN 1820
```

Figure 5.7. (continued)

```
1960 REM ***************************************
1970 REM * ROUTINE TO GAIN THE COMPUTER'S MOVE *
1980 REM ***************************************
1990 MOVE = MOVE + 1
2000 VPOS=22:HPOS=7
2010 PRINT "I'M DECIDING HOW MANY MATCHES TO REMOVE.   ";
2020 FOR Z = 1 TO 1500:NEXT Z
2030 IF (MATCHES > 3) AND (MATCHES < 5) THEN 2120
2040 REMOVE = INT(RND(MATCHES)*10)
2050 IF (REMOVE > 3) OR (REMOVE < 1) THEN 2040
2060 MATCHES = MATCHES - REMOVE
2070 PRINT "I WILL REMOVE";REMOVE;
2080 IF REMOVE = 1 THEN PRINT "MATCH.";:GOTO 2110
2090 PRINT "MATCHES.";
2100 GOSUB 2150
2110 FOR Z = 1 TO 1500:NEXT Z:RETURN
2120 REMOVE = MATCHES - 1
2130 MATCHES = 1
2140 GOTO 2070
2150 REM *******************
2160 REM * SCORING ROUTINE *
2170 REM *******************
2180 IF (PLAYER$ = "X") AND (MATCHES < 2) THEN 2210
2190 IF (COMPUTER$ = "X") AND (MATCHES < 2) THEN 2240
2200 RETURN
2210 GOSUB 1260:GOSUB 1570
2220 VPOS=24:HPOS=1
2230 PRINT "THE PLAYER WINS";:GOTO 2270
2240 GOSUB 1260:GOSUB 1570
2250 VPOS=24:HPOS=1
2260 PRINT "THE COMPUTER WINS";
2270 VPOS=25:HPOS=1
2280 PRINT "DO YOU WISH TO PLAY AGAIN (Y/N)? ";
2290 GET Z$
2300 PRINT Z$
2310 IF Z$ = "Y" THEN 1000
2320 CLOSE #1
2330 CHAIN .D2/APPLE-5-1
```

Figure 5.7. (continued)

As you can see, we have adapted one of the graphics programs which we did in the last chapter to this program, beginning with statement 1290. The general concept of operation is that the matches are removed by you or by the computer, and then the entire field of matches (at an appropriate number) is redrawn. You are allowed to remove from 1 to 4 matches. Likewise, the computer. You can select. The computer must go through some gyration to select, using a random number.

Enter and play this game, and you'll find that it's not particularly difficult, partly because complex strategy has been kept out of it. The game itself is a very old one. In England it is known as *Nim,* and a junior high school teacher named Leo Christopherson is reputed to have changed its matches to robots, animated them, added sound, published *Android Nim,* and become quite wealthy in the process. You never know where the most simple game will lead.

Before we can use the Grade School Math program within the frame program, there is some work to be done. The general intent is to place two or more programs together into one program. In the examples which follow, each section is uniquely numbered, a requirement for combining programs. There are two ways to combine programs on the Apple III, and they are both part of the RENUMBERing program we discussed in an earlier chapter. The general format is:

```
INVOKE RENUMBER.INV
PERFORM APPEND (@FIRST$,@SECOND$,@OUT$)
```

or

```
INVOKE RENUMBER.INV
PERFORM MERGE (@FIRST$,@SECOND$,@OUT$)
```

The differences in these examples are slight, but important. APPEND adds SECOND$ to the end of FIRST$, and if there is a statement number overlap, you have a problem. MERGE adds new code from SECOND$ to existing code in FIRST$, and if there are duplicate statement numbers, statements from SECOND$ overlay identically numbered statements from FIRST$. FIRST$ and SECOND$ are the names of the files containing your programs. OUT$ contains the name of where you would like to file the result. Thus, to take the root program of Figure 5.8 and add to it the program of Figure 5.9, which we'll call ADD, it would be done like this:

```
INVOKE RENUMBER.INV
APPEND (@.D2/APPLE-5-5,@.D2/ADD,@.D2/APPLE-5-5)
```

You would then repeat the process for each program element, collecting it to the program APPLE-5-5.

```
10 HOME
20 PRINT "HELLO, ";USER.NAME$
30 A$ = "                                    "
40 VPOS=4:HPOS=5
50 PRINT "THIS IS A MATH EXERCISE BASED ON ";
60 PRINT "WHOLE NUMBERS IN THE RANGE OF 0 - 12";
70 VPOS=6:HPOS=8
80 PRINT "IT ALSO SHOWS HOW PROGRAMS WHICH";
90 PRINT "ARE ENTITIES MAY BE COMBINED";
100 VPOS=8:HPOS=23
110 PRINT "SELECT EXERCISE YOU WISH TO USE ";
120 VPOS=10:HPOS=30
130 PRINT "<A>DDITION";
140 VPOS=12:HPOS=30
150 PRINT "<S>UBTRACTION";
160 VPOS=14:HPOS=30
170 PRINT "<M>ULTIPLICATION";
180 VPOS=16:HPOS=30
190 PRINT "<D>IVISION";
200 VPOS=18:HPOS=29
210 PRINT "E<X>IT THE PROGRAM";
220 VPOS=20:HPOS=23
230 PRINT "SELECT: ";
240 GET Z$
250 IF Z$ = "A" THEN PRINT Z$:GOTO 1000
260 IF Z$ = "S" THEN PRINT Z$:GOTO 2000
270 IF Z$ = "M" THEN PRINT Z$:GOTO 3000
280 IF Z$ = "D" THEN PRINT Z$:GOTO 4000
290 IF Z$ = "X" THEN PRINT Z$:CHAIN .D2/APPLE-5-1
300 GOTO 240
310 REM ************************
320 REM * THE NUMBER GENERATOR *
330 REM ************************
340 X = 1:Y = 2
350 A = INT(RND(X) * 20)
360 IF (A < 1) OR (A > 12) THEN 350
370 B = INT(RND(Y) * 20)
380 IF (B < 1) OR (B > 12) THEN 370
390 X = X + 1:Y = Y + 2
400 RETURN
```

Figure 5.8.

```
1000 REM ************************
1010 REM * THE ADDITION ROUTINE *
1020 REM ************************
1030 FOR Z = 1 TO 1000:NEXT Z
1040 GOSUB 310
1050 HOME
1060 VPOS=10:HPOS=10
1070 PRINT "ADD: ";A;" + ";B;" = ";CHR$(219);CHR$(219);
1080 VPOS=15:HPOS=10
1090 PRINT "WHAT IS YOUR ANSWER? ";:INPUT "",C
1100 IF ABS(C) < > A + B THEN 1170
1110 VPOS=20:HPOS=10
1120 PRINT "CORRECT";A$;
```

Figure 5.9.

```
1130 VPOS=24:HPOS=10
1140 PRINT "DO YOU WISH TO DO ANOTHER ADDITION PROBLEM (Y/N)? ";
1150 GET Z$
1160 IF Z$ = "Y" THEN 1040 ELSE 10
1170 VPOS=20:HPOS=10
1180 PRINT "NOT CORRECT - TRY AGAIN";
1190 VPOS=15:HPOS=1
1200 FOR N = 1 TO 79:PRINT " ";:NEXT N
1210 GOTO 1080
```

Figure 5.9. (continued)

The subtraction routine is Figure 5.10, the multiplication routine is Figure 5.11, and the division routine is Figure 5.12.

```
2000 REM ***************************
2010 REM * THE SUBTRACTION ROUTINE *
2020 REM ***************************
2030 FOR Z = 1 TO 1000:NEXT Z
2040 GOSUB 310
2050 HOME
2060 IF B > A THEN SWAP A,B
2070 VPOS=10:HPOS=10
2080 PRINT "SUBTRACT: ";A;" - ";B;" = ";CHR$(219);CHR$(219);
2090 VPOS=15:HPOS=10
2100 PRINT "WHAT IS YOUR ANSWER? ";:INPUT "",C
2110 IF ABS(C) < > A - B THEN 2180
2120 VPOS=20:HPOS=10
2130 PRINT "CORRECT";A$;
2140 VPOS=24:HPOS=10
2150 PRINT "DO YOU WISH TO DO ANOTHER SUBTRACTION PROBLEM (Y/N)? ";
2160 GET Z$
2170 IF Z$ = "Y" THEN 2040 ELSE 10
2180 VPOS=20:HPOS=10
2190 PRINT "NOT CORRECT - TRY AGAIN";
2200 VPOS=15:HPOS=1
2210 FOR N = 1 TO 79:PRINT " ";:NEXT N
2220 GOTO 2090
```

Figure 5.10.

```
3000 REM ******************************
3010 REM * THE MULTIPLICATION ROUTINE *
3020 REM ******************************
3030 FOR Z = 1 TO 1000:NEXT Z
3040 GOSUB 310
3050 HOME
3060 VPOS=10:HPOS=10
3070 PRINT "MULTIPLY: ";A;" * ";B;" = ";CHR$(219);CHR$(219);
3080 VPOS=15:HPOS=10
3090 PRINT "WHAT IS YOUR ANSWER? ";:INPUT "",C
3100 IF ABS(C) < > A * B THEN 3170
```

Figure 5.11.

```
3110 VPOS=20:HPOS=10
3120 PRINT "CORRECT";A$;
3130 VPOS=24:HPOS=10
3140 PRINT "DO YOU WISH TO DO ANOTHER MULTIPLICATION PROBLEM (Y/N)? ";
3150 GET Z$
3160 IF Z$ = "Y" THEN 3040 ELSE 10
3170 VPOS=20:HPOS=10
3180 PRINT "NOT CORRECT - TRY AGAIN";
3190 VPOS=15:HPOS=1
3200 FOR N = 1 TO 79:PRINT " ";:NEXT N
3210 GOTO 3080
```

Figure 5.11. (continued)

```
4000 REM ***********************
4010 REM * THE DIVISION ROUTINE *
4020 REM ***********************
4030 FOR Z = 1 TO 1000:NEXT Z
4040 GOSUB 310
4050 HOME
4060 IF B > A THEN SWAP A,B
4070 VPOS=10:HPOS=10
4080 PRINT "DIVIDE: ";A;" / ";B;" = ";CHR$(219);CHR$(219);
4090 PRINT "  QUOTIENT,  ";CHR$(219);CHR$(219);"  REMAINDER";
4100 VPOS=15:HPOS=10
4110 PRINT "WHAT IS THE QUOTIENT? ";:INPUT Q:Q = ABS(Q)
4120 VPOS=16:HPOS=10
4130 PRINT "WHAT IS THE REMAINDER? ";:INPUT R:R = ABS(R)
4140 IF A < > ((Q * B) + R) THEN 4210
4150 VPOS=20:HPOS=10
4160 PRINT "CORRECT";A$;
4170 VPOS=24:HPOS=10
4180 PRINT "DO YOU WISH TO DO ANOTHER DIVISION PROBLEM (Y/N)? ";
4190 GET Z$
4200 IF Z$ = "Y" THEN 4040 ELSE 10
4210 VPOS=20:HPOS=10
4220 PRINT "NOT CORRECT - TRY AGAIN";
4230 VPOS=15:HPOS=1
4240 FOR N = 1 TO 79:PRINT " ";:NEXT N
4250 VPOS=16:HPOS=1
4260 FOR N = 1 TO 79:PRINT " ";:NEXT N
4270 GOTO 4100
```

Figure 5.12.

Again, each of these exist as separate programs to be combined into one which looks like Figure 5.13.

```
10 HOME
20 PRINT "HELLO, ";USER.NAME$
30 A$ = "
40 VPOS=4:HPOS=5
50 PRINT "THIS IS A MATH EXERCISE BASED ON ";
```

Figure 5.13.

```
60 PRINT "WHOLE NUMBERS IN THE RANGE OF 0 - 12";
70 VPOS=6:HPOS=8
80 PRINT "IT ALSO SHOWS HOW PROGRAMS WHICH";
90 PRINT "ARE ENTITIES MAY BE COMBINED";
100 VPOS=8:HPOS=23
110 PRINT "SELECT EXERCISE YOU WISH TO USE ";
120 VPOS=10:HPOS=30
130 PRINT "<A>DDITION";
140 VPOS=12:HPOS=30
150 PRINT "<S>UBTRACTION";
160 VPOS=14:HPOS=30
170 PRINT "<M>ULTIPLICATION";
180 VPOS=16:HPOS=30
190 PRINT "<D>IVISION";
200 VPOS=18:HPOS=29
210 PRINT "E<X>IT THE PROGRAM";
220 VPOS=20:HPOS=23
230 PRINT "SELECT: ";
240 GET Z$
250 IF Z$ = "A" THEN PRINT Z$:GOTO 1000
260 IF Z$ = "S" THEN PRINT Z$:GOTO 2000
270 IF Z$ = "M" THEN PRINT Z$:GOTO 3000
280 IF Z$ = "D" THEN PRINT Z$:GOTO 4000
290 IF Z$ = "X" THEN PRINT Z$:CHAIN .D2/APPLE-5-1
300 GOTO 240
310 REM ************************
320 REM * THE NUMBER GENERATOR *
330 REM ************************
340 X = 1:Y = 2
350 A = INT(RND(X) * 20)
360 IF (A < 1) OR (A > 12) THEN 350
370 B = INT(RND(Y) * 20)
380 IF (B < 1) OR (B > 12) THEN 370
390 X = X + 1:Y = Y + 2
400 RETURN
1000 REM ************************
1010 REM * THE ADDITION ROUTINE *
1020 REM ************************
1030 FOR Z = 1 TO 1000:NEXT Z
1040 GOSUB 310
1050 HOME
1060 VPOS=10:HPOS=10
1070 PRINT "ADD: ";A;" + ";B;" = ";CHR$(219);CHR$(219);
1080 VPOS=15:HPOS=10
1090 PRINT "WHAT IS YOUR ANSWER? ";:INPUT "",C
1100 IF ABS(C) < > A + B THEN 1170
1110 VPOS=20:HPOS=10
1120 PRINT "CORRECT";A$;
1130 VPOS=24:HPOS=10
1140 PRINT "DO YOU WISH TO DO ANOTHER ADDITION PROBLEM (Y/N)? ";
1150 GET Z$
1160 IF Z$ = "Y" THEN 1040 ELSE 10
1170 VPOS=20:HPOS=10
1180 PRINT "NOT CORRECT - TRY AGAIN";
1190 VPOS=15:HPOS=1
1200 FOR N = 1 TO 79:PRINT " ";:NEXT N
```

Figure 5.13. (continued)

```
1210 GOTO 1080
2000 REM ***************************
2010 REM * THE SUBTRACTION ROUTINE *
2020 REM ***************************
2030 FOR Z = 1 TO 1000:NEXT Z
2040 GOSUB 310
2050 HOME
2060 IF B > A THEN SWAP A,B
2070 VPOS=10:HPOS=10
2080 PRINT "SUBTRACT: ";A;" - ";B;" = ";CHR$(219);CHR$(219);
2090 VPOS=15:HPOS=10
2100 PRINT "WHAT IS YOUR ANSWER? ";:INPUT "",C
2110 IF ABS(C) < > A - B THEN 2180
2120 VPOS=20:HPOS=10
2130 PRINT "CORRECT";A$;
2140 VPOS=24:HPOS=10
2150 PRINT "DO YOU WISH TO DO ANOTHER SUBTRACTION PROBLEM (Y/N)? ";
2160 GET Z$
2170 IF Z$ = "Y" THEN 2040 ELSE 10
2180 VPOS=20:HPOS=10
2190 PRINT "NOT CORRECT - TRY AGAIN";
2200 VPOS=15:HPOS=1
2210 FOR N = 1 TO 79:PRINT " ";:NEXT N
2220 GOTO 2090
3000 REM ******************************
3010 REM * THE MULTIPLICATION ROUTINE *
3020 REM ******************************
3030 FOR Z = 1 TO 1000:NEXT Z
3040 GOSUB 310
3050 HOME
3060 VPOS=10:HPOS=10
3070 PRINT "MULTIPLY: ";A;" * ";B;" = ";CHR$(219);CHR$(219);
3080 VPOS=15:HPOS=10
3090 PRINT "WHAT IS YOUR ANSWER? ";:INPUT "",C
3100 IF ABS(C) < > A * B THEN 3170
3110 VPOS=20:HPOS=10
3120 PRINT "CORRECT";A$;
3130 VPOS=24:HPOS=10
3140 PRINT "DO YOU WISH TO DO ANOTHER MULTIPLICATION PROBLEM (Y/N)? ";
3150 GET Z$
3160 IF Z$ = "Y" THEN 3040 ELSE 10
3170 VPOS=20:HPOS=10
3180 PRINT "NOT CORRECT - TRY AGAIN";
3190 VPOS=15:HPOS=1
3200 FOR N = 1 TO 79:PRINT " ";:NEXT N
3210 GOTO 3080
4000 REM ************************
4010 REM * THE DIVISION ROUTINE *
4020 REM ************************
4030 FOR Z = 1 TO 1000:NEXT Z
4040 GOSUB 310
4050 HOME
4060 IF B > A THEN SWAP A,B
4070 VPOS=10:HPOS=10
4080 PRINT "DIVIDE: ";A;" / ";B;" = ";CHR$(219);CHR$(219);
4090 PRINT "  QUOTIENT,  ";CHR$(219);CHR$(219);"  REMAINDER";
4100 VPOS=15:HPOS=10
```

Figure 5.13. (continued)

```
4110 PRINT "WHAT IS THE QUOTIENT? ";:INPUT Q:Q = ABS(Q)
4120 VPOS=16:HPOS=10
4130 PRINT "WHAT IS THE REMAINDER? ";:INPUT R:R = ABS(R)
4140 IF A < > ((Q * B) + R) THEN 4210
4150 VPOS=20:HPOS=10
4160 PRINT "CORRECT";A$;
4170 VPOS=24:HPOS=10
4180 PRINT "DO YOU WISH TO DO ANOTHER DIVISION PROBLEM (Y/N)? ";
4190 GET Z$
4200 IF Z$ = "Y" THEN 4040 ELSE 10
4210 VPOS=20:HPOS=10
4220 PRINT "NOT CORRECT - TRY AGAIN";
4230 VPOS=15:HPOS=1
4240 FOR N = 1 TO 79:PRINT " ";:NEXT N
4250 VPOS=16:HPOS=1
4260 FOR N = 1 TO 79:PRINT " ";:NEXT N
4270 GOTO 4100
```

Figure 5.13. (continued)

DISK APPLICATIONS

We can now begin to concentrate on using the disk for applications useful to business purposes. The program that follows is a scheduling program for a golf course. Faced with having to keep a book of reservations, the Lazy Daze Golf Course has decided to use an Apple III to computerize a day's schedule. As you review this program, please keep in mind that we are inventorying players in a slot called *tee-off time.* We could just as easily be inventorying widgets in a slot called *part number,* people in a slot called *airplane seats,* or haircut hopefuls in a shop called the Clip Joint. You get the picture.

Before we start, a few thoughts about using disk in a *random* fashion: "Random" is technically a misnomer for this system, for the simple reason that its capability is *finite.* Every record placed on a disk has some common identifying feature, usually a sequence number close enough to other similar numbers to allow efficient allocation of the storage. In an employee personnel file, for instance, a small business might have ten people, numbered from 1 (the owner) to 10 (the latest trainee). Ten years have passed, however, since the company was formed, and the current crop of employees are numbered 1000 to 1100; but numbers 1, 2, and 3 still exist. The numbers in the sequence would obviously contain a large hole. When holes are present in a sequence, a different method of accounting must be used. Figure 5.14 shows the list of tee-off times for the Lazy Daze Golf Course (LDGC).

```
2190 '******************
2200 '* STARTING TIMES *
2210 '******************
2220 DATA 0800,0815,0830,0845
2230 DATA 0900,0915,0930,0945
2240 DATA 1000,1015,1030,1045
2250 DATA 1100,1115,1130,1145
2260 DATA 1200,1215,1230,1245
2270 DATA 1300,1315,1330,1345
2280 DATA 1400,1415,1430,1445
2290 DATA 1500,1515,1530,1545
2300 DATA 1600,1615,1630,1645
2310 DATA 1700,1715,1730,1745
2320 DATA 9999,9999,9999,9999
```

Figure 5.14.

Note that there are 40 starting times, staggered in 15-minute intervals, commencing at 0800 (8 a.m.) and ending at 1745 (5:45 p.m.). For convenience, 24-hour clock time is used in this program. Note also that there is a sentinel row at the end. As we will see later, these numbers are READ as integer types but must be converted to string variables, producing curious attributes of length. That subject will be discussed later.

Now, if the file were set up on a time basis, the key field range would require nearly 1800 records (sequence number 0001 to 1745), only 40 of which would have to be used. If we place these times in DATA statements, thereby creating a table of starting times, we can use only 40 records on the disk and thus save much space and search time. The key field 0800 is relative record 1 and 0815 is relative record 2. By "relative record" we mean that records are counted from zero. More on that as necessary.

In order to write to disk or read from it, its file must be OPENed. Recall that a RESTORE must be used to initialize the pointer to DATA lines. The concept is the same. You may open the file AS INPUT or AS OUTPUT, and thereby designate the direction of flow in the specified direction *only*. Or you may simply OPEN the file and allow the selected random disk verbs (READ# and WRITE#) to be used.

Business BASIC allows you up to ten buffers. A *buffer* is a temporary storage space for data targeted either for the disk or for a recent arrival – a sort of Ellis Island for data. The OPEN command must therefore specify a buffer. Disks are organized in sectors. Each sector will accept 512 characters or *bytes.* Since we need only 63 bytes in the LDGC problem, the buffer size can be shortened, giving SOS more room to pack data. The OPEN statement used is shown in Figure 5.15.

```
10 HOME
20 CREATE ".D2/TEEOFF",TEXT,63
30 SP15$ = "               "
40 REM ***************************
50 REM * OPEN AND DEFINE THE FILE *
60 REM ***************************
70 OPEN #1,".D2/TEEOFF"
```

Figure 5.15.

The CREATE is SOS' way to establish the file size and type. The size we will use is 63 characters and the type is TEXT, which will give us an ASCII file. That is, all numbers and characters will occupy character positions. Examining the OPEN, we see that it is for buffer 1, and the data file is on drive 2 and is called TEEOFF. Because the Apple III is driver oriented, it is not necessary to use specialized instructions for loading the buffer. It will be done for you.

Figure 5.16 shows the opening menu of the LDGC program and the selection routine. For simplicity, we have isolated the upper case and lower case responses. The purpose of the whole menu testing mechanism is to develop a value which will be useful to the ON ... GOSUB of statement 470. Note the first four instructions. These set the name fields to null. A null ("") is the lowest value in the ASCII character set.

```
80 REM ******************************
90 REM * PRESENT THE SELECTION MENU *
100 REM ******************************
110 HOME
120 NAME.1$ = ""
130 NAME.2$ = ""
140 NAME.3$ = ""
150 NAME.4$ = ""
160 PRINT:PRINT TAB(30);"LAZY DAZE GOLF COURSE"
170 FOR N = 1 TO 79:PRINT "-";:NEXT N
180 PRINT :PRINT TAB(36);"OPTIONS:"
190 PRINT:PRINT TAB(18);"<I>NITIALIZE THE FILE (CAUTION: REMOVES ALL DATA)"
200 PRINT:PRINT TAB(18);"<C>REATE A NEW STARTING TIME"
210 PRINT:PRINT TAB(18);"<D>ISPLAY A STARTING TIME"
220 PRINT:PRINT TAB(18);"<A>DD (OR DELETE) A PERSON'S STARTING TIME"
230 PRINT:PRINT TAB(18);"<R>EMOVE A FOURSOME FROM A STARTING TIME"
```

Figure 5.16.

```
240 PRINT:PRINT TAB(18);"<L>IST RESERVATIONS WITH FEWER THAN FOUR PLAYERS"
250 PRINT:PRINT TAB(18);"<P>RINT AND DISPLAY THE DAY'S SCHEDULE"
260 PRINT:PRINT TAB(18);"<E>ND THE PROGRAM"
270 PRINT:PRINT "SELECT: ";
280 GET Z$
290 PRINT Z$;
300 IF Z$ = "I" THEN PRINT "NITIALIZE":SELECTION = 1:GOTO 470
310 IF Z$ = "i" THEN PRINT "nitialize":SELECTION = 1:GOTO 470
320 IF Z$ = "C" THEN PRINT "REATE":SELECTION = 2:GOTO 470
330 IF Z$ = "c" THEN PRINT "reate":SELECTION = 2:GOTO 470
340 IF Z$ = "D" THEN PRINT "ISPLAY":SELECTION = 3:GOTO 470
350 IF Z$ = "d" THEN PRINT "isplay":SELECTION = 3:GOTO 470
360 IF Z$ = "A" THEN PRINT "DD":SELECTION = 4:GOTO 470
370 IF Z$ = "a" THEN PRINT "dd":SELECTION = 4:GOTO 470
380 IF Z$ = "R" THEN PRINT "EPLACE":SELECTION = 5:GOTO 470
390 IF Z$ = "r" THEN PRINT "eplace":SELECTION = 5:GOTO 470
400 IF Z$ = "L" THEN PRINT "IST":SELECTION = 6:GOTO 470
410 IF Z$ = "l" THEN PRINT "ist":SELECTION = 6:GOTO 470
420 IF Z$ = "P" THEN PRINT "RINT":SELECTION = 7:GOTO 470
430 IF Z$ = "p" THEN PRINT "rint":SELECTION = 7:GOTO 470
440 IF Z$ = "E" THEN PRINT "ND":SELECTION = 8:GOTO 470
450 IF Z$ = "e" THEN PRINT "nd":SELECTION = 8:GOTO 470
460 GOTO 110
470 ON SELECTION GOSUB 1990,510,880,1060,1520,1650,2600,2150
480 PRINT "PRESS ANY KEY TO CONTINUE";
490 GET Z$
500 GOTO 110
```

Figure 5.16. (continued)

This, like previous programs, has an alphabetically controlled menu. Statements 120 to 150 define what the four main input and display variables will be, and then the heading is placed onto the screen. Statements 300 to 450 require the operator to respond in either upper or lower case. Each statement completes the word, establishes a value which can be used by the ON ... GOSUB, and then branches to 470.

Since the purpose of this program is to allocate a golf foursome to a specific playing time, we'll deal first with the routine that accepts and then uses the entered time. Refer to Figure 5.17.

```
1840 REM ****************************
1850 REM * OBTAIN THE PLAYING TIME *
1860 REM ****************************
1870 NO.FIND.SWITCH = 0
1880 INPUT "PLAYING TIME";PLAYTIME%
1890      TIME.TIME$ = STR$(PLAYTIME%)
1900      TIME.TIME$ = RIGHT$(TIME.TIME$,4)
1910      TEE.TIME$=LEFT$(TIME.TIME$,2)+":"+RIGHT$(TIME.TIME$,2)
1920 GOSUB 2330
1930 IF NO.FIND.SWITCH = 1 THEN 1960
1940 IF (PLAYTIME% < 1) OR (PLAYTIME% > 40) THEN 1960
1950 READ #1,PLAYTIME%;F$,N1$,N2$,N3$,N4$,NR:RETURN
1960 PRINT "BAD STARTING TIME"
1970 NO.FIND.SWITCH = 0
1980 GOTO 1880
```

Figure 5.17.

The first thing in the routine is the setting of the NO.FIND.SWITCH, which occurs when the DATA table is searched and the desired value (argument) is not located. The setting of this switch permits the program to learn, elsewhere, that a specific argument has not been located in the table (that is, that the specified starting time is invalid). You'll be able to recognize that once you have the program running.

Look at statement 1880. It seems straightforward enough, but wait a minute. Why the integer specification of PLAYTIME? Remember that when you're using diskette in TEXT mode, numeric values end up being string variables. The % indicates that the numeric variable with which you're dealing is in integer mode. The specification of TEXT mode in the CREATE statement, by the way, tells the Apple III that you want an ASCII file. If you specify it as a DATA file the program will still work – except that the only way you'll be able to get at the file will be through the program. With a TEXT file you can see it in a variety of ways.

Study statements 1820 through 1910 before we discuss them. Remember that PLAYTIME% has come directly from the keyboard in response to an INPUT statement that requests a *numeric* value. Since we are using 24-hour clock time, the response will be in four digits, ranging from 0800 to 1745. The first thing we do, therefore, is to get the playtime into a string variable with the STR$ instruction. A curious transformation takes place when this occurs, however. You may very well have entered 1245 at the keyboard, but when statement 1820 is executed, variable TIME.TIME$ has a length of 5. You must realize that every number has an intrinsic *positive* sign, even though it has not been specified. When a signed numeric is converted to a string variable, *it brings the sign position with it.* We get rid of that position with statement 1830. In other words, what *was* +1245 is now simply 1245. The function of statement 1910 is simply to insert a colon between the left two characters and the right two characters of the time. Statements 1820 to 1910 are duplicated in other parts of the program, as required.

We'll get to statement 2330 in a minute. It is a routine that selects a relative record number on the basis of the starting time in the DATA table. What isn't immediately obvious is that PLAYTIME% has received a new value in the range of 1 to 40 (see statement 2470, SWAP), the latter of which, you will recall, is the number of records in the file. If there were no find in the DATA statements, the switch would be tested, a message given, and the process repeated. In any event, when you come back from statement 2330, PLAYTIME% has the number of the record that contains the corresponding starting time, and that record will be obtained in statement 1950. Now let us proceed to statement 2330, which initiates the routine that determines the relative position of the starting time and allows that position to be used at statement 1950. Refer to Figure 5.18.

```
2330 REM ***********************************************************
2340 REM * ROUTINE TO SELECT RECORD NUMBER BASED ON STARTING TIME *
2350 REM ***********************************************************
2360 RESTORE
2370 FOR CHECK.RECORD% = 1 TO 100
2380     READ WHICH.RECORD%;F$,N1$,N2$,N3$,N4$,NR
2390     IF WHICH.RECORD% = 9999 THEN 2440
2400     IF WHICH.RECORD% = PLAYTIME% THEN 2470
2410 NEXT CHECK.RECORD%
2420 PRINT "BAD TIME TABLE IN PROGRAM"
2430 END
2440 PRINT "TIME NOT AVAILABLE AS A STARTING TIME"
2450 NO.FIND.SWITCH = 1
2460 RETURN
2470 SWAP CHECK.RECORD%,PLAYTIME%
2480 GOTO 2460
2490 REM ***********************************************************
2500 REM * ROUTINE TO SELECT STARTING TIME BASED ON RECORD NUMBER *
2510 REM ***********************************************************
2520 RESTORE
2530 FOR CHECK.RECORD% = 1 TO FILE.NUMBER
2540     READ #1,WHICH.RECORD%;F$,N1$,N2$,N3$,N4$
2550     IF WHICH.RECORD% = 9999 THEN 2580
2560 NEXT CHECK.RECORD%
2570 RETURN
2580 PRINT "BAD TIME TABLE IN PROGRAM"
2590 END
```

Figure 5.18.

The RESTORE in statement 2520 sets the pointer to the head of the DATA statements. The movement that will take place in the FOR ... NEXT loop of statements 2530 to 2560 will be strictly linear, and although the file number may not be on the table, we're also looking for the sentinel (9999) in statement 2550 to tell us when to stop. That way we can add new values to the table, assuming that we make the proper changes elsewhere. Values that arrive from the DATA lines do so as integer variables (WHICH.RECORD%). In a later routine the same values will be read as string variables. In any event, the selected DATA element is matched against the entered PLAYTIME%. If no find is made, we are notified. If a hit is encountered, however, we merely exchange the value of the count (which contains the DATA element number that matches the value of the time). We could have gotten away with making both of them equal to the value of CHECK.RECORD%, but that would have prevented us from using a nifty little instruction – SWAP.

The first option on the menu is to initialize the file. Technically, when a file is initialized, everything must be cleared. It would be simple enough merely to flag the F$ with 255 to indicate that a record is inoperative. We've gone one step further and cleared the entire record. As a result, if you need to review your files, they will be free of garbage. We do indeed flag F$ with 255 and then we clear N1$ through N4$. Irrespective of the number of characters you store in these variables, all of them consist of 15 bytes *as far as the disk is concerned.* Note that the buffer is set *once,* and then forty consecutive blank records are written (WRITE #). Because you should have a chance to confirm a desire to blank a disk, that question is asked in statement 2020. The initializing routine is given in Figure 5.19.

```
1990 REM ***********************
2000 REM * INITIALIZE THE FILE *
2010 REM ***********************
2020 PRINT "ARE YOU SURE(Y/N)? ";
2030 GET Z$
2040 PRINT Z$
2050 IF Z$ < > "Y" THEN RETURN
2060 F$=CHR$(255)
2070 N1$ = SP15$
2080 N2$ = SP15$
2090 N3$ = SP15$
2100 N4$ = SP15$
2110 FOR FILE.NUMBER = 1 TO 40
2120      WRITE #1,FILE.NUMBER;F$,N1$,N2$,N3$,N4$,NR
2130      NEXT FILE.NUMBER
2140 RETURN
```

Figure 5.19.

Next comes the creation option. Recall that the record on the disk file has already been initialized, and now we will select it by a record number based upon the starting time. That routine is given in Figure 5.20.

```
510 REM ******************
520 REM * BUILD NEW ENTRY *
530 REM ******************
540 GOSUB 1880
550 IF ASC(F$) = 255 THEN 600
560 PRINT "THE RECORD EXISTS - DO YOU WISH TO OVERWRITE (Y/N)?";
570 GET Z$
580 PRINT Z$
590 IF Z$ < > "Y" THEN RETURN
600 HOME
610 PRINT:PRINT TAB(30);"LAZY DAZE GOLF COURSE"
620 FOR N = 1 TO 79:PRINT "-";:NEXT N
630 PRINT
640 TEE.TIME$=LEFT$(TIME.TIME$,2)+":"+RIGHT$(TIME.TIME$,2)
650 PRINT "RESERVATION TIME: ";TEE.TIME$
660 PRINT
670 NAME.1$ = ""
680 NAME.2$ = ""
690 NAME.3$ = ""
700 NAME.4$ = ""
710 F$=CHR$(0)
720 INPUT " FIRST PLAYER: ";NAME.1$
730 N1$ = NAME.1$
740 INPUT "SECOND PLAYER: ";NAME.2$
750 N2$ = NAME.2$
760 INPUT " THIRD PLAYER: ";NAME.3$
770 N3$ = NAME.3$
780 INPUT "FOURTH PLAYER: ";NAME.4$
790 N4$ = NAME.4$
800 IF NAME.1$ < > "" THEN NUMBER.OF.PLAYERS% = NUMBER.OF.PLAYERS% + 1
810 IF NAME.2$ < > "" THEN NUMBER.OF.PLAYERS% = NUMBER.OF.PLAYERS% + 1
820 IF NAME.3$ < > "" THEN NUMBER.OF.PLAYERS% = NUMBER.OF.PLAYERS% + 1
830 IF NAME.4$ < > "" THEN NUMBER.OF.PLAYERS% = NUMBER.OF.PLAYERS% + 1
840 NR$ = CONV$(NUMBER.OF.PLAYERS%)
850 NUMBER.OF.PLAYERS% = 0
860 WRITE #1,PLAYTIME%
870 RETURN
```

Figure 5.20.

Because it would be theoretically possible to enter an incorrect time and destroy a previously entered record, once you have determined that a record already exists, you are asked if you wish to overwrite it. If you respond with N, the main menu will be brought back. If your response is Y, the new record will overwrite the old one.

Because new names will be received, all name fields are set to null in statements 670–700. The presence or absence of these null codes will be the basis for counting how many players are registered by statements 800–830. One by one the names of the players are gained. Because an INPUT statement is used, there must be no imbedded commas in the name which is entered.

The buffer is loaded in statements 720–790, using the INPUT statements and those which follow immediately. In a similar manner, the integer variable is set into the buffer with the CONV$ instruction of statement 840. The player count is reset in statement 850, and then the record is written in statement 860.

The DISPLAY option functions are to get the desired starting time, select the record required, and present the data on the screen. Using the buffer for display is sufficient. In the modification routine, however, the buffer names are set back into the variable names. The CONV% instruction allows the number obtained from the disk to be presented. See Figure 5.21.

```
880 REM ********************
890 REM * DISPLAY THE ENTRY *
900 REM ********************
910 GOSUB 1880
920 IF ASC(F$) = 255 THEN PRINT "NOT RESERVED":RETURN
930 HOME
940 PRINT:PRINT TAB(30);"LAZY DAZE GOLF COURSE"
950 FOR N = 1 TO 79:PRINT "-";:NEXT N
960 PRINT:PRINT TAB(30);"STARTING TIME:  ";TEE.TIME$
970 PRINT:PRINT TAB(20);"PERSON #1:     ";N1$:NAME.1$ = N1$
980 PRINT:PRINT TAB(20);"PERSON #2:     ";N2$:NAME.2$ = N2$
990 PRINT:PRINT TAB(20);"PERSON #3:     ";N3$:NAME.3$ = N3$
1000 PRINT:PRINT TAB(20);"PERSON #4:     ";N4$:NAME.4$ = N4$
1010 PRINT:PRINT TAB(20);"SIZE OF GROUP:     ";CONV%(NR$)
1020 PRINT
1030 FOR N = 1 TO 79:PRINT "-";:NEXT N
1040 PRINT
1050 RETURN
```

Figure 5.21.

The replace (ADD or DELETE) option allows you to add or subtract a person from the foursome. All names are displayed and you are asked which you wish to modify (1, 2, 3, or 4). You can exit from this section by entering 9 to the question posed at statement 1300. The determination of the size of the group for display purposes is a little more difficult since the name may be coming from either the disk or the keyboard and there will be a length difference. Therefore a compound logical is used in statements 1210–1270 to ask for either a blank line of 15 characters (from the disk) or a length of zero (from the keyboard). The remainder of the routine is as before. The complete routine is shown in Figure 5.22.

```
1060 REM ********************************************
1070 REM * ADD TO OR DELETE FROM AN EXISTING FOURSOME *
1080 REM ********************************************
1090 GOSUB 1880
1100 IF ASC(F$) = 255 THEN PRINT "NOT RESERVED":RETURN
1110 NAME.1$ = N1$
1120 NAME.2$ = N2$
1130 NAME.3$ = N3$
1140 NAME.4$ = N4$
1150 HOME
1160 PRINT:PRINT TAB(30);"LAZY DAZE GOLF COURSE"
1170 FOR N = 1 TO 79:PRINT "-";:NEXT N
1180 PRINT:PRINT TAB(30);"STARTING TIME: ";TEE.TIME$
1190 SIZE.OF.GROUP% = 0
1200 PRINT:PRINT TAB(20);"PERSON #1:   ";NAME.1$
1210 IF (NAME.1$ < > SP15$) AND (LEN(NAME.1$) < > 0)
      THEN SIZE.OF.GROUP% = SIZE.OF.GROUP% + 1
1220 PRINT:PRINT TAB(20);"PERSON #2:   ";NAME.2$
1230 IF (NAME.2$ < > SP15$) AND (LEN(NAME.2$) < > 0)
      THEN SIZE.OF.GROUP% = SIZE.OF.GROUP% + 1
1240 PRINT:PRINT TAB(20);"PERSON #3:   ";NAME.3$
1250 IF (NAME.3$ < > SP15$) AND (LEN(NAME.3$) < > 0)
      THEN SIZE.OF.GROUP% = SIZE.OF.GROUP% + 1
1260 PRINT:PRINT TAB(20);"PERSON #4:   ";NAME.4$
1270 IF (NAME.4$ < > SP15$) AND (LEN(NAME.4$) < > 0)
      THEN SIZE.OF.GROUP% = SIZE.OF.GROUP% + 1
1280 PRINT:PRINT TAB(20);"SIZE OF GROUP:   ";SIZE.OF.GROUP%
1290 PRINT
1300 PRINT:INPUT "WHICH NAME TO CHANGE (9 WHEN COMPLETE): ",WHICH.NAME
1310 PRINT
1320 IF WHICH.NAME = 9 THEN 1390
1330 IF WHICH.NAME = 1 THEN INPUT "ENTER PERSON #1: ";NAME.1$:GOTO 1150
1340 IF WHICH.NAME = 2 THEN INPUT "ENTER PERSON #2: ";NAME.2$:GOTO 1150
1350 IF WHICH.NAME = 3 THEN INPUT "ENTER PERSON #3: ";NAME.3$:GOTO 1150
1360 IF WHICH.NAME = 4 THEN INPUT "ENTER PERSON #4: ";NAME.4$:GOTO 1150
1370 HOME
1380 GOTO 1130
1390 PRINT
1400 NUMBER.OF.PLAYERS% = 0
1410 IF NAME.1$ < > "" THEN NUMBER.OF.PLAYERS% = NUMBER.OF.PLAYERS% + 1
1420 IF NAME.2$ < > "" THEN NUMBER.OF.PLAYERS% = NUMBER.OF.PLAYERS% + 1
1430 IF NAME.3$ < > "" THEN NUMBER.OF.PLAYERS% = NUMBER.OF.PLAYERS% + 1
1440 IF NAME.4$ < > "" THEN NUMBER.OF.PLAYERS% = NUMBER.OF.PLAYERS% + 1
1450 NR$ = CONV$(NUMBER.OF.PLAYERS%)
1460 N1$ = NAME.1$
1470 N2$ = NAME.2$
1480 N3$ = NAME.3$
1490 N4$ = NAME.4$
1500 WRITE #1,PLAYTIME%
1510 RETURN
```

Figure 5.22.

Occasionally an entire foursome may cancel its scheduled time. The routine of Figure 5.23 will remove this foursome from the file. Although it would have been sufficient simply to perform 1570 followed by 1630, it's generally good practice to neutralize the entire record. Whenever the time comes to print the entire file, extraneous information in the record might prove confusing.

```
1520 REM *********************************
1530 REM * REMOVE FOURSOME FROM THE FILE *
1540 REM *********************************
1550 GOSUB 1880
1560 IF ASC(F$) = 255 THEN PRINT "NOT RESERVED":RETURN
1570 F$=CHR$(255)
1580 NR$ = "  "
1590 N1$ = SP15$
1600 N2$ = SP15$
1610 N3$ = SP15$
1620 N4$ = SP15$
1630 WRITE #1,PLAYTIME%
1640 RETURN
```

Figure 5.23.

Suppose that you're busy at work and a customer comes in and asks, "Have you got an open time and a foursome I can join?" You tell him, "Sure" and press the "L" option of your menu, invoking a routine whose only function is to survey the file for foursomes with fewer than four people. Refer to Figure 5.24. As presently programed, statement 1770 does not permit the listing of the totally open times. You may wish to change that limitation. In any event, with this option, your customer can join a developing foursome.

```
1650 REM *******************************************
1660 REM * LIST FOURSOMES WITHOUT FULL COMPLEMENTS *
1670 REM *******************************************
1680 HOME
1690 PRINT:PRINT TAB(30);"LAZY DAZE GOLF COURSE"
1700 FOR N = 1 TO 79:PRINT "-";:NEXT N
1710 PRINT:PRINT TAB(20);"FOURSOMES WITHOUT FULL COMPLEMENTS"
1720 FOR N = 1 TO 79:PRINT "-";:NEXT N
1730 PRINT
1740 FOR FILE.NUMBER = 1 TO 40
1750      GOSUB 2490
1760      READ #1,FILE.NUMBER;F$,N1$,N2$,N3$,N4$,NR
1770      IF F$ = CHR$(255) THEN 1820
1780      TIME.TIME$ = STR$(WHICH.RECORD%)
1790      TIME.TIME$ = RIGHT$(TIME.TIME$,4)
1800      TEE.TIME$=LEFT$(TIME.TIME$,2)+":"+RIGHT$(TIME.TIME$,2)
1810      IF CONV%(NR$) < 4 THEN PRINT
              "TEE TIME: ";TEE.TIME$,"NR OF PLAYERS: ";CONV%(NR$)
1820      NEXT FILE.NUMBER
1830 RETURN
```

Figure 5.24.

Finally, the program provides a printed schedule by selecting menu option "P." The schedule looks like Figure 5.25.

```
LAZY DAZE GOLF COURSE TEE-OFF SCHEDULE FOR: 01-17-1983

1                 08:00              MERRILL
                                     LYNCH
                                     PIERCE
                                     FENNER

2                 09:00              SMITH
                                     KLINE
                                     FRENCH

9                 10:00              WINKIN
                                     BLINKIN
                                     NOD

13                11:00              DASHER
                                     DANCER
                                     PRANCER
                                     VIXEN

17                12:00              COMET
                                     CUPID
                                     DONDER
                                     BLITZEN
```

Figure 5.25.

The coding for the schedule is given in Figure 5.26.

```
2600 REM ***********************************************************
2610 REM * ROUTINE TO DISPLAY AND HARDCOPY PRINT A DAY'S SCHEDULE *
2620 REM ***********************************************************
2630 OPEN #2,".PRINTER"
2640 OUTPUT #2
2650 PRINT "LAZY DAZE GOLF COURSE TEE-OFF SCHEDULE FOR: ";DATE$
2660 PRINT
2670 CLOSE #2
2680 OPEN #1,".D2/TEEOFF"
2690 RESTORE
2700 FOR FILE.NUMBER = 1 TO 40
2710     READ #1,FILE.NUMBER;F$,N1$,N2$,N3$,N4$,NR
2720     READ DISPLAY.TIME$
2730     TEE.TIME$ = RIGHT$(DISPLAY.TIME$,4)
2740     TEE.TIME$ = LEFT$(TEE.TIME$,2) + ":" + RIGHT$(TEE.TIME$,2)
2750     IF F$ = CHR$(255) THEN 2890
2760     PRINT FILE.NUMBER,TEE.TIME$,N1$
2770     PRINT ,,N2$
2780     PRINT ,,N3$
2790     PRINT ,,N4$
```

Figure 5.26.

```
2800        PRINT
2810        OPEN #2,".PRINTER"
2820        PRINT FILE.NUMBER,TEE.TIME$,N1$
2830        OUTPUT #2
2840        PRINT ,,N2$
2850        PRINT ,,N3$
2860        PRINT ,,N4$
2870        PRINT
2880        CLOSE #2
2890        NEXT FILE.NUMBER
2900 OPEN #2,".PRINTER"
2910 OUTPUT #2
2920 PRINT CHR$(12)
2930 CLOSE #2
2940 RETURN
```

Figure 5.26. (continued)

This coding completes the discussion of the LAZY DAZE GOLF COURSE reservation system. The entire program is given as Figure 5.27.

```
10 HOME
20 CREATE ".D2/TEEOFF",TEXT,63
30 SP15$ = "               "
40 REM ****************************
50 REM * OPEN AND DEFINE THE FILE *
60 REM ****************************
70 OPEN #1,".D2/TEEOFF"
80 REM ******************************
90 REM * PRESENT THE SELECTION MENU *
100 REM ******************************
110 HOME
120 NAME.1$ = ""
130 NAME.2$ = ""
140 NAME.3$ = ""
150 NAME.4$ = ""
160 PRINT:PRINT TAB(30);"LAZY DAZE GOLF COURSE"
170 FOR N = 1 TO 79:PRINT "-";:NEXT N
180 PRINT :PRINT TAB(36);"OPTIONS:"
190 PRINT:PRINT TAB(18);"<I>NITIALIZE THE FILE (CAUTION: REMOVES ALL DATA)"
200 PRINT:PRINT TAB(18);"<C>REATE A NEW STARTING TIME"
210 PRINT:PRINT TAB(18);"<D>ISPLAY A STARTING TIME"
220 PRINT:PRINT TAB(18);"<A>DD (OR DELETE) A PERSON'S STARTING TIME"
230 PRINT:PRINT TAB(18);"<R>EMOVE A FOURSOME FROM A STARTING TIME"
240 PRINT:PRINT TAB(18);"<L>IST RESERVATIONS WITH FEWER THAN FOUR PLAYERS"
250 PRINT:PRINT TAB(18);"<P>RINT AND DISPLAY THE DAY'S SCHEDULE"
260 PRINT:PRINT TAB(18);"<E>ND THE PROGRAM"
270 PRINT:PRINT "SELECT: ";
280 GET Z$
290 PRINT Z$;
300 IF Z$ = "I" THEN PRINT "NITIALIZE":SELECTION = 1:GOTO 470
310 IF Z$ = "i" THEN PRINT "nitialize":SELECTION = 1:GOTO 470
320 IF Z$ = "C" THEN PRINT "REATE":SELECTION = 2:GOTO 470
330 IF Z$ = "c" THEN PRINT "reate":SELECTION = 2:GOTO 470
340 IF Z$ = "D" THEN PRINT "ISPLAY":SELECTION = 3:GOTO 470
350 IF Z$ = "d" THEN PRINT "isplay":SELECTION = 3:GOTO 470
360 IF Z$ = "A" THEN PRINT "DD":SELECTION = 4:GOTO 470
```

Figure 5.27.

```
370 IF Z$ = "a" THEN PRINT "dd":SELECTION = 4:GOTO 470
380 IF Z$ = "R" THEN PRINT "EPLACE":SELECTION = 5:GOTO 470
390 IF Z$ = "r" THEN PRINT "eplace":SELECTION = 5:GOTO 470
400 IF Z$ = "L" THEN PRINT "IST":SELECTION = 6:GOTO 470
410 IF Z$ = "l" THEN PRINT "ist":SELECTION = 6:GOTO 470
420 IF Z$ = "P" THEN PRINT "RINT":SELECTION = 7:GOTO 470
430 IF Z$ = "p" THEN PRINT "rint":SELECTION = 7:GOTO 470
440 IF Z$ = "E" THEN PRINT "ND":SELECTION = 8:GOTO 470
450 IF Z$ = "e" THEN PRINT "nd":SELECTION = 8:GOTO 470
460 GOTO 110
470 ON SELECTION GOSUB 1990,510,880,1060,1520,1650,2600,2150
480 PRINT "PRESS ANY KEY TO CONTINUE";
490 GET Z$
500 GOTO 110
510 REM ******************
520 REM * BUILD NEW ENTRY *
530 REM ******************
540 GOSUB 1880
550 IF ASC(F$) = 255 THEN 600
560 PRINT "THE RECORD EXISTS - DO YOU WISH TO OVERWRITE (Y/N)?";
570 GET Z$
580 PRINT Z$
590 IF Z$ < > "Y" THEN RETURN
600 HOME
610 PRINT:PRINT TAB(30);"LAZY DAZE GOLF COURSE"
620 FOR N = 1 TO 79:PRINT "-";:NEXT N
630 PRINT
640 TEE.TIME$=LEFT$(TIME.TIME$,2)+":"+RIGHT$(TIME.TIME$,2)
650 PRINT "RESERVATION TIME: ";TEE.TIME$
660 PRINT
670 NAME.1$ = ""
680 NAME.2$ = ""
690 NAME.3$ = ""
700 NAME.4$ = ""
710 F$=CHR$(0)
720 INPUT " FIRST PLAYER: ";NAME.1$
730 N1$ = NAME.1$
740 INPUT "SECOND PLAYER: ";NAME.2$
750 N2$ = NAME.2$
760 INPUT " THIRD PLAYER: ";NAME.3$
770 N3$ = NAME.3$
780 INPUT "FOURTH PLAYER: ";NAME.4$
790 N4$ = NAME.4$
800 IF NAME.1$ < > "" THEN NUMBER.OF.PLAYERS% = NUMBER.OF.PLAYERS% + 1
810 IF NAME.2$ < > "" THEN NUMBER.OF.PLAYERS% = NUMBER.OF.PLAYERS% + 1
820 IF NAME.3$ < > "" THEN NUMBER.OF.PLAYERS% = NUMBER.OF.PLAYERS% + 1
830 IF NAME.4$ < > "" THEN NUMBER.OF.PLAYERS% = NUMBER.OF.PLAYERS% + 1
840 NR$ = CONV$(NUMBER.OF.PLAYERS%)
850 NUMBER.OF.PLAYERS% = 0
860 WRITE #1,PLAYTIME%
870 RETURN
880 REM *********************
890 REM * DISPLAY THE ENTRY *
900 REM *********************
910 GOSUB 1880
920 IF ASC(F$) = 255 THEN PRINT "NOT RESERVED":RETURN
930 HOME
940 PRINT:PRINT TAB(30);"LAZY DAZE GOLF COURSE"
950 FOR N = 1 TO 79:PRINT "-";:NEXT N
960 PRINT:PRINT TAB(30);"STARTING TIME: ";TEE.TIME$
970 PRINT:PRINT TAB(20);"PERSON #1:  ";N1$:NAME.1$ = N1$
980 PRINT:PRINT TAB(20);"PERSON #2:  ";N2$:NAME.2$ = N2$
990 PRINT:PRINT TAB(20);"PERSON #3:  ";N3$:NAME.3$ = N3$
1000 PRINT:PRINT TAB(20);"PERSON #4:  ";N4$:NAME.4$ = N4$
```

Figure 5.27. (continued)

```
1010 PRINT:PRINT TAB(20);"SIZE OF GROUP:  ";CONV%(NR$)
1020 PRINT
1030 FOR N = 1 TO 79:PRINT "-";:NEXT N
1040 PRINT
1050 RETURN
1060 REM ********************************************
1070 REM * ADD TO OR DELETE FROM AN EXISTING FOURSOME *
1080 REM ********************************************
1090 GOSUB 1880
1100 IF ASC(F$) = 255 THEN PRINT "NOT RESERVED":RETURN
1110 NAME.1$ = N1$
1120 NAME.2$ = N2$
1130 NAME.3$ = N3$
1140 NAME.4$ = N4$
1150 HOME
1160 PRINT:PRINT TAB(30);"LAZY DAZE GOLF COURSE"
1170 FOR N = 1 TO 79:PRINT "-";:NEXT N
1180 PRINT:PRINT TAB(30);"STARTING TIME: ";TEE.TIME$
1190 SIZE.OF.GROUP% = 0
1200 PRINT:PRINT TAB(20);"PERSON #1:  ";NAME.1$
1210 IF (NAME.1$ < > SP15$) AND (LEN(NAME.1$) < > 0)
     THEN SIZE.OF.GROUP% = SIZE.OF.GROUP% + 1
1220 PRINT:PRINT TAB(20);"PERSON #2:  ";NAME.2$
1230 IF (NAME.2$ < > SP15$) AND (LEN(NAME.2$) < > 0)
     THEN SIZE.OF.GROUP% = SIZE.OF.GROUP% + 1
1240 PRINT:PRINT TAB(20);"PERSON #3:  ";NAME.3$
1250 IF (NAME.3$ < > SP15$) AND (LEN(NAME.3$) < > 0)
     THEN SIZE.OF.GROUP% = SIZE.OF.GROUP% + 1
1260 PRINT:PRINT TAB(20);"PERSON #4:  ";NAME.4$
1270 IF (NAME.4$ < > SP15$) AND (LEN(NAME.4$) < > 0)
     THEN SIZE.OF.GROUP% = SIZE.OF.GROUP% + 1
1280 PRINT:PRINT TAB(20);"SIZE OF GROUP:  ";SIZE.OF.GROUP%
1290 PRINT
1300 PRINT:INPUT "WHICH NAME TO CHANGE (9 WHEN COMPLETE): ",WHICH.NAME
1310 PRINT
1320 IF WHICH.NAME = 9 THEN 1390
1330 IF WHICH.NAME = 1 THEN INPUT "ENTER PERSON #1: ";NAME.1$:GOTO 1150
1340 IF WHICH.NAME = 2 THEN INPUT "ENTER PERSON #2: ";NAME.2$:GOTO 1150
1350 IF WHICH.NAME = 3 THEN INPUT "ENTER PERSON #3: ";NAME.3$:GOTO 1150
1360 IF WHICH.NAME = 4 THEN INPUT "ENTER PERSON #4: ";NAME.4$:GOTO 1150
1370 HOME
1380 GOTO 1130
1390 PRINT
1400 NUMBER.OF.PLAYERS% = 0
1410 IF NAME.1$ < > "" THEN NUMBER.OF.PLAYERS% = NUMBER.OF.PLAYERS% + 1
1420 IF NAME.2$ < > "" THEN NUMBER.OF.PLAYERS% = NUMBER.OF.PLAYERS% + 1
1430 IF NAME.3$ < > "" THEN NUMBER.OF.PLAYERS% = NUMBER.OF.PLAYERS% + 1
1440 IF NAME.4$ < > "" THEN NUMBER.OF.PLAYERS% = NUMBER.OF.PLAYERS% + 1
1450 NR$ = CONV$(NUMBER.OF.PLAYERS%)
1460 N1$ = NAME.1$
1470 N2$ = NAME.2$
1480 N3$ = NAME.3$
1490 N4$ = NAME.4$
1500 WRITE #1,PLAYTIME%
1510 RETURN
1520 REM ********************************
1530 REM * REMOVE FOURSOME FROM THE FILE *
1540 REM ********************************
1550 GOSUB 1880
1560 IF ASC(F$) = 255 THEN PRINT "NOT RESERVED":RETURN
1570 F$=CHR$(255)
1580 NR$ = "  "
1590 N1$ = SP15$
1600 N2$ = SP15$
```

Figure 5.27. (continued)

```
1610 N3$ = SP15$
1620 N4$ = SP15$
1630 WRITE #1,PLAYTIME%
1640 RETURN
1650 REM ******************************************
1660 REM * LIST FOURSOMES WITHOUT FULL COMPLEMENTS *
1670 REM ******************************************
1680 HOME
1690 PRINT:PRINT TAB(30);"LAZY DAZE GOLF COURSE"
1700 FOR N = 1 TO 79:PRINT "-";:NEXT N
1710 PRINT:PRINT TAB(20);"FOURSOMES WITHOUT FULL COMPLEMENTS"
1720 FOR N = 1 TO 79:PRINT "-";:NEXT N
1730 PRINT
1740 FOR FILE.NUMBER = 1 TO 40
1750      GOSUB 2490
1760      READ #1,FILE.NUMBER;F$,N1$,N2$,N3$,N4$,NR
1770      IF F$ = CHR$(255) THEN 1820
1780      TIME.TIME$ = STR$(WHICH.RECORD%)
1790      TIME.TIME$ = RIGHT$(TIME.TIME$,4)
1800      TEE.TIME$=LEFT$(TIME.TIME$,2)+":"+RIGHT$(TIME.TIME$,2)
1810      IF CONV%(NR$) < 4 THEN PRINT
             "TEE TIME: ";TEE.TIME$,"NR OF PLAYERS: ";CONV%(NR$)
1820      NEXT FILE.NUMBER
1830 RETURN
1840 REM **************************
1850 REM * OBTAIN THE PLAYING TIME *
1860 REM **************************
1870 NO.FIND.SWITCH = 0
1880 INPUT "PLAYING TIME";PLAYTIME%
1890      TIME.TIME$ = STR$(PLAYTIME%)
1900      TIME.TIME$ = RIGHT$(TIME.TIME$,4)
1910      TEE.TIME$=LEFT$(TIME.TIME$,2)+":"+RIGHT$(TIME.TIME$,2)
1920 GOSUB 2330
1930 IF NO.FIND.SWITCH = 1 THEN 1960
1940 IF (PLAYTIME% < 1) OR (PLAYTIME% > 40) THEN 1960
1950 READ #1,PLAYTIME%;F$,N1$,N2$,N3$,N4$,NR:RETURN
1960 PRINT "BAD STARTING TIME"
1970 NO.FIND.SWITCH = 0
1980 GOTO 1880
1990 REM **********************
2000 REM * INITIALIZE THE FILE *
2010 REM **********************
2020 PRINT "ARE YOU SURE(Y/N)? ";
2030 GET Z$
2040 PRINT Z$
2050 IF Z$ < > "Y" THEN RETURN
2060 F$-CHR$(255)
2070 N1$ = SP15$
2080 N2$ = SP15$
2090 N3$ = SP15$
2100 N4$ = SP15$
2110 FOR FILE.NUMBER = 1 TO 40
2120      WRITE #1,FILE.NUMBER;F$,N1$,N2$,N3$,N4$,NR
2130      NEXT FILE.NUMBER
2140 RETURN
2150 REM **********************
2160 REM * END THE APPLICATION *
2170 REM **********************
2180 CLOSE:END
2190 REM *****************
2200 REM * STARTING TIMES *
2210 REM *****************
2220 DATA 0800,0815,0830,0845
2230 DATA 0900,0915,0930,0945
2240 DATA 1000,1015,1030,1045
```

Figure 5.27. (continued)

```
2250 DATA 1100,1115,1130,1145
2260 DATA 1200,1215,1230,1245
2270 DATA 1300,1315,1330,1345
2280 DATA 1400,1415,1430,1445
2290 DATA 1500,1515,1530,1545
2300 DATA 1600,1615,1630,1645
2310 DATA 1700,1715,1730,1745
2320 DATA 9999,9999,9999,9999
2330 REM ***********************************************************
2340 REM * ROUTINE TO SELECT RECORD NUMBER BASED ON STARTING TIME *
2350 REM ***********************************************************
2360 RESTORE
2370 FOR CHECK.RECORD% = 1 TO 100
2380      READ WHICH.RECORD%;F$,N1$,N2$,N3$,N4$,NR
2390      IF WHICH.RECORD% = 9999 THEN 2440
2400      IF WHICH.RECORD% = PLAYTIME% THEN 2470
2410      NEXT CHECK.RECORD%
2420 PRINT "BAD TIME TABLE IN PROGRAM"
2430 END
2440 PRINT "TIME NOT AVAILABLE AS A STARTING TIME"
2450 NO.FIND.SWITCH = 1
2460 RETURN
2470 SWAP CHECK.RECORD%,PLAYTIME%
2480 GOTO 2460
2490 REM ***********************************************************
2500 REM * ROUTINE TO SELECT STARTING TIME BASED ON RECORD NUMBER *
2510 REM ***********************************************************
2520 RESTORE
2530 FOR CHECK.RECORD% = 1 TO FILE.NUMBER
2540      READ #1,WHICH.RECORD%;F$,N1$,N2$,N3$,N4$
2550      IF WHICH.RECORD% = 9999 THEN 2580
2560      NEXT CHECK.RECORD%
2570 RETURN
2580 PRINT "BAD TIME TABLE IN PROGRAM"
2590 END
2600 REM ***********************************************************
2610 REM * ROUTINE TO DISPLAY AND HARDCOPY PRINT A DAY'S SCHEDULE *
2620 REM ***********************************************************
2630 OPEN #2,".PRINTER"
2640 OUTPUT #2
2650 PRINT "LAZY DAZE GOLF COURSE TEE-OFF SCHEDULE FOR: ";DATE$
2660 PRINT
2670 CLOSE #2
2680 OPEN #1,".D2/TEEOFF"
2690 RESTORE
2700 FOR FILE.NUMBER = 1 TO 40
2710      READ #1,FILE.NUMBER;F$,N1$,N2$,N3$,N4$,NR
2720      READ DISPLAY.TIME$
2730      TEE.TIME$ = RIGHT$(DISPLAY.TIME$,4)
2740      TEE.TIME$ = LEFT$(TEE.TIME$,2) + ":" + RIGHT$(TEE.TIME$,2)
2750      IF F$ = CHR$(255) THEN 2890
2760      PRINT FILE.NUMBER,TEE.TIME$,N1$
2770      PRINT ,,N2$
2780      PRINT ,,N3$
2790      PRINT ,,N4$
2800      PRINT
2810      OPEN #2,".PRINTER"
2820      PRINT FILE.NUMBER,TEE.TIME$,N1$
2830      OUTPUT #2
2840      PRINT ,,N2$
2850      PRINT ,,N3$
2860      PRINT ,,N4$
2870      PRINT
2880      CLOSE #2
2070      NEXT FILE.NUMBER
```

Figure 5.27. (continued)

```
2900 OPEN #2,".PRINTER"
2910 OUTPUT #2
2920 PRINT CHR$(12)
2930 CLOSE #2
2940 RETURN
```

Figure 5.27. (continued)

SLEAZE, PLEASE

The Lazy Daze Golf Course problem was an inventory program in which the inventory numbers were not contiguous but the record numbers had to be. Unless we have a considerable amount of media available, the use of noncontiguous product codes, inventory numbers, or the like can lead to a great deal of wasted space. Therefore, building a DATA table of starting times and using their relative position within the table as the location of the record corresponding to that time on the disk was our wisest possible move. What if it were indeed part or inventory numbers that concerned us and if adding or deleting a part number would mean modifying our program with each change? That wouldn't seem to be the wisest thing to do, and it isn't. Changes in approach would have to be made. A second file of part numbers would be necessary, with a record of part numbers and their relative locations on the inventory file. These techniques will be dealt with in the next chapter, which is devoted to a small business system.

For the balance of this chapter we will concentrate on a bonafide inventory application that is randomly organized. Imagine that you have just become the Quartermaster of Camp Sleazy and that when you turn on your Apple III, Figure 5.28 is what you see.

In this example we do not find the inventory record by a two step process as we did in the Lazy Daze Golf Course problem. Instead, we're assuming the presence of one hundred items, numbered sequentially from 1 to 100. Our discussion of this program will not be on a module by module basis because its similarities to the Lazy Daze program are great. The differences will be pointed out by reference to the program listing at the end of the discussion (Figure 5.31).

In this program we want to determine the quantity of items on hand, the reorder level, the unit price, and the location of each. *Important note:* No routines have been included to change anything

```
                    CAMP SLEAZY QUARTERMASTER
    ------------------------------------------------------------
                            OPTIONS:

    <I>NITIALIZE THE FILE - (CAUTION: REMOVES ALL DATA)

    <C>REATE A NEW ENTRY

    <D>ISPLAY INVENTORY FOR ONE ITEM

    <A>DD TO STOCK

    <S>UBTRACT FROM STOCK

    <L>IST ITEMS BELOW REORDER LEVEL

    <P>RINT THE ENTIRE INVENTORY LIST

    <E>ND THE PROGRAM

SELECT:
```

Figure 5.28.

other than the quantity on hand. The inclusion of such options would not be a difficult task since it would follow precisely the technique by which the players names were substituted in the Lazy Daze program.

The output from menu option "P" is given in Figure 5.29. The output from menu option "L" is given in Figure 5.30.

```
          CAMP SLEAZY QUARTERMASTER
  --------------------------------------------------
              INVENTORY FILE LIST
  --------------------------------------------------
          ITEM NUMBER    1

              ITEM:  COMBAT BOOTS

              QUANTITY ON HAND        100
              REORDER LEVEL            75
              UNIT PRICE            $5.55
              BIN LOCATION            A45

          ITEM NUMBER    3

              ITEM:  BLANKETS, O.D.

              QUANTITY ON HAND        100
              REORDER LEVEL           500
              UNIT PRICE            $6.66
              BIN LOCATION            C78
```

Figure 5.29.

```
            ITEM NUMBER  5

                 ITEM:   PONCHO

                 QUANTITY ON HAND        10
                 REORDER LEVEL           20
                 UNIT PRICE           $4.44
                 BIN LOCATION:          B23
```

Figure 5.29. (continued)

```
                 CAMP SLEAZY QUARTERMASTER
-------------------------------------------------------------------------------
BLANKETS, O.D.   QUANTITY 100    REORDER LEVEL 500
PONCHO           QUANTITY 10     REORDER LEVEL 20
PRESS ANY KEY TO CONTINUE
```

Figure 5.30.

The complete program is shown in Figure 5.31. There are a few more figures involved in the data stored on disk (and converted both ways) and in the calculations. You'll notice that in particular when you stop to study the addition and subtraction routines. The difference in both routines is that after a change has been made, *a portion* of the display routine is invoked, allowing the change to be presented before the program goes back to the main menu again.

```
10 HOME
20 CREATE ".D2/ITEMS",TEXT,43
30 REM ****************************
40 REM * OPEN AND DEFINE THE FILE *
50 REM ****************************
60 OPEN #1,".D2/ITEMS"
70 REM ******************************
80 REM * PRESENT THE SELECTION MENU *
90 REM ******************************
100 HOME
110 PRINT:PRINT TAB(30);"CAMP SLEAZY QUARTERMASTER"
120 FOR N = 1 TO 79:PRINT " ";:NEXT N
130 PRINT:PRINT TAB(36);"OPTIONS:"
140 PRINT:PRINT TAB(18);"<I>NITIALIZE THE FILE - (CAUTION: REMOVES ALL DATA)"
150 PRINT:PRINT TAB(18);"<C>REATE A NEW ENTRY"
160 PRINT:PRINT TAB(18);"<D>ISPLAY INVENTORY FOR ONE ITEM"
170 PRINT:PRINT TAB(18);"<A>DD TO STOCK"
180 PRINT:PRINT TAB(18);"<S>UBTRACT FROM STOCK"
190 PRINT:PRINT TAB(18);"<L>IST ITEMS BELOW REORDER LEVEL"
200 PRINT:PRINT TAB(18);"<P>RINT THE ENTIRE INVENTORY LIST"
210 PRINT:PRINT TAB(18);"<E>ND THE PROGRAM"
220 PRINT:PRINT "SELECT: ";
230 GET Z$
240 PRINT Z$;
250 IF Z$ = "I" THEN PRINT "NITIALIZE":SELECTION = 1:GOTO 420
```

Figure 5.31.

```
260 IF Z$ = "i" THEN PRINT "nitialize":SELECTION = 1:GOTO 420
270 IF Z$ = "C" THEN PRINT "REATE":SELECTION = 2:GOTO 420
280 IF Z$ = "c" THEN PRINT "reate":SELECTION = 2:GOTO 420
290 IF Z$ = "D" THEN PRINT "ISPLAY":SELECTION = 3:GOTO 420
300 IF Z$ = "d" THEN PRINT "isplay":SELECTION = 3:GOTO 420
310 IF Z$ = "A" THEN PRINT "DD":SELECTION = 4:GOTO 420
320 IF Z$ = "a" THEN PRINT "dd":SELECTION = 4:GOTO 420
330 IF Z$ = "S" THEN PRINT "UBTRACT":SELECTION = 5:GOTO 420
340 IF Z$ = "s" THEN PRINT "ubtract":SELECTION = 5:GOTO 420
350 IF Z$ = "L" THEN PRINT "IST":SELECTION = 6:GOTO 420
360 IF Z$ = "l" THEN PRINT "ist":SELECTION = 6:GOTO 420
370 IF Z$ = "P" THEN PRINT "RINT":SELECTION = 7:GOTO 420
380 IF Z$ = "p" THEN PRINT "rint":SELECTION = 7:GOTO 420
390 IF Z$ = "E" THEN PRINT "ND":SELECTION = 8:GOTO 420
400 IF Z$ = "e" THEN PRINT "nd":SELECTION = 8:GOTO 420
410 GOTO 100
420 ON SELECTION GOSUB 1450,460,770,960,1100,1280,1570,1850
430 PRINT "PRESS ANY KEY TO CONTINUE";
440 GET Z$
450 GOTO 100
460 REM *******************
470 REM * BUILD NEW ENTRY *
480 REM *******************
490 HOME
500 PRINT:PRINT TAB(30);"CAMP SLEAZY QUARTERMASTER"
510 FOR N = 1 TO 79:PRINT " ";:NEXT N
520 GOSUB 1430
530 IF ASC(FLAG$) = 255 THEN 580
540 PRINT "THE RECORD EXISTS - DO YOU WISH TO OVERWRITE (Y/N)? ";
550 GET Z$
560 PRINT Z$
570 IF Z$ < > "Y" THEN RETURN
580 FLAG$=CHR$(0)
590 PRINT
600 INPUT "ITEM DESCRIPTION: ";ITEM.DESCRIPTION$
610 FILE.DESCRIPTION$ = ITEM.DESCRIPTION$
620 PRINT
630 INPUT "QUANTITY IN STOCK: ",QUANTITY.IN.STOCK%
640 FILE.QUANTITY$ = CONV$(QUANTITY.IN.STOCK%)
650 PRINT
660 INPUT "REORDER POINT: ",REORDER.POINT%
670 FILE.REORDER.POINT$ = CONV$(REORDER.POINT%)
680 PRINT
690 INPUT "UNIT PRICE: $",UNIT.PRICE
700 FILE.UNIT.PRICE$ =CONV$(UNIT.PRICE)
710 PRINT
720 INPUT "BIN LOCATION: ";BIN.LOCATION$
730 FILE.BIN.LOCATION$ = BIN.LOCATION$
740 PRINT
750 WRITE #1,ITEM%
760 RETURN
770 REM *********************
780 REM * DISPLAY THE ENTRY *
790 REM *********************
800 HOME
810 PRINT:PRINT TAB(30);"CAMP SLEAZY QUARTERMASTER"
820 FOR N = 1 TO 79:PRINT " ";:NEXT N
830 GOSUB 1430
840 IF ASC(FLAG$)= 255 THEN PRINT "NULL ENTRY":RETURN
850 PRINT
860 PRINT USING "ITEM NUMBER 3&";ITEM%
870 PRINT
880 PRINT TAB(5);"ITEM: ";FILE.DESCRIPTION$
890 PRINT
```

Figure 5.31. (continued)

```
900 PRINT TAB(5);"";:PRINT USING "QUANTITY ON HAND 5&";
          CONV%(FILE.QUANTITY$)
910 PRINT TAB(5);"";:PRINT USING "REORDER LEVEL     5&";
          CONV%(FILE.REORDER.POINT$)
920 PRINT TAB(5);"";:PRINT USING "UNIT PRICE      $2&.2&";
          CONV(FILE.UNIT.PRICE$)
930 PRINT TAB(5);"";:PRINT "BIN LOCATION:       ";FILE.BIN.LOCATION$
940 PRINT
950 RETURN
960 REM ****************
970 REM * ADD TO STOCK *
980 REM ****************
990 HOME
1000 PRINT:PRINT TAB(30);"CAMP SLEAZY QUARTERMASTER"
1010 FOR N = 1 TO 79:PRINT " ";:NEXT N
1020 GOSUB 1430
1030 IF ASC(FLAG$) = 255 THEN PRINT "NULL ENTRY":RETURN
1040 PRINT FILE.DESCRIPTION$:INPUT "QUANTITY TO ADD ";QUANTITY.TO.ADD%
1050 QUANTITY% = CONV%(FILE.QUANTITY$) + QUANTITY.TO.ADD%
1060 FILE.QUANTITY$=CONV$(QUANTITY%)
1070 WRITE #1,ITEM%
1080 GOSUB 850                    :REM USE PART OF THE DISPLAY ROUTINE
1090 RETURN
1100 REM *********************
1110 REM * REMOVE FROM STOCK *
1120 REM *********************
1130 HOME
1140 PRINT:PRINT TAB(30);"CAMP SLEAZY QUARTERMASTER"
1150 FOR N = 1 TO 79:PRINT " ";:NEXT N
1160 GOSUB 1430
1170 IF ASC(FLAG$) = 255 THEN PRINT "NULL ENTRY":RETURN
1180 PRINT FILE.DESCRIPTION$
1190 INPUT "QUANTITY TO SUBTRACT";QUANTITY.TO.SUBTRACT%
1200 QUANTITY%=CONV%(FILE.QUANTITY$)
1210 IF (QUANTITY% - QUANTITY.TO.SUBTRACT%) < 0
        THEN PRINT "INSUFFICIENT QUANTITY - ONLY";QUANTITY%;
             " IN STOCK":GOTO 1190
1220 QUANTITY% = QUANTITY% - QUANTITY.TO.SUBTRACT%
1230 IF QUANTITY% = < CONV%(FILE.REORDER.POINT$) THEN PRINT
        "QUANTITY NOW";QUANTITY%;" REORDER LEVEL";
             CONV%(FILE.REORDER.POINT$)
1240 FILE.QUANTITY$=CONV$(QUANTITY%)
1250 WRITE #1,ITEM%
1260 GOSUB 850                    :REM USE PART OF THE DISPLAY ROUTINE
1270 RETURN
1280 REM **********************************
1290 REM * LIST ITEMS BELOW REORDER LEVEL *
1300 REM **********************************
1310 HOME
1320 PRINT:PRINT TAB(30);"CAMP SLEAZY QUARTERMASTER"
1330 FOR N = 1 TO 79:PRINT " ";:NEXT N
1340 PRINT
1350 FOR I = 1 TO 100
1360     READ #1,I
1370     IF CONV%(FILE.QUANTITY$) < CONV%(FILE.REORDER.POINT$)
            THEN PRINT FILE.DESCRIPTION$;"QUANTITY";
                 CONV%(FILE.QUANTITY$);TAB(50);"REORDER LEVEL";
                      CONV%(FILE.REORDER.POINT$)
1380     NEXT I
1390 RETURN
1400 REM **************************
1410 REM * OBTAIN THE ITEM NUMBER *
1420 REM **************************
1430 PRINT:INPUT "ITEM NUMBER";ITEM%
1440 IF (ITEM% < 1) OR (ITEM% > 100) THEN PRINT "BAD PART NUMBER":
        GOTO 1430:ELSE READ #1,ITEM%:RETURN
```

Figure 5.31. (continued)

```
1450 REM ************************
1460 REM * INITIALIZE THE FILE *
1470 REM ************************
1480 PRINT "ARE YOU SURE (Y/N)? ";
1490 GET Z$
1500 PRINT Z$
1510 IF Z$ < > "Y" THEN RETURN
1520 FLAG$ = CHR$(255)
1530 FOR I = 1 TO 100
1540      WRITE #1,I
1550      NEXT I
1560 RETURN
1570 REM ****************************
1580 REM * PRINT THE INVENTORY FILE *
1590 REM ****************************
1600 HOME
1610 PRINT:PRINT TAB(30);"CAMP SLEAZY QUARTERMASTER"
1620 FOR N = 1 TO 79:PRINT " ";:NEXT N
1630 PRINT
1640 PRINT:PRINT TAB(33);"INVENTORY FILE LIST"
1650 FOR N = 1 TO 79:PRINT " ";:NEXT N
1660 PRINT
1670 FOR I = 1 TO 100
1680      READ #1,I
1690      IF FLAG$ = CHR$(255) THEN 1800
1700      PRINT USING "ITEM NUMBER 3&";I
1710      PRINT
1720      PRINT TAB(5);"ITEM: ";FILE.DESCRIPTION$
1730      PRINT
1740      PRINT TAB(5);"";:PRINT USING "QUANTITY ON HAND 5&";
                  CONV%(FILE.QUANTITY$)
1750      PRINT TAB(5);"";:PRINT USING "REORDER LEVEL    5&";
                  CONV%(FILE.REORDER.POINT$)
1760      PRINT TAB(5);"";:PRINT USING "UNIT PRICE      $2&.2&";
                  CONV(FILE.UNIT.PRICE$)
1770      PRINT TAB(5);"";:PRINT "BIN LOCATION:        ";FILE.BIN.LOCATION$
1780      PRINT
1790      GOSUB 1860
1800      NEXT I
1810 RETURN
1820 REM ***********************
1830 REM * END THE APPLICATION *
1840 REM ***********************
1850 CLOSE:END
1860 REM ***********************
1870 REM * PRINTER SUBROUTINE  *
1880 REM ***********************
1890 OPEN #2,".PRINTER"
1900 OUTPUT #2
1910 PRINT:PRINT TAB(30);"CAMP SLEAZY QUARTERMASTER"
1920 PRINT FOR N = 1 TO 79:PRINT " ";:NEXT N
1930 PRINT
1940 PRINT:PRINT TAB(33);"INVENTORY FILE LIST"
1950 PRINT
1960 FOR I = 1 TO 100
1970      READ #1,I
1980      IF FLAG$ = CHR$(255) THEN 1800
1990      PRINT USING "ITEM NUMBER 3&";I
2000      PRINT
2010      PRINT TAB(5);"ITEM: ";FILE.DESCRIPTION$
2020      PRINT
2030      PRINT TAB(5);"";:PRINT USING "QUANTITY ON HAND 5&";
                  CONV%(FILE.QUANTITY$)
2040      PRINT TAB(5);"";:PRINT USING "REORDER LEVEL    5&";
                  CONV%(FILE.REORDER.POINT$)
```

Figure 5.31. (continued)

```
2050      PRINT TAB(5);"";:PRINT USING "UNIT PRICE      $2&.2&";
                CONV(FILE.UNIT.PRICE$)
2060      PRINT TAB(5);"";:PRINT "BIN LOCATION:       ";FILE.BIN.LOCATION$
2070      PRINT
2080      NEXT I
2090 PRINT CHR$(12)
2100 CLOSE #2
2110 RETURN
```

Figure 5.31. (continued)

Unlike in COBOL, which is an English-like programing language, references to BASIC statements are by line number, not symbolic label. This means that if you choose to remove a line in BASIC, it disappears. If another instruction references that line, however, you'll be able to find the line only when you renumber or use that instruction.

SUMMARY

These are the new commands used in this chapter:

ASC	Converts an ASCII character to its numeric value.
CHAIN	Loads and transfers control to another program, passing all variables.
CONV(	Converts an expression to a real number value.
CONV$	Converts an expression to a string variable.
CONV&	Converts an expression to a long integer.
CONV%	Converts an expression to an integer.
ERR	Used as part on an ON ERR instruction to give direction when an error has been detected.
ERRLIN	Details the line number where an error, having been anticipated, has occurred.
READ #	Used in the reading of random files.

REM	REMarks.
SWAP	Exchanges variables of like type.
WRITE #	Used to write random files.

6
A Small Business System

We have now reached the point at which this book was designed to arrive. The Apple III is basically a business machine, any way you look at it. The machine can be used in a variety of business uses.

Insofar as Apple III technique is concerned, most of it has already been conveyed. There are a few new things in this chapter, but its major purpose is to walk you through the development of a small business system.

The system that we will consider is not a simple one. It has aspects that will make you think differently about your business and about how you may wish to employ a computer to support it. Furthermore, no two businesses are exactly alike because they have differing needs for information. The system presented here, then, is only the skeletal structure of what yours should be. Therefore, as we dissect each piece, we will take note of where the program(s) can serve your purposes and where they should be modified for a closer fit.

Our system consists of eleven major building blocks, some of which have several small component building blocks. The major blocks are as follows:

BUSINESS — This is the frame program – the one that operates the menu which provides access to the other blocks of the system. It is *the one* place where the name of the organization is placed. That name is then carried throughout the entire system.

CHART — This program is used to build the chart of accounts. The chart of accounts is required essentially for income statement and balance sheet purposes, but also serves as the repository of account types and titles as required by the accounts receivable operation. The feeds exist to do the same in the accounts payable operation. This file is used jointly with the account file discussed next.

VALUE

As the system is set up, there is an account file for every period to be considered. This account file is the one file whose name must be specified to the program. In order for it to work with the income statement and the balance sheet programs, values must be loaded into it. The important thing to remember is that this is a *small business* system and therefore requires certain manual operations and interfaces. One of the things not built into it is an ability to combine account files over a long period. You may wish to develop such a program. More probably, other programs will be modified for multiple file input.

CUSTOMER

If you are to have an accounts receivable system, then it is necessary to have a customer file. This program is used to develop a sequential customer file. For purposes of this book, only rudimentary information is designed into the system. You may wish to modify the system to gather more information about your customers.

VENDOR

The accounts payable portion of the system is not a full-fledged A/P system and for a very basic reason: The small business simply does not have enough accounts payable to have to worry about discount dates and automated generation of checks. However, in anticipation of such an activity, a vendor file has been established. Later, when you get into the accounts payable subsystem, you may wish to change the given approach to tie it to the vendor file in much the same manner as the accounts receivable application is tied to the customer file.

MAILLIST — As the name implies, this program allows selection of either the customer file or the vendor file for the purposes of preparing mailing labels. The spacing worked into the program will fit popular-size labels.

PRODUCT — The system includes a rudimentary inventory control mechanism. This file is used with accounts receivable invoices and statements. It might further be used should you wish to develop purchase order, inventory movement, and replenishment reports.

RECIVBLE — The accounts receivable system is perhaps the most important of all to the small business. Therefore, the A/R subsystem of the small business system is quite extensive. This program provides three of the seven services incorporated into the system: Initial entry, addition of invoices, and the production of invoices. On the smallest Apple III system there is plenty of room for these applications, but because of simplicity of design, we have broken down some of the services into callable submodules. The remaining four services called by this program include the production of A/R reports, the posting of account records, the production of monthly statements, and the aging of accounts.

PAYABLE — The accounts payable implemented here is *not* a complete accounts payable subsystem. Having been in a small business for many years, the author has found that the accounts payable features required by a larger company are not really relevant to the small business. What *is* relevant is the ability to control the cash *outflow.* For that reason, the accounts payable application as contained here is devoted entirely to checkbook entry (what a larger company would call the "purchases journal"), maintenance, reporting, and balancing.

INCOME — This program simply produces an income statement using the prestored totals from the account file selected and using the titles from the chart of accounts. As previously stated, the system is designed to accept one data file at a time. Changing it to accept others is not difficult.

BALANCE — This program produces the accompanying balance sheet. All considerations that are applicable to the income statement also apply here.

The interrelationship of these building blocks is shown in Figure 6.1.

PRELUDE

Important point: Because the author wanted the Business Basic diskette to remain in Drive .D1, strictly as a matter of convenience for testing, all references to program and to data are to .D2. Keep the same arrangement so long as you are entering and testing. When your testing is complete, change the *program* references only to Drive .D1. Thus, after Business BASIC is loaded, you can swap diskettes and the program disk can occupy drive .D1 and the data disk can occupy drive .D2.

BUSINESS

The entire process begins with this program – BUSINESS – which is simply a frame program. If you will examine it now – the program immediately follows this discussion – what is to be said here will be far more meaningful.

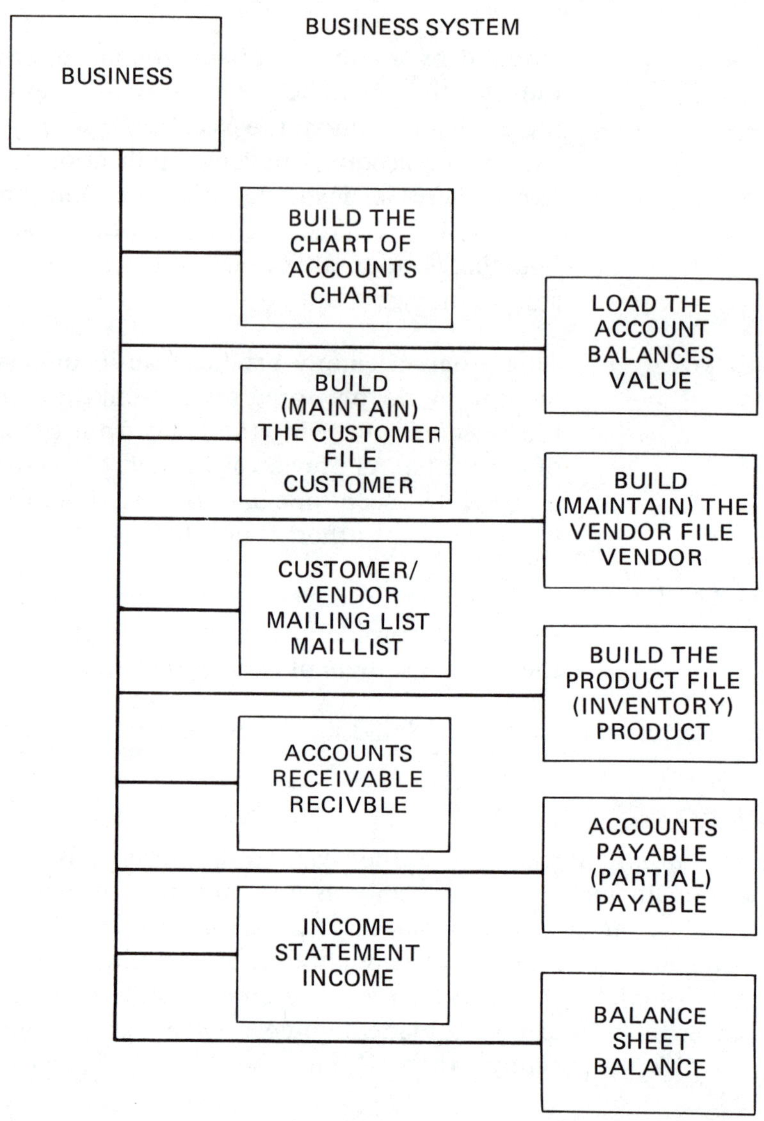

Figure 6.1.

Statement 30 establishes COMPANY.NAME$ as the vehicle to carry the name to other subprograms. We've selected a very pertinent company name – SMALL BUSINESS ENTERPRISE, INC. That name is centered by the instruction in 40. We know that the screen is 80 characters wide. Statement 40 determines the difference in length of the screen line and the entered name, divides it by two, and centers it.

There are ten options plus a termination option. As the system is entirely integrated, the latter will be the only exit from the system, unless, of course, a program ceases to function or you purposely interrupt it. At statement 250 the response of "X" will terminate the program.

Look at statement 260. The ASCII value of the letter "A" is 65. The ON ... GOTO of statement 280 must make the varying branch on the basis of a *numeric value.* It is therefore necessary to take the alphabetic response of A through J and transmute it to a number that will work with that variable (called PROGRAM). Therefore, if the letter "A" is the response, 65 (A) less 64 will leave the result of 1, producing a branch to 300. The same is true for the letter "B" – a response of 2 – the letter C – a response of 3, etc. There is an error trap in statement 270 that will not allow anything less than 1 or more than 10 to pass. Protection is also provided by the fact that there are but 10 branching addresses in 260. Statement 270 is an unnecessary instruction; it is entered for clarity and further protection – just in case.

Statements 300 through 390 are CHAINs to carry you to the selected program. Again, statement 400 will undoubtedly never occur. It is not a bad idea to occasionally include an instruction whose necessity you doubt. In 20 years in the business, the author has learned that Murphy's Law is omnipresent. The idea of the CHAIN is that the selected program is drawn into memory, *replacing the program that CHAINed to it* – in this case, BUSINESS. All that will remain of BUSINESS until it is recalled will be the COMPANY.NAME$, Small Business Enterprise, Inc. The other variables will be carried forward, of course, but are quickly replaced. Again, remember to keep your programs assigned to drive .D2 until you are prepared to run them regularly.

Figure 6.2 shows the program BUSINESS:

```
10 HOME
20 CLEAR
30 COMPANY.NAME$ = "SMALL BUSINESS ENTERPRISE, INC."
40 X = ((80 - LEN(COMPANY.NAME$)) / 2)
50 HOME
60 VPOS=2:HPOS=X
70 PRINT COMPANY.NAME$;
80 FOR N = 1 TO 79:PRINT CHR$(220);:NEXT N
```

Figure 6.2.

```
90 PRINT:PRINT TAB(20);"A.  CHART OF ACCOUNTS"
100 PRINT TAB(20);"B.  LOAD ACCOUNT BALANCES"
110 PRINT TAB(20);"C.  CREATE (MAINTAIN) CUSTOMER FILE"
120 PRINT TAB(20);"D.  CREATE (MAINTAIN) VENDOR FILE"
130 PRINT TAB(20);"E.  CUSTOMER/VENDOR MAILING LIST"
140 PRINT TAB(20);"F.  CREATE (MAINTAIN) PRODUCT (INVENTORY) FILE"
150 PRINT TAB(20);"G.  ACCOUNTS RECEIVABLE"
160 PRINT TAB(20);"H.  ACCOUNTS PAYABLE"
170 PRINT TAB(20);"I.  INCOME STATEMENT"
180 PRINT TAB(20);"J.  BALANCE SHEET"
190 VPOS=25:HPOS=1
200 PRINT "PRESS 'X' TO TERMINATE PROGRAM";
210 VPOS=22:HPOS=10
220 PRINT "SELECT: ";
230 GET Z$
240 PRINT Z$;
250 IF Z$ = "X" THEN END
260 PROGRAM = ASC(Z$) - 64
270 IF (PROGRAM < 1) OR (PROGRAM > 10) THEN 410
280 ON PROGRAM GOTO 300,310,320,330,340,350,360,370,380,390
290 GOTO 410
300 CHAIN .D2/CHART
310 CHAIN .D2/VALUE
320 CHAIN .D2/CUSTOMER
330 CHAIN .D2/VENDOR
340 CHAIN .D2/MAILLIST
350 CHAIN .D2/PRODUCT
360 CHAIN .D2/RECIVBLE
370 CHAIN .D2/PAYABLE
380 CHAIN .D2/INCOME
390 CHAIN .D2/BALANCE
400 GOTO 10
410 PRINT CHR$(7)
420 VPOS=22:HPOS=1
430 FOR N = 1 TO 79:PRINT " ";:NEXT N
440 GOTO 210
```

Figure 6.2. (continued)

CHART

Since the entire system is built around the Chart of Accounts, that's where the process must begin. The user has the opportunity to enter one or more account types and titles using this program. They must fall within five distinct categories: Asset, Liability, Capital, Income, and Expense; it can be seen that these are the headings that will appear on the Income Statement and Balance Sheet.

Like every system, there is a first time option and a second and subsequent time option. If you respond to the program that this is an entirely new file, you will build the file from scratch. It is built in memory and not written to disk until you state that you've entered all the data. Therefore, if you have inadvertently begun a new file when one already exists, you can either interrupt the process or replace the disk.

Throughout this chapter the programs will contain reference to both programs and data on Drive .D2. As previously stated, you should separate programs to Drive .D1 before going into "production." In any event, *always copy critical data files before beginning any work on them.* It's always wise to have backup copies of the programs, as well. It's very difficult to reconstruct old data once it's been changed. The cost of a few extra diskettes is far less than the cost of the time necessary to correct a 10-second mistake.

The program will accept keyboard input from the keyboard only (when no file previously exists) or input from an existing file plus the keyboard. It then writes the initial file or updates the previous file and, of course, displays the results of its work.

Figure 6.3 shows a block diagram of the Chart of Accounts program. The program accepts input from the keyboard, or from the file and keyboard combined, and uses it to develop a new Chart of Accounts. Each account is coded with A (Asset), L (Liability), C (Capital), I (Income), or E (Expense), and is given an account title. These account titles will be used throughout the system and when income statements and balance sheets are prepared.

BUILD THE CHART OF ACCOUNTS

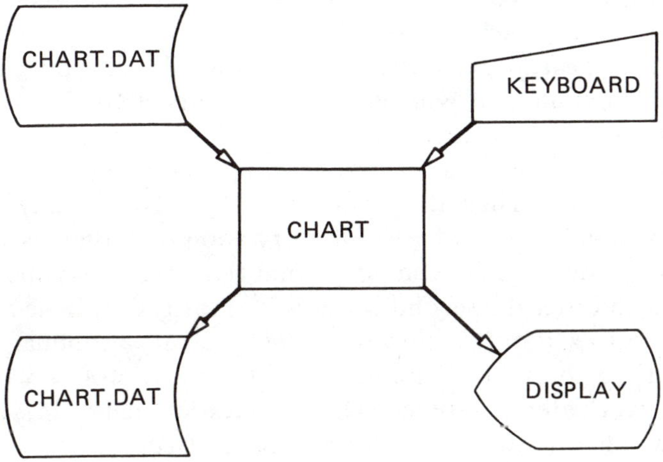

CHART.DAT

KEYBOARD

CHART

CHART.DAT

DISPLAY

Figure 6.3.

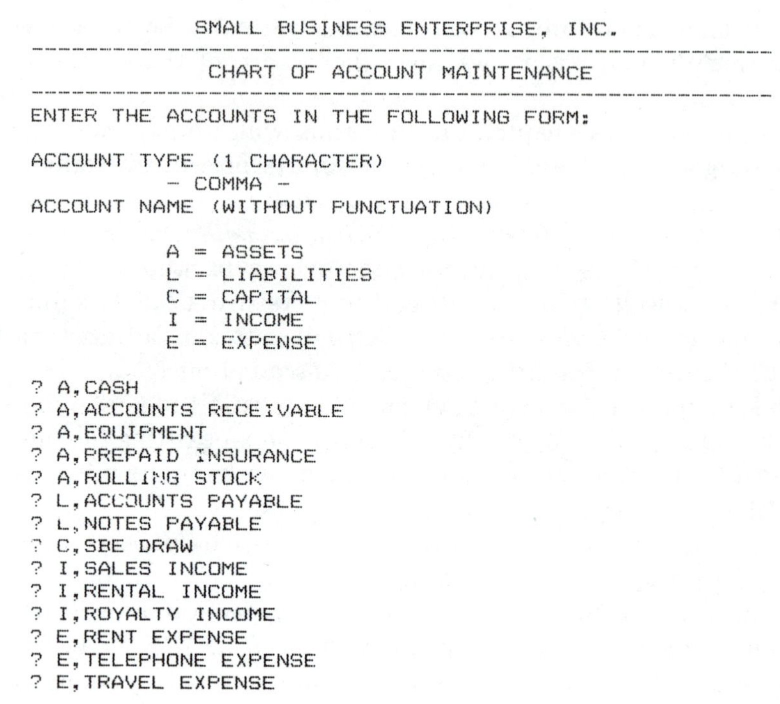

```
                 SMALL BUSINESS ENTERPRISE, INC.
------------------------------------------------------------------
                  CHART OF ACCOUNT MAINTENANCE
------------------------------------------------------------------
ENTER THE ACCOUNTS IN THE FOLLOWING FORM:

ACCOUNT TYPE (1 CHARACTER)
           - COMMA -
ACCOUNT NAME (WITHOUT PUNCTUATION)

            A = ASSETS
            L = LIABILITIES
            C = CAPITAL
            I = INCOME
            E = EXPENSE

? A,CASH
? A,ACCOUNTS RECEIVABLE
? A,EQUIPMENT
? A,PREPAID INSURANCE
? A,ROLLING STOCK
? L,ACCOUNTS PAYABLE
? L,NOTES PAYABLE
? C,SBE DRAW
? I,SALES INCOME
? I,RENTAL INCOME
? I,ROYALTY INCOME
? E,RENT EXPENSE
? E,TELEPHONE EXPENSE
? E,TRAVEL EXPENSE
```

Figure 6.4.

Before we show you the program, we should present its two major displays. Refer to Figures 6.4 and 6.5.

As usual, a little explanation is required. When you get to the complete program you will note that a paired INPUT statement is used. This means that titles must be devoid of punctuation. It also means that the program anticipates *two* responses before it can interpret the first one. Thus, the request for END,END is really a request for two operands. However, as for every good rule, there is an exception. Study the program and you'll find that it searches out only the first END and that the second could just as easily be satisfied by pressing the return key only – however, *after* entering a comma. If you'll look back to the first of the previous pair of printouts, you'll note that the data entered is preceded by a question mark. It is a feature of Business BASIC that the question mark be suppressed. In this instance, we decided not to do so, so that it would be perfectly obvious

```
             SMALL BUSINESS ENTERPRISE, INC.
-----------------------------------------------------------
              CHART OF ACCOUNT MAINTENANCE
-----------------------------------------------------------
ACCOUNT #          TYPE          NAME
1                   A        CASH
2                   A        ACCOUNTS RECEIVABLE
3                   A        EQUIPMENT
4                   A        PREPAID INSURANCE
5                   A        ROLLING STOCK
6                   L        ACCOUNTS PAYABLE
7                   L        NOTES PAYABLE
8                   C        SBE DRAW
9                   I        SALES INCOME
10                  I        RENTAL INCOME
11                  I        ROYALTY INCOME
12                  E        RENT EXPENSE
13                  E        TELEPHONE EXPENSE
14                  E        TRAVEL EXPENSE

ARE THERE OTHER ACCOUNTS TO BE ADDED (Y/N)
```

Figure 6.5.

that an input was requested. The first response is one of the five codes A, L, C, I, or E. Those codes could be entered in any order.

In this example, fourteen accounts have been created. In a later program, you will note that the number of accounts has grown to 15, as the program itself adds a new account, INTEREST INCOME. The Account Number given represents the record number of the account in the sequential file CHART.DAT. That file exists as a part of internal program design and is written with the record that you see plus one additional record that precedes the whole thing – the first record, which contains the count of the records to follow. Sequential files are written with the PRINT # instruction and are read with the INPUT # instruction. There are some similarities in the CREATE and OPEN statements, owing to the design of the Apple III's drivers.

Throughout this entire small business system, the disk files are organized sequentially (they're not large enough to require random access), and they each have an initial record that specifies the number of records to follow. This arrangement is possible because all the work is done in arrays and the record count is known before the file is written. In some cases throughout this discussion you will note that the DIMensioning of the array used to handle the data will not take place at the beginning of the program but is delayed until the size of the file is known.

Figure 6.6 gives the program CHART.

```
10 HOME
20 GOSUB 1360
30 REM *************************************************************************
40 REM * T$ HOLDS THE ACCOUNT TYPE; N$ HOLDS THE ACCOUNT NAME.  BS$ IS USED   *
50 REM * TO DETERMINE THE SEQUENCE IN WHICH THE ACCOUNTS ARE WRITTEN TO DISK.*
60 REM * THIS WILL BE IMPORTANT FOR THE CONSTRUCTION OF A BALANCE SHEET.      *
70 REM *************************************************************************
80 DIM T$(25),N$(25),BS$(5)
90 BS$(1) = "A"
100 BS$(2) = "L"
110 BS$(3) = "C"
120 BS$(4) = "I"
130 BS$(5) = "E"
140 REM *********
150 PRINT
160 PRINT
170 PRINT "WILL THE CHART OF ACCOUNTS BE ENTERED FROM THE FILE (Y/N) ";
180 GET Z$
190 PRINT Z$
200 IF Z$ < > "Y" THEN 230
210 GOSUB 1140
220 GOTO 500
230 REM **********************************
240 REM * ENTER ACCOUNTS FROM THE KEYBOARD *
250 REM **********************************
260 PRINT
270 HOME
280 GOSUB 1360
290 PRINT "ENTER THE ACCOUNTS IN THE FOLLOWING FORM (INCLUDE THE COMMA): "
300 PRINT TAB(5);"ACCOUNT TYPE (ONE LETTER), ACCOUNT NAME (NO PUNCTUATION)
310 PRINT
320 PRINT "TYPES  A=ASSETS, L=LIABILITIES, C=CAPITAL, I=INCOME, E=EXPENSE"
330 PRINT "EXAMPLE INPUTS: A,CASH  OR  L,ACCOUNTS PAYABLE"
340 PRINT
350 PRINT "ENTER INFORMATION NOW - TYPE 'END,END' TO TERMINATE INPUT"
360 I = 1
370      T$(I)=""
380      INPUT T$(I),N$(I)
390      IF T$(I) = "END" THEN 480
400      IF T$(I) = "A" THEN 460
410      IF T$(I) = "L" THEN 460
420      IF T$(I) = "C" THEN 460
430      IF T$(I) = "I" THEN 460
440      IF T$(I) = "E" THEN 460
450      PRINT "ENTRY NOT ACCEPTABLE - REPEAT":GOTO 690
460      I = I + 1
470 GOTO 370
480 N = I - 1    :REM THIS COUNT WILL BE WRITTEN AS THE FIRST RECORD
490 REM **************************
500 REM * PRINT THE ACCOUNT NAMES *
510 REM **************************
520 HOME
530 GOSUB 1360
540 PRINT
550 PRINT " ACCOUNT #     TYPE          NAME"
560 FOR I = 1 TO N
570      PRINT I;TAB(17);T$(I);TAB(23);N$(I)
580      NEXT I
```

Figure 6.6.

```
590 REM ***********************
600 REM * ADDING NEW ACCOUNTS *
610 REM ***********************
620 PRINT
630 PRINT "ARE THERE OTHER ACCOUNTS TO BE ADDED (Y/N) ";
640 GET Z$
650 PRINT Z$
660 IF Z$ < > "Y" THEN 820
670 PRINT "ENTER NEW ACCOUNTS - TYPE 'END,END' WHEN FINISHED"
680 N = N + 1
690 T$(N) = " "
700 INPUT T$(N),N$(N)
710 IF T$(N) = "END" THEN 790
720      IF T$(N) = "A" THEN 780
730      IF T$(N) = "L" THEN 780
740      IF T$(N) = "C" THEN 780
750      IF T$(N) = "I" THEN 780
760      IF T$(N) = "E" THEN 780
770      PRINT "ENTRY NOT ACCEPTABLE - REPEAT":GOTO 690
780 GOTO 680
790 N = N - 1    :REM THIS COUNT WILL BE WRITTEN AS THE FIRST RECORD
800 GOTO 500
810 REM ******************************
820 REM * CHANGING EXISTING ACCOUNTS *
830 REM ******************************
840 PRINT "ARE THERE ANY ITEMS TO CHANGE (Y/N)? ";
850 GET Z$
860 PRINT Z$
870 IF Z$ < > "Y" THEN 1000
880 PRINT "ENTER THE ACCOUNT # TO BE CHANGED FOLLOWED BY (COMMA),"
890 PRINT " THE NEW TYPE (COMMA), THE ACCOUNT NAME"
900 INPUT Z,T$(Z),N$(Z)
910 HOME
920 GOSUB 1360
930 PRINT
940 PRINT " #     TYPE         NAME"
950 FOR I = 1 TO N
960      PRINT I;TAB(9);T$(I);TAB(15);N$(I)
970      NEXT I
980 GOTO 840
990 REM ***********************
1000 REM * SAVING ARRAY IN FILE *
1010 REM ***********************
1020 FILE.NAME$ = ".D2/CHART.DAT"
1030 GOSUB 1230
1040 REM ***********************
1050 REM * PROGRAM TERMINATION *
1060 REM ***********************
1070 PRINT
1080 PRINT
1090 PRINT "CHART OF ACCOUNTS IS COMPLETE"
1100 CHAIN .D2/BUSINESS
1110 REM ***********************
1120 REM * SUBROUTINES FOLLOW *
1130 REM ****************************
1140 REM * OPEN AND INPUT NAME FILE *
1150 REM ****************************
1160 OPEN #1,FILE.NAME$
1170 INPUT #1,N   :REM OBTAIN THE RECORD COUNT PREVIOUSLY STORED
1180 FOR I = 1 TO N
1190      INPUT #1,T$(I),N$(I)
1200      NEXT I
1210 CLOSE #1
1220 RETURN
```

Figure 6.6. (continued)

```
1230 REM **************************
1240 REM * OPEN AND WRITE TO FILE *
1250 REM **************************
1260 CREATE ".D2/CHART.DAT",TEXT
1270 OPEN #2,FILE.NAME$
1280 PRINT #2,N          :REM WRITE THE RECORD COUNT
1290 FOR J = 1 TO 5
1300     FOR I = 1 TO N
1310         IF BS$(J) = T$(I) THEN PRINT #2,T$(I);",";N$(I)
1320         NEXT I
1330     NEXT J
1340 CLOSE #2
1350 RETURN
1360 REM ********************************
1370 REM * HEADING USED FOR THE DISPLAY *
1380 REM ********************************
1390 X = ((80 - LEN(COMPANY.NAME$)) / 2)
1400 VPOS=2:HPOS=X
1410 PRINT COMPANY.NAME$
1420 FOR N = 1 TO 79:PRINT "-";:NEXT N:PRINT
1430 PRINT TAB(27);"CHART OF ACCOUNT MAINTENANCE"
1440 FOR N = 1 TO 79:PRINT "-";:NEXT N
1450 RETURN
```

Figure 6.6. (continued)

In this program, there are three tables: T$, which will permit up to 25 account codes; N$, which will permit up to 25 account names; B$, which will hold the five acceptable code types loaded 90 through 130.

Examine the routine from 360 through 470. You'll note that it *looks* like a traditional FOR ... NEXT loop, and it is – almost. Because we knew that T$ was DIMensioned at 25, we could have used a 1 to 25 FOR ... NEXT loop. Suppose, however, that you wish to have 37 accounts? Two different methods are possible. The FOR ... NEXT loop can be established as a number larger than would ever be possible, as we do in a later program, or it can be established merely linearly, with "I" being set initially at 1 (statement 360) and then being incremented with each iteration of the loop (460). (*Iteration* is a computerese term that simply means a movement through the loop). When the last entry has been made and the END is received, the count (less 1, as it will have been incremented *beyond* – the count exceeds the FOR) is stored in the variable N to permit it to be used later.

Some mention must be made of the one-letter variables that find their way into common use. Such variables as Z$, Z, N, I, J, K, L, etc., are frequently used by programers as *work variables.* By themselves, the variables have no specific meaning, such as a variable like COMPANY.NAME$ would. There are times however, when a utility variable is required as a means to count. Generally in this programming, the variable "I" is used for *I*ndexing through an array. Where there are several arrays in concurrent or simultaneous use, the variables J, K, etc., will be used. In a later program discussion we will show you how to compress the contents of an array while indexing through the *source* array with one variable and through the *destination* array with a second. Interestingly enough, we'll find that we're using the same array.

At this point, the variable N contains the size of the loaded arrays. It then becomes the maximum to which any further work on the arrays will range. In this application, when a file is read into the program and records are added to the end, it becomes necessary to go beyond the current ending. Now, a word of caution: Look through the program and you will see that the file reading routine at statements 1130 to 1220 reads the size of the file in records at 1170 and then reads *that many* records in the loop 1180 to 1200. The variable N here has the same use as the variable N in statement 480. In later programs we will substitute a name for N – xxxx.FILE.SIZE, with a name replacing xxxx.

There is an interesting concept in statement 1310. Statement 1310 says that if the entry to the array contains one of the codes in array B$, then it may be written to the file. Although protection is provided to the entry process, if for some reason that protection is changed, only the values loaded into B$ may be used. The routine from statements 1290 to 1330 demonstrates the two-variable J is used to move through the five-position array B$ while variable I moves through the range of 1 to N, previously discussed).

VALUE

The Chart of Accounts is noting more than a pattern to be used for corresponding data on one or more account files. It's important to note that both the Chart of Accounts file and the account files (which could more properly be called *account value files*) are in the same configuration *as far as the account value file goes.* As mentioned before, the Chart of Accounts has 14 records. Thus, it's possible that you will develop data on 14 accounts for several months before you suddenly discover that a new one is needed. From that point on, 15 accounts will be required, *but the first 14 will always be the same.* Thus, you can see that it's not very good business to change the sequence of accounts in the Chart of Accounts once the process has begun. It's not important what sequence the Chart of Accounts is in originally. When the Income Statement and Balance Sheet are developed, they'll be in the proper sequence.

The block diagram in Figure 6.7 summarizes the capabilities for the file load we call VALUE. This program passes the Chart of Accounts file for the purpose of developing an account file with balances that correspond to the accounts listed in the chart. This function will be particularly useful when the INCOME statement and BALANCE sheet are prepared. The name of the output file must be specified from the keyboard, will be combined with ".DAT" within the program (and with .D2/ pending your shift to Drive .D1), and will then produce a file that will be used in the referenced runs and also with the Accounts Receivable subsystem.

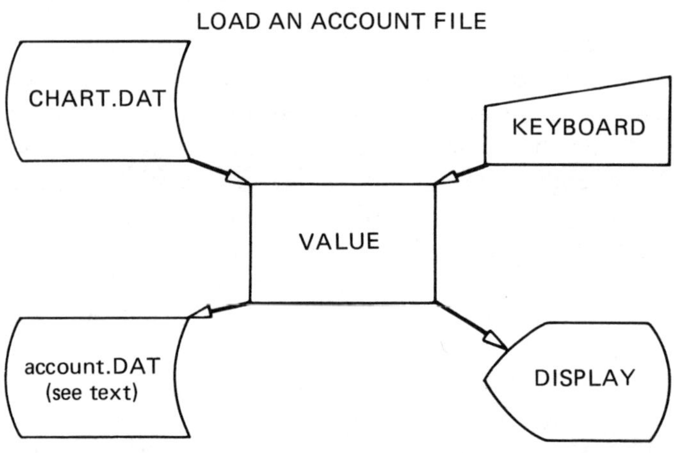

Figure 6.7.

The Chart File records are read and loaded into array T$ and N$. Then, one by one, they are passed upon the screen, and the operator is asked to give a value to them. In practice, the opening balances should be where your accountant says they should be. Since there is no transition from period to period (e.g., month to quarter), then the final balances of one period become the opening balances of the new period. You can accomplish this with either a value load or a copy of the file with the name changed. Thus, if the present file is MAY83.DAT you need only copy it to JUN83.DAT to have a new file with which to begin the new period – in this case, a month.

Using this application, changes may be made to existing codes and account titles, and, of course, the amounts are added to the array. Then, when the process is complete, you are asked for the *stub* of the file name. It is the convention of this system that data files are suffixed with .DAT.

The program VALUE is given in Figure 6.8.

```
10 HOME
20 GOSUB 800
30 REM ************************************************************************
40 REM * T$ HOLDS THE ACCOUNT TYPE; N$ HOLDS THE ACCOUNT NAME.  A IS USED     *
50 REM * TO STORE THE BALANCE OF THE ACCOUNTS WHICH HAVE BEEN ENTERED BY THE *
60 REM * PROGRAM CHART.                                                       *
70 REM ************************************************************************
80 DIM T$(25),N$(25),A(25)
90 PRINT
100 GOSUB 580
110 PRINT "ENTER AMOUNTS FOR THE ACCOUNTS SHOWN"
120 PRINT
130 FOR I = 1 TO N
140     PRINT T$(I),N$(I),"$";
150     INPUT "",A(I)
160     NEXT I
170 REM *********************
180 REM * PRINT THE RESULTS *
190 REM *********************
200 GOSUB 800
210 PRINT
220 PRINT "ACCOUNT #";TAB(15);"ACCOUNT TYPE";TAB(30);
230 PRINT "ACCOUNT TITLE";TAB(55);"AMOUNT"
240 PRINT
250 FOR I = 1 TO N
260     PRINT I;TAB(20);T$(I);TAB(30);N$(I);TAB(55);A(I)
270     NEXT I
280 PRINT
290 REM ******************************
300 REM * CHANGING EXISTING ACCOUNTS *
310 REM ******************************
320 PRINT
330 PRINT "ARE THERE ANY ITEMS TO CHANGE (Y/N)? ";
340 GET Z$
350 PRINT Z$
360 IF Z$ < > "Y" THEN 410
370 PRINT "ENTER THE ACCOUNT # TO BE CHANGED FOLLOWED BY (COMMA AND)";
380 PRINT " THE NEW AMOUNT"
390 INPUT Z,A(Z)
400 GOTO 170
410 REM ************************
420 REM * SAVING ARRAY IN FILE *
430 REM ************************
440 PRINT "ENTER THE FILE NAME FOR THIS DATA (I WILL COMBINE WITH .DAT)";
```

Figure 6.8.

```
450 INPUT "",FILE.NAME$
460 FILE.NAME$ = ".D2/" + FILE.NAME$ + ".DAT"
470 GOSUB 670
480 REM ***********************
490 REM * PROGRAM TERMINATION *
500 REM ***********************
510 PRINT
520 PRINT
530 PRINT "LOADING OF ACCOUNT VALUES IS COMPLETE"
540 CHAIN .D2/BUSINESS
550 REM **********************
560 REM * SUBROUTINES FOLLOW *
570 REM ****************************
580 REM * OPEN AND INPUT NAME FILE *
590 REM ****************************
600 OPEN #1,.D2/CHART.DAT
610 INPUT #1,N   :REM OBTAIN THE RECORD COUNT PREVIOUSLY STORED
620 FOR I = 1 TO N
630     INPUT #1,T$(I),N$(I)
640     NEXT I
650 CLOSE #1
660 RETURN
670 REM *************************
680 REM * OPEN AND WRITE TO FILE *
690 REM *************************
700 CREATE FILENAME$,TEXT
710 OPEN #2,FILE.NAME$
720 PRINT #2,N          :REM WRITE THE RECORD COUNT
740 FOR I = 1 TO N
750     PRINT #2,A(I)
760     NEXT I
780 CLOSE #2
790 RETURN
800 REM ********************************
810 REM * HEADING USED FOR THE DISPLAY *
820 REM ********************************
830 HOME
840 X = ((80 - LEN(COMPANY.NAME$)) / 2)
850 VPOS=2:HPOS=X
860 PRINT COMPANY.NAME$
870 FOR N = 1 TO 79:PRINT "-";:NEXT N:PRINT
880 PRINT TAB(28);"ACCOUNT BALANCE DATA ENTRY"
890 FOR N = 1 TO 79:PRINT "-";:NEXT N:PRINT
900 RETURN
```

Figure 6.8. (continued)

CUSTOMER

A small business has a customer list – particularly if it is in the business of selling something, which makes it, by definition, a business. Such a list ordinarily proves to be extremely useful. In the small business system presented here, it's essential, because without it accounts receivable subsystem cannot function. If you have a small number of customers, the list may be very informal, and the Apple III and this book will probably not mean very much to you.

There are many ways to develop a customer list. The most expeditious is to use a devoted application to develop and maintain a customer list, which may then be used in other applications. Our particular application allows for initial development of the file, additions to the file, and changes to the file. It does not allow for the removal of a customer from the file as it's currently constituted. There are a couple of reasons for this omission, the chief one being that since a small business needs all the customers it can get, it seldom gives up on any client. This application also stores the names onto a file that will be used for later mail list purposes.

A block diagram for building and maintaining the customer file is shown in Figure 6.9. The program accepts input from the keyboard, or from the file and keyboard combined, and uses it to develop a Customer Master File. This Customer Master File is used in several other places in the system, specifically in the Accounts Receivable subsystem. A list of customers and pertinent data may be obtained. You may wish to augment the customer file with other pertinent data.

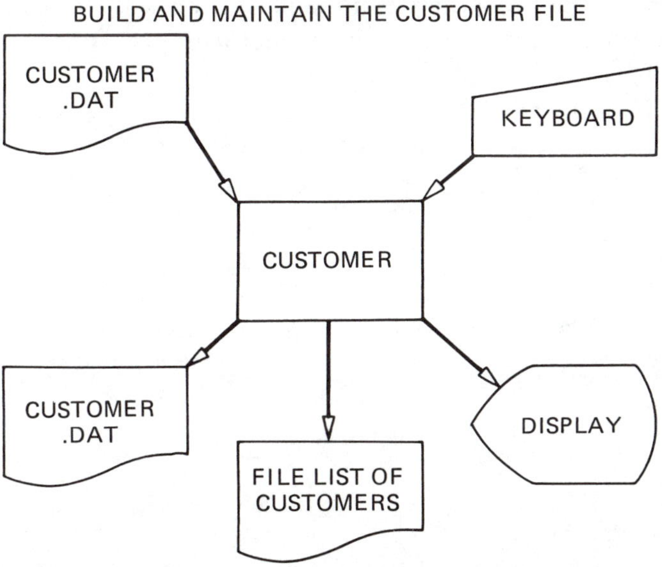

Figure 6.9.

The opening message of the program is extremely important. If you respond that the file has never been built before, then the program will create a new file with the same name. So long as you are entering information from a keyboard, you need not be concerned about interrupting or changing the disk. When input is terminated, however, the new file is written. As in other examples, the data is handled through arrays.

When the file does exist, the proper response will cause the current CUSTOMER.DAT to be read into memory, and additions are made by increasing the length of the array. For safety's sake, the file size and array sizes are reserved at 1000 elements each, even though that much space may not be needed. In this particular program, 1000 elements are set aside. In a later application it is trimmed (in one instance) to 800, and DIMensioned as a function of the file size (in another). Both approaches work well and are illustrated to show you the variety possible.

Observe the FOR ... NEXT loop at statements 220–290. In this instance, we have asked for a name, four lines of address, and customer terms. Each of the items requested exists in its own array (as DIMensioned in the routine in statements 410–470). Only rudimentary information is asked for; there is no request for a telephone number or other information. Moreover, the item Customer Terms is given as

```
RECORD NUMBER:  1

CUSTOMER NAME:       MR. BENJAMIN WATERS
CUSTOMER ADDRESS:    IMAGINATION INTERPRETED
                     327 PAGE ROAD
                     WATERTOWN,
                     PENNSYLVANIA 17743
CUSTOMER TERMS:      2/10 NET 30

----------------------------------------------------------

RECORD NUMBER:  2

CUSTOMER NAME:       MRS. MARGUERITE ALLISON
CUSTOMER ADDRESS:    COMPUTER INSTITUTE
                     830 TAMARACK LANE
                     METARIE,
                     LOUISIANA 34769
CUSTOMER TERMS:      CASH ON DELIVERY

----------------------------------------------------------

RECORD NUMBER:  3

CUSTOMER NAME:       PURCHASING AGENT
CUSTOMER ADDRESS:    SILICON VALLEY CHIPS
                     TRANSISTOR LANE
                     CUPERTINO,
                     CALIFORNIA 94377

CUSTOMER TERMS:      CREDIT IS ACCEPTABLE

----------------------------------------------------------
```

Figure 6.10.

an alphabetic string, allowing text but not a numeric value upon which calculations can be performed. If you wish to use the customer terms as a calculation variable (this system uses a fixed 1.5% factor), then you must change the customer terms variable and build it into your programs.

This application, as programed, allows for the listing of the file. The system is currently programed to print four customer records per page of printed output, the printed output looking like Figure 6.10. The program CUSTOMER is given in Figure 6.11.

```
10 GOSUB 2170
20 ARRAY.SIZE = 1000
30 FILE.SIZE = 1000
40 GOSUB 410
50 BASE = 1
60 PRINT
70 PRINT "TWO FORMS OF INPUT ARE POSSIBLE IN THIS PROGRAM: INPUT
          FROM EITHER"
80 PRINT "DISK OR THE KEYBOARD.  IF YOU CHOOSE NOT TO OBTAIN THE
          INPUT FROM"
90 PRINT "THE DISK, THE PROGRAM WILL ASSUME THAT YOU WISH TO ENTER
          FROM THE"
100 PRINT "KEYBOARD, DESTROYING ANY DISK FILE.  IF YOU WISH TO ADD
          TO THE FILE"
110 PRINT "WHICH ALREADY EXISTS, YOU MUST ANSWER 'Y' TO THIS
          QUESTION:"
120 PRINT:PRINT "WILL INPUT BE FROM THE DISK FILE (Y/N)? ";
130 GET Z$
140 PRINT Z$
150 IF Z$ < > "Y" THEN 530
160 REM ****************************
170 REM * OPEN AND INPUT NAME FILE *
180 REM ****************************
190 FILE.NAME$ = ".D2/CUSTOMER.DAT"
200 OPEN #1,FILE.NAME$
210 INPUT #1,FILE.SIZE       :REM OBTAIN THE RECORD COUNT
220 FOR I = 1 TO FILE.SIZE
230     INPUT #1,CUSTOMER.NAME$(I)
240     INPUT #1,CUSTOMER.ADDR.1$(I)
250     INPUT #1,CUSTOMER.ADDR.2$(I)
260     INPUT #1,CUSTOMER.ADDR.3$(I)
270     INPUT #1,CUSTOMER.ADDR.4$(I)
280     INPUT #1,CUSTOMER.TERMS$(I)
290     NEXT I
300 RECORD.COUNT = I - 1
310 CLOSE #1
320 PRINT:PRINT "WILL THERE BE ADDITIONS TO THE FILE (Y/N)? ";
330 GET Z$
340 PRINT Z$
350 IF Z$ < > "Y" THEN 830
```

Figure 6.11.

```
360 BASE = I
370 GOTO 530
380 REM ***********************************************************
390 REM * THE DIMENSIONING IS ESTABLISHED AS A THOUSAND RECORDS. *
400 REM ***********************************************************
410 DIM CUSTOMER.NAME$(ARRAY.SIZE)
420 DIM CUSTOMER.ADDR.1$(ARRAY.SIZE)
430 DIM CUSTOMER.ADDR.2$(ARRAY.SIZE)
440 DIM CUSTOMER.ADDR.3$(ARRAY.SIZE)
450 DIM CUSTOMER.ADDR.4$(ARRAY.SIZE)
460 DIM CUSTOMER.TERMS$(ARRAY.SIZE)
470 RETURN
480 REM *****************************************************************
490 REM * THIS IS THE ROUTINE TO ACCEPT TOTAL INPUT OF THE FILE FROM  *
500 REM * THE KEYBOARD.  IT IS NOT THE ROUTINE TO ADD TO AN EXISTING  *
510 REM * FILE.  FILE SIZE IS DEFAULTED TO 1000 RECORDS MAXIMUM.      *
520 REM *****************************************************************
530 FOR I = BASE TO ARRAY.SIZE
540     GOSUB 2170
550     PRINT
560     PRINT "ENTER 'END' UNDER CUSTOMER NAME TO TERMINATE ENTRY."
570     PRINT
580     INPUT "CUSTOMER NAME:                    ";CUSTOMER.NAME$(I)
590     IF (CUSTOMER.NAME$(I) = "END") AND RECORD.COUNT < 1 THEN 690
600     IF CUSTOMER.NAME$(I) = "END" THEN 760
610     INPUT "CUSTOMER ADDRESS LINE 1:          ";CUSTOMER.ADDR.1$(I)
620     INPUT "CUSTOMER ADDRESS LINE 2:          ";CUSTOMER.ADDR.2$(I)
630     INPUT "CUSTOMER ADDRESS LINE 3:          ";CUSTOMER.ADDR.3$(I)
640     INPUT "CUSTOMER ADDRESS LINE 4:          ";CUSTOMER.ADDR.4$(I)
650     INPUT "CUSTOMER TERMS:                   ",CUSTOMER.TERMS$(I)
660     PRINT:PRINT "ACCEPTABLE (Y/N)? "
670     GET Z$
680     IF Z$ = "Y" THEN 740
690     VPOS=25:HPOS=1
700     PRINT "ENTRY REJECTED";
710     PRINT CHR$(7)
720     FOR Z = 1 TO 1000:NEXT Z
730     GOTO 540
740     RECORD.COUNT = RECORD.COUNT + 1
750     NEXT I
760 FILE.SIZE = I - 1
770 GOSUB 2020            :REM ROUTINE TO WRITE THE FILE
780 REM *****************************************************************
790 REM * THE FILE IS WRITTEN AND CLOSED.  IT MUST BE OPENED AGAIN IF *
800 REM * THE USER DETERMINES TO GET A LISTING OF THE FILE EITHER IN  *
810 REM * DISPLAY FORM ON IN HARDCOPY FORM.                           *
820 REM *****************************************************************
830 GOSUB 2170
840 FOUR.TO.A.PAGE = 0
850 PRINT:PRINT "DO YOU WISH TO SEE THE CONTENTS OF THE FILE (Y/N)? ";
860 GET Z$
870 PRINT Z$
880 IF Z$ < > "Y" THEN 1740
890 PRINT "DO YOU WISH A HARDCOPY OUTPUT (Y/N)? ";
900 GET Z$
```

Figure 6.11. (continued)

```
910 PRINT Z$
920 IF Z$ < > "Y" THEN HARDCOPY$ = "NO":GOTO 940
930 HARDCOPY$ = "YES"
940 PRINT "UNINTERRUPTED PRINTING - 'N' CAUSES PAUSE WITH EACH - (Y/N)? ";
950 GET Z$
960 PRINT Z$
970 IF Z$ < > "Y" THEN CONTINUE$ = "NO":GOTO 990
980 CONTINUE$ = "YES"
990 FILE.NAME$ = ".D2/CUSTOMER.DAT"
1000 OPEN #1,FILE.NAME$
1010 INPUT #1,FILE.SIZE       :REM OBTAIN THE RECORD COUNT
1020 FOR I = 1 TO FILE.SIZE
1030      INPUT #1,CUSTOMER.NAME$(I)
1040      INPUT #1,CUSTOMER.ADDR.1$(I)
1050      INPUT #1,CUSTOMER.ADDR.2$(I)
1060      INPUT #1,CUSTOMER.ADDR.3$(I)
1070      INPUT #1,CUSTOMER.ADDR.4$(I)
1080      INPUT #1,CUSTOMER.TERMS$(I)
1090      NEXT I
1100 CLOSE #1
1110 FOR I = 1 TO FILE.SIZE
1120      IF CONTINUE$ = "YES" THEN 1140
1130      GET Z$
1140      PRINT
1150      FOR N = 1 TO 79:PRINT "-";:NEXT N
1160      PRINT
1170      PRINT "RECORD NUMBER:  ";I
1180      PRINT "CUSTOMER NAME:";TAB(20);CUSTOMER.NAME$(I)
1190      PRINT "CUSTOMER ADDRESS:";TAB(20);CUSTOMER.ADDR.1$(I)
1200      PRINT TAB(20);CUSTOMER.ADDR.2$(I)
1210      PRINT TAB(20);CUSTOMER.ADDR.3$(I)
1220      PRINT TAB(20);CUSTOMER.ADDR.4$(I)
1230      PRINT "CUSTOMER TERMS:";TAB(20);CUSTOMER.TERMS$(I)
1240      PRINT
1250      PRINT
1260      IF HARDCOPY$ = "NO" THEN 1450
1270      OPEN #3,".PRINTER"
1280      OUTPUT #3
1290      PRINT "RECORD NUMBER:  ";I
1300      PRINT
1310      PRINT "CUSTOMER NAME:";TAB(20);CUSTOMER.NAME$(I)
1320      PRINT "CUSTOMER ADDRESS:";TAB(20);CUSTOMER.ADDR.1$(I)
1330      PRINT TAB(20);CUSTOMER.ADDR.2$(I)
1340      PRINT TAB(20);CUSTOMER.ADDR.3$(I)
1350      PRINT TAB(20);CUSTOMER.ADDR.4$(I)
1360      PRINT "CUSTOMER TERMS:";TAB(20);CUSTOMER.TERMS$(I)
1370      PRINT
1380      PRINT
1390      FOR N = 1 TO 79:PRINT "-";:NEXT N
1400      PRINT
1410      PRINT
1420      FOUR.TO.A.PAGE = FOUR.TO.A.PAGE +1
1430      IF FOUR.TO.A.PAGE = 4 THEN PRINT CHR$(12):FOUR.TO.A.PAGE = 0
1440      CLOSE #3
1450      NEXT I
```

Figure 6.11. (continued)

```
1460 GOSUB 2170
1470 PRINT:PRINT "DO YOU WISH TO MAKE CORRECTIONS (Y/N)? ";
1480 GET Z$
1490 PRINT Z$
1500 IF Z$ < > "Y" THEN GOSUB 2010:GOTO 1740
1510 PRINT:INPUT "WHICH RECORD DO YOU WISH TO CHANGE? ";I
1520 PRINT
1530 INPUT "CUSTOMER NAME:                   ",TEMPORARY.CUSTOMER.NAME$
1540 INPUT "CUSTOMER ADDRESS LINE 1:         ",TEMPORARY.CUSTOMER.ADDR.1$
1550 INPUT "CUSTOMER ADDRESS LINE 2:         ",TEMPORARY.CUSTOMER.ADDR.2$
1560 INPUT "CUSTOMER ADDRESS LINE 3:         ",TEMPORARY.CUSTOMER.ADDR.3$
1570 INPUT "CUSTOMER ADDRESS LINE 4:         ",TEMPORARY.CUSTOMER.ADDR.4$
1580 INPUT "CUSTOMER TERMS:                  ",TEMPORARY.CUSTOMER.TERMS$
1590 PRINT:PRINT "ACCEPTABLE (Y/N)? ";
1600 GET Z$
1610 PRINT Z$
1620 IF Z$ < > "Y" THEN 1460
1630 CUSTOMER.NAME$(I) = TEMPORARY.CUSTOMER.NAME$
1640 CUSTOMER.ADDR.1$(I) = TEMPORARY.CUSTOMER.ADDR.1$
1650 CUSTOMER.ADDR.2$(I) = TEMPORARY.CUSTOMER.ADDR.2$
1660 CUSTOMER.ADDR.3$(I) = TEMPORARY.CUSTOMER.ADDR.3$
1670 CUSTOMER.ADDR.4$(I) = TEMPORARY.CUSTOMER.ADDR.4$
1680 CUSTOMER.TERMS$(I) = TEMPORARY.CUSTOMER.TERMS$
1690 GOTO 1460
1700 REM ***********************************************
1710 REM * ALL CORRECTIONS ARE MADE - REWRITE THE FILE *
1720 REM ***********************************************
1730 GOSUB 2020
1740 REM ***********************
1750 REM * PROGRAM TERMINATION *
1760 REM ***********************
1770 PRINT
1780 PRINT "LOADING OF CUSTOMER FILE IS COMPLETE"
1790 PRINT
1800 PRINT "DO YOU WISH TO REVIEW THE FILE (Y/N)? ";
1810 GET Z$
1820 PRINT Z$
1830 IF Z$ = "Y" THEN 830
1840 PRINT
1850 PRINT "DO YOU WISH TO REPEAT THE PROGRAM (Y/N)? ";
1860 GET Z$
1870 PRINT Z$
1880 IF Z$ < > "Y" THEN 1980
1890 FOR N = 1 TO ARRAY.SIZE
1900     CUSTOMER.NAME$(N) = ""
1910     CUSTOMER.ADDR.1$(N) = ""
1920     CUSTOMER.ADDR.2$(N) = ""
1930     CUSTOMER.ADDR.3$(N) = ""
1940     CUSTOMER.ADDR.4$(N) = ""
1950     CUSTOMER.TERMS$(N) = ""
1960     NEXT N
1970 GOTO 10
1980 CHAIN .D2/BUSINESS
```

Figure 6.11. (continued)

```
1990 REM **********************
2000 REM * SUBROUTINES FOLLOW *
2010 REM **************************
2020 REM * OPEN AND WRITE TO FILE *
2030 REM **************************
2040 CREATE ".D2/CUSTOMER.DAT",TEXT
2050 OPEN #2,"CUSTOMER.DAT"
2060 PRINT #2,FILE.SIZE          :REM WRITE THE RECORD COUNT
2070 FOR I = 1 TO FILE.SIZE
2080      PRINT #2,CUSTOMER.NAME$(I)
2090      PRINT #2,CUSTOMER.ADDR.1$(I)
2100      PRINT #2,CUSTOMER.ADDR.2$(I)
2110      PRINT #2,CUSTOMER.ADDR.3$(I)
2120      PRINT #2,CUSTOMER.ADDR.4$(I)
2130      PRINT #2,CUSTOMER.TERMS$(I)
2140      NEXT I
2150 CLOSE #2
2160 RETURN
2170 REM ********************************
2180 REM * HEADING USED FOR THE DISPLAY *
2190 REM ********************************
2200 HOME
2210 X = ((80 - LEN(COMPANY.NAME$)) / 2)
2220 VPOS=2:HPOS=X
2230 PRINT COMPANY.NAME$
2240 FOR N = 1 TO 79:PRINT "-";:NEXT N:PRINT
2250 PRINT TAB(29);"CUSTOMER FILE DATA ENTRY"
2260 FOR N = 1 TO 79:PRINT "-";:NEXT N
2270 RETURN
```

Figure 6.11. (continued)

VENDOR

If you'll look at VENDOR carefully, you'll notice some similarities between it and CUSTOMER. You'll also notice similarities between it and PRODUCT, a program that will come along later in the discussion. A close inspection will show a valid reason for this: they're the same program. Well, not entirely the same, of course, but close enough to be near copies, which, of course, they are. Recall that in our discussion of MERGE in a previous chapter we said that we could store commonly used routines and combine them with a program being developed in order to save a lot of time. The same is true with direct copies and minor changes.

A block diagram for the building and maintenance of the vendor file is shown in Figure 6.12. The program accepts input from the keyboard, or from the file and keyboard combined, and uses it to develop a Vendor file.

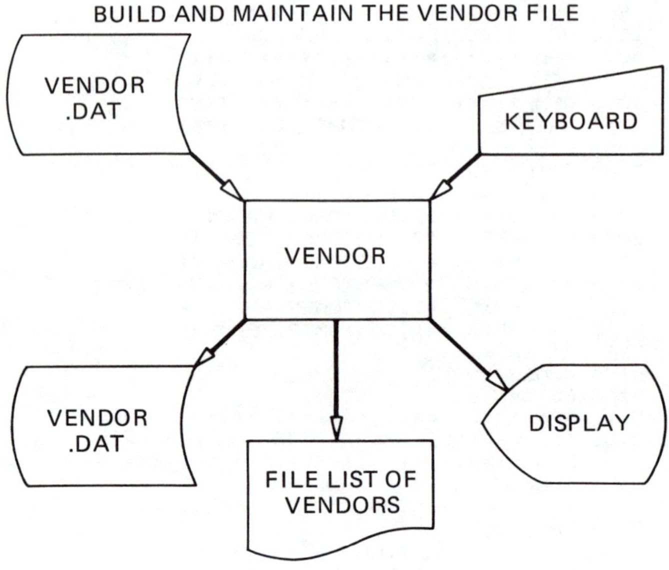

Figure 6.12.

This Vendor File is used in other places in the system and is structured for use should the Accounts Payable subsystem be expanded. You may wish to augment the Vendor File with other pertinent data.

```
RECORD NUMBER:   1

VENDOR NAME:           MR. BENJAMIN WATERS
VENDOR ADDRESS:        IMAGINATION INTERPRETED
                       327 PAGE ROAD
                       WATERTOWN,
                       PENNSYLVANIA 17743
VENDOR TERMS:          CASH
----------------------------------------------------------------

RECORD NUMBER:   2

VENDOR NAME:           MRS. MARGUERITE ALLISON
VENDOR ADDRESS:        COMPUTER INSTITUTE
                       830 TAMARACK LANE
                       METARIE,
                       LOUISIANA 34769
VENDOR TERMS:          NET 30 DAYS
----------------------------------------------------------------
```

Figure 6.13.

```
RECORD NUMBER:  3

VENDOR NAME:           PURCHASING AGENT
VENDOR ADDRESS:        SILICON VALLEY CHIPS
                       TRANSISTOR LANE
                       CUPERTINO,
                       CALIFORNIA 94377

VENDOR TERMS:          1.5% ON UNPAID BALANCE

----------------------------------------------------------------
```

Figure 6.13. (continued)

The similarity in the output with that of the Customer File can be seen in Figure 6.13. (For simplicity, we have used the same people as both customers and vendors.)

Because the program is a near copy of the previous one, we'll not chew our cabbage a second time, but we would like to draw your attention to statements 1890–1960. The DIMensioning of arrays is done where needed. The Apple III has no means to erase the dimensioning of an array, however, so be aware that you may have to go back into the program BUSINESS to achieve a bypass of the dimensioning of the array. Each of these programs have been written to function as called. On the return to the frame, however, a duplicate dimensioning will cause problems. We have not attempted to bypass that problem in this coding.

By the way, should you choose to interrupt the process via a Control-C, you may restart the program that is in memory. If you do, you will lose the COMPANY.NAME$ that had been supplied by the program BUSINESS.

The program VENDOR is given in Figure 6.14.

```
10 GOSUB 2170
20 ARRAY.SIZE = 1000
30 FILE.SIZE = 1000
40 GOSUB 410
50 BASE = 1
60 PRINT
70 PRINT "TWO FORMS OF INPUT ARE POSSIBLE IN THIS PROGRAM: INPUT
         FROM EITHER"
80 PRINT "DISK OR THE KEYBOARD.  IF YOU CHOOSE NOT TO OBTAIN THE
         INPUT FROM"
90 PRINT "THE DISK, THE PROGRAM WILL ASSUME THAT YOU WISH TO ENTER
         FROM THE"
```

Figure 6.14.

```
100 PRINT "KEYBOARD, DESTROYING ANY DISK FILE.  IF YOU WISH TO ADD
        TO THE FILE"
110 PRINT "WHICH ALREADY EXISTS, YOU MUST ANSWER 'Y' TO THIS
        QUESTION:"
120 PRINT:PRINT "WILL INPUT BE FROM THE DISK FILE (Y/N)? ";
130 GET Z$
140 PRINT Z$
150 IF Z$ < > "Y" THEN 530
160 REM ***************************
170 REM * OPEN AND INPUT NAME FILE *
180 REM ***************************
190 FILE.NAME$ = ".D2/VENDOR.DAT"
200 OPEN #1,FILE.NAME$
210 INPUT #1,FILE.SIZE      :REM OBTAIN THE RECORD COUNT
220 FOR I = 1 TO FILE.SIZE
230      INPUT #1,VENDOR.NAME$(I)
240      INPUT #1,VENDOR.ADDR.1$(I)
250      INPUT #1,VENDOR.ADDR.2$(I)
260      INPUT #1,VENDOR.ADDR.3$(I)
270      INPUT #1,VENDOR.ADDR.4$(I)
280      INPUT #1,VENDOR.TERMS$(I)
290      NEXT I
300 RECORD.COUNT = I - 1
310 CLOSE #1
320 PRINT:PRINT "WILL THERE BE ADDITIONS TO THE FILE (Y/N)? ";
330 GET Z$
340 PRINT Z$
350 IF Z$ < > "Y" THEN 830
360 BASE = I
370 GOTO 530
380 REM ****************************************************
390 REM * THE DIMENSIONING IS ESTABLISHED AS A THOUSAND RECORDS. *
400 REM ****************************************************
410 DIM VENDOR.NAME$(ARRAY.SIZE)
420 DIM VENDOR.ADDR.1$(ARRAY.SIZE)
430 DIM VENDOR.ADDR.2$(ARRAY.SIZE)
440 DIM VENDOR.ADDR.3$(ARRAY.SIZE)
450 DIM VENDOR.ADDR.4$(ARRAY.SIZE)
460 DIM VENDOR.TERMS$(ARRAY.SIZE)
470 RETURN
480 REM ************************************************************
490 REM * THIS IS THE ROUTINE TO ACCEPT TOTAL INPUT OF THE FILE FROM  *
500 REM * THE KEYBOARD.  IT IS NOT THE ROUTINE TO ADD TO AN EXISTING  *
510 REM * FILE.  FILE SIZE IS DEFAULTED TO 1000 RECORDS MAXIMUM.      *
520 REM ************************************************************
530 FOR I = BASE TO ARRAY.SIZE
540      GOSUB 2170
550      PRINT
560      PRINT "ENTER 'END' UNDER VENDOR NAME TO TERMINATE ENTRY."
570      PRINT
580      INPUT "VENDOR NAME:                   ";VENDOR.NAME$(I)
590      IF (VENDOR.NAME$(I) = "END") AND RECORD.COUNT < 1 THEN 690
600      IF VENDOR.NAME$(I) = "END" THEN 760
610      INPUT "VENDOR ADDRESS LINE 1:         ";VENDOR.ADDR.1$(I)
620      INPUT "VENDOR ADDRESS LINE 2:         ";VENDOR.ADDR.2$(I)
```

Figure 6.14. (continued)

```
630       INPUT "VENDOR ADDRESS LINE 3:        ";VENDOR.ADDR.3$(I)
640       INPUT "VENDOR ADDRESS LINE 4:        ";VENDOR.ADDR.4$(I)
650       INPUT "VENDOR TERMS:                 ",VENDOR.TERMS$(I)
660       PRINT:PRINT "ACCEPTABLE (Y/N)? "
670       GET Z$
680       IF Z$ = "Y" THEN 740
690       VPOS=25:HPOS=1
700       PRINT "ENTRY REJECTED";
710       PRINT CHR$(7)
720       FOR Z = 1 TO 1000:NEXT Z
730       GOTO 540
740       RECORD.COUNT = RECORD.COUNT + 1
750       NEXT I
760 FILE.SIZE = I - 1
770 GOSUB 2020             :REM ROUTINE TO WRITE THE FILE
780 REM ***********************************************************
790 REM * THE FILE IS WRITTEN AND CLOSED.  IT MUST BE OPENED AGAIN IF *
800 REM * THE USER DETERMINES TO GET A LISTING OF THE FILE EITHER IN  *
810 REM * DISPLAY FORM ON IN HARDCOPY FORM.                           *
820 REM ***********************************************************
830 GOSUB 2170
840 FOUR.TO.A.PAGE = 0
850 PRINT:PRINT "DO YOU WISH TO SEE THE CONTENTS OF THE FILE (Y/N)? ";
860 GET Z$
870 PRINT Z$
880 IF Z$ < > "Y" THEN 1740
890 PRINT "DO YOU WISH A HARDCOPY OUTPUT (Y/N)? ";
900 GET Z$
910 PRINT Z$
920 IF Z$ < > "Y" THEN HARDCOPY$ = "NO":GOTO 940
930 HARDCOPY$ = "YES"
940 PRINT "UNINTERRUPTED PRINTING - 'N' CAUSES PAUSE WITH EACH - (Y/N)? ";
950 GET Z$
960 PRINT Z$
970 IF Z$ < > "Y" THEN CONTINUE$ = "NO":GOTO 990
980 CONTINUE$ = "YES"
990 FILE.NAME$ = ".D2/VENDOR.DAT"
1000 OPEN #1,FILE.NAME$
1010 INPUT #1,FILE.SIZE        :REM OBTAIN THE RECORD COUNT
1020 FOR I = 1 TO FILE.SIZE
1030      INPUT #1,VENDOR.NAME$(I)
1040      INPUT #1,VENDOR.ADDR.1$(I)
1050      INPUT #1,VENDOR.ADDR.2$(I)
1060      INPUT #1,VENDOR.ADDR.3$(I)
1070      INPUT #1,VENDOR.ADDR.4$(I)
1080      INPUT #1,VENDOR.TERMS$(I)
1090      NEXT I
1100 CLOSE #1
1110 FOR I = 1 TO FILE.SIZE
1120      IF CONTINUE$ = "YES" THEN 1140
1130      GET Z$
1140      PRINT
1150      FOR N = 1 TO 79:PRINT "-";:NEXT N
1160      PRINT
1170      PRINT "RECORD NUMBER: ";I
```

Figure 6.14. (continued)

```
1180     PRINT "VENDOR NAME:";TAB(20);VENDOR.NAME$(I)
1190     PRINT "VENDOR ADDRESS:";TAB(20);VENDOR.ADDR.1$(I)
1200     PRINT TAB(20);VENDOR.ADDR.2$(I)
1210     PRINT TAB(20);VENDOR.ADDR.3$(I)
1220     PRINT TAB(20);VENDOR.ADDR.4$(I)
1230     PRINT "VENDOR TERMS:";TAB(20);VENDOR.TERMS$(I)
1240     PRINT
1250     PRINT
1260     IF HARDCOPY$ = "NO" THEN 1450
1270     OPEN #3,".PRINTER"
1280     OUTPUT #3
1290     PRINT "RECORD NUMBER: ";I
1300     PRINT
1310     PRINT "VENDOR NAME:";TAB(20);VENDOR.NAME$(I)
1320     PRINT "VENDOR ADDRESS:";TAB(20);VENDOR.ADDR.1$(I)
1330     PRINT TAB(20);VENDOR.ADDR.2$(I)
1340     PRINT TAB(20);VENDOR.ADDR.3$(I)
1350     PRINT TAB(20);VENDOR.ADDR.4$(I)
1360     PRINT "VENDOR TERMS:";TAB(20);VENDOR.TERMS$(I)
1370     PRINT
1380     PRINT
1390     FOR N = 1 TO 79:PRINT "-";:NEXT N
1400     PRINT
1410     PRINT
1420     FOUR.TO.A.PAGE = FOUR.TO.A.PAGE +1
1430     IF FOUR.TO.A.PAGE = 4 THEN PRINT CHR$(12):FOUR.TO.A.PAGE = 0
1440     CLOSE #3
1450     NEXT I
1460 GOSUB 2170
1470 PRINT:PRINT "DO YOU WISH TO MAKE CORRECTIONS (Y/N)? ";
1480 GET Z$
1490 PRINT Z$
1500 IF Z$ < > "Y" THEN GOSUB 2010:GOTO 1740
1510 PRINT:INPUT "WHICH RECORD DO YOU WISH TO CHANGE? ";I
1520 PRINT
1530 INPUT "VENDOR NAME:               ",TEMPORARY.VENDOR.NAME$
1540 INPUT "VENDOR ADDRESS LINE 1:     ",TEMPORARY.VENDOR.ADDR.1$
1550 INPUT "VENDOR ADDRESS LINE 2:     ",TEMPORARY.VENDOR.ADDR.2$
1560 INPUT "VENDOR ADDRESS LINE 3:     ",TEMPORARY.VENDOR.ADDR.3$
1570 INPUT "VENDOR ADDRESS LINE 4:     ",TEMPORARY.VENDOR.ADDR.4$
1580 INPUT "VENDOR TERMS:              ",TEMPORARY.VENDOR.TERMS$
1590 PRINT:PRINT "ACCEPTABLE (Y/N)? ";
1600 GET Z$
1610 PRINT Z$
1620 IF Z$ < > "Y" THEN 1460
1630 VENDOR.NAME$(I) = TEMPORARY.VENDOR.NAME$
1640 VENDOR.ADDR.1$(I) = TEMPORARY.VENDOR.ADDR.1$
1650 VENDOR.ADDR.2$(I) = TEMPORARY.VENDOR.ADDR.2$
1660 VENDOR.ADDR.3$(I) = TEMPORARY.VENDOR.ADDR.3$
1670 VENDOR.ADDR.4$(I) = TEMPORARY.VENDOR.ADDR.4$
1680 VENDOR.TERMS$(I) = TEMPORARY.VENDOR.TERMS$
1690 GOTO 1460
1700 REM ***********************************************
1710 REM * ALL CORRECTIONS ARE MADE - REWRITE THE FILE *
1720 REM ***********************************************
```

Figure 6.14. (continued)

```
1730 GOSUB 2020
1740 REM ***********************
1750 REM * PROGRAM TERMINATION *
1760 REM ***********************
1770 PRINT
1780 PRINT "LOADING OF VENDOR FILE IS COMPLETE"
1790 PRINT
1800 PRINT "DO YOU WISH TO REVIEW THE FILE (Y/N)? ";
1810 GET Z$
1820 PRINT Z$
1830 IF Z$ = "Y" THEN 830
1840 PRINT
1850 PRINT "DO YOU WISH TO REPEAT THE PROGRAM (Y/N)? ";
1860 GET Z$
1870 PRINT Z$
1880 IF Z$ < > "Y" THEN 1980
1890 FOR N = 1 TO ARRAY.SIZE
1900      VENDOR.NAME$(N) = ""
1910      VENDOR.ADDR.1$(N) = ""
1920      VENDOR.ADDR.2$(N) = ""
1930      VENDOR.ADDR.3$(N) = ""
1940      VENDOR.ADDR.4$(N) = ""
1950      VENDOR.TERMS$(N) = ""
1960      NEXT N
1970 GOTO 10
1980 CHAIN .D2/BUSINESS
1990 REM **********************
2000 REM * SUBROUTINES FOLLOW *
2010 REM *************************
2020 REM * OPEN AND WRITE TO FILE *
2030 REM *************************
2040 CREATE ".D2/VENDOR.DAT",TEXT
2050 OPEN #2,"VENDOR.DAT"
2060 PRINT #2,FILE.SIZE          :REM WRITE THE RECORD COUNT
2070 FOR I = 1 TO FILE.SIZE
2080      PRINT #2,VENDOR.NAME$(I)
2090      PRINT #2,VENDOR.ADDR.1$(I)
2100      PRINT #2,VENDOR.ADDR.2$(I)
2110      PRINT #2,VENDOR.ADDR.3$(I)
2120      PRINT #2,VENDOR.ADDR.4$(I)
2130      PRINT #2,VENDOR.TERMS$(I)
2140      NEXT I
2150 CLOSE #2
2160 RETURN
2170 REM ********************************
2180 REM * HEADING USED FOR THE DISPLAY *
2190 REM ********************************
2200 HOME
2210 X = ((80 - LEN(COMPANY.NAME$)) / 2)
2220 VPOS=2:HPOS=X
2230 PRINT COMPANY.NAME$
2240 FOR N = 1 TO 79:PRINT "-";:NEXT N:PRINT
2250 PRINT TAB(29);"VENDOR FILE DATA ENTRY"
2260 FOR N = 1 TO 79:PRINT "-";:NEXT N
2270 RETURN
```

Figure 6.14. (continued)

MAILLIST

This program contains the one joke in the entire system; it asks if you want a hardcopy. Of course, there would be no point in running a mail list program were it not for the purpose of acquiring a hardcopy list or labels. Throughout the design of this system, the author placed the output listings on the screen as well as the printer. Occasionally, it may be necessary to run a program when the printer has slipped a cog and gone into the shop for a cog-replacement. It's generally good programing practice to allow the user to specify if a printer is to be used. There are, of course, sophisticated error-trapping routines that allow a programer to determine if, in fact, a system has no printer attached (either physically or electronically) at the time it is needed. The Apple III, however, is a one-user system. It's assumed the user will know if a printer is required. If a printer is not available and it has been *selected* (computer term for *demanded*), you'll know it soon enough, as everything grinds to a halt.

This is not a complex program to understand. It merely reads the file into an array and then works its way through the array producing output to the display and/or printer. The block diagram for this program is shown in Figure 6.15. The program takes the Customer File

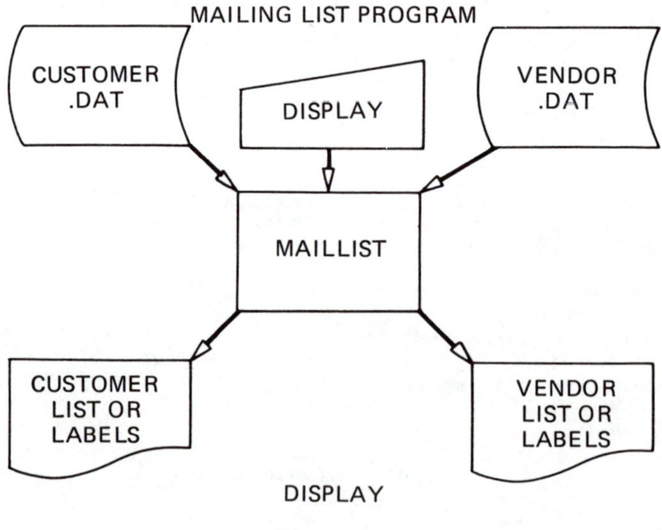

Figure 6.15.

and Vendor File and, with a menu selection, produces a display and, if one is selected, either of the lists. Proper spacing is established in the program to permit use of commonly available pressure-sensitive labels. The program will work for your Christmas card list so long as your friends are loaded as customers or vendors.

The program MAILLIST is given in Figure 6.16.

```
10 GOSUB 1040
20 PRINT
30 PRINT "TWO DIFFERENT MAILING LISTS MAY BE OBTAINED WITH THIS PROGRAM."
40 PRINT "YOU MAY PRODUCE A MAILING LIST FOR EITHER YOUR CUSTOMERS OR YOUR"
50 PRINT "VENDORS.  YOU HAVE THE OPPORTUNITY TO VIEW THEM ON THE SCREEN AND"
60 PRINT "TO OBTAIN A HARDCOPY REPORT ON PAPER (OR LABELS) FOR YOUR USE."
70 PRINT
80 PRINT "YOU MAY SELECT EITHER THE <C>USTOMER FILE OR THE <V>ENDOR FILE"
90 PRINT "MERELY BY PRESSING THE LETTER."
100 PRINT
110 GET Z$
120 PRINT Z$;
130 IF Z$ = "C" THEN PRINT "USTOMER FILE WAS SELECTED":PRINT
140 IF Z$ = "V" THEN PRINT "ENDOR FILE WAS SELECTED":PRINT
150 IF Z$ = "C" THEN FILE.NAME$ = ".D2/CUSTOMER.DAT":GOTO 230
160 IF Z$ = "V" THEN FILE.NAME$ = ".D2/VENDOR.DAT":GOTO 230
170 VPOS=25:HPOS=1
180 PRINT "INVALID CODE";
190 PRINT CHR$(7)
200 FOR Z = 1 TO 1000:NEXT Z
210 GOSUB 1040
220 GOTO 20
230 REM ****************************
240 REM * OPEN AND INPUT NAME FILE *
250 REM ****************************
260 OPEN #1,FILE.NAME$
270 INPUT #1,FILE.SIZE        :REM OBTAIN THE RECORD COUNT PREVIOUSLY STORED
280 REM ******************************************************************
290 REM * THE DIMENSIONING IS ESTABLISHED ON THE BASIS OF THE FIRST RECORD *
300 REM ******************************************************************
310 DIM LABEL.NAME$(FILE.SIZE)
320 DIM LABEL.ADDR.1$(FILE.SIZE)
330 DIM LABEL.ADDR.2$(FILE.SIZE)
340 DIM LABEL.ADDR.3$(FILE.SIZE)
350 DIM LABEL.ADDR.4$(FILE.SIZE)
360 DIM LABEL.TERMS$(FILE.SIZE)
370 FOR I = 1 TO FILE.SIZE
380       INPUT #1,LABEL.NAME$(I)
390       INPUT #1,LABEL.ADDR.1$(I)
400       INPUT #1,LABEL.ADDR.2$(I)
410       INPUT #1,LABEL.ADDR.3$(I)
420       INPUT #1,LABEL.ADDR.4$(I)
430       INPUT #1,LABEL.TERMS$(I)
440       NEXT I
450 CLOSE #1
460 REM **************************
470 REM * LABEL PRINTING ROUTINE *
480 REM **************************
490 GOSUB 1040
500 PRINT
510 PRINT "DO YOU WISH A HARDCOPY OUTPUT (Y/N)? ";
520 GET Z$
530 PRINT Z$
```

Figure 6.16.

```
540 IF Z$ < > "Y" THEN HARDCOPY$ = "NO":GOTO 560
550 HARDCOPY$ = "YES"
560 PRINT "UNINTERRUPTED PRINTING - 'N' CAUSES PAUSE WITH EACH - (Y/N)? ";
570 GET Z$
580 PRINT Z$
590 IF Z$ < > "Y" THEN CONTINUE$ = "NO":GOTO 610
600 CONTINUE$ = "YES"
610 FOR I = 1 TO FILE.SIZE
620      PRINT
630      PRINT
640      PRINT LABEL.NAME$(I)
650      PRINT LABEL.ADDR.1$(I)
660      PRINT LABEL.ADDR.2$(I)
670      PRINT LABEL.ADDR.3$(I)
680      PRINT LABEL.ADDR.4$(I)
690      IF CONTINUE$ = "YES" THEN 730
700      GET Z$
710      OPEN #2,".PRINTER"
720      OUTPUT #2
730      IF HARDCOPY$ = "NO" THEN 810
740      PRINT
750      PRINT
760      PRINT LABEL.NAME$(I)
770      PRINT LABEL.ADDR.1$(I)
780      PRINT LABEL.ADDR.2$(I)
790      PRINT LABEL.ADDR.3$(I)
800      PRINT LABEL.ADDR.4$(I)
810      NEXT I
820 CLOSE #2
830 REM ***********************
840 REM * PROGRAM TERMINATION *
850 REM ***********************
860 PRINT
870 IF FILE.NAME$ = ".D2/CUSTOMER.DAT" THEN
         PRINT "PRINTING OF THE CUSTOMER FILE IS COMPLETE"
880 IF FILE.NAME$ = ".D2/VENDOR.DAT" THEN
         PRINT "PRINTING OF THE VENDOR FILE IS COMPLETE"
890 PRINT
900 PRINT "DO YOU WISH TO REPEAT THE PROGRAM (Y/N)? ";
910 GET Z$
920 PRINT Z$
930 IF Z$ < > "Y" THEN 1030
940 FOR N = 1 TO FILE.SIZE
950      LABEL.NAME$(N)=""
960      LABEL.ADDR.1$(N)=""
970      LABEL.ADDR.2$(N)=""
980      LABEL.ADDR.3$(N)=""
990      LABEL.ADDR.4$(N)=""
1000     LABEL.TERMS$(N)=""
1010     NEXT N
1020 GOTO 10
1030 CHAIN .D2/BUSINESS
1040 REM ********************************
1050 REM * HEADING USED FOR THE DISPLAY *
1060 REM ********************************
1070 HOME
1080 X = ((80 - LEN(COMPANY.NAME$)) / 2)
1090 VPOS=2:HPOS=X
1100 PRINT COMPANY.NAME$
1110 FOR N = 1 TO 79:PRINT "-";:NEXT N:PRINT
1120 PRINT TAB(25);"MAILING LIST PRINT PROGRAM"
1130 FOR N = 1 TO 79:PRINT "-";:NEXT N
1140 RETURN
```

Figure 6.16. (continued)

PRODUCT

As if we haven't had enough inventory programs in this book, here is yet another. This one is integrated with the system and uses sequential files. A block diagram is shown in Figure 6.17. The program accepts input from the keyboard, or from the file and keyboard combined, and uses it to develop a Product (Inventory) File. This file is used with the Accounts Receivable subsystem. At the moment, since it contains the bare minimum of information needed, you may wish to augment it for further use.

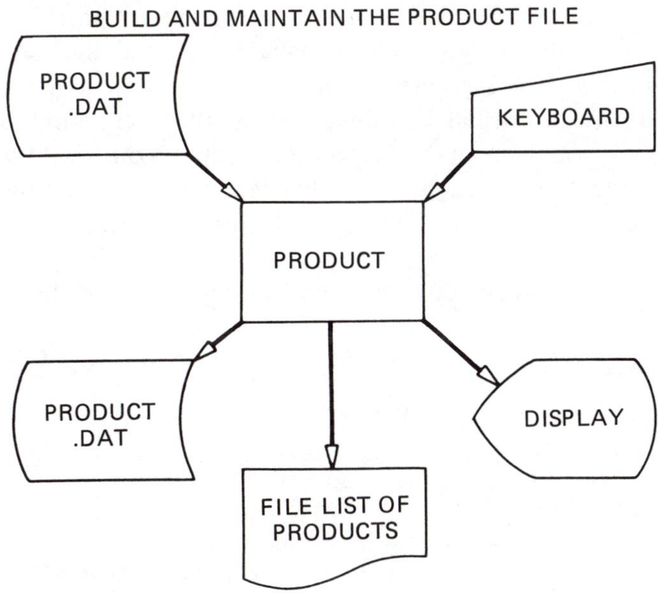

Figure 6.17.

An inventory file is, of course, a suitable place for storing information about double-sided, framistan-oriented widgets and octagonal, centrifugal gizmos, as we shall demonstrate. More importantly, it is a place where you can store descriptive information *once* and call upon it forever after, as required. If you are able to reduce the number of keystrokes, your operation cannot help but be improved. If your business involves products and inventory, this file is the way to save the labor of typing each invoice individually. You need only to ensure the initial accuracy of the descriptive information and it will be accurate until all the purple cows come home.

Some additional information appears in this application. We've included a unit of measure, a location within your storage facility, the quantity on hand, the reorder point, and room for any special shipping instructions. Although it wasn't brought up during the discussion of the customer file, you might want to include a mechanism to separate *types* of product *by shipping method.* Thus, you might wish to invoice on one piece of paper all products to be shipped by mail in order to distinguish them from those to be shipped by motor transport, for instance. That facility is not present in this system as designed. To add it, you would have to replace the narrative included in the shipping instructions with some standardized code: "A" could mean special handling; "B" could mean ship by motor freight; "C" could mean dangerous cargo, etc. You would need only to string together enough codes to describe the shipping method required and then use the INSTRing facility to determine the codes stored there.

Figure 6.18 shows a couple examples of an inventory listing:

```
ITEM NUMBER:    1

PRODUCT:                     WIDGET

PRODUCT DESCRIPTION:         DOUBLE-SIDED, FRAMISTAN-ORIENTED
UNIT OF MEASURE:             100 BUSHEL
LOCATION:                    B45
QUANTITY ON HAND:             500
REORDER POINT:                200
SHIPPING INSTR:              SHIP ONLY IN GLASS CONTAINER

-------------------------------------------------------------

ITEM NUMBER:    2

PRODUCT:                     GIZMO

PRODUCT DESCRIPTION:         OCTAGONAL, CENTRIFUGAL
UNIT OF MEASURE:             1 EACH
LOCATION:                    REAR WAREHOUSE, BIN 10
QUANTITY ON HAND:             5
REORDER POINT:                10
SHIPPING INSTR:              AIR MAIL SPECIAL DELIVERY
```

Figure 6.18.

And now, the program. The assumption has been made that your inventory file will not exceed 1,000 items. As in previous programs, you are given a first time option. If you respond incorrectly, you will develop a new file that will destroy the previous file. The work is done in the array, as before, and the new file will not be written until you indicate that no more input will be received. As a matter of practice, daily backup copies of critical files are an absolute must. You'll find that a minimum of three cycles will be required. In the industry, that is known as the grandfather, father, son approach to protection.

As with previous programs also, there is the opportunity to obtain a listing of the inventory – either to the display or to hardcopy. Perhaps it should be mentioned – lest anybody get the wrong impression – that the author can't actually vouch for a high degree of mortality among cogs in a printer, but the cogs (which are the teeth of a gear) in most of the printers available nowadays are made of nylon. Cogs being wear parts, you can therefore expect that some wear will occur, depending upon how heavily you use the equipment.

There is one concept in this program that deserves special consideration. Look at statements 1620–1680. Whenever you are making changes to previously entered information in an array (information that you are now entering), it's always wise to withhold the update of that information until such time as you are absolutely certain that the replacement record is accurate and that the change is indeed desirable. Everything else within the program conforms to what we have previously discussed.

The program PRODUCT is given in Figure 6.19.

```
10 GOSUB 2300
20 ARRAY.SIZE = 1000
30 FILE.SIZE = 1000
40 GOSUB 420
50 BASE = 1
60 PRINT
70 PRINT "TWO FORMS OF INPUT ARE POSSIBLE IN THIS PROGRAM: FROM EITHER"
80 PRINT "DISK OR THE KEYBOARD.  IF YOU CHOOSE NOT TO OBTAIN INPUT FROM"
90 PRINT "THE DISK, THE PROGRAM WILL ASSUME ENTRY FROM THE KEYBOARD,"
100 PRINT "DESTROYING ANY DISK FILE.  IF YOU WISH TO ADD TO THE FILE"
110 PRINT "WHICH ALREADY EXISTS, YOU MUST ANSWER 'Y' TO THIS QUESTION:"
120 PRINT:PRINT "WILL INPUT BE FROM THE DISK FILE (Y/N)? ";
130 GET Z$
```

Figure 6.19.

```
140 PRINT Z$
150 IF Z$ < > "Y" THEN 550
160 REM ****************************
170 REM * OPEN AND INPUT NAME FILE *
180 REM ****************************
190 FILE.NAME$ = ".D2/PRODUCT.DAT"
200 OPEN #1,FILE.NAME$
210 INPUT #1,FILE.SIZE      :REM OBTAIN THE RECORD COUNT PREVIOUSLY STORED
220 FOR I = 1 TO FILE.SIZE
230     INPUT #1,PRODUCT.NAME$(I)
240     INPUT #1,PRODUCT.DESCR$(I)
250     INPUT #1,PRODUCT.UNIT$(I)
260     INPUT #1,PRODUCT.LOCATION$(I)
270     INPUT #1,PRODUCT.Q.O.H(I)
280     INPUT #1,PRODUCT.R.O.P(I)
290     INPUT #1,PRODUCT.SHIP.INSTR$(I)
300     NEXT I
310 RECORD.COUNT = I - 1
320 CLOSE #1
330 PRINT:PRINT "WILL THERE BE ADDITIONS TO THE FILE (Y/N)? ";
340 GET Z$
350 PRINT Z$
360 IF Z$ < > "Y" THEN 860
370 BASE = I
380 GOTO 550
390 REM **********************************************************
400 REM * THE DIMENSIONING IS ESTABLISHED AS A THOUSAND RECORDS. *
410 REM **********************************************************
420 DIM PRODUCT.NAME$(ARRAY.SIZE)
430 DIM PRODUCT.DESCR$(ARRAY.SIZE)
440 DIM PRODUCT.UNIT$(ARRAY.SIZE)
450 DIM PRODUCT.LOCATION$(ARRAY.SIZE)
460 DIM PRODUCT.Q.O.H(ARRAY.SIZE)
470 DIM PRODUCT.R.O.P(ARRAY.SIZE)
480 DIM PRODUCT.SHIP.INSTR$(ARRAY.SIZE)
490 RETURN
500 REM ***************************************************************
510 REM * THIS IS THE ROUTINE TO ACCEPT TOTAL INPUT OF THE FILE FROM  *
520 REM * THE KEYBOARD.  IT IS NOT THE ROUTINE TO ADD TO AN EXISTING  *
530 REM * FILE.  FILE SIZE IS DEFAULTED TO 1000 RECORDS MAXIMUM.      *
540 REM ***************************************************************
550 FOR I = BASE TO ARRAY.SIZE
560     GOSUB 2300
570     PRINT
580     PRINT "ENTER 'END' UNDER PRODUCT NAME TO TERMINATE ENTRY."
590     PRINT
600     INPUT "PRODUCT NAME:                ";PRODUCT.NAME$(I)
610     IF (PRODUCT.NAME$(I) = "END") AND RECORD.COUNT < 1 THEN 720
620     IF PRODUCT.NAME$(I) = "END" THEN 790
630     INPUT "PRODUCT DESCRIPTION:         ";PRODUCT.DESCR$(I)
640     INPUT "PRODUCT UNIT OF MEASURE:     ";PRODUCT.UNIT$(I)
650     INPUT "PRODUCT LOCATION:            ";PRODUCT.LOCATION$(I)
660     INPUT "PRODUCT QTY ON HAND:         ",PRODUCT.Q.O.H(I)
670     INPUT "PRODUCT REORDER POINT:       ",PRODUCT.R.O.P(I)
680     INPUT "SPECIAL SHIPPING INSTR:      ",PRODUCT.SHIP.INSTR$(I)
690     PRINT:PRINT "ACCEPTABLE (Y/N)? "
700     GET Z$
710     IF Z$ = "Y" THEN 770
720     VPOS=25:HPOS=1
730     PRINT "ENTRY REJECTED";
740     PRINT CHR$(7)
750     FOR Z = 1 TO 1000:NEXT Z
760     GOTO 560
770     RECORD.COUNT = RECORD.COUNT + 1
780     NEXT I
```

Figure 6.19. (continued)

```
790 FILE.SIZE = I - 1
800 GOSUB 2140              :REM ROUTINE TO WRITE THE FILE
810 REM ***********************************************************
820 REM * THE FILE IS WRITTEN AND CLOSED.  IT MUST BE OPENED AGAIN IF *
830 REM * THE USER DETERMINES TO GET A LISTING OF THE FILE EITHER IN  *
840 REM * DISPLAY FORM ON IN HARDCOPY FORM.                           *
850 REM ***********************************************************
860 GOSUB 2300
870 FOUR.TO.A.PAGE = 0
880 PRINT:PRINT "DO YOU WISH TO SEE THE CONTENTS OF THE FILE (Y/N)? ";
890 GET Z$
900 PRINT Z$
910 IF Z$ < > "Y" THEN 1850
920 PRINT "DO YOU WISH A HARDCOPY OUTPUT (Y/N)? ";
930 GET Z$
940 PRINT Z$
950 IF Z$ < > "Y" THEN HARDCOPY$ = "NO":GOTO 970
960 HARDCOPY$ = "YES"
970 PRINT "UNINTERRUPTED PRINTING - 'N' CAUSES PAUSE WITH EACH - (Y/N)? ";
980 GET Z$
990 PRINT Z$
1000 IF Z$ < > "Y" THEN CONTINUE$ = "NO":GOTO 1020
1010 CONTINUE$ = "YES"
1020 FILE.NAME$ = ".D2/PRODUCT.DAT"
1030 OPEN #1,FILE.NAME$
1040 INPUT #1,FILE.SIZE        :REM OBTAIN THE RECORD COUNT PREVIOUSLY STORED
1050 FOR I = 1 TO FILE.SIZE
1060     INPUT #1,PRODUCT.NAME$(I)
1070     INPUT #1,PRODUCT.DESCR$(I)
1080     INPUT #1,PRODUCT.UNIT$(I)
1090     INPUT #1,PRODUCT.LOCATION$(I)
1100     INPUT #1,PRODUCT.Q.O.H(I)
1110     INPUT #1,PRODUCT.R.O.P(I)
1120     INPUT #1,PRODUCT.SHIP.INSTR$(I)
1130      NEXT I
1140 CLOSE #1
1150 FOR I = 1 TO FILE.SIZE
1160      IF CONTINUE$ = "YES" THEN 1180
1170      GET Z$
1180      PRINT
1190      FOR N = 1 TO 79:PRINT "-";:NEXT N
1200      PRINT
1210      PRINT "ITEM NUMBER: ";I
1220      PRINT
1230      PRINT "PRODUCT:";TAB(25);PRODUCT.NAME$(I)
1240      PRINT
1250      PRINT "PRODUCT DESCRIPTION:";TAB(25);PRODUCT.DESCR$(I)
1260      PRINT "UNIT OF MEASURE:";TAB(25);PRODUCT.UNIT$(I)
1270      PRINT "LOCATION:";TAB(25);PRODUCT.LOCATION$(I)
1280      PRINT "QUANTITY ON HAND:";TAB(25);PRODUCT.Q.O.H(I)
1290      PRINT "REORDER POINT:";TAB(25);PRODUCT.R.O.P(I)
1300      PRINT "SHIPPING INSTR:";TAB(25);PRODUCT.SHIP.INSTR$(I)
1310      PRINT
1320      PRINT
1330      IF HARDCOPY$ = "NO" THEN 1540
1340      OPEN #3,".PRINTER"
1350      OUTPUT #3
1360      PRINT "ITEM NUMBER: ";I
1370      PRINT
1380      PRINT "PRODUCT:";TAB(25);PRODUCT.NAME$(I)
1390      PRINT
1400      PRINT "PRODUCT DESCRIPTION:";TAB(25);PRODUCT.DESCR$(I)
1410      PRINT "UNIT OF MEASURE:";TAB(25);PRODUCT.UNIT$(I)
1420      PRINT "LOCATION:";TAB(25);PRODUCT.LOCATION$(I)
1430      PRINT "QUANTITY ON HAND:";TAB(25);PRODUCT.Q.O.H(I)
```

Figure 6.19. (continued)

```
1440      PRINT "REORDER POINT:";TAB(25);PRODUCT.R.O.P(I)
1450      PRINT "SHIPPING INSTR:";TAB(25);PRODUCT.SHIP.INSTR$(I)
1460      PRINT
1470      PRINT
1480      FOR N = 1 TO 79:PRINT "-";:NEXT N
1490      PRINT
1500      PRINT
1510      FOUR.TO.A.PAGE = FOUR.TO.A.PAGE +1
1520      IF FOUR.TO.A.PAGE = 4 THEN PRINT CHR$(12):FOUR.TO.A.PAGE = 0
1530      CLOSE #3
1540      NEXT I
1550 GOSUB 2300
1560 PRINT:PRINT "DO YOU WISH TO MAKE CORRECTIONS (Y/N)? ";
1570 GET Z$
1580 PRINT Z$
1590 IF Z$ < > "Y" THEN GOSUB 2130:GOTO 1850
1600 PRINT:INPUT "WHICH RECORD DO YOU WISH TO CHANGE? ";I
1610 PRINT
1620 INPUT "PRODUCT NAME:                     ",TEMPORARY.PRODUCT.NAME$
1630 INPUT "PRODUCT DESCRIPTION:              ",TEMPORARY.PRODUCT.DESCR$
1640 INPUT "PRODUCT UNIT OF MEASURE:          ",TEMPORARY.PRODUCT.UNIT$
1650 INPUT "PRODUCT LOCATION:                 ",TEMPORARY.PRODUCT.LOCATION$
1660 INPUT "PRODUCT QUANTITY ON HAND:         ",TEMPORARY.PRODUCT.Q.O.H
1670 INPUT "PRODUCT REORDER POINT:            ",TEMPORARY.PRODUCT.R.O.P
1680 INPUT "PRODUCT SHIPPING INSTR:           ",TEMPORARY.PRODUCT.SHIP.INSTR$
1690 PRINT:PRINT "ACCEPTABLE (Y/N)? ";
1700 GET Z$
1710 PRINT Z$
1720 IF Z$ < > "Y" THEN 1550
1730 PRODUCT.NAME$(I) = TEMPORARY.PRODUCT.NAME$
1740 PRODUCT.DESCR$(I) = TEMPORARY.PRODUCT.DESCR$
1750 PRODUCT.UNIT$(I) = TEMPORARY.PRODUCT.UNIT$
1760 PRODUCT.LOCATION$(I) = TEMPORARY.PRODUCT.LOCATION$
1770 PRODUCT.Q.O.H(I) = TEMPORARY.PRODUCT.Q.O.H
1780 PRODUCT.R.O.P(I) = TEMPORARY.PRODUCT.R.O.P
1790 PRODUCT.SHIP.INSTR$(I) = TEMPORARY.PRODUCT.SHIP.INSTR$
1800 GOTO 1550
1810 REM ***********************************************
1820 REM * ALL CORRECTIONS ARE MADE - REWRITE THE FILE *
1830 REM ***********************************************
1840 GOSUB 2140
1850 REM ************************
1860 REM * PROGRAM TERMINATION *
1870 REM ************************
1880 PRINT
1890 PRINT "LOADING OF PRODUCT FILE IS COMPLETE"
1900 PRINT
1910 PRINT "DO YOU WISH TO REVIEW THE FILE (Y/N)? ";
1920 GET Z$
1930 PRINT Z$
1940 IF Z$ = "Y" THEN 860
1950 PRINT
1960 PRINT "DO YOU WISH TO REPEAT THE PROGRAM (Y/N)? ";
1970 GET Z$
1980 PRINT Z$
1990 IF Z$ < > "Y" THEN 2100
2000 FOR N = 1 TO FILE.SIZE
2010      PRODUCT.NAME$(N)=""
2020      PRODUCT.DESCR$(N)=""
2030      PRODUCT.UNIT$(N)=""
2040      PRODUCT.LOCATION$(N)=""
2050      PRODUCT.Q.O.H(N)=""
2060      PRODUCT.R.O.P(N)=""
2070      PRODUCT.SHIP.INSTR$(N)=""
2080      NEXT N
```

Figure 6.19. (continued)

```
2090 GOTO 10
2100 CHAIN .D2/BUSINESS
2110 REM ***********************
2120 REM * SUBROUTINES FOLLOW *
2130 REM ***************************
2140 REM * OPEN AND WRITE TO FILE *
2150 REM ***************************
2160 CREATE ".D2/PRODUCT.DAT",TEXT
2170 OPEN #2,.D2/PRODUCT.DAT
2180 PRINT #2,FILE.SIZE              :REM WRITE THE RECORD COUNT
2190 FOR I = 1 TO FILE.SIZE
2200      PRINT #2,PRODUCT.NAME$(I)
2210      PRINT #2,PRODUCT.DESCR$(I)
2220      PRINT #2,PRODUCT.UNIT$(I)
2230      PRINT #2,PRODUCT.LOCATION$(I)
2240      PRINT #2,PRODUCT.Q.O.H(I)
2250      PRINT #2,PRODUCT.R.O.P(I)
2260      PRINT #2,PRODUCT.SHIP.INSTR$(I)
2270      NEXT I
2280 CLOSE #2
2290 RETURN
2300 REM ********************************
2310 REM * HEADING USED FOR THE DISPLAY *
2320 REM ********************************
2330 HOME
2340 X = ((80 - LEN(COMPANY.NAME$)) / 2)
2350 VPOS=2:HPOS=X
2360 PRINT COMPANY.NAME$
2370 FOR N = 1 TO 79:PRINT "-";:NEXT N:PRINT
2380 PRINT TAB(26);"PRODUCT (INVENTORY) PROCESSING"
2390 FOR N = 1 TO 79:PRINT "-";:NEXT N
2400 RETURN
```

Figure 6.19. (continued)

RECIVBLE

The Accounts Receivable subsystem of the small business system is the largest, and by definition, the most complex of them all. While the Apple III has sufficient memory to accommodate all programs in the subsystem, we have broken down several of them for ease of handling. Those have been placed into CHAINable programs. Throughout the book the programs have taken advantage of the documentation capabilities of Business BASIC as implemented on the Apple III. The statements have been made as simple as possible. Multiple statements have generally been separated, except where they were required to be on a single line. Sometimes, for printing purposes, the line has been broken, but will still work, as the machine will compress the spaces.

The Accounts Receivable application provides the following services:

1. Initial entry of data for an A/R file.
2. Adding entries to the A/R file.

3. Posting of payments to the A/R file.
4. Production of invoices.
5. Production of statements.
6. Production of A/R reports.
7. Aging the accounts.

The seven services are distributed in this manner:

RECIVBLE	Initial entry of data.
	Additional entry of data.
	Production of A/R.
INVOICE	Production of invoices.
POSTREC	Posting the payment of accounts.
STATMENT	Production of the monthly statement.
AGING	Aging the accounts.

The opening menu to the application, which we arrive at as a result of a selection made in BUSINESS, is shown in Figure 6.20.

```
THIS APPLICATION WILL ALLOW:

   1.   A/R DATA ENTRY TO A/R FILE
   2.   ADD INVOICE ENTRIES TO A/R FILE
   3.   REMOVE INVOICE ENTRIES WHEN PAID
   4.   PRODUCE CUSTOMER INVOICES
   5.   PRODUCE CUSTOMER MONTHLY STATEMENTS
   6.   PRODUCE A/R REPORTS
   7.   AGE A/R AND APPLY INTEREST
   8.   TERMINATE THE PROGRAM
```

Figure 6.20.

The big difficulty, of course, of having to subdivide a large program is that commonly used subroutines, such as those used in the loading or writing of files or of displaying data on the screen, must be copied into the new program. That is true of this program; and you will find routines in INVOICE, POSTREC, STATMENT, and AGING appearing in each other, as well as in RECIVBLE, probably at entirely different sequence numbers.

The first two options differ only in the manner in which they are entered. In the program following this discussion, follow them through the ON ... GOTO. You will see that the only difference between the two is that in the case of the first, no file is read into the program, whereas in the second, the file is read into the array and the new data is then added to the end.

Figure 6.21 is a *linear screen* - that is, the first portion appears and then the screen builds one statement at a time, until completed. It is presented here in its entirety.

```
                 SMALL BUSINESS ENTERPRISE, INC.
-----------------------------------------------------------------------
            ACCOUNTS RECEIVABLE PROCESSING PROGRAM
-----------------------------------------------------------------------
A TERMINATION QUESTION IS ASKED

DO YOU NEED TO REVIEW THE CUSTOMER FILE (Y/N) N

ENTER CUSTOMER NUMBER:      1
CUSTOMER NAME:              MR. BENJAMIN WATERS
CUSTOMER ADDRESS:           IMAGINATION INTERPRETED
                            327 PAGE ROAD
                            WATERTOWN,
                            PENNSYLVANIA 17743

CORRECT (Y/N)? Y

DO YOU NEED TO REVIEW THE PRODUCT FILE (Y/N) N

HOW MANY ITEMS ON THIS INVOICE (MAXIMUM 4)? 2

ENTER PRODUCT NUMBER:       1
PRODUCT NAME:               WIDGET
DESCRIPTION:                DOUBLE-SIDED, FRAMISTAN-ORIENTED
SHIPPING INSTRUCTIONS:      SHIP ONLY IN GLASS CONTAINER

CORRECT (Y/N)? Y
HOW MANY WILL BE INVOICED? 1
UNIT PRICE? $111.11

ENTER PRODUCT NUMBER:       2
PRODUCT NAME:               GIZMO
DESCRIPTION:                OCTAGONAL, CENTRIFUGAL
SHIPPING INSTRUCTINS:       AIR MAIL SPECIAL DELIVERY

CORRECT (Y/N)? Y
HOW MANY WILL BE INVOICED? 2
UNIT PRICE? $222.22
```

Figure 6.21.

The screen's development, of course, traces the development of the program. The opening entry advises the operator that there will be a question at the end of each entry as to whether or not the process will be terminated, which it does after the entered record has been accepted.

Next, the operator is asked if it is necessary to review the customer file. If it is, the routines necessary to pass the customer file onto the screen (with a hardcopy option) are invoked, before returning to the opening entry. The whole purpose is to allow the mechanism to determine the customer number before proceeding to the next required entry, which is, coincidentally, where you will enter the customer number. When you have entered the customer number, the customer information is displayed and you are given the opportunity to confirm that it pertains to the customer to whom this invoice is to be assigned.

The program now asks if you wish to review the product file. If you do, then a side trip is taken to allow you to determine which products to request without having to specify them. You are then asked how many products are to be listed on the invoice (the maximum is set at four). Having responded to that question, you may enter the product number for each in turn. As each is selected, the product name, description, and shipping instructions are displayed. You are then asked to confirm that each item is the one you wish to invoice. Once you do, you are asked how many will be invoiced and at what price.

In the design of any system, some fundamental questions must be asked. One of these is whether or not a small business offers the same price to every client for a product. If the product is tangible, it often happens that it's against the law to sell it at a different price to different clients. In this case, the unit price could be made a part of the product master file. Some small businesses get around this restriction by charging the same basic unit price but adding a mark-up based on customer terms. In this case, the invoicing would have to be tied to the customer terms of the customer file. If charges are made on the basis of estimate or proposal and therefore differ among clients, an override must be built into the application. The author chose to avoid any question of this possibility simply by building the request for the unit price into the invoicing application itself.

In this process, you are asked to assign an invoice number. Although not prevented from using a previous invoice number, you are advised of the highest number currently on file. This arrangement could lead to a problem. Suppose that invoice 555 is presented as being the highest number in the file, that you had generated invoice 556, and that it had already been paid. In this case, you might inadvertently use 556 again. Again, there was a design choice. It would have been easy enough to store the latest number in the area of the file where the number of records in the file is stored, but there would also be maintenance requirements for changing it. Thus, it was decided that most small businesses no doubt keep a register of invoices or at least duplicate invoices and would therefore know what the next invoice number in the sequence would be.

Once completed, the invoice is prepared, and the operator is asked if it is acceptable. If it is acceptable, then the invoice may be printed. Again, it will be necessary to shift the screen to view the entire invoice. See Figure 6.22.

```
DATE: 02-24-1983                                                 INVOICE NUMBER: 555
CUSTOMER NAME:                MR. BENJAMIN WATERS
CUSTOMER ADDRESS:             IMAGINATION INTERPRETED
                              327 PAGE ROAD
                              WATERTOWN,
                              PENNSYLVANIA 17743

ITEM       QUANTITY           DESCRIPTION                    PRICE   EXTENSION
---------------------------------------------------------------------------------
 1             1              WIDGET                        111.11      111.11
 2             2              GIZMO                         222.22      444.44
AMOUNT DUE:                                                             555.55
                                                                     ============

ACCEPTABLE (Y/N)? Y
```

Figure 6.22.

As stated, since the second option is the first option entered without first loading the file, there is nothing new to say about it. The same is almost true of the A/R reports. If you'll look at the program, you'll note that a list of invoice data and customer data is produced. In this instance, it is a work list; no care has been taken to make it a fancy report. The invoice number is presented, its date, and its amount, followed by the customer's name and address. Itemized purchases are not a part of this report. As before, you are given the option of reviewing this report either on the display screen or with a hardcopy added. At the end, the total number of invoices produced is given.

The program RECIVBLE is given in Figure 6.23.

```
10 GOSUB 3530
20 INVOICE.MONTH$ = LEFT$(DATE$,2)
30 INVOICE.DAY$ = MID$(DATE$,4,2)
40 INVOICE.YEAR$ = RIGHT$(DATE$,4)
50 IF VAL(INVOICE.MONTH$) = 1 THEN INVOICE.MONTH$ = "JANUARY"
60 IF VAL(INVOICE.MONTH$) = 2 THEN INVOICE.MONTH$ = "FEBRUARY"
70 IF VAL(INVOICE.MONTH$) = 3 THEN INVOICE.MONTH$ = "MARCH"
80 IF VAL(INVOICE.MONTH$) = 4 THEN INVOICE.MONTH$ = "APRIL"
90 IF VAL(INVOICE.MONTH$) = 5 THEN INVOICE.MONTH$ = "MAY"
100 IF VAL(INVOICE.MONTH$) = 6 THEN INVOICE.MONTH$ = "JUNE"
110 IF VAL(INVOICE.MONTH$) = 7 THEN INVOICE.MONTH$ = "JULY"
120 IF VAL(INVOICE.MONTH$) = 8 THEN INVOICE.MONTH$ = "AUGUST"
130 IF VAL(INVOICE.MONTH$) = 9 THEN INVOICE.MONTH$ = "SEPTEMBER"
140 IF VAL(INVOICE.MONTH$) = 10 THEN INVOICE.MONTH$ = "OCTOBER"
150 IF VAL(INVOICE.MONTH$) = 11 THEN INVOICE.MONTH$ = "NOVEMBER"
160 IF VAL(INVOICE.MONTH$) = 12 THEN INVOICE.MONTH$ = "DECEMBER"
170 INVOICE.MONTH$ = INVOICE.MONTH$ + " "
180 INVOICE.DATE$ = INVOICE.MONTH$ + INVOICE.DAY$ + ", " + INVOICE.YEAR$
190 PRINT
200 PRINT INVOICE.DATE$
210 REM ***********************************
220 REM * DIMENSION THE RECEIVABLES FILE. *
230 REM ***********************************
240 DIM CUSTOMER.NUMBER(100)
250 DIM DATE.OF.INVOICE$(100)
260 DIM DOCUMENT.NUMBER(100)
270 DIM ITEM.1.NUMBER(100)
280 DIM ITEM.1.QTY(100)
290 DIM ITEM.1.UNIT.PRICE(100)
300 DIM ITEM.2.NUMBER(100)
310 DIM ITEM.2.QTY(100)
320 DIM ITEM.2.UNIT.PRICE(100)
330 DIM ITEM.3.NUMBER(100)
340 DIM ITEM.3.QTY(100)
350 DIM ITEM.3.UNIT.PRICE(100)
360 DIM ITEM.4.NUMBER(100)
370 DIM ITEM.4.QTY(100)
380 DIM ITEM.4.UNIT.PRICE(100)
390 DIM AMOUNT.OF.INVOICE(100)
400 DIM AMOUNT.LESS.THAN.30.DAYS(100)
410 DIM AMOUNT.AT.30.DAYS(100)
420 DIM AMOUNT.AT.60.DAYS(100)
430 DIM AMOUNT.AT.90.DAYS(100)
440 REM *******************************
450 REM * DIMENSION THE PRODUCT FILE. *
460 REM *******************************
470 DIM PRODUCT.NAME$(100)
480 DIM PRODUCT.DESCR$(100)
490 DIM PRODUCT.UNIT$(100)
500 DIM PRODUCT.LOCATION$(100)
510 DIM PRODUCT.Q.O.H(100)
520 DIM PRODUCT.R.O.P(100)
530 DIM PRODUCT.SHIP.INSTR$(100)
540 REM ********************************
550 REM * DIMENSION THE CUSTOMER FILE. *
560 REM ********************************
570 DIM CUSTOMER.NAME$(100)
580 DIM CUSTOMER.ADDR.1$(100)
590 DIM CUSTOMER.ADDR.2$(100)
600 DIM CUSTOMER.ADDR.3$(100)
610 DIM CUSTOMER.ADDR.4$(100)
620 DIM CUSTOMER.TERMS$(100)
630 REM *******************************
640 REM * DIMENSION THE ACCOUNT FILE. *
650 REM *******************************
```

Figure 6.23.

```
660 DIM T$(100)
670 DIM N$(100)
680 DIM A(100)
690 REM ****************
700 REM * OPENING MENU *
710 REM ****************
720 PRINT
730 PRINT "THIS APPLICATION WILL ALLOW :"
740 PRINT
750 PRINT "     1.  INITIAL ENTRY OF DATA FOR AN ACCOUNTS RECEIVABLE FILE."
760 PRINT "     2.  ADDING INVOICE ENTRIES TO THE ACCOUNTS RECEIVABLE FILE."
770 PRINT "     3.  REMOVAL OF INVOICE ENTRIES FROM THE FILES WHEN PAID."
780 PRINT "     4.  PRODUCING THE INVOICE TO BE SENT TO THE CUSTOMER."
790 PRINT "     5.  PRODUCING THE CUSTOMERS' MONTHLY STATEMENTS"
800 PRINT "     6.  PRODUCING REPORTS OF ACCOUNTS RECEIVABLE."
810 PRINT "     7.  AGING THE ACCOUNTS RECEIVABLE FILE/APPLYING INTEREST."
820 PRINT "     8.  TERMINATE THE PROGRAM"
830 PRINT
840 REM ************
850 PRINT:PRINT "SELECT: ";
860 GET Z$
870 PRINT Z$:PRINT
880 IF Z$ = "1" THEN PRINT "INITIAL ENTRY OF A/R DATA":PRINT
890 IF Z$ = "2" THEN PRINT "ADD INVOICE ENTRIES TO THE A/R FILE":PRINT
900 IF Z$ = "3" THEN PRINT "POST PAYMENTS TO A/R FILE":PRINT
910 IF Z$ = "4" THEN PRINT "PRODUCE CUSTOMER INVOICE":PRINT
920 IF Z$ = "5" THEN PRINT "PRODUCE CUSTOMER STATEMENTS":PRINT
930 IF Z$ = "6" THEN PRINT "PRODUCE A/R REPORTS":PRINT
940 IF Z$ = "7" THEN PRINT "AGE THE ACCOUNTS":PRINT
950 IF Z$ = "8" THEN 3040
960 FOR Z = 1 TO 1000:NEXT Z
970 MENU.SELECTION = VAL(Z$)
980 IF (MENU.SELECTION > 0) AND (MENU.SELECTION < 8) THEN 1050
990 VPOS=25:HPOS=1
1000 PRINT "INVALID CODE";
1010 PRINT CHR$(7)
1020 FOR Z = 1 TO 1000:NEXT Z
1030 GOSUB 3530
1040 GOTO 720
1050 ON MENU.SELECTION GOTO 1150,1210,2880,3000,2920,2380,2960
1060 GOTO 990
1070 REM ***********************************************************
1080 REM * THIS IS THE ROUTINE FOR ENTRY OF ACCOUNTS RECEIVABLE.  THE *
1090 REM * POINT OF ENTRY TO THE ROUTINE DETERMINES IF A NEW FILES IS *
1100 REM * BEING CREATED OR IF AN EXISTING FILE IS TO BE USED.        *
1110 REM ***********************************************************
1120 REM * ENTRY HERE (NEW FILE) REQUIRES ARRAY COUNT TO BE SET TO 0  *
1130 REM * TO ALLOW RELATIVE INCREMENTATION (RFS).                    *
1140 REM ***********************************************************
1150 RECEIVE.FILE.SIZE = 0
1160 GOTO 1250
1170 REM ***********************************************************
1180 REM * ENTRY HERE (ADD TO FILE) REQUIRES ARRAY COUNT TO BE SET TO *
1190 REM * FILE SIZE TO ALLOW RELATIVE INCREMENTATION (RFS).          *
1200 REM ***********************************************************
1210 GOSUB 3640            :REM GET THE RECEIVABLES FILE
1220 FOR I = 1 TO RECEIVE.FILE.SIZE
1230      IF DOCUMENT.NUMBER(I) > HIGHEST.NUMBER THEN
               HIGHEST.NUMBER = DOCUMENT.NUMBER(I)
1240      NEXT I
1250 GOSUB 3530            :REM GET THE DISPLAY HEADING
1260 PRINT:PRINT "HIGHEST INVOICE IN THE FILE IS: ";HIGHEST.NUMBER
1270 PRINT:INPUT "ENTER THE BEGINNING INVOICE NUMBER: ",INVOICE.NUMBER
1280 IF INVOICE.NUMBER = 0 THEN PRINT CHR$(7):GOTO 1250
1290 IF INVOICE.NUMBER < = HIGHEST.NUMBER THEN PRINT CHR$(7):GOTO 1250
```

Figure 6.23. (continued)

```
1300 INVOICE.NUMBER = INT(INVOICE.NUMBER)
1310 PRINT:PRINT "CORRECT (Y/N)? ";
1320 GET Z$
1330 PRINT Z$
1340 IF Z$ < > "Y" THEN PRINT CHR$(7):GOTO 1250
1350 GOSUB 4420            :REM GET THE CUSTOMER FILE
1360 GOSUB 4250            :REM GET THE PRODUCT FILE
1370 GOSUB 3530            :REM GET THE DISPLAY HEADING
1380 PRINT:PRINT "INPUT IS TERMINATED BY QUESTION AT THE END OF EACH ENTRY"
1390 PRINT:PRINT "DO YOU NEED TO REVIEW THE CUSTOMER FILE (Y/N)? ";
1400 GET Z$
1410 PRINT Z$
1420 IF Z$ = "Y" THEN GOSUB 4730:GOTO 1370
1430 PRINT
1440 PRINT "ENTER CUSTOMER NUMBER:";TAB(25);:INPUT "",WHICH.CUSTOMER
1450 IF (WHICH.CUSTOMER < 1) OR (WHICH.CUSTOMER > CUSTOMER.FILE.SIZE)
      THEN PRINT "CUSTOMER NUMBER INVALID":GOTO 1430
1460 GOSUB 5690
1470 IF ALREADY.ACCEPTED$ = "YES" THEN ALREADY.ACCEPTED$ = "NO":GOTO 1530
1480 PRINT:PRINT "CORRECT (Y/N)? ";
1490 GET Z$
1500 PRINT Z$
1510 IF Z$ < > "Y" THEN PRINT CHR$(7):GOTO 1370
1520 ALREADY.ACCEPTED$ = "YES"
1530 PRINT:PRINT "DO YOU NEED TO REVIEW THE PRODUCT FILE (Y/N)? ";
1540 GET Z$
1550 PRINT Z$
1560 IF Z$ = "Y" THEN GOSUB 5200:GOSUB 3530:GOSUB 5690:GOTO 1470
1570 PRINT
1580 INPUT "HOW MANY ITEMS ON THIS INVOICE (MAXIMUM 4)? ",INVOICE.ITEMS
1590 IF (INVOICE.ITEMS < 1) OR (INVOICE.ITEMS > 4) THEN
      PRINT "INVALID ENTRY - REPEAT":GOTO 1580
1600 BILLED.ITEMS = 1
1610 RFS = RECEIVE.FILE.SIZE + 1
1620 PRINT
1630 PRINT "ENTER PRODUCT NUMBER:";TAB(25);:INPUT "",WHICH.PROD
1640 IF (WHICH.PROD < 1) OR (WHICH.PROD > PRODUCT.FILE.SIZE) THEN
      PRINT "INVALID PRODUCT NUMBER - REPEAT":GOTO 1620
1650 PRINT "PRODUCT.NAME:";TAB(25);PRODUCT.NAME$(WHICH.PROD)
1660 PRINT "DESCRIPTION:";TAB(25);PRODUCT.DESCR$(WHICH.PROD)
1670 PRINT "SHIPPING INSTRUCTIONS:";TAB(25);PRODUCT.SHIP.INSTR$(WHICH.PROD)
1680 PRINT:PRINT "CORRECT (Y/N)? ";
1690 GET Z$
1700 PRINT Z$
1710 IF Z$ < > "Y" THEN PRINT CHR$(7):GOTO 1620
1720 IF BILLED.ITEMS = 2 THEN 1850
1730 IF BILLED.ITEMS = 3 THEN 1950
1740 IF BILLED.ITEMS = 4 THEN 2050
1750 ITEM.1.NUMBER(RFS) = WHICH.PROD
1760 ITEM.NAME.1$ = PRODUCT.NAME$(WHICH.PROD)
1770 INPUT "HOW MANY WILL BE INVOICED? ",ITEM.1.QTY(RFS)
1780 IF ITEM.1.QTY(RFS) = 0 THEN 1770
1790 ITEM.1.QTY = INT(ITEM.1.QTY(RFS))
1800 INPUT "UNIT PRICE? $",ITEM.1.UNIT.PRICE(RFS)
1810 IF ITEM.1.UNIT.PRICE(RFS) = 0 THEN 1800
1820 IF BILLED.ITEMS = INVOICE.ITEMS THEN 2120
1830 BILLED.ITEMS = BILLED.ITEMS + 1
1840 GOTO 1620
1850 ITEM.2.NUMBER(RFS) = WHICH.PROD
1860 ITEM.NAME.2$ = PRODUCT.NAME$(WHICH.PROD)
1870 INPUT "HOW MANY WILL BE INVOICED? ",ITEM.2.QTY(RFS)
1880 IF ITEM.2.QTY(RFS) = 0 THEN 1870
1890 ITEM.2.QTY = INT(ITEM.2.QTY(RFS))
1900 INPUT "UNIT PRICE? $",ITEM.2.UNIT.PRICE(RFS)
1910 IF ITEM.2.UNIT.PRICE(RFS) = 0 THEN 1900
```

Figure 6.23. (continued)

```
1920 IF BILLED.ITEMS = INVOICE.ITEMS THEN 2120
1930 BILLED.ITEMS = BILLED.ITEMS + 1
1940 GOTO 1620
1950 ITEM.3.NUMBER(RFS) = WHICH.PROD
1960 ITEM.NAME.3$ = PRODUCT.NAME$(WHICH.PROD)
1970 INPUT "HOW MANY WILL BE INVOICED? ",ITEM.3.QTY(RFS)
1980 IF ITEM.3.QTY(RFS) = 0 THEN 1970
1990 ITEM.3.QTY = INT(ITEM.3.QTY(RFS))
2000 INPUT "UNIT PRICE? $",ITEM.3.UNIT.PRICE(RFS)
2010 IF ITEM.3.UNIT.PRICE(RFS) = 0 THEN 2000
2020 IF BILLED.ITEMS = INVOICE.ITEMS THEN 2120
2030 BILLED.ITEMS = BILLED.ITEMS + 1
2040 GOTO 1620
2050 ITEM.4.NUMBER(RFS) = WHICH.PROD
2060 ITEM.NAME.4$ = PRODUCT.NAME$(WHICH.PROD)
2070 INPUT "HOW MANY WILL BE INVOICED? ",ITEM.4.QTY(RFS)
2080 IF ITEM.4.QTY(RFS) = 0 THEN 2070
2090 ITEM.4.QTY = INT(ITEM.4.QTY(RFS))
2100 INPUT "UNIT PRICE? $",ITEM.4.UNIT.PRICE(RFS)
2110 IF ITEM.4.UNIT.PRICE(RFS) = 0 THEN 2100
2120 REM ************************************************************
2130 REM * NOW THE INVOICE IS ASSEMBLED.  IT IS SHOWN FOR ACCEPTANCE *
2140 REM ************************************************************
2150 PRINT CHR$(12)
2160 DATE.OF.INVOICE$(RFS) = INVOICE.DATE$
2170 DOCUMENT.NUMBER(RFS) = INVOICE.NUMBER
2180 CUSTOMER.NUMBER(RFS) = WHICH.CUSTOMER
2190 PRINT "DATE: ";DATE$;TAB(50);"INVOICE NUMBER: ";INVOICE.NUMBER
2200 GOSUB 5690
2210 PRINT
2220 GOSUB 5900
2230 PRINT "ACCEPTABLE (Y/N)? ";
2240 GET Z$
2250 PRINT Z$
2260 IF Z$ < > "Y" THEN 1370
2270 RECEIVE.FILE.SIZE = RFS
2280 PRINT "DO YOU NOW WISH TO TERMINATE INPUT (Y/N)? ";
2290 GET Z$
2300 PRINT Z$
2310 IF Z$ = "Y" THEN 2350
2320 INVOICE.NUMBER = INVOICE.NUMBER + 1
2330 GOTO 1370
2340 REM **********
2350 GOSUB 3940                    :REM WRITE THE A/R FILE
2360 GOSUB 3530                    :REM GET THE HEADING
2370 GOTO 690                      :REM RETURN TO MAIN MENU
2380 REM **************************************************
2390 REM * ROUTINE TO PRODUCE ACCOUNTS RECEIVABLE REPORTS *
2400 REM **************************************************
2410 GOSUB 4420           :REM GET THE CUSTOMER FILE
2420 GOSUB 3640           :REM GET THE RECEIVABLE FILE
2430 GOSUB 3530           :REM GET THE HEADING
2440 PRINT:PRINT "ACCOUNTS RECEIVABLE REPORT - WANT A HARDCOPY (Y/N)? ";
2450 GET Z$
2460 PRINT Z$
2470 IF Z$ < > "Y" THEN HARDCOPY$ = "NO":GOTO 2490
2480 HARDCOPY$ = "YES"
2490 PRINT
2500 FOR I = 1 TO RECEIVE.FILE.SIZE
2510     TOTAL.AMT.OF.INVOICES=TOTAL.AMT.OF.INVOICES+AMOUNT.OF.INVOICE(I)
2520     PRINT DOCUMENT.NUMBER(I),DATE.OF.INVOICE$(I),;
2530     PRINT USING "$5&.2&";AMOUNT.OF.INVOICE(I)
2540     PRINT
2550     PRINT CUSTOMER.NAME$(CUSTOMER.NUMBER(I))
2560     PRINT CUSTOMER.ADDR.1$(CUSTOMER.NUMBER(I))
```

Figure 6.23. (continued)

```
2570      PRINT CUSTOMER.ADDR.2$(CUSTOMER.NUMBER(I))
2580      PRINT CUSTOMER.ADDR.3$(CUSTOMER.NUMBER(I))
2590      PRINT CUSTOMER.ADDR.4$(CUSTOMER.NUMBER(I))
2600      PRINT
2610      FOR N = 1 TO 79:PRINT "-";:NEXT N
2620      PRINT
2630      IF HARDCOPY$ = "YES" THEN 2650
2640      FOR Z = 1 TO 1500:NEXT Z:GOTO 2790
2650      OPEN #3,".PRINTER"
2660      OUTPUT #3
2670      PRINT DOCUMENT.NUMBER(I),DATE.OF.INVOICE$(I),;
2680      PRINT USING "$5&.2&";AMOUNT.OF.INVOICE(I)
2690      PRINT
2700      PRINT CUSTOMER.NAME$(CUSTOMER.NUMBER(I))
2710      PRINT CUSTOMER.ADDR.1$(CUSTOMER.NUMBER(I))
2720      PRINT CUSTOMER.ADDR.2$(CUSTOMER.NUMBER(I))
2730      PRINT CUSTOMER.ADDR.3$(CUSTOMER.NUMBER(I))
2740      PRINT CUSTOMER.ADDR.4$(CUSTOMER.NUMBER(I))
2750      PRINT
2760      FOR N = 1 TO 79:PRINT "-";:NEXT N
2770      PRINT
2780      CLOSE #3
2790      NEXT I
2800      PRINT USING "TOTAL VALUE OF INVOICES: $5&.2&";
               TOTAL.AMT.OF.INVOICES
2810      IF HARDCOPY$ = "NO" THEN 2860
2820      OPEN #3,".PRINTER"
2830      OUTPUT #3
2840      PRINT USING "TOTAL VALUE OF INVOICES: $5&.2&";
               TOTAL.AMT OF.INVOICES:PRINT CHR$(12)
2850      CLOSE #3
2860 GOSUB 3530                       :REM GET THE HEADING
2870 GOTO 690                         :REM RETURN TO MAIN MENU
2880 REM ***************************
2890 REM * ROUTINE TO POST PAYMENTS *
2900 REM ***************************
2910 CHAIN .D2/POSTREC
2920 REM *********************************
2930 REM * ROUTINE TO PRODUCE A STATEMENT *
2940 REM *********************************
2950 CHAIN .D2/STATMENT
2960 REM ******************************
2970 REM * ROUTINE TO AGE THE ACCOUNTS *
2980 REM ******************************
2990 CHAIN .D2/AGING
3000 REM ****************************************
3010 REM * INVOICE DISPLAY AND PRINTING ROUTINE *
3020 REM ****************************************
3030 CHAIN .D2/INVOICE
3040 REM **********************
3050 REM * PROGRAM TERMINATION *
3060 REM **********************
3070 PRINT
3080 PRINT "INVOICE PREPARATION IS COMPLETE"
3090 PRINT
3100 PRINT "DO YOU WISH TO REPEAT THE PROGRAM (Y/N)? ";
3110 GET Z$
3120 PRINT Z$
3130 IF Z$ < > "Y" THEN 3520
3140 FOR N = 1 TO 100
3150     CUSTOMER.NUMBER(N) = 0
3160     DATE.OF.INVOICE$(N) = ""
3170     DOCUMENT.NUMBER(N) = 0
3180     ITEM.1.NUMBER(N) = 0
3190     ITEM.1.QTY(N) = 0
```

Figure 6.23. (continued)

```
3200      ITEM.1.UNIT.PRICE(N) = 0
3210      ITEM.2.NUMBER(N) = 0
3220      ITEM.2.UNIT.PRICE(N) = 0
3230      ITEM.3.NUMBER(N) = 0
3240      ITEM.3.QTY(N) = 0
3250      ITEM.3.UNIT.PRICE(N) = 0
3260      ITEM.4.NUMBER(N) = 0
3270      ITEM.4.QTY(N) = 0
3280      ITEM.4.UNIT.PRICE(N) = 0
3290      AMOUNT.OF.INVOICE(N) = 0
3300      AMOUNT.LESS.THAN.30.DAYS(N) = 0
3310      AMOUNT.AT.30.DAYS(N) = 0
3320      AMOUNT.AT.60.DAYS(N) = 0
3330      AMOUNT.AT.90.DAYS(N) = 0
3340      PRODUCT.NAME$(N) = ""
3350      PRODUCT.DESCR$(N) = ""
3360      PRODUCT.UNIT$(N) = ""
3370      PRODUCT.LOCATION$(N) = ""
3380      PRODUCT.Q.O.H(N) = 0
3390      PRODUCT.R.O.P(N) = 0
3400      PRODUCT.SHIP.INSTR$(N) = ""
3410      CUSTOMER.NAME$(N) = ""
3420      CUSTOMER.ADDR.1$(N) = ""
3430      CUSTOMER.ADDR.2$(N) = ""
3440      CUSTOMER.ADDR.3$(N) = ""
3450      CUSTOMER.ADDR.4$(N) = ""
3460      CUSTOMER.TERMS$(N) = ""
3470      T$(N) = ""
3480      N$(N) = ""
3490      A(N) = 0
3500      NEXT N
3510 GOTO 10
3520 CHAIN .D2/BUSINESS
3530 REM *******************************
3540 REM * HEADING USED FOR THE DISPLAY *
3550 REM *******************************
3560 HOME
3570 X = ((80 - LEN(COMPANY.NAME$)) / 2)
3580 VPOS=2:HPOS=X
3590 PRINT COMPANY.NAME$
3600 FOR N = 1 TO 79:PRINT "-";:NEXT N:PRINT
3610 PRINT TAB(19);"ACCOUNTS RECEIVABLE PROCESSING PROGRAM"
3620 FOR N = 1 TO 79:PRINT "-";:NEXT N
3630 RETURN
3640 REM **********************************
3650 REM * OPEN AND INPUT RECEIVABLE FILE *
3660 REM **********************************
3670 PRINT:PRINT "LOADING THE RECEIVABLES FILE"
3680 OPEN #1,.D2/RECEIVE.DAT
3690 INPUT #1,RECEIVE.FILE.SIZE      :REM OBTAIN THE RECORD COUNT
3700 FOR I = 1 TO RECEIVE.FILE.SIZE
3710      INPUT #1,CUSTOMER.NUMBER(I)
3720      INPUT #1,DATE.OF.INVOICE$(I)
3730      INPUT #1,DOCUMENT.NUMBER(I)
3740      INPUT #1,ITEM.1.NUMBER(I)
3750      INPUT #1,ITEM.1.QTY(I)
3760      INPUT #1,ITEM.1.UNIT.PRICE(I)
3770      INPUT #1,ITEM.2.NUMBER(I)
3780      INPUT #1,ITEM.2.QTY(I)
3790      INPUT #1,ITEM.2.UNIT.PRICE(I)
3800      INPUT #1,ITEM.3.NUMBER(I)
3810      INPUT #1,ITEM.3.QTY(I)
3820      INPUT #1,ITEM.3.UNIT.PRICE(I)
3830      INPUT #1,ITEM.4.NUMBER(I)
3840      INPUT #1,ITEM.4.QTY(I)
```

Figure 6.23. (continued)

```
3850      INPUT #1,ITEM.4.UNIT.PRICE(I)
3860      INPUT #1,AMOUNT.OF.INVOICE(I)
3870      INPUT #1,AMOUNT.LESS.THAN.30.DAYS(I)
3880      INPUT #1,AMOUNT.AT.30.DAYS(I)
3890      INPUT #1,AMOUNT.AT.60.DAYS(I)
3900      INPUT #1,AMOUNT.AT.90.DAYS(I)
3910      NEXT I
3920 CLOSE #1
3930 RETURN
3940 REM **********************************
3950 REM * OPEN AND OUTPUT RECEIVABLE FILE *
3960 REM **********************************
3970 PRINT:PRINT "WRITING THE RECEIVABLES FILE"
3980 CREATE ".D2/RECEIVE.DAT",TEXT
3990 OPEN #1,.D2/RECEIVE.DAT
4000 PRINT #1,RECEIVE.FILE.SIZE        :REM STORE THE RECORD COUNT
4010 FOR I = 1 TO RECEIVE.FILE.SIZE
4020      PRINT #1,CUSTOMER.NUMBER(I)
4030      PRINT #1,DATE.OF.INVOICE$(I)
4040      PRINT #1,DOCUMENT.NUMBER(I)
4050      PRINT #1,ITEM.1.NUMBER(I)
4060      PRINT #1,ITEM.1.QTY(I)
4070      PRINT #1,ITEM.1.UNIT.PRICE(I)
4080      PRINT #1,ITEM.2.NUMBER(I)
4090      PRINT #1,ITEM.2.QTY(I)
4100      PRINT #1,ITEM.2.UNIT.PRICE(I)
4110      PRINT #1,ITEM.3.NUMBER(I)
4120      PRINT #1,ITEM.3.QTY(I)
4130      PRINT #1,ITEM.3.UNIT.PRICE(I)
4140      PRINT #1,ITEM.4.NUMBER(I)
4150      PRINT #1,ITEM.4.QTY(I)
4160      PRINT #1,ITEM.4.UNIT.PRICE(I)
4170      PRINT #1,AMOUNT.OF.INVOICE(I)
4180      PRINT #1,AMOUNT.LESS.THAN.30.DAYS(I)
4190      PRINT #1,AMOUNT.AT.30.DAYS(I)
4200      PRINT #1,AMOUNT.AT.60.DAYS(I)
4210      PRINT #1,AMOUNT.AT.90.DAYS(I)
4220      NEXT I
4230 CLOSE #1
4240 RETURN
4250 REM ******************************
4260 REM * OPEN AND INPUT PRODUCT FILE *
4270 REM ******************************
4280 PRINT:PRINT "LOADING THE PRODUCT FILE"
4290 OPEN #1,.D2/PRODUCT.DAT
4300 INPUT #1,PRODUCT.FILE.SIZE        :REM OBTAIN THE RECORD COUNT
4310 FOR J = 1 TO PRODUCT.FILE.SIZE
4320      INPUT #1,PRODUCT.NAME$(J)
4330      INPUT #1,PRODUCT.DESCR$(J)
4340      INPUT #1,PRODUCT.UNIT$(J)
4350      INPUT #1,PRODUCT.LOCATION$(J)
4360      INPUT #1,PRODUCT.Q.O.H(J)
4370      INPUT #1,PRODUCT.R.O.P(J)
4380      INPUT #1,PRODUCT.SHIP.INSTR$(J)
4390      NEXT J
4400 CLOSE #1
4410 RETURN
4420 REM *******************************
4430 REM * OPEN AND INPUT CUSTOMER FILE *
4440 REM *******************************
4450 PRINT:PRINT "LOADING THE CUSTOMER FILE"
4460 OPEN #1,.D2/CUSTOMER.DAT
4470 INPUT #1,CUSTOMER.FILE.SIZE     :REM OBTAIN THE RECORD COUNT
4480 FOR K = 1 TO CUSTOMER.FILE.SIZE
4490      INPUT #1,CUSTOMER.NAME$(K)
```

Figure 6.23. (continued)

```
4500       INPUT #1,CUSTOMER.ADDR.1$(K)
4510       INPUT #1,CUSTOMER.ADDR.2$(K)
4520       INPUT #1,CUSTOMER.ADDR.3$(K)
4530       INPUT #1,CUSTOMER.ADDR.4$(K)
4540       INPUT #1,CUSTOMER.TERMS$(K)
4550       NEXT K
4560 CLOSE #1
4570 RETURN
4580 REM ******************************
4590 REM * OPEN AND INPUT ACCOUNT FILE *
4600 REM *******************************
4610 PRINT:PRINT "LOADING THE ACCOUNT FILE"
4620 PRINT:INPUT "SPECIFY THE ACCOUNT FILE TO BE USED: ",SPECIFIED.FILE$
4630 SPECIFIED.FILE$ = ".D2/" + SPECIFIED.FILE$ + ".DAT"
4640 OPEN #1,SPECIFIED.FILE$
4650 INPUT #1,SPECIFIED.FILE.SIZE     :REM OBTAIN THE RECORD COUNT
4660 FOR L = 1 TO SPECIFIED.FILE.SIZE
4670       INPUT #1,T$(L)
4680       INPUT #1,N$(L)
4690       INPUT #1,A(L)
4700       NEXT L
4710 CLOSE #1
4720 RETURN
4730 REM *************************************************************
4740 REM * REVIEW THE MATRIX IN WHICH THE CUSTOMER FILE HAS BEEN STORED *
4750 REM *************************************************************
4760 PRINT:PRINT "DO YOU WISH CONTINUOUS DISPLAY (Y/N)? ";
4770 GET Z$
4780 PRINT Z$
4790 IF Z$ = "Y" THEN CONTINUE$ = "YES":GOTO 4810
4800 CONTINUE$ = "NO"
4810 PRINT:PRINT "DO YOU WISH TO OBTAIN A HARD COPY (Y/N)? ";
4820 GET Z$
4830 PRINT Z$
4840 IF Z$ = "Y" THEN HARDCOPY$ = "YES":GOTO 4860
4850 HARDCOPY$ = "NO"
4860 FOR I = 1 TO CUSTOMER.FILE.SIZE
4870       PRINT
4880       PRINT "CUSTOMER NUMBER: ";I
4890       PRINT
4900       PRINT "CUSTOMER NAME:";TAB(25);CUSTOMER.NAME$(I)
4910       PRINT
4920       PRINT "CUSTOMER ADDRESS:";TAB(25);CUSTOMER.ADDR.1$(I)
4930       PRINT TAB(25);CUSTOMER.ADDR.2$(I)
4940       PRINT TAB(25);CUSTOMER.ADDR.3$(I)
4950       PRINT TAB(25);CUSTOMER.ADDR.4$(I)
4960       PRINT
4970       IF CONTINUE$ = "YES" THEN 5010
4980       PRINT "PRESS 'X' TO EXIT -- ANY OTHER KEY TO CONTINUE"
4990       GET Z$
5000       IF Z$ = "X" THEN 5190
5010       IF (HARDCOPY$ = "NO") AND (CONTINUE$ = "NO") THEN 5030
5020       FOR Z = 1 TO 1500:NEXT Z
5030       IF HARDCOPY$ = "NO" THEN 5180
5040       OPEN #3,".PRINTER"
5050       OUTPUT #3
5060       PRINT
5070       PRINT
5080       PRINT "CUSTOMER NUMBER: ";I
5090       PRINT
5100       PRINT "CUSTOMER NAME:";TAB(25);CUSTOMER.NAME$(I)
5110       PRINT
5120       PRINT "CUSTOMER ADDRESS:";TAB(25);CUSTOMER.ADDR.1$(I)
5130       PRINT TAB(25);CUSTOMER.ADDR.2$(I)
5140       PRINT TAB(25);CUSTOMER.ADDR.3$(I)
```

Figure 6.23. (continued)

```
5150       PRINT TAB(25);CUSTOMER.ADDR.4$(I)
5160       PRINT
5170       CLOSE #3
5180       NEXT I
5190 RETURN
5200 REM ***********************************************************************
5210 REM * REVIEW THE MATRIX IN WHICH THE PRODUCT FILE HAS BEEN STORED *
5220 REM ***********************************************************************
5230 PRINT:PRINT "DO YOU WISH CONTINUOUS DISPLAY (Y/N)? ";
5240 GET Z$
5250 PRINT Z$
5260 IF Z$ = "Y" THEN CONTINUE$ = "YES":GOTO 5280
5270 CONTINUE$ = "NO"
5280 PRINT:PRINT "DO YOU WISH TO OBTAIN A HARD COPY (Y/N)? ";
5290 GET Z$
5300 PRINT Z$
5310 IF Z$ = "Y" THEN HARDCOPY$ = "YES":GOTO 5330
5320 HARDCOPY$ = "NO"
5330 FOR J = 1 TO PRODUCT.FILE.SIZE
5340       PRINT
5350       PRINT "PRODUCT NUMBER: ";J
5360       PRINT
5370       PRINT "PRODUCT NAME:";TAB(25);PRODUCT.NAME$(J)
5380       PRINT
5390       PRINT "DESCRIPTION:";TAB(25);PRODUCT.DESCR$(J)
5400       PRINT "UNIT OF MEASURE:";TAB(25);PRODUCT.UNIT$(J)
5410       PRINT "LOCATION:";TAB(25);PRODUCT.UNIT$(J)
5420       PRINT "QUANTITY ON HAND:";TAB(25);PRODUCT.Q.O.H(J)
5430       PRINT "REORDER POINT:";TAB(25);PRODUCT.R.O.P(J)
5440       PRINT "SHIPPING INSTRUCTIONS:";TAB(25);PRODUCT.SHIP.INSTR$(J)
5450       PRINT
5460       IF CONTINUE$ = "YES" THEN 5500
5470       PRINT "PRESS 'X' TO EXIT -- ANY OTHER KEY TO CONTINUE"
5480       GET Z$
5490       IF Z$ = "X" THEN 5680
5500       IF (HARDCOPY$ = "NO") AND (CONTINUE$ = "NO") THEN 5520
5510       FOR Z = 1 TO 1500:NEXT Z
5520       IF HARDCOPY$ = "NO" THEN 5670
5530       OPEN #3,".PRINTER"
5540       OUTPUT #3
5550       PRINT
5560       PRINT
5570       PRINT "PRODUCT NAME:";TAB(25);PRODUCT.NAME$(J)
5580       PRINT
5590       PRINT "DESCRIPTION:";TAB(25);PRODUCT.DESCR$(J)
5600       PRINT "UNIT OF MEASURE:";TAB(25);PRODUCT.UNIT$(J)
5610       PRINT "LOCATION:";TAB(25);PRODUCT.UNIT$(J)
5620       PRINT "QUANTITY ON HAND:";TAB(25);PRODUCT.Q.O.H(J)
5630       PRINT "REORDER POINT:";TAB(25);PRODUCT.R.O.P(J)
5640       PRINT "SHIPPING INSTRUCTIONS:";TAB(25);PRODUCT.SHIP.INSTR$(J)
5650       PRINT
5660       CLOSE #3
5670       NEXT J
5680 RETURN
5690 REM ********************************************************************
5700 REM * ROUTINE USED MORE THAN ONCE TO DISPLAY THE CUSTOMER INFO *
5710 REM ********************************************************************
5720 PRINT "CUSTOMER.NAME:";TAB(25);CUSTOMER.NAME$(WHICH.CUSTOMER)
5730 PRINT "CUSTOMER ADDRESS:";TAB(25);CUSTOMER.ADDR.1$(WHICH.CUSTOMER)
5740 PRINT TAB(25);CUSTOMER.ADDR.2$(WHICH.CUSTOMER)
5750 PRINT TAB(25);CUSTOMER.ADDR.3$(WHICH.CUSTOMER)
5760 PRINT TAB(25);CUSTOMER.ADDR.4$(WHICH.CUSTOMER)
5770 RETURN
5780 REM ******************************************************************
5790 REM * ROUTINE USED MORE THAN ONCE TO PRINT THE CUSTOMER INFO *
5800 REM ******************************************************************
```

Figure 6.23. (continued)

```
5810 OPEN #3,".PRINTER"
5820 OUTPUT #3
5830 PRINT "CUSTOMER.NAME:";TAB(25);CUSTOMER.NAME$(WHICH.CUSTOMER)
5840 PRINT "CUSTOMER ADDRESS:";TAB(25);CUSTOMER.ADDR.1$(WHICH.CUSTOMER)
5850 PRINT TAB(25);CUSTOMER.ADDR.2$(WHICH.CUSTOMER)
5860 PRINT TAB(25);CUSTOMER.ADDR.3$(WHICH.CUSTOMER)
5870 PRINT TAB(25);CUSTOMER.ADDR.4$(WHICH.CUSTOMER)
5880 CLOSE #3
5890 RETURN
5900 REM ****************************************
5910 REM * ROUTINE TO DISPLAY THE INVOICE DETAIL *
5920 REM ****************************************
5930 PRINT "ITEM";TAB(10);"QUANTITY";TAB(30);"DESCRIPTION";
5940 PRINT TAB(60);"PRICE";TAB(70);"EXTENSION"
5950 ITEM.1.EXTENSION = (ITEM.1.QTY(RFS) * ITEM.1.UNIT.PRICE(RFS))
5960 ITEM.2.EXTENSION = (ITEM.2.QTY(RFS) * ITEM.2.UNIT.PRICE(RFS))
5970 ITEM.3.EXTENSION = (ITEM.3.QTY(RFS) * ITEM.3.UNIT.PRICE(RFS))
5980 ITEM.4.EXTENSION = (ITEM.4.QTY(RFS) * ITEM.4.UNIT.PRICE(RFS))
5990 FOR N = 1 TO 79:PRINT "-";:NEXT N
6000 PRINT ITEM.1.NUMBER(RFS);TAB(13);ITEM.1.QTY(RFS);TAB(30);
6010 PRINT ITEM.NAME.1$;TAB(55);
6020 PRINT USING "5&.2&";ITEM.1.UNIT.PRICE(RFS);
6030 PRINT TAB(70);"";:PRINT USING "5&.2&";ITEM.1.EXTENSION
6040 IF ITEM.NAME.2$ = "" THEN 6200
6050 PRINT ITEM.2.NUMBER(RFS);TAB(13);ITEM.2.QTY(RFS);TAB(30);
6060 PRINT ITEM.NAME.2$;TAB(55);
6070 PRINT USING "5&.2&";ITEM.2.UNIT.PRICE(RFS);
6080 PRINT TAB(70);"";:PRINT USING "5&.2&";ITEM.2.EXTENSION
6090 IF ITEM.NAME.3$ = "" THEN 6200
6100 PRINT ITEM.3.NUMBER(RFS);TAB(13);ITEM.3.QTY(RFS);TAB(30);
6110 PRINT ITEM.NAME.3$;TAB(55);
6120 PRINT USING "5&.2&";ITEM.3.UNIT.PRICE(RFS);
6130 PRINT TAB(70);"";:PRINT USING "5&.2&";ITEM.3.EXTENSION
6140 IF ITEM.NAME.4$ = "" THEN 6200
6150 PRINT ITEM.4.NUMBER(RFS);TAB(13);ITEM.4.QTY(RFS);TAB(30);
6160 PRINT ITEM.NAME.4$;TAB(55);
6170 PRINT USING "5&.2&";ITEM.4.UNIT.PRICE(RFS);
6180 PRINT TAB(70);"";:PRINT USING "5&.2&";ITEM.4.EXTENSION
6190 PRINT TAB(68);"------------"
6200 AMOUNT.OF.INVOICE(RFS) = 0
6210 AMOUNT.OF.INVOICE(RFS) = AMOUNT.OF.INVOICE(RFS) + ITEM.1.EXTENSION
6220 AMOUNT.OF.INVOICE(RFS) = AMOUNT.OF.INVOICE(RFS) + ITEM.2.EXTENSION
6230 AMOUNT.OF.INVOICE(RFS) = AMOUNT.OF.INVOICE(RFS) + ITEM.3.EXTENSION
6240 AMOUNT.OF.INVOICE(RFS) = AMOUNT.OF.INVOICE(RFS) + ITEM.4.EXTENSION
6250 PRINT "AMOUNT DUE:";
6260 PRINT TAB(68);"";:PRINT USING "$5&.2&";AMOUNT.OF.INVOICE(RFS)
6270 AMOUNT.LESS.THAN.30.DAYS(RFS) = AMOUNT.OF.INVOICE(RFS)
6280 PRINT TAB(68);"============"
6290 RETURN
6300 REM ****************************************
6310 REM * ROUTINE TO PRINT THE INVOICE DETAIL *
6320 REM ****************************************
6330 OPEN #3,".PRINTER"
6340 OUTPUT #3
6350 PRINT "ITEM";TAB(10);"QUANTITY";TAB(30);"DESCRIPTION";
6360 PRINT TAB(60);"PRICE";TAB(70);"EXTENSION"
6370 ITEM.1.EXTENSION = (ITEM.1.QTY(RFS) * ITEM.1.UNIT.PRICE(RFS))
6380 ITEM.2.EXTENSION = (ITEM.2.QTY(RFS) * ITEM.2.UNIT.PRICE(RFS))
6390 ITEM.3.EXTENSION = (ITEM.3.QTY(RFS) * ITEM.3.UNIT.PRICE(RFS))
6400 ITEM.4.EXTENSION = (ITEM.4.QTY(RFS) * ITEM.4.UNIT.PRICE(RFS))
6410 FOR N = 1 TO 79:PRINT "-";:NEXT N
6420 PRINT ITEM.1.NUMBER(RFS);TAB(13);ITEM.1.QTY(RFS);TAB(30);
6430 PRINT ITEM.NAME.1$;TAB(55);
6440 PRINT USING "5&.2&";ITEM.1.UNIT.PRICE(RFS);
6450 PRINT TAB(70);"";:PRINT USING "5&.2&";ITEM.1.EXTENSION
6460 IF ITEM.NAME.2$ = "" THEN 6640
```

Figure 6.23. (continued)

```
6470 PRINT
6480 PRINT ITEM.2.NUMBER(RFS);TAB(13);ITEM.2.QTY(RFS);TAB(30);
6490 PRINT ITEM.NAME.2$;TAB(55);
6500 PRINT USING "5&.2&";ITEM.2.UNIT.PRICE(RFS);
6510 PRINT TAB(70);"";:PRINT USING "5&.2&";ITEM.2.EXTENSION
6520 IF ITEM.NAME.3$ = "" THEN 6640
6530 PRINT
6540 PRINT ITEM.3.NUMBER(RFS);TAB(13);ITEM.3.QTY(RFS);TAB(30);
6550 PRINT ITEM.NAME.3$;TAB(55);
6560 PRINT USING "5&.2&";ITEM.3.UNIT.PRICE(RFS);
6570 PRINT TAB(70);"";:PRINT USING "5&.2&";ITEM.3.EXTENSION
6580 IF ITEM.NAME.4$ = "" THEN 6640
6590 PRINT
6600 PRINT ITEM.4.NUMBER(RFS);TAB(13);ITEM.4.QTY(RFS);TAB(30);
6610 PRINT ITEM.NAME.4$;TAB(55);
6620 PRINT USING "5&.2&";ITEM.4.UNIT.PRICE(RFS);
6630 PRINT TAB(70);"";:PRINT USING "5&.2&";ITEM.4.EXTENSION
6640 PRINT TAB(68);"-------------"
6650 PRINT
6660 AMOUNT.OF.INVOICE(RFS) = 0
6670 AMOUNT.OF.INVOICE(RFS) = AMOUNT.OF.INVOICE(RFS) + ITEM.1.EXTENSION
6680 AMOUNT.OF.INVOICE(RFS) = AMOUNT.OF.INVOICE(RFS) + ITEM.2.EXTENSION
6690 AMOUNT.OF.INVOICE(RFS) = AMOUNT.OF.INVOICE(RFS) + ITEM.3.EXTENSION
6700 AMOUNT.OF.INVOICE(RFS) = AMOUNT.OF.INVOICE(RFS) + ITEM.4.EXTENSION
6710 PRINT "AMOUNT DUE:";
6720 PRINT TAB(68);"";:PRINT USING "$5&.2&";AMOUNT.OF.INVOICE(RFS)
6730 AMOUNT.LESS.THAN.30.DAYS(RFS) = AMOUNT.OF.INVOICE(RFS)
6740 PRINT TAB(68);"============="
6750 CLOSE #3
6760 RETURN
6770 REM ***************************************
6780 REM * ROUTINE TO DISPLAY THE AGING DETAIL *
6790 REM ***************************************
6800 FOR N = 1 TO 79:PRINT "-";:NEXT N
6810 PRINT "30 DAYS OR LESS";TAB(20);"30 - 60 DAYS";TAB(40);
6820 PRINT "60 - 90 DAYS";TAB(60);"90 DAYS AND OVER"
6830 PRINT USING "$5&.2&";AMOUNT.LESS.THAN.30.DAYS(I);
6840 PRINT TAB(20);"";
6850 PRINT USING "$5&.2&";AMOUNT.AT.30.DAYS(I);
6860 PRINT TAB(37);"";
6870 PRINT USING "$5&.2&";AMOUNT.AT.60.DAYS(I);
6880 PRINT TAB(57);"";
6890 PRINT USING "$5&.2&";AMOUNT.AT.90.DAYS(I)
6900 FOR N = 1 TO 79:PRINT "-";:NEXT N
6910 RETURN
6920 REM *************************************
6930 REM * ROUTINE TO PRINT THE AGING DETAIL *
6940 REM *************************************
6950 OPEN #3,".PRINTER"
6960 OUTPUT #3
6970 FOR N = 1 TO 79:PRINT "-";:NEXT N
6980 PRINT "30 DAYS OR LESS";TAB(20);"30 - 60 DAYS";TAB(40);
6990 PRINT "60 - 90 DAYS";TAB(60);"90 DAYS AND OVER"
7000 PRINT USING "$5&.2&";AMOUNT.LESS.THAN.30.DAYS(I);
7010 PRINT TAB(20);"";
7020 PRINT USING "$5&.2&";AMOUNT.AT.30.DAYS(I);
7030 PRINT TAB(37);"";
7040 PRINT USING "$5&.2&";AMOUNT.AT.60.DAYS(I);
7050 PRINT TAB(57);"";
7060 PRINT USING "$5&.2&";AMOUNT.AT.90.DAYS(I)
7070 PRINT
7080 FOR N = 1 TO 79:PRINT "-";:NEXT N
7090 CLOSE #3
7100 RETURN
```

Figure 6.23. (continued)

The opening of this program asks for a date which can be used on invoices. Recall that a system date can be established for the Apple III. You may wish to use it here. Until then, it's incumbent upon you to enter the date *as you would like it to appear.* Once entered, it is presented for your confirmation.

In statements 880–940, the words corresponding to the line number selected are displayed, and the display is frozen. The response is then changed from a string variable to a numeric variable and used both in the range check of statement 980 and in the ON ... GOTO of statement 1050.

The CHAIN statements to call programs that are not incorporated are located in statements 2940–3060. It is possible to repeat the program, but the dimensioning must be removed to do so. If the program is terminated, the frame program is called in statement 3520.

The commonly used routines begin in statement 3530. Note the contents of the receivables file. There is a customer number (which can be different from the record number, as we have previously discussed), the date of the invoice, the number of the invoice, and the provision for four items. Again, the design maximum was set at four items – a design choice made because of the size of the system and the available media. You may wish to change the posting program so that it will merely separate records to a dead file rather than cancel them. If you do so, then you will have the basis for developing sales statistics over an extended and cyclical period.

The aging information is part of the record. Note that the aging is performed at the invoice level. You will see later that it is done within category and that the accumulated interest is reflected as an additional line item to the statement. We'll have more to say about that when the POSTREC, STATMENT, and AGING programs are discussed.

The rest of this program is fairly straightforward and easily understood. Figure 6.24 is a block diagram of the RECIVBLE program. Figure 6.25 shows the logical relationship of the subordinated programs.

The program either builds RECEIVE.DAT from scratch or adds to it. The invoice data combines information from the customer and product files in the preparation of invoice data. The actual production of the invoice takes place in INVOICE. In like manner, statements are produced in STATMENT. Records are posted and aged in the subordinate programs POSTREC and AGING, respectively.

ACCOUNTS RECEIVABLE SUBSYSTEM
RECIVBLE
INITIAL ENTRY
RECIVBLE
ADDING INVOICES
RECIVBLE
PRODUCING INVOICES
INVOICE
PRODUCING REPORTS
RECIVBLE
POSTING PAYMENTS
POSTREC
PRODUCING STATEMENTS
STATMENT
AGE THE ACCOUNTS-
AGING

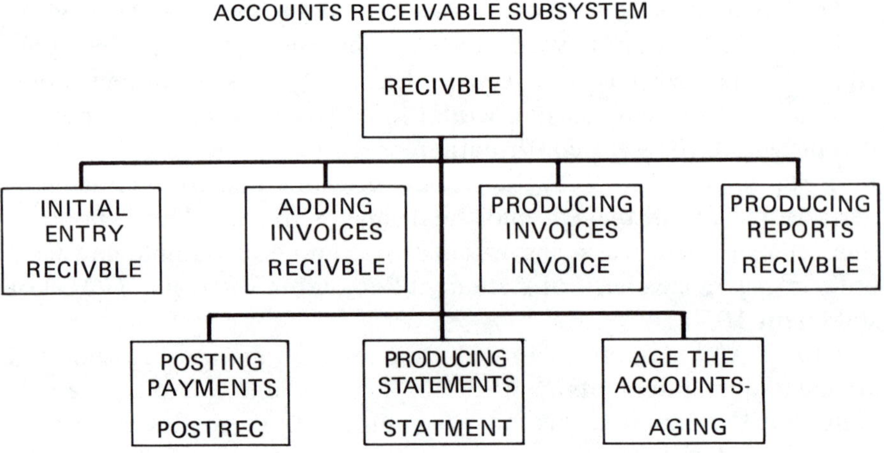

Figure 6.24.

ACCOUNTS RECEIVABLE SUBSYSTEM
RECEIVE .DAT
CUSTOMER .DAT
KEYBOARD
PRODUCT .DAT
DISPLAY
RECIVBLE
INVOICE
UPDATED RECEIVE .DAT
ACCOUNTS RECEIVABLE REPORTS
POSTREC
STATMENT
AGING

Figure 6.25.

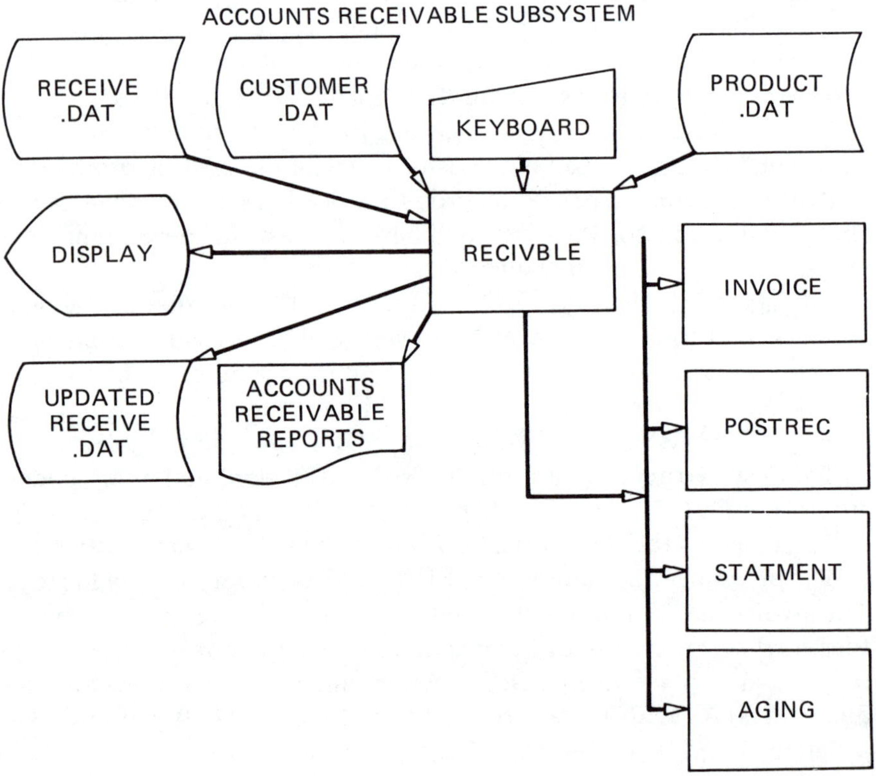

INVOICE

The invoicing program takes the file developed in RECIVBLE and transfers it to paper. You'll see the date is entered and affirmed, as before. In the illustration which follows, a narrative date is entered.

It is possible to specify a beginning place: either those invoices that have been produced on the date of the run or a beginning invoice number if you are unable to run the invoices on the day they are prepared.

In the same manner as the invoices are displayed on the screen, they are transferred to paper, with the exception that the paper is ejected between invoices. That is the purpose of the PRINT CHR$(12). A block diagram for the invoicing application appears in Figure 6.26.

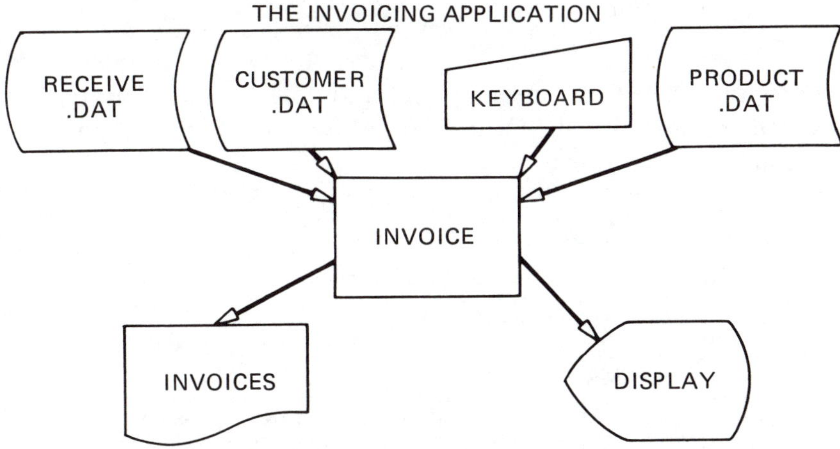

Figure 6.26.

This program, which is subordinate to RECIVBLE, takes the information written to file by that program and produces display and paper output. If a given starting place is desired, it may be specified; otherwise, the invoices for the entire file are produced.

The invoice produced looks like Figure 6.27.

One of the things you learn as you do more and more programing is that you must plan for many contingencies. Since there is a possibility that the invoice application will become tied to the statement application, a routine has been included to obtain input from the specified account file. That routine is not invoked in the program; it is merely there in case it is needed.

```
INVOICE NUMBER: 555                                         DATE: MAY 24, 1983

CUSTOMER NAME:                  MR. BENJAMIN WATERS
CUSTOMER ADDRESS:               IMAGINATION INTERPRETED
                                327 PAGE ROAD
                                WATERTOWN,
                                PENNSYLVANIA 17443

-------------------------------------------------------------------------------
ITEM      QUANTITY              DESCRIPTION                  PRICE     EXTENSION
 1            1                 WIDGET                      111.11        111.11

 2            2                 GIZMO                       222.22        444.44
                                                                     -----------

AMOUNT DUE                                                                555.55
                                                                     ===========

-------------------------------------------------------------------------------
30 DAYS OR LESS     30 - 60 DAYS      60 - 90 DAYS      90 DAYS AND OVER
   $555.55            $0.00             $0.00              $0.00

-------------------------------------------------------------------------------
```

Figure 6.27.

Note that when the program is complete, it CHAINs back to RECIVBLE, *not* to BUSINESS. In other words, the chain is followed in both directions.

The program INVOICE is given in Figure 6.28.

```
10 GOSUB 1760
20 INVOICE.MONTH$ = LEFT$(DATE$,2)
30 INVOICE.DAY$ = MID$(DATE$,4,2)
40 INVOICE.YEAR$ = RIGHT$(DATE$,4)
50 IF VAL(INVOICE.MONTH$) = 1 THEN INVOICE.MONTH$ = "JANUARY"
60 IF VAL(INVOICE.MONTH$) = 2 THEN INVOICE.MONTH$ = "FEBRUARY"
70 IF VAL(INVOICE.MONTH$) = 3 THEN INVOICE.MONTH$ = "MARCH"
80 IF VAL(INVOICE.MONTH$) = 4 THEN INVOICE.MONTH$ = "APRIL"
90 IF VAL(INVOICE.MONTH$) = 5 THEN INVOICE.MONTH$ = "MAY"
100 IF VAL(INVOICE.MONTH$) = 6 THEN INVOICE.MONTH$ = "JUNE"
110 IF VAL(INVOICE.MONTH$) = 7 THEN INVOICE.MONTH$ = "JULY"
120 IF VAL(INVOICE.MONTH$) = 8 THEN INVOICE.MONTH$ = "AUGUST"
130 IF VAL(INVOICE.MONTH$) = 9 THEN INVOICE.MONTH$ = "SEPTEMBER"
140 IF VAL(INVOICE.MONTH$) = 10 THEN INVOICE.MONTH$ = "OCTOBER"
150 IF VAL(INVOICE.MONTH$) = 11 THEN INVOICE.MONTH$ = "NOVEMBER"
160 IF VAL(INVOICE.MONTH$) = 12 THEN INVOICE.MONTH$ = "DECEMBER"
170 INVOICE.MONTH$ = INVOICE.MONTH$ + " "
180 INVOICE.DATE$ = INVOICE.MONTH$ + INVOICE.DAY$ + ", " + INVOICE.YEAR$
190 PRINT
200 PRINT INVOICE.DATE$
210 REM ***********************************
220 REM * DIMENSION THE RECEIVABLES FILE. *
230 REM ***********************************
240 DIM CUSTOMER.NUMBER(100)
250 DIM DATE.OF.INVOICE$(100)
260 DIM DOCUMENT.NUMBER(100)
270 DIM ITEM.1.NUMBER(100)
280 DIM ITEM.1.QTY(100)
```

Figure 6.28.

```
290 DIM ITEM.1.UNIT.PRICE(100)
300 DIM ITEM.2.NUMBER(100)
310 DIM ITEM.2.QTY(100)
320 DIM ITEM.2.UNIT.PRICE(100)
330 DIM ITEM.3.NUMBER(100)
340 DIM ITEM.3.QTY(100)
350 DIM ITEM.3.UNIT.PRICE(100)
360 DIM ITEM.4.NUMBER(100)
370 DIM ITEM.4.QTY(100)
380 DIM ITEM.4.UNIT.PRICE(100)
390 DIM AMOUNT.OF.INVOICE(100)
400 DIM AMOUNT.LESS.THAN.30.DAYS(100)
410 DIM AMOUNT.AT.30.DAYS(100)
420 DIM AMOUNT.AT.60.DAYS(100)
430 DIM AMOUNT.AT.90.DAYS(100)
440 REM ******************************
450 REM * DIMENSION THE PRODUCT FILE. *
460 REM ******************************
470 DIM PRODUCT.NAME$(100)
480 DIM PRODUCT.DESCR$(100)
490 DIM PRODUCT.UNIT$(100)
500 DIM PRODUCT.LOCATION$(100)
510 DIM PRODUCT.Q.O.H(100)
520 DIM PRODUCT.R.O.P(100)
530 DIM PRODUCT.SHIP.INSTR$(100)
540 REM *******************************
550 REM * DIMENSION THE CUSTOMER FILE. *
560 REM *******************************
570 DIM CUSTOMER.NAME$(100)
580 DIM CUSTOMER.ADDR.1$(100)
590 DIM CUSTOMER.ADDR.2$(100)
600 DIM CUSTOMER.ADDR.3$(100)
610 DIM CUSTOMER.ADDR.4$(100)
620 DIM CUSTOMER.TERMS$(100)
630 REM ******************************
640 REM * DIMENSION THE ACCOUNT FILE. *
650 REM ******************************
660 DIM T$(100)
670 DIM N$(100)
680 DIM A(100)
690 REM ***************************************
700 REM * INVOICE DISPLAY AND PRINTING ROUTINE *
710 REM ***************************************
720 GOSUB 2480          :REM GET THE PRODUCT FILE
730 GOSUB 2650          :REM GET THE CUSTOMER FILE
740 GOSUB 1870          :REM GET THE RECEIVABLES FILE
750 PRINT:PRINT "DO YOU WISH TO BEGIN WITH TODAY'S INVOICE (Y/N)? ";
760 GET Z$
770 PRINT Z$
780 IF Z$ < > "Y" THEN SPECIFIED.INVOICE$ = "NO":GOTO 800
790 SPECIFIED.INVOICE$ = "YES"
800 GOSUB 1760          :REM GET THE HEADING
810 PRINT
820 PRINT "DO YOU WISH A HARDCOPY OUTPUT (Y/N)? ";
830 GET Z$
840 PRINT Z$
850 IF Z$ < > "Y" THEN HARDCOPY$ = "NO":GOTO 870
860 HARDCOPY$ = "YES"
870 PRINT "UNINTERRUPTED PRINTING - 'N' CAUSES PAUSE WITH EACH - (Y/N)? ";
880 GET Z$
890 PRINT Z$
900 IF Z$ < > "Y" THEN CONTINUE$ = "NO":GOTO 920
910 CONTINUE$ = "YES"
920 FOR I = 1 TO RECEIVE.FILE.SIZE
930     ITEM.NAME.1$ = PRODUCT.NAME$(ITEM.1.NUMBER(I))
```

Figure 6.28. (continued)

```
940       ITEM.NAME.2$ = PRODUCT.NAME$(ITEM.2.NUMBER(I))
950       ITEM.NAME.3$ = PRODUCT.NAME$(ITEM.3.NUMBER(I))
960       ITEM.NAME.4$ = PRODUCT.NAME$(ITEM.4.NUMBER(I))
970       WHICH.CUST = I
980       RFS = I
990       IF SPECIFIED.INVOICE$ = "NO" THEN 1010
1000      IF DOCUMENT.NUMBER(I) < INVOICE.NUMBER THEN 1240
1010      PRINT
1020      PRINT "ACCOUNT NUMBER: ";I
1030      PRINT "INVOICE.NUMBER";DOCUMENT.NUMBER(I);
1040      PRINT TAB(50);"DATE: ";DATE.OF.INVOICE$(I)
1050      GOSUB 2960
1060      FOR N = 1 TO 79:PRINT "-";:NEXT N
1070      GOSUB 3170
1080      GOSUB 4050
1090      IF CONTINUE$ = "YES" THEN 1110
1100      GET Z$
1110      IF HARDCOPY$ = "NO" THEN 1240
1120      PRINT
1130      PRINT
1140      PRINT "INVOICE.NUMBER";DOCUMENT.NUMBER(I);
1150      PRINT TAB(50);"DATE: ";DATE.OF.INVOICE$(I)
1160      GOSUB 3050
1170      PRINT
1180      FOR N = 1 TO 79:PRINT "-";:NEXT N
1190      PRINT
1200      GOSUB 3570
1210      PRINT
1220      GOSUB 4200
1230      PRINT CHR$(12)
1240      NEXT I
1250 GOSUB 1760                       :REM GET THE HEADING
1260 REM ***********************
1270 REM * PROGRAM TERMINATION *
1280 REM ***********************
1290 PRINT
1300 PRINT "INVOICE PREPARATION IS COMPLETE"
1310 PRINT
1320 PRINT "DO YOU WISH TO REPEAT THE PROGRAM (Y/N)? ";
1330 GET Z$
1340 PRINT Z$
1350 IF Z$ < > "Y" THEN 1750
1360 FOR N = 1 TO 100
1370      CUSTOMER.NUMBER(N) = 0
1380      DATE.OF.INVOICE$(N) = ""
1390      DOCUMENT.NUMBER(N) = 0
1400      ITEM.1.NUMBER(N) = 0
1410      ITEM.1.QTY(N) = 0
1420      ITEM.1.UNIT.PRICE(N) = 0
1430      ITEM.2.NUMBER(N) = 0
1440      ITEM.2.QTY(N) = 0
1450      ITEM.2.UNIT.PRICE(N) = 0
1460      ITEM.3.NUMBER(N) = 0
1470      ITEM.3.QTY(N) = 0
1480      ITEM.3.UNIT.PRICE(N) = 0
1490      ITEM.4.NUMBER(N) = 0
1500      ITEM.4.QTY(N) = 0
1510      ITEM.4.UNIT.PRICE(N) = 0
1520      AMOUNT.OF.INVOICE(N) = 0
1530      AMOUNT.LESS.THAN.30.DAYS(N) = 0
1540      AMOUNT.AT.30.DAYS(N) = 0
1550      AMOUNT.AT.60.DAYS(N) = 0
1560      AMOUNT.AT.90.DAYS(N) = 0
1570      PRODUCT.NAME$(N) = ""
1580      PRODUCT.DESCR$(N) = ""
```

Figure 6.28. (continued)

```
1590      PRODUCT.UNIT$(N) = ""
1600      PRODUCT.LOCATION$(N) = ""
1610      PRODUCT.Q.O.H(N) = 0
1620      PRODUCT.R.O.P(N) = 0
1630      PRODUCT.SHIP.INSTR$(N) = ""
1640      CUSTOMER.NAME$(N) = ""
1650      CUSTOMER.ADDR.1$(N) = ""
1660      CUSTOMER.ADDR.2$(N) = ""
1670      CUSTOMER.ADDR.3$(N) = ""
1680      CUSTOMER.ADDR.4$(N) = ""
1690      CUSTOMER.TERMS$(N) = ""
1700      T$(N) = ""
1710      N$(N) = ""
1720      A(N) = 0
1730      NEXT N
1740 GOTO 10
1750 CHAIN .D2/RECIVBLE
1760 REM ********************************
1770 REM * HEADING USED FOR THE DISPLAY *
1780 REM ********************************
1790 HOME
1800 X = ((80 - LEN(COMPANY.NAME$)) / 2)
1810 VPOS=2:HPOS=X
1820 PRINT COMPANY.NAME$
1830 FOR N = 1 TO 79:PRINT "-";:NEXT N:PRINT
1840 PRINT TAB(19);"ACCOUNTS RECEIVABLE PROCESSING PROGRAM"
1850 FOR N = 1 TO 79:PRINT "-";:NEXT N
1860 RETURN
1870 REM **********************************
1880 REM * OPEN AND INPUT RECEIVABLE FILE *
1890 REM **********************************
1900 PRINT:PRINT "LOADING THE RECEIVABLES FILE"
1910 OPEN #1,.D2/RECEIVE.DAT
1920 INPUT #1,RECEIVE.FILE.SIZE       :REM OBTAIN THE RECORD COUNT
1930 FOR I = 1 TO RECEIVE.FILE.SIZE
1940      INPUT #1,CUSTOMER.NUMBER(I)
1950      INPUT #1,DATE.OF.INVOICE$(I)
1960      INPUT #1,DOCUMENT.NUMBER(I)
1970      INPUT #1,ITEM.1.NUMBER(I)
1980      INPUT #1,ITEM.1.QTY(I)
1990      INPUT #1,ITEM.1.UNIT.PRICE(I)
2000      INPUT #1,ITEM.2.NUMBER(I)
2010      INPUT #1,ITEM.2.QTY(I)
2020      INPUT #1,ITEM.2.UNIT.PRICE(I)
2030      INPUT #1,ITEM.3.NUMBER(I)
2040      INPUT #1,ITEM.3.QTY(I)
2050      INPUT #1,ITEM.3.UNIT.PRICE(I)
2060      INPUT #1,ITEM.4.NUMBER(I)
2070      INPUT #1,ITEM.4.QTY(I)
2080      INPUT #1,ITEM.4.UNIT.PRICE(I)
2090      INPUT #1,AMOUNT.OF.INVOICE(I)
2100      INPUT #1,AMOUNT.LESS.THAN.30.DAYS(I)
2110      INPUT #1,AMOUNT.AT.30.DAYS(I)
2120      INPUT #1,AMOUNT.AT.60.DAYS(I)
2130      INPUT #1,AMOUNT.AT.90.DAYS(I)
2140      NEXT I
2150 CLOSE #1
2160 RETURN
2170 REM ***********************************
2180 REM * OPEN AND OUTPUT RECEIVABLE FILE *
2190 REM ***********************************
2200 PRINT:PRINT "WRITING THE RECEIVABLES FILE"
2210 CREATE ".D2/RECEIVE.DAT",TEXT
2220 OPEN #1,.D2/RECEIVE.DAT
2230 PRINT #1,RECEIVE.FILE.SIZE       :REM STORE THE RECORD COUNT
```

Figure 6.28. (continued)

```
2240 FOR I = 1 TO RECEIVE.FILE.SIZE
2250      PRINT #1,CUSTOMER.NUMBER(I)
2260      PRINT #1,DATE.OF.INVOICE$(I)
2270      PRINT #1,DOCUMENT.NUMBER(I)
2280      PRINT #1,ITEM.1.NUMBER(I)
2290      PRINT #1,ITEM.1.QTY(I)
2300      PRINT #1,ITEM.1.UNIT.PRICE(I)
2310      PRINT #1,ITEM.2.NUMBER(I)
2320      PRINT #1,ITEM.2.QTY(I)
2330      PRINT #1,ITEM.2.UNIT.PRICE(I)
2340      PRINT #1,ITEM.3.NUMBER(I)
2350      PRINT #1,ITEM.3.QTY(I)
2360      PRINT #1,ITEM.3.UNIT.PRICE(I)
2370      PRINT #1,ITEM.4.NUMBER(I)
2380      PRINT #1,ITEM.4.QTY(I)
2390      PRINT #1,ITEM.4.UNIT.PRICE(I)
2400      PRINT #1,AMOUNT.OF.INVOICE(I)
2410      PRINT #1,AMOUNT.LESS.THAN.30.DAYS(I)
2420      PRINT #1,AMOUNT.AT.30.DAYS(I)
2430      PRINT #1,AMOUNT.AT.60.DAYS(I)
2440      PRINT #1,AMOUNT.AT.90.DAYS(I)
2450      NEXT I
2460 CLOSE #1
2470 RETURN
2480 REM ********************************
2490 REM * OPEN AND INPUT PRODUCT FILE *
2500 REM ********************************
2510 PRINT:PRINT "LOADING THE PRODUCT FILE"
2520 OPEN #1,.D2/PRODUCT.DAT
2530 INPUT #1,PRODUCT.FILE.SIZE       :REM OBTAIN THE RECORD COUNT
2540 FOR J = 1 TO PRODUCT.FILE.SIZE
2550      INPUT #1,PRODUCT.NAME$(J)
2560      INPUT #1,PRODUCT.DESCR$(J)
2570      INPUT #1,PRODUCT.UNIT$(J)
2580      INPUT #1,PRODUCT.LOCATION$(J)
2590      INPUT #1,PRODUCT.Q.O.H(J)
2600      INPUT #1,PRODUCT.R.O.P(J)
2610      INPUT #1,PRODUCT.SHIP.INSTR$(J)
2620      NEXT J
2630 CLOSE #1
2640 RETURN
2650 REM *********************************
2660 REM * OPEN AND INPUT CUSTOMER FILE *
2670 REM *********************************
2680 PRINT:PRINT "LOADING THE CUSTOMER FILE"
2690 OPEN #1,.D2/CUSTOMER.DAT
2700 INPUT #1,CUSTOMER.FILE.SIZE     :REM OBTAIN THE RECORD COUNT
2710 FOR K = 1 TO CUSTOMER.FILE.SIZE
2720      INPUT #1,CUSTOMER.NAME$(K)
2730      INPUT #1,CUSTOMER.ADDR.1$(K)
2740      INPUT #1,CUSTOMER.ADDR.2$(K)
2750      INPUT #1,CUSTOMER.ADDR.3$(K)
2760      INPUT #1,CUSTOMER.ADDR.4$(K)
2770      INPUT #1,CUSTOMER.TERMS$(K)
2780      NEXT K
2790 CLOSE #1
2800 RETURN
2810 REM ********************************
2820 REM * OPEN AND INPUT ACCOUNT FILE *
2830 REM ********************************
2840 PRINT:PRINT "LOADING THE ACCOUNT FILE"
2850 PRINT:INPUT "SPECIFY THE ACCOUNT FILE TO BE USED: ",SPECIFIED.FILE$
2860 SPECIFIED.FILE$ = ".D2/" + SPECIFIED.FILE$ + ".DAT"
2870 OPEN #1,SPECIFIED.FILE$
2880 INPUT #1,SPECIFIED.FILE.SIZE     :REM OBTAIN THE RECORD COUNT
```

Figure 6.28. (continued)

```
2890 FOR L = 1 TO SPECIFIED.FILE.SIZE
2900      INPUT #1,T$(L)
2910      INPUT #1,N$(L)
2920      INPUT #1,A(L)
2930      NEXT L
2940 CLOSE #1
2950 RETURN
2960 REM ************************************************************
2970 REM * ROUTINE USED MORE THAN ONCE TO DISPLAY THE CUSTOMER INFO *
2980 REM ************************************************************
2990 PRINT "CUSTOMER.NAME:";TAB(25);CUSTOMER.NAME$(WHICH.CUST)
3000 PRINT "CUSTOMER ADDRESS:";TAB(25);CUSTOMER.ADDR.1$(WHICH.CUST)
3010 PRINT TAB(25);CUSTOMER.ADDR.2$(WHICH.CUST)
3020 PRINT TAB(25);CUSTOMER.ADDR.3$(WHICH.CUST)
3030 PRINT TAB(25);CUSTOMER.ADDR.4$(WHICH.CUST)
3040 RETURN
3050 REM **********************************************************
3060 REM * ROUTINE USED MORE THAN ONCE TO PRINT THE CUSTOMER INFO *
3070 REM **********************************************************
3080 OPEN #3,".PRINTER"
3090 OUTPUT #3
3100 PRINT "CUSTOMER.NAME:";TAB(25);CUSTOMER.NAME$(WHICH.CUST)
3110 PRINT "CUSTOMER ADDRESS:";TAB(25);CUSTOMER.ADDR.1$(WHICH.CUST)
3120 PRINT TAB(25);CUSTOMER.ADDR.2$(WHICH.CUST)
3130 PRINT TAB(25);CUSTOMER.ADDR.3$(WHICH.CUST)
3140 PRINT TAB(25);CUSTOMER.ADDR.4$(WHICH.CUST)
3150 CLOSE #3
3160 RETURN
3170 REM *****************************************
3180 REM * ROUTINE TO DISPLAY THE INVOICE DETAIL *
3190 REM *****************************************
3200 PRINT "ITEM";TAB(10);"QUANTITY";TAB(30);"DESCRIPTION";
3210 PRINT TAB(60);"PRICE";TAB(70);"EXTENSION"
3220 ITEM.1.EXTENSION = (ITEM.1.QTY(RFS) * ITEM.1.UNIT.PRICE(RFS))
3230 ITEM.2.EXTENSION = (ITEM.2.QTY(RFS) * ITEM.2.UNIT.PRICE(RFS))
3240 ITEM.3.EXTENSION = (ITEM.3.QTY(RFS) * ITEM.3.UNIT.PRICE(RFS))
3250 ITEM.4.EXTENSION = (ITEM.4.QTY(RFS) * ITEM.4.UNIT.PRICE(RFS))
3260 FOR N = 1 TO 79:PRINT "-";:NEXT N
3270 PRINT ITEM.1.NUMBER(RFS);TAB(13);ITEM.1.QTY(RFS);TAB(30);
3280 PRINT ITEM.NAME.1$;TAB(55);
3290 PRINT USING "5&.2&";ITEM.1.UNIT.PRICE(RFS);
3300 PRINT TAB(70);"";:PRINT USING "5&.2&";ITEM.1.EXTENSION
3310 IF ITEM.NAME.2$ = "" THEN 3470
3320 PRINT ITEM.2.NUMBER(RFS);TAB(13);ITEM.2.QTY(RFS);TAB(30);
3330 PRINT ITEM.NAME.2$;TAB(55);
3340 PRINT USING "5&.2&";ITEM.2.UNIT.PRICE(RFS);
3350 PRINT TAB(70);"";:PRINT USING "5&.2&";ITEM.2.EXTENSION
3360 IF ITEM.NAME.3$ = "" THEN 3470
3370 PRINT ITEM.3.NUMBER(RFS);TAB(13);ITEM.3.QTY(RFS);TAB(30);
3380 PRINT ITEM.NAME.3$;TAB(55);
3390 PRINT USING "5&.2&";ITEM.3.UNIT.PRICE(RFS);
3400 PRINT TAB(70);"";:PRINT USING "5&.2&";ITEM.3.EXTENSION
3410 IF ITEM.NAME.4$ = "" THEN 3470
3420 PRINT ITEM.4.NUMBER(RFS);TAB(13);ITEM.4.QTY(RFS);TAB(30);
3430 PRINT ITEM.NAME.4$;TAB(55);
3440 PRINT USING "5&.2&";ITEM.4.UNIT.PRICE(RFS);
3450 PRINT TAB(70);"";:PRINT USING "5&.2&";ITEM.4.EXTENSION
3460 PRINT TAB(68);"-----------"
3470 AMOUNT.OF.INVOICE(RFS) = 0
3480 AMOUNT.OF.INVOICE(RFS) = AMOUNT.OF.INVOICE(RFS) + ITEM.1.EXTENSION
3490 AMOUNT.OF.INVOICE(RFS) = AMOUNT.OF.INVOICE(RFS) + ITEM.2.EXTENSION
3500 AMOUNT.OF.INVOICE(RFS) = AMOUNT.OF.INVOICE(RFS) + ITEM.3.EXTENSION
3510 AMOUNT.OF.INVOICE(RFS) = AMOUNT.OF.INVOICE(RFS) + ITEM.4.EXTENSION
3520 PRINT "AMOUNT DUE:";
3530 PRINT TAB(68);"";:PRINT USING "$5&.2&";AMOUNT.OF.INVOICE(RFS)
```

Figure 6.28. (continued)

```
3540 AMOUNT.LESS.THAN.30.DAYS(RFS) = AMOUNT.OF.INVOICE(RFS)
3550 PRINT TAB(68);"============="
3560 RETURN
3570 REM ****************************************
3580 REM * ROUTINE TO PRINT THE INVOICE DETAIL *
3590 REM ****************************************
3600 OPEN #3,".PRINTER"
3610 OUTPUT #3
3620 PRINT "ITEM";TAB(10);"QUANTITY";TAB(30);"DESCRIPTION";
3630 PRINT TAB(60);"PRICE";TAB(70);"EXTENSION"
3640 FOR N = 1 TO 79:PRINT "-";:NEXT N
3650 ITEM.1.EXTENSION = (ITEM.1.QTY(RFS) * ITEM.1.UNIT.PRICE(RFS))
3660 ITEM.2.EXTENSION = (ITEM.2.QTY(RFS) * ITEM.2.UNIT.PRICE(RFS))
3670 ITEM.3.EXTENSION = (ITEM.3.QTY(RFS) * ITEM.3.UNIT.PRICE(RFS))
3680 ITEM.4.EXTENSION = (ITEM.4.QTY(RFS) * ITEM.4.UNIT.PRICE(RFS))
3690 FOR N = 1 TO 79:PRINT "-";:NEXT N
3700 PRINT ITEM.1.NUMBER(RFS);TAB(13);ITEM.1.QTY(RFS);TAB(30);
3710 PRINT ITEM.NAME.1$;TAB(55);
3720 PRINT USING "5&.2&";ITEM.1.UNIT.PRICE(RFS);
3730 PRINT TAB(70);"";:PRINT USING "5&.2&";ITEM.1.EXTENSION
3740 IF ITEM.NAME.2$ = "" THEN 3920
3750 PRINT
3760 PRINT ITEM.2.NUMBER(RFS);TAB(13);ITEM.2.QTY(RFS);TAB(30);
3770 PRINT ITEM.NAME.2$;TAB(55);
3780 PRINT USING "5&.2&";ITEM.2.UNIT.PRICE(RFS);
3790 PRINT TAB(70);"";:PRINT USING "5&.2&";ITEM.2.EXTENSION
3800 IF ITEM.NAME.3$ = "" THEN 3920
3810 PRINT
3820 PRINT ITEM.3.NUMBER(RFS);TAB(13);ITEM.3.QTY(RFS);TAB(30);
3830 PRINT ITEM.NAME.3$;TAB(55);
3840 PRINT USING "5&.2&";ITEM.3.JNIT.PRICE(RFS);
3850 PRINT TAB(70);"";:PRINT USING "5&.2&";ITEM.3.EXTENSION
3860 IF ITEM.NAME.4$ = "" THEN 3920
3870 PRINT
3880 PRINT ITEM.4.NUMBER(RFS);TAB(13);ITEM.4.QTY(RFS);TAB(30);
3890 PRINT ITEM.NAME.4$;TAB(55);
3900 PRINT USING "5&.2&";ITEM.4.UNIT.PRICE(RFS);
3910 PRINT TAB(70);"";:PRINT USING "5&.2&";ITEM.4.EXTENSION
3920 PRINT TAB(68);"-------------"
3930 PRINT
3940 AMOUNT.OF.INVOICE(RFS) = 0
3950 AMOUNT.OF.INVOICE(RFS) = AMOUNT.OF.INVOICE(RFS) + ITEM.1.EXTENSION
3960 AMOUNT.OF.INVOICE(RFS) = AMOUNT.OF.INVOICE(RFS) + ITEM.2.EXTENSION
3970 AMOUNT.OF.INVOICE(RFS) = AMOUNT.OF.INVOICE(RFS) + ITEM.3.EXTENSION
3980 AMOUNT.OF.INVOICE(RFS) = AMOUNT.OF.INVOICE(RFS) + ITEM.4.EXTENSION
3990 PRINT "AMOUNT DUE:";
4000 PRINT TAB(68);"";:PRINT USING "$5&.2&";AMOUNT.OF.INVOICE(RFS)
4010 AMOUNT.LESS.THAN.30.DAYS(RFS) = AMOUNT.OF.INVOICE(RFS)
4020 PRINT TAB(68);"============="
4030 CLOSE #3
4040 RETURN
4050 REM ****************************************
4060 REM * ROUTINE TO DISPLAY THE AGING DETAIL *
4070 REM ****************************************
4080 FOR N = 1 TO 79:PRINT "-";:NEXT N
4090 PRINT "30 DAYS OR LESS";TAB(20);"30 - 60 DAYS";TAB(40);
4100 PRINT "60 - 90 DAYS";TAB(60);"90 DAYS AND OVER"
4110 PRINT USING "$5&.2&";AMOUNT.LESS.THAN.30.DAYS(I);
4120 PRINT TAB(20);"";
4130 PRINT USING "$5&.2&";AMOUNT.AT.30.DAYS(I);
4140 PRINT TAB(37);"";
4150 PRINT USING "$5&.2&";AMOUNT.AT.60.DAYS(I);
4160 PRINT TAB(57);"";
4170 PRINT USING "$5&.2&";AMOUNT.AT.90.DAYS(I)
4180 FOR N = 1 TO 79:PRINT "-";:NEXT N
```

Figure 6.28. (continued)

```
4190 RETURN
4200 REM ************************************
4210 REM * ROUTINE TO PRINT THE AGING DETAIL *
4220 REM ************************************
4230 OPEN #3,".PRINTER"
4240 OUTPUT #3
4250 FOR N = 1 TO 79:PRINT "-";:NEXT N
4260 PRINT "30 DAYS OR LESS";TAB(20);"30 - 60 DAYS";TAB(40);
4270 PRINT "60 - 90 DAYS";TAB(60);"90 DAYS AND OVER"
4280 PRINT USING "$5&.2&";AMOUNT.LESS.THAN.30.DAYS(I);
4290 PRINT TAB(20);"";
4300 PRINT USING "$5&.2&";AMOUNT.AT.30.DAYS(I);
4310 PRINT TAB(37);"";
4320 PRINT USING "$5&.2&";AMOUNT.AT.60.DAYS(I);
4330 PRINT TAB(57);"";
4340 PRINT USING "$5&.2&";AM
4350 CLOSE #3
4360 RETURN
```

Figure 6.28. (continued)

POSTREC

The posting of the payments involves the same files as the other programs and its opening menu provides the key to the way it works. Refer to Figure 6.29.

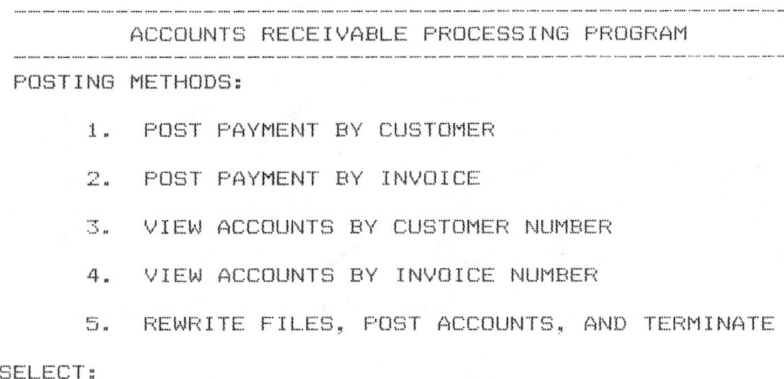

```
                SMALL BUSINESS ENTERPRISE, INC
--------------------------------------------------------------
            ACCOUNTS RECEIVABLE PROCESSING PROGRAM
--------------------------------------------------------------
POSTING METHODS:

     1.   POST PAYMENT BY CUSTOMER

     2.   POST PAYMENT BY INVOICE

     3.   VIEW ACCOUNTS BY CUSTOMER NUMBER

     4.   VIEW ACCOUNTS BY INVOICE NUMBER

     5.   REWRITE FILES, POST ACCOUNTS, AND TERMINATE

SELECT:
```

Figure 6.29.

Looking at options 3 and 4 first, let's simply state that all payments are against invoice. However, on the possibility that you don't know what the invoice number and amount are, option 3 will summarize the outstanding invoices by customer number. Each invoice can then be viewed separately. The same is true of the posting. If the posting is done by invoice, then the invoice number is specified. If it's done by customer, then you apply toward the customer's invoice. However you slice it, the payment will be made by invoice. When you tell the computer how much money it has to spend, it will continue to process payment requests until it runs out of money. If the payment is the right amount, the program simply adjusts its balances towards zero. If interest is paid, the accumulated interest is posted to the INTEREST INCOME account. If there is no such account, the program creates one for you. If the payment is too small, posting of the account attacks the oldest money first, leaving the unpaid balance in the youngest money. As you will find when we discuss the aging process, the money is aged and incremented where it is.

A block diagram for the posting application is shown in Figure 6.30.

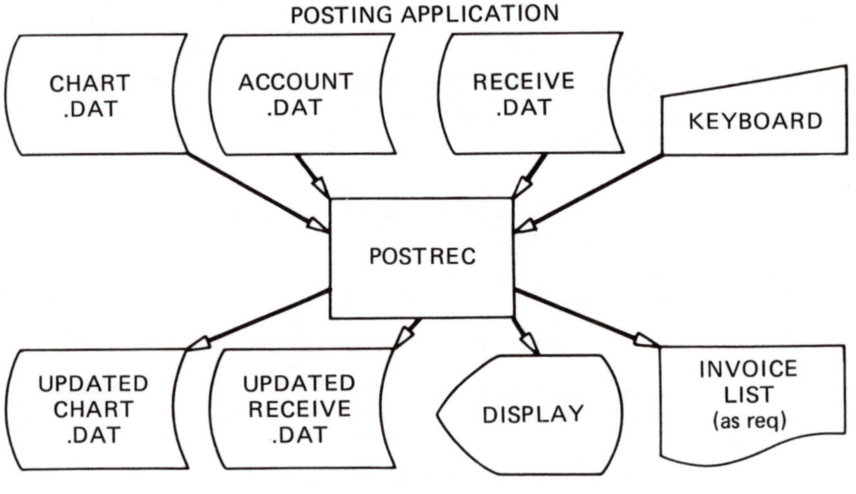

Figure 6.30.

This program takes the Chart of Accounts, the Receivables File, and the Account File for the period and allows the operator to post against the files. Payments are then posted individually or in groups. When all payments have been posted, the updated files are written back to media. Posting of accounts is detailed in the display and before and after application balances are shown to the operator.

When the program opens, an important message is presented: a display of those accounts on the Chart of Accounts and the balances from the Account File. The program will create new accounts for Cash Income and for Interest Income. For the present, no other accounts are needed if you take the specific approach offered by this system. If, however, you wish to do something more complex and want other accounts to be posted, it will be necessary to ensure that the proper account type and title have been loaded into the Chart of Accounts. Remember that the balances on the account file must be in the same sequence. A typical display of accounts and balances is shown in Figure 6.31.

The invoice is presented as in Figure 6.32.

```
                SMALL BUSINESS ENTERPRISE, INC
 -------------------------------------------------------
            ACCOUNTS RECEIVABLE PROCESSING PROGRAM
-------------------------------------------------------
I M P O R T A N T ! ! !
IF PAYMENT CANNOT BE POSTED TO THESE ACCOUNTS
YOU MUST TERMINATE HERE AND RETURN TO CHART,
FOLLOWED BY VALUE, TO ESTABLISH THE ACCOUNT.
-------------------------------------------------------
A,CASH                                       101.23
A,ACCOUNTS RECEIVABLE                      1,000.47
A,EQUIPMENT                                  200.00
A,PREPAID INSURANCE                          400.00
A,ROLLING STOCK                            4,000.00
L,ACCOUNTS PAYABLE                           637.34
L,NOTES PAYABLE                            1,245.78
C,SBE DRAW                                   209.88
I,SALES INCOME                            30,000.00
I,RENTAL INCOME                              473.00
I,ROYALTY INCOME                          20,000.00
E,RENT EXPENSE                               600.00
E,TELEPHONE EXPENSE                          225.00
E,TRAVEL EXPENSE                             110.47

DO YOU WISH TO TERMINATE (Y/N)?
```

Figure 6.31.

```
                SMALL BUSINESS ENTERPRISE, INC.
-------------------------------------------------------
            ACCOUNTS RECEIVABLE PROCESSING PROGRAM
-------------------------------------------------------
ENTER THE INVOICE NUMBER: 555

ENTER CUSTOMER NUMBER:    1
CUSTOMER NAME:            MR. BENJAMIN WATERS
CUSTOMER ADDRESS:         IMAGINATION INTERPRETED
                          327 PAGE ROAD
                          WATERTOWN,
                          PENNSYLVANIA 17743

DATE OF INVOICE: MAY 24, 1983      INVOICE NUMBER:555

AMOUNT OF INVOICE:                   5.55
ACCUMULATED INTEREST:                0.00

TOTAL DUE:                           5.55
-------------------------------------------------------
PRESS ANY KEY TO CONTINUE
```

Figure 6.32.

The program POSTREC is given in Figure 6.33.

```
10 REM **********************************
20 REM * DIMENSION THE RECEIVABLES FILE. *
30 REM **********************************
40 DIM CUSTOMER.NUMBER(100)
50 DIM DATE.OF.INVOICE$(100)
60 DIM DOCUMENT.NUMBER(100)
70 DIM ITEM.1.NUMBER(100)
80 DIM ITEM.1.QTY(100)
90 DIM ITEM.1.UNIT.PRICE(100)
100 DIM ITEM.2.NUMBER(100)
110 DIM ITEM.2.QTY(100)
120 DIM ITEM.2.UNIT.PRICE(100)
130 DIM ITEM.3.NUMBER(100)
140 DIM ITEM.3.QTY(100)
150 DIM ITEM.3.UNIT.PRICE(100)
160 DIM ITEM.4.NUMBER(100)
170 DIM ITEM.4.QTY(100)
180 DIM ITEM.4.UNIT.PRICE(100)
190 DIM AMOUNT.OF.INVOICE(100)
200 DIM AMOUNT.LESS.THAN.30.DAYS(100)
210 DIM AMOUNT.AT.30.DAYS(100)
220 DIM AMOUNT.AT.60.DAYS(100)
230 DIM AMOUNT.AT.90.DAYS(100)
240 REM *******************************
250 REM * DIMENSION THE CUSTOMER FILE. *
260 REM *******************************
270 DIM CUSTOMER.NAME$(100)
280 DIM CUSTOMER.ADDR.1$(100)
290 DIM CUSTOMER.ADDR.2$(100)
300 DIM CUSTOMER.ADDR.3$(100)
310 DIM CUSTOMER.ADDR.4$(100)
320 DIM CUSTOMER.TERMS$(100)
330 REM ***************************************
340 REM * DIMENSION THE CHART OF ACCOUNTS FILE *
350 REM ***************************************
360 DIM T$(25),N$(25)
370 REM ******************************
380 REM * DIMENSION THE ACCOUNT FILE *
390 REM ******************************
400 DIM A(25)
410 REM ****************************
420 REM * ROUTINE TO POST PAYMENTS *
430 REM ****************************
440 GOSUB 5040
450 PRINT TAB(17);"P O S T   P A Y M E N T S   R E C E I V E D"
460 GOSUB 4210          :REM GET THE CUSTOMER FILE
470 GOSUB 3600          :REM GET THE RECEIVABLES FILE
480 GOSUB 4370          :REM GET THE CHART OF ACCOUNTS FILE
490 PRINT:INPUT "ENTER THE ACCOUNT FILE NAME (I'LL ADD .DAT): ",ACCOUNT.FILE$
500 ACCOUNT.FILE$ = ".D2/" + ACCOUNT.FILE$ + ".DAT"
510 GOSUB 4600          :REM GET THE ACCOUNT FILE
520 GOSUB 5040
530 PRINT:PRINT"I M P O R T A N T ! ! !"
540 PRINT "IF THE PAYMENT CANNOT BE POSTED TO THESE ACCOUNTS, YOU MUST ";
550 PRINT "TERMINATE HERE"
560 PRINT "AND RETURN TO CHART, FOLLOWED BY VALUE, TO ESTABLISH ";
570 PRINT "THE ACCOUNT:"
580 FOR N = 1 TO 79:PRINT "-";:NEXT N
590 FOR I = 1 TO CHART.FILE.SIZE
600     PRINT T$(I);TAB(30);
610     PRINT USING "5&.2&";A(I)
620     NEXT I
```

Figure 6.33.

```
630 PRINT
640 PRINT "DO YOU WISH TO TERMINATE (Y/N)? ";
650 GET Z$
660 IF Z$ = "Y" THEN 3590
670 GOSUB 5040
680 PRINT:PRINT "POSTING METHODS:"
690 PRINT
700 PRINT TAB(5);"1.  POST PAYMENT BY CUSTOMER"
710 PRINT
720 PRINT TAB(5);"2.  POST PAYMENT BY INVOICE"
730 PRINT
740 PRINT TAB(5);"3.  VIEW ACCOUNTS BY CUSTOMER NUMBER"
750 PRINT
760 PRINT TAB(5);"4.  VIEW ACCOUNTS BY INVOICE NUMBER"
770 PRINT
780 PRINT TAB(5);"5.  REWRITE FILES, POST ACCOUNTS, AND TERMINATE"
790 PRINT
800 PRINT "SELECT: ";
810 GET Z$
820 IF Z$ = "1" THEN PRINT "POST PAYMENT BY CUSTOMER"
830 IF Z$ = "2" THEN PRINT "POST PAYMENT BY INVOICE"
840 IF Z$ = "3" THEN PRINT "VIEW ACCOUNTS BY CUSTOMER NUMBER"
850 IF Z$ = "4" THEN PRINT "VIEW ACCOUNTS BY INVOICE NUMBER"
860 IF Z$ = "5" THEN PRINT "POSTING ACCOUNTS"
870 FOR Z = 1 TO 1500:NEXT Z
880 A = VAL(Z$)
890 ON A GOSUB 910,1270,2050,2950,3300
900 GOTO 670
910 REM ****************************
920 REM * POST PAYMENT BY CUSTOMER *
930 REM ****************************
940 GOSUB 5040
950 PRINT:INPUT "ENTER THE CUSTOMER NUMBER: ",WHICH.CUST
960 PRINT
970 GOSUB 4840
980 PRINT:PRINT "CORRECT (Y/N)? ";
990 GET Z$
1000 PRINT Z$
1010 IF Z$ < > "Y" THEN 440
1020 PRINT:INPUT "ENTER THE AMOUNT OF THE PAYMENT: ",AMOUNT.OF.PAYMENT
1030 CASH.ADJUSTMENT = CASH.ADJUSTMENT + AMOUNT.OF.PAYMENT
1040 GOSUB 5040
1050 PRINT "THESE ARE THE INVOICES FOR THIS CUSTOMER:":PRINT
1060 PRINT "PERHAPS YOU SHOULD TAKE NOTES":PRINT
1070 FOR J = 1 TO RECEIVE.FILE.SIZE
1080      IF CUSTOMER.NUMBER(J) < > WHICH.CUST THEN 1180
1090      PRINT "CUSTOMER: ";J;TAB(18);"DATE: ";DATE.OF.INVOICE$(J);
1100      PRINT TAB(42);"INVOICE: ";DOCUMENT.NUMBER(J);
1110      PRINT TAB(60);"AMOUNT: ";
1120      TOTAL.AGING = 0
1130      TOTAL.AGING = TOTAL.AGING + AMOUNT.LESS.THAN.30.DAYS(J)
1140      TOTAL.AGING = TOTAL.AGING + AMOUNT.AT.30.DAYS(J)
1150      TOTAL.AGING = TOTAL.AGING + AMOUNT.AT.60.DAYS(J)
1160      TOTAL.AGING = TOTAL.AGING + AMOUNT.AT.90.DAYS(J)
1170      PRINT USING "5&.2&";TOTAL.AGING
1180      NEXT J
1190 IF AMOUNT.OF.PAYMENT < 1 THEN AMOUNT.OF.PAYMENT = 0
1200 PRINT:PRINT "YOU HAVE ";
1210 PRINT USING "$5&.2&";AMOUNT.OF.PAYMENT;
1220 PRINT " TO APPLY"
1230 FOR Z = 1 TO 1000:NEXT Z
1240 IF AMOUNT.OF.PAYMENT < = 0 THEN RETURN
1250 GOSUB 1330          :REM JUMP INTO MIDDLE OF POST PAYMENT BY INVOICE
1260 GOTO 1190
```

Figure 6.33. (continued)

```
1270 REM ***************************
1280 REM * POST PAYMENT BY INVOICE *
1290 REM ***************************
1300 GOSUB 5040
1310 PRINT:INPUT "ENTER THE AMOUNT OF THE PAYMENT: ",AMOUNT.OF.PAYMENT
1320 CASH.ADJUSTMENT = CASH.ADJUSTMENT + AMOUNT.OF.PAYMENT
1330 PRINT
1340 GOSUB 2990          :REM ENTER REVIEW ROUTINE AFTER THE BEGINNING
1350 INTEREST.DUE = (TOTAL.AGING - AMOUNT.OF.INVOICE(J))
1360 PRINT
1370 PRINT "ACCOUNT BEFORE APPLYING PAYMENT"
1380 PRINT
1390 PRINT USING "  90 DAYS: 5&.2&";AMOUNT.AT.90.DAYS(J)
1400 PRINT USING "  60 DAYS: 5&.2&";AMOUNT.AT.60.DAYS(J)
1410 PRINT USING "  30 DAYS: 5&.2&";AMOUNT.AT.30.DAYS(J)
1420 PRINT USING "< 30 DAYS: 5&.2&";AMOUNT.LESS.THAN.30.DAYS(J)
1430 IF AMOUNT.OF.PAYMENT > = TOTAL.AGING THEN 1960
1440 IF AMOUNT.OF.PAYMENT < AMOUNT.AT.90.DAYS(J) THEN 1510
1450 AMOUNT.OF.PAYMENT = (AMOUNT.OF.PAYMENT - AMOUNT.AT.90.DAYS(J))
1460 A.R.ADJUSTMENT = 0
1470 A.R.ADJUSTMENT = A.R.ADJUSTMENT + AMOUNT.AT.90.DAYS(J)
1480 AMOUNT.OF.INVOICE(J) = AMOUNT.OF.INVOICE(J) - AMOUNT.AT.90.DAYS(J)
1490 AMOUNT.AT.90.DAYS = 0
1500 GOTO 1540
1510 AMOUNT.AT.90.DAYS(J) = (AMOUNT.AT.90.DAYS(J) - AMOUNT.OF.PAYMENT)
1520 AMOUNT.OF.PAYMENT = 0
1530 GOTO 1770
1540 IF AMOUNT.OF.PAYMENT < AMOUNT.AT.60.DAYS(J) THEN 1600
1550 AMOUNT.OF.PAYMENT = (AMOUNT.OF.PAYMENT - AMOUNT.AT.60.DAYS(J))
1560 A.R.ADJUSTMENT = A.R.ADJUSTMENT + AMOUNT.AT.60.DAYS(J)
1570 AMOUNT.OF.INVOICE(J) = AMOUNT.OF.INVOICE(J) - AMOUNT.AT.60.DAYS(J)
1580 AMOUNT.AT.60.DAYS = 0
1590 GOTO 1630
1600 AMOUNT.AT.60.DAYS(J) = (AMOUNT.AT.60.DAYS(J) - AMOUNT.OF.PAYMENT)
1610 AMOUNT.OF.PAYMENT = 0
1620 GOTO 1770
1630 IF AMOUNT.OF.PAYMENT < AMOUNT.AT.30.DAYS(J) THEN 1690
1640 AMOUNT.OF.PAYMENT = (AMOUNT.OF.PAYMENT - AMOUNT.AT.30.DAYS(J))
1650 A.R.ADJUSTMENT = A.R.ADJUSTMENT + AMOUNT.AT.30.DAYS(J)
1660 AMOUNT.OF.INVOICE(J) = AMOUNT.OF.INVOICE(J) - AMOUNT.AT.30.DAYS(J)
1670 AMOUNT.AT.30.DAYS = 0
1680 GOTO 1720
1690 AMOUNT.AT.30.DAYS(J) = (AMOUNT.AT.30.DAYS(J) - AMOUNT.OF.PAYMENT)
1700 AMOUNT.OF.PAYMENT = 0
1710 GOTO 1770
1720 IF AMOUNT.OF.PAYMENT < AMOUNT.LESS.THAN.30.DAYS(J) THEN PRINT CHR$(7):
       PRINT "AMOUNT OF PAYMENT INSUFFICIENT - REJECTED":GOTO 1870
1730 AMOUNT.OF.PAYMENT = (AMOUNT.OF.PAYMENT - AMOUNT.LESS.THAN.30.DAYS(J))
1740 A.R.ADJUSTMENT = A.R.ADJUSTMENT + AMOUNT.LESS.THAN.30.DAYS(J)
1750 AMOUNT.OF.INVOICE(J) = AMOUNT.OF.INVOICE(J) - AMOUNT.LESS.THAN.30.DAYS(J)
1760 AMOUNT.LESS.THAN.30.DAYS = 0
1770 RECAST.INVOICE.AMOUNT = 0
1780 RECAST.INVOICE.AMOUNT = (RECAST.INVOICE.AMOUNT + AMOUNT.AT.90.DAYS(J))
1790 RECAST.INVOICE.AMOUNT = (RECAST.INVOICE.AMOUNT + AMOUNT.AT.60.DAYS(J))
1800 RECAST.INVOICE.AMOUNT = (RECAST.INVOICE.AMOUNT + AMOUNT.AT.30.DAYS(J))
1810 RECAST.INVOICE.AMOUNT =
       (RECAST.INVOICE.AMOUNT + AMOUNT.LESS.THAN.30.DAYS(J))
1820 INVOICE.AMOUNT(J) = RECAST.INVOICE.AMOUNT
1830 INTEREST.ADJUSTMENT = TOTAL.AGING - A.R.ADJUSTMENT
1840 PRINT "INTEREST.ADJUSTMENT: ";INTEREST.ADJUSTMENT
1850 PRINT "TOTAL AGING: ";TOTAL.AGING
1860 PRINT "A.R. ADJUSTMENT: ";A.R.ADJUSTMENT
1870 PRINT
1880 PRINT "ACCOUNT AFTER APPLYING PAYMENT"
1890 PRINT
```

Figure 6.33. (continued)

```
1900 PRINT USING "  90 DAYS:  5&.2&";AMOUNT.AT.90.DAYS(J)
1910 PRINT USING "  60 DAYS:  5&.2&";AMOUNT.AT.60.DAYS(J)
1920 PRINT USING "  30 DAYS:  5&.2&";AMOUNT.AT.30.DAYS(J)
1930 PRINT USING "< 30 DAYS:  5&.2&";AMOUNT.LESS.THAN.30.DAYS(J)
1940 FOR Z = 1 TO 1500:NEXT Z
1950 RETURN
1960 AMOUNT.OF.PAYMENT = (AMOUNT.OF.PAYMENT - TOTAL.AGING)
1970 A.R.ADJUSTMENT = A.R.ADJUSTMENT + TOTAL.AGING
1980 INTEREST.RECEIVED = (TOTAL.AGING - AMOUNT.OF.INVOICE(J))
1990 AMOUNT.AT.90.DAYS(J) = 0
2000 AMOUNT.AT.60.DAYS(J) = 0
2010 AMOUNT.AT.30.DAYS(J) = 0
2020 AMOUNT.LESS.THAN.30.DAYS(J) = 0
2030 AMOUNT.OF.INVOICE(J) = 0
2040 GOTO 1870
2050 REM *************************************
2060 REM * REVIEW ACCOUNTS BY CUSTOMER NUMBER *
2070 REM *************************************
2080 GOSUB 5040
2090 PRINT "TO SEE ENTIRE FILE, ENTER FIRST CUSTOMER NUMBER AND MOVE FORWARD"
2100 PRINT:INPUT "ENTER THE CUSTOMER NUMBER: ",WHICH.CUST
2110 PRINT
2120 GOSUB 4840
2130 PRINT:PRINT "CORRECT (Y/N)? ";
2140 GET Z$
2150 PRINT Z$
2160 IF Z$ = "Y" THEN 2230
2170 PRINT
2180 PRINT "DO YOU WISH TO REVIEW THE FILE (Y/N)? ";
2190 GET Z$
2200 PRINT Z$
2210 IF Z$ = "Y" THEN 2230
2220 GOTO 2080
2230 PRINT
2240 PRINT "DO YOU WANT A HARD COPY (Y/N)? ";
2250 GET Z$
2260 PRINT Z$
2270 PRINT
2280 IF Z$ = "Y" THEN HARDCOPY$ = "YES":GOTO 2300
2290 HARDCOPY$ = "NO"
2300 FOR I = 1 TO CUSTOMER.FILE.SIZE
2310      PRINT "CUSTOMER NUMBER:";TAB(20);I
2320      GOSUB 4840
2330      PRINT
2340      IF HARDCOPY$ = "NO" THEN 2410
2350      OPEN #3,".PRINTER"
2360      OUTPUT #3
2370      PRINT "CUSTOMER NUMBER:";TAB(20);I
2380      GOSUB 4930
2390      PRINT
2400      CLOSE #3
2410      PRINT:PRINT "PRESS 'A' TO ACCEPT"
2420      PRINT "PRESS 'X' TO ESCAPE"
2430      PRINT "PRESS ANY OTHER KEY TO CONTINUE"
2440      PRINT
2450      GET Z$
2460      IF Z$ = "A" THEN 2500
2470      IF Z$ = "X" THEN 2080
2480      NEXT I
2490 GOTO 2080
2500 PRINT
2510 PRINT:PRINT "NOTE THE ACCOUNT NUMBERS":PRINT
2520 FOR J = 1 TO RECEIVE.FILE.SIZE
2530      IF CUSTOMER.NUMBER(J) < > WHICH.CUST THEN 2930
2540      PRINT CUSTOMER.NUMBER(J),;
```

Figure 6.33. (continued)

```
2550      PRINT CUSTOMER.NAME$(I)
2560      PRINT
2570      PRINT "DATE OF INVOICE: ";DATE.OF.INVOICE$(J),;
2580      PRINT "INVOICE NUMBER: ";DOCUMENT.NUMBER(J)
2590      PRINT
2600      PRINT "AMOUNT OF INVOICE:";TAB(40);
2610      PRINT USING "5&.2&";AMOUNT.OF.INVOICE(J)
2620      PRINT "ACCUMULATED INTEREST:";TAB(40);
2630      TOTAL.AGING = 0
2640      TOTAL.AGING = TOTAL.AGING + AMOUNT.LESS.THAN.30.DAYS(J)
2650      TOTAL.AGING = TOTAL.AGING + AMOUNT.AT.30.DAYS(J)
2660      TOTAL.AGING = TOTAL.AGING + AMOUNT.AT.60.DAYS(J)
2670      TOTAL.AGING = TOTAL.AGING + AMOUNT.AT.90.DAYS(J)
2680      ACCUMULATED.INTEREST = TOTAL.AGING - AMOUNT.OF.INVOICE(J)
2690      PRINT USING "5&.2&";ACCUMULATED.INTEREST
2700      PRINT
2710      PRINT "TOTAL DUE:";TAB(38);
2720      PRINT USING "$5&.2&";TOTAL.AGING
2730      FOR N = 1 TO 79:PRINT "-";:NEXT N
2740      PRINT "PRESS ANY KEY TO CONTINUE"
2750      GET Z$
2760      IF HARDCOPY$ = "NO" THEN 2930
2770      OPEN #3,".PRINTER"
2780      OUTPUT #3
2790      PRINT CUSTOMER.NUMBER(J),;
2800      PRINT CUSTOMER.NAME$(I)
2810      PRINT
2820      PRINT "DATE OF INVOICE: ";DATE.OF.INVOICE$(J),;
2830      PRINT "INVOICE NUMBER: ";DOCUMENT.NUMBER(J)
2840      PRINT "AMOUNT OF INVOICE:";TAB(30);
2850      PRINT USING "5&.2&";AMOUNT.OF.INVOICE(J)
2860      PRINT "ACCUMULATED INTEREST:";TAB(30);
2870      PRINT USING "5&.2&";ACCUMULATED.INTEREST
2880      PRINT
2890      PRINT "TOTAL DUE:";TAB(28);
2900      PRINT USING "$5&.2&";ACCUMULATED.INTEREST
2910      FOR N = 1 TO 79:PRINT "-";:NEXT N
2920      CLOSE #3
2930      NEXT J
2940 RETURN
2950 REM ************************************
2960 REM * REVIEW ACCOUNTS BY INVOICE NUMBER *
2970 REM ************************************
2980 GOSUB 5040
2990 PRINT:INPUT "ENTER THE INVOICE NUMBER: ",WHICH.INVOICE
3000 PRINT
3010 FOR J = 1 TO RECEIVE.FILE.SIZE
3020      IF DOCUMENT.NUMBER(J) = WHICH.INVOICE THEN 3070
3030      NEXT J
3040 PRINT "THE INVOICE NUMBER DOES NOT EXIST"
3050 FOR Z = 1 TO 1000:NEXT Z
3060 GOTO 670
3070 WHICH.CUST = CUSTOMER.NUMBER(J)
3080 PRINT "CUSTOMER: ";CUSTOMER.NUMBER(J)
3090 GOSUB 4840
3100 PRINT
3110 PRINT "DATE OF INVOICE: ";DATE.OF.INVOICE$(J),;
3120 PRINT "INVOICE NUMBER: ";DOCUMENT.NUMBER(J)
3130 PRINT:PRINT "AMOUNT OF INVOICE:";TAB(40);
3140 PRINT USING "5&.2&";AMOUNT.OF.INVOICE(J)
3150 PRINT "ACCUMULATED INTEREST:";TAB(40);
3160 TOTAL.AGING = 0
3170 TOTAL.AGING = TOTAL.AGING + AMOUNT.LESS.THAN.30.DAYS(J)
3180 TOTAL.AGING = TOTAL.AGING + AMOUNT.AT.30.DAYS(J)
3190 TOTAL.AGING = TOTAL.AGING + AMOUNT.AT.60.DAYS(J)
```

Figure 6.33. (continued)

```
3200 TOTAL.AGING = TOTAL.AGING + AMOUNT.AT.90.DAYS(J)
3210 ACCUMULATED.INTEREST = TOTAL.AGING - AMOUNT.OF.INVOICE(J)
3220 PRINT USING "5&.2&";ACCUMULATED.INTEREST
3230 PRINT
3240 PRINT "TOTAL DUE:";TAB(38);
3250 PRINT USING "$5&.2&";TOTAL.AGING
3260 FOR N = 1 TO 79:PRINT "-";:NEXT N
3270 PRINT "PRESS ANY KEY TO CONTINUE"
3280 GET Z$
3290 RETURN
3300 REM ******************************************************
3310 REM * POST THE ACCOUNT FILE, REWRITE THE RECEIVABLES FILE *
3320 REM ******************************************************
3330 FOR J = 1 TO CHART.FILE.SIZE
3340     IF T$(J) = "A,ACCOUNTS RECEIVABLE" THEN 3400
3350     NEXT J
3360 PRINT "NO ACCOUNTS RECEIVABLE ENTRY TO CHART FILE - BEING ADDED"
3370 CHART.FILE.SIZE = J
3380 ACCOUNT.FILE.SIZE = J
3390 T$(J) = "A,ACCOUNTS RECEIVABLE"
3400 A(J) = A.R.ADJUSTMENT
3410 FOR J = 1 TO CHART.FILE.SIZE
3420     IF T$(J) = "A,CASH" THEN 3480
3430     NEXT J
3440 PRINT "NO ACCOUNTS RECEIVABLE ENTRY TO CHART FILE - BEING ADDED"
3450 CHART.FILE.SIZE = J
3460 ACCOUNT.FILE.SIZE = J
3470 T$(J) = "A,CASH"
3480 A(J) = CASH.ADJUSTMENT
3490 FOR J = 1 TO CHART.FILE.SIZE
3500     IF T$(J) = "I,INTEREST INCOME" THEN 3530
3510     NEXT J
3520 CHART.FILE.SIZE = J
3530 ACCOUNT.FILE.SIZE = J
3540 T$(J) = "I,INTEREST INCOME"
3550 A(J) = INTEREST.ADJUSTMENT
3560 GOSUB 4480                    :REM REWRITE CHART FILE
3570 GOSUB 4710                    :REM REWRITE ACCOUNT FILE
3580 GOSUB 3900                    :REM REWRITE RECEIVABLE FILE
3590 CHAIN .D2/RECIVBLE
3600 REM ************************************************
3610 REM * ROUTINE TO OPEN AND INPUT THE RECEIVABLES FILE *
3620 REM ************************************************
3630 PRINT:PRINT "LOADING THE RECEIVABLES FILE"
3640 OPEN #1,.D2/RECEIVE.DAT
3650 INPUT #1,RECEIVE.FILE.SIZE        :REM OBTAIN THE RECORD COUNT
3660 FOR I = 1 TO RECEIVE.FILE.SIZE
3670      INPUT #1,CUSTOMER.NUMBER(I)
3680      INPUT #1,DATE.OF.INVOICE$(I)
3690      INPUT #1,DOCUMENT.NUMBER(I)
3700      INPUT #1,ITEM.1.NUMBER(I)
3710      INPUT #1,ITEM.1.QTY(I)
3720      INPUT #1,ITEM.1.UNIT.PRICE(I)
3730      INPUT #1,ITEM.2.NUMBER(I)
3740      INPUT #1,ITEM.2.QTY(I)
3750      INPUT #1,ITEM.2.UNIT.PRICE(I)
3760      INPUT #1,ITEM.3.NUMBER(I)
3770      INPUT #1,ITEM.3.QTY(I)
3780      INPUT #1,ITEM.3.UNIT.PRICE(I)
3790      INPUT #1,ITEM.4.NUMBER(I)
3800      INPUT #1,ITEM.4.QTY(I)
3810      INPUT #1,ITEM.4.UNIT.PRICE(I)
3820      INPUT #1,AMOUNT.OF.INVOICE(I)
3830      INPUT #1,AMOUNT.LESS.THAN.30.DAYS(I)
3840      INPUT #1,AMOUNT.AT.30.DAYS(I)
```

Figure 6.33. (continued)

```
3850      INPUT #1,AMOUNT.AT.60.DAYS(I)
3860      INPUT #1,AMOUNT.AT.90.DAYS(I)
3870      NEXT I
3880 CLOSE #1
3890 RETURN
3900 REM *************************************************
3910 REM * ROUTINE TO OPEN AND OUTPUT THE RECEIVABLES FILE *
3920 REM *************************************************
3930 PRINT:PRINT "WRITING THE RECEIVABLES FILE"
3940 CREATE ".D2/RECEIVE.DAT",TEXT
3950 OPEN #1,.D2/RECEIVE.DAT
3960 PRINT #1,CUSTOMER.FILE.SIZE        :REM WRITE THE RECORD COUNT
3970 FOR I = 1 TO RECEIVE.FILE.SIZE
3980      PRINT #1,CUSTOMER.NUMBER(I)
3990      PRINT #1,DATE.OF.INVOICE$(I)
4000      PRINT #1,DOCUMENT.NUMBER(I)
4010      PRINT #1,ITEM.1.NUMBER(I)
4020      PRINT #1,ITEM.1.QTY(I)
4030      PRINT #1,ITEM.1.UNIT.PRICE(I)
4040      PRINT #1,ITEM.2.NUMBER(I)
4050      PRINT #1,ITEM.2.QTY(I)
4060      PRINT #1,ITEM.2.UNIT.PRICE(I)
4070      PRINT #1,ITEM.3.NUMBER(I)
4080      PRINT #1,ITEM.3.QTY(I)
4090      PRINT #1,ITEM.3.UNIT.PRICE(I)
4100      PRINT #1,ITEM.4.NUMBER(I)
4110      PRINT #1,ITEM.4.QTY(I)
4120      PRINT #1,ITEM.4.UNIT.PRICE(I)
4130      PRINT #1,AMOUNT.OF.INVOICE(I)
4140      PRINT #1,AMOUNT.LESS.THAN.30.DAYS(I)
4150      PRINT #1,AMOUNT.AT.30.DAYS(I)
4160      PRINT #1,AMOUNT.AT.60.DAYS(I)
4170      PRINT #1,AMOUNT.AT.90.DAYS(I)
4180      NEXT I
4190 CLOSE #1
4200 RETURN
4210 REM *********************************
4220 REM * OPEN AND INPUT CUSTOMER FILE *
4230 REM *********************************
4240 PRINT:PRINT "LOADING THE CUSTOMER FILE"
4250 OPEN #1,.D2/CUSTOMER.DAT
4260 INPUT #1,CUSTOMER.FILE.SIZE        :REM OBTAIN THE RECORD COUNT
4270 FOR K = 1 TO CUSTOMER.FILE.SIZE
4280      INPUT #1,CUSTOMER.NAME$(K)
4290      INPUT #1,CUSTOMER.ADDR.1$(K)
4300      INPUT #1,CUSTOMER.ADDR.2$(K)
4310      INPUT #1,CUSTOMER.ADDR.3$(K)
4320      INPUT #1,CUSTOMER.ADDR.4$(K)
4330      INPUT #1,CUSTOMER.TERMS$(K)
4340      NEXT K
4350 CLOSE #1
4360 RETURN
4370 REM *******************************************
4380 REM * OPEN AND INPUT CHART OF ACCOUNTS FILE *
4390 REM *******************************************
4400 PRINT:PRINT "LOADING THE CHART OF ACCOUNTS"
4410 OPEN #1,.D2/CHART.DAT
4420 INPUT #1,CHART.FILE.SIZE        :REM OBTAIN THE RECORD COUNT
4430 FOR J = 1 TO CHART.FILE.SIZE
4440      INPUT #1,T$(J)
4450      NEXT J
4460 CLOSE #1
4470 RETURN
4480 REM ********************************************
4490 REM * OPEN AND OUTPUT CHART OF ACCOUNTS FILE *
4500 REM ********************************************
```

Figure 6.33. (continued)

```
4510 PRINT:PRINT "WRITING THE CHART OF ACCOUNTS"
4520 CREATE ".D2/CHART.DAT",TEXT
4530 OPEN #1,.D2/CHART.DAT
4540 PRINT #1,CHART.FILE.SIZE          :REM WRITE THE RECORD COUNT
4550 FOR J = 1 TO CHART.FILE.SIZE
4560      PRINT #1,T$(J)
4570      NEXT J
4580 CLOSE #1
4590 RETURN
4600 REM ***********************************
4610 REM * OPEN AND INPUT THE ACCOUNT FILE *
4620 REM ***********************************
4630 PRINT:PRINT "LOADING THE ACCOUNT FILE"
4640 OPEN #1,ACCOUNT.FILE$
4650 INPUT #1,ACCOUNT.FILE.SIZE
4660 FOR J = 1 TO ACCOUNT.FILE.SIZE
4670      INPUT #1,A(J)
4680      NEXT J
4690 CLOSE #1
4700 RETURN
4710 REM ************************************
4720 REM * OPEN AND OUTPUT THE ACCOUNT FILE *
4730 REM ************************************
4740 PRINT:PRINT "WRITING THE ACCOUNT FILE"
4750 PREFIX$ = ".D2/"
4760 CREATE ACCOUNT.FILE$,TEXT
4770 OPEN #1,ACCOUNT.FILE$
4780 PRINT #1,ACCOUNT.FILE.SIZE
4790 FOR J = 1 TO ACCOUNT.FILE.SIZE
4800      PRINT #1,A(J)
4810      NEXT J
4820 CLOSE #1
4830 RETURN
4840 REM ************************************************************
4850 REM * ROUTINE USED MORE THAN ONCE TO DISPLAY THE CUSTOMER INFO *
4860 REM ************************************************************
4870 PRINT "CUSTOMER NAME:";TAB(25);CUSTOMER.NAME$(WHICH.CUST)
4880 PRINT "CUSTOMER ADDRESS:";TAB(25);CUSTOMER.ADDR.1$(WHICH.CUST)
4890 PRINT TAB(25);CUSTOMER.ADDR.2$(WHICH.CUST)
4900 PRINT TAB(25);CUSTOMER.ADDR.3$(WHICH.CUST)
4910 PRINT TAB(25);CUSTOMER.ADDR.4$(WHICH.CUST)
4920 RETURN
4930 REM **********************************************************
4940 REM * ROUTINE USED MORE THAN ONCE TO PRINT THE CUSTOMER INFO *
4950 REM **********************************************************
4960 OUTPUT #3
4970 PRINT "CUSTOMER NAME:";TAB(25);CUSTOMER.NAME$(WHICH.CUST)
4980 PRINT "CUSTOMER ADDRESS:";TAB(25);CUSTOMER.ADDR.1$(WHICH.CUST)
4990 PRINT TAB(25);CUSTOMER.ADDR.2$(WHICH.CUST)
5000 PRINT TAB(25);CUSTOMER.ADDR.3$(WHICH.CUST)
5010 PRINT TAB(25);CUSTOMER.ADDR.4$(WHICH.CUST)
5020 CLOSE #3
5030 RETURN
5040 REM ********************************
5050 REM * HEADING USED FOR THE DISPLAY *
5060 REM ********************************
5070 HOME
5080 X = ((80 - LEN(COMPANY.NAME$)) / 2)
5090 VPOS=2:HPOS=X
5100 PRINT COMPANY.NAME$
5110 FOR N = 1 TO 79:PRINT "-";:NEXT N:PRINT
5120 PRINT TAB(19);"ACCOUNTS RECEIVABLE PROCESSING PROGRAM"
5130 FOR N = 1 TO 79:PRINT "-";:NEXT N
5140 RETURN
```

Figure 6.33. (continued)

STATMENT

The production of a statement is not unlike the production of an invoice, but there are some significant differences:

1. It is usually done monthly or for some other fiscal period.
2. It will list *all* invoices that are current to that date.
3. It will list any accumulated interest (which is the difference between the total developed in the aging figures and the original amount of the invoice).
4. It will usually be run *after* the account aging has been accomplished.

The statement shown in Figure 6.34 involves only one invoice, since only one was left on file at the time the statement was made. Note, however, that the aging has been accomplished (incremented by 1.5%) and that the invoice has developed $8.33 in interest.

```
                          S T A T E M E N T

CUSTOMER NAME:            MR. BENJAMIN WATERS
CUSTOMER ADDRESS:         IMAGINATION INTERPRETED
                          327 PAGE ROAD
                          WATERTOWN,
                          PENNSYLVANIA 17743

 555     MAY 17, 1983             555.00

ACCUMULATED INTEREST:              $8.33

TOTAL DUE:                       $563.33

--------------------------------------------------------------------------------
30 DAYS OR LESS      30 - 60 DAYS      60 - 90 DAYS      90 DAYS AND OVER
    $0.00              $563.33            $0.00              $0.00
--------------------------------------------------------------------------------
```

Figure 6.34.

A block diagram of the statement production is shown in Figure 6.35.

Using the input from the Receivables File and from the Customer File, this program will produce statements reflecting the balance status of the account. The invoices on which charges remain are presented, along with their respective balances. The difference is the aging charges and the amount of the invoice(s) reflect the accumulated interest charges.

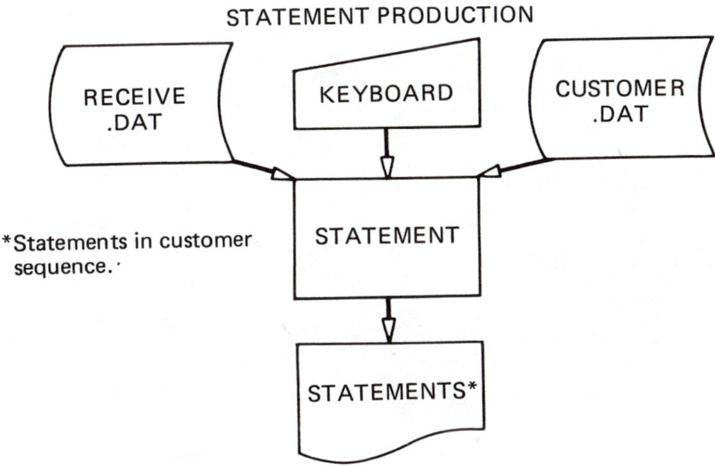

Figure 6.35.

The program STATMENT is given in Figure 6.36.

```
10 REM ***********************************
20 REM * DIMENSION THE RECEIVABLES FILE. *
30 REM ***********************************
40 DIM CUSTOMER.NUMBER(100)
50 DIM DATE.OF.INVOICE$(100)
60 DIM DOCUMENT.NUMBER(100)
70 DIM ITEM.1.NUMBER(100)
80 DIM ITEM.1.QTY(100)
90 DIM ITEM.1.UNIT.PRICE(100)
100 DIM ITEM.2.NUMBER(100)
110 DIM ITEM.2.QTY(100)
120 DIM ITEM.2.UNIT.PRICE(100)
130 DIM ITEM.3.NUMBER(100)
140 DIM ITEM.3.QTY(100)
150 DIM ITEM.3.UNIT.PRICE(100)
160 DIM ITEM.4.NUMBER(100)
170 DIM ITEM.4.QTY(100)
180 DIM ITEM.4.UNIT.PRICE(100)
190 DIM AMOUNT.OF.INVOICE(100)
200 DIM AMOUNT.LESS.THAN.30.DAYS(100)
210 DIM AMOUNT.AT.30.DAYS(100)
220 DIM AMOUNT.AT.60.DAYS(100)
230 DIM AMOUNT.AT.90.DAYS(100)
```

Figure 6.36.

```
240 REM *********************************
250 REM * DIMENSION THE CUSTOMER FILE. *
260 REM *********************************
270 DIM CUSTOMER.NAME$(100)
280 DIM CUSTOMER.ADDR.1$(100)
290 DIM CUSTOMER.ADDR.2$(100)
300 DIM CUSTOMER.ADDR.3$(100)
310 DIM CUSTOMER.ADDR.4$(100)
320 DIM CUSTOMER.TERMS$(100)
330 REM ************************************
340 REM * ROUTINE TO PRODUCE A STATEMENT *
350 REM ************************************
360 PRINT TAB(20);"S T A T E M E N T   P R E P A R A T I O N"
370 GOSUB 1580          :REM GET THE CUSTOMER FILE
380 GOSUB 1280          :REM GET THE RECEIVABLES FILE
390 FOR I = 1 TO CUSTOMER.FILE.SIZE
400     BYPASS$ = "OFF"
410     GOSUB 1950
420     STATEMENT.AMOUNT = 0
430     WHICH.CUST = I
440     PRINT:PRINT
450     OPEN #3,".PRINTER"
460     OUTPUT #3
470     PRINT
480     FOR J = 1 TO RECEIVE.FILE.SIZE
490         IF CUSTOMER.NUMBER(J) < > I THEN 700
500         IF AMOUNT.OF.INVOICE(J) = 0 THEN 700
510         IF BYPASS$ = "ON" THEN 580
520         PRINT TAB(30);"S T A T E M E N T"
530         PRINT:PRINT
540         GOSUB 1740      :REM DISPLAY NAME INFORMATION
550         GOSUB 1830      :REM PRINT NAME INFORMATION
560         PRINT:PRINT
570         BYPASS$ = "ON"
580         STATEMENT.AMOUNT = STATEMENT.AMOUNT + AMOUNT.OF.INVOICE(J)
590         PRINT DOCUMENT.NUMBER(J),DATE.OF.INVOICE$(J),;
600         PRINT USING "  5&.2&";AMOUNT.OF.INVOICE(J)
610         AGING.FIGURE = 0
620         AGING.FIGURE = AGING.FIGURE + AMOUNT.LESS.THAN.30.DAYS(J)
630         AGING.FIGURE = AGING.FIGURE + AMOUNT.AT.30.DAYS(J)
640         AGING.FIGURE = AGING.FIGURE + AMOUNT.AT.60.DAYS(J)
650         AGING.FIGURE = AGING.FIGURE + AMOUNT.AT.90.DAYS(J)
660         CLOSE #3
670         PRINT:PRINT
680         PRINT DOCUMENT.NUMBER(J),DATE.OF.INVOICE$(J),;
690         PRINT USING "  5&.2&";AMOUNT.OF.INVOICE(J)
700     NEXT J
710     IF BYPASS$ = "OFF" THEN 1230
720     PRINT
730     ACCUMULATED.INTEREST = (AGING.FIGURE - STATEMENT.AMOUNT)
740     PRINT "ACCUMULATED INTEREST: ",;
750     PRINT USING "$5&.2&";ACCUMULATED.INTEREST
760     PRINT
770     PRINT "TOTAL DUE:",,;
780     PRINT USING "$5&.2&";STATEMENT.AMOUNT + ACCUMULATED.INTEREST
790     PRINT
800     FOR N = 1 TO 79:PRINT "-";:NEXT N
810     PRINT "30 DAYS OR LESS";TAB(20);"30 - 60 DAYS";TAB(40);
820     PRINT "60 - 90 DAYS";TAB(60);"90 DAYS AND OVER"
830     PRINT USING "$5&.2&";AMOUNT.LESS.THAN.30.DAYS(I);
840     PRINT TAB(18);"";
850     PRINT USING "$5&.2&";AMOUNT.AT.30.DAYS(I);
860     PRINT TAB(38);"";
870     PRINT USING "$5&.2&";AMOUNT.AT.60.DAYS(I);
880     PRINT TAB(60);"";
```

Figure 6.36. (continued)

```
890      PRINT USING "$5&.2&";AMOUNT.AT.90.DAYS(I)
900      FOR N = 1 TO 79:PRINT "-";:NEXT N
910      FOR N = 1 TO 79:PRINT "-";:NEXT N
920      OPEN #3,".PRINTER"
930      OUTPUT #3
940      PRINT
950      PRINT "ACCUMULATED INTEREST: ",;
960      PRINT USING "$5&.2&";ACCUMULATED.INTEREST
970      PRINT
980      PRINT
990      PRINT "TOTAL DUE:",,;
1000      PRINT USING "$5&.2&";STATEMENT.AMOUNT
1010      PRINT USING "$5&.2&";ACCUMULATED.INTEREST
1020      PRINT
1030      FOR N = 1 TO 79:PRINT "-";:NEXT N
1040      PRINT "30 DAYS OR LESS";TAB(20);"30 - 60 DAYS";TAB(40);
1050      PRINT "60 - 90 DAYS";TAB(60);"90 DAYS AND OVER"
1060      PRINT USING "$5&.2&";AMOUNT.LESS.THAN.30.DAYS(I);
1070      PRINT TAB(18);"";
1080      PRINT USING "$5&.2&";AMOUNT.AT.30.DAYS(I);
1090      PRINT TAB(38);"";
1100      PRINT USING "$5&.2&";AMOUNT.AT.60.DAYS(I);
1110      PRINT TAB(60);"";
1120      PRINT USING "$5&.2&";AMOUNT.AT.90.DAYS(I)
1130      FOR N = 1 TO 79:PRINT "-";:NEXT N
1140      IF J > 10 THEN 1160
1150      FOR N = 1 TO (10 - J):PRINT:NEXT N      :REM TO PREVENT TIMEOUT
1160      PRINT CHR$(12)
1170      FOR N = 1 TO 30:PRINT:NEXT N        :REM THWART THE PRINTER TIMEOUT
1180      PRINT CHR$(12)
1190      PRINT "TOTAL VALUE OF STATEMENTS:",,;
1200      PRINT USING "$5&.2&";GRAND.TOTAL
1210      CLOSE #3
1220      GRAND.TOTAL = GRAND.TOTAL + STATEMENT.AMOUNT
1230 NEXT I
1240 FOR N = 1 TO 30:PRINT:NEXT N        :REM THWART THE PRINTER TIMEOUT
1250 PRINT "TOTAL VALUE OF STATEMENTS:",,;
1260 PRINT USING "$5&.2&";GRAND.TOTAL
1270 CHAIN .D2/RECIVBLE
1280 REM ********************************
1290 REM * OPEN AND INPUT RECEIVABLE FILE *
1300 REM ********************************
1310 PRINT:PRINT "LOADING THE RECEIVABLES FILE"
1320 OPEN #1,.D2/RECEIVE.DAT
1330 INPUT #1,RECEIVE.FILE.SIZE       :REM OBTAIN THE RECORD COUNT
1340 FOR I = 1 TO RECEIVE.FILE.SIZE
1350      INPUT #1,CUSTOMER.NUMBER(I)
1360      INPUT #1,DATE.OF.INVOICE$(I)
1370      INPUT #1,DOCUMENT.NUMBER(I)
1380      INPUT #1,ITEM.1.NUMBER(I)
1390      INPUT #1,ITEM.1.QTY(I)
1400      INPUT #1,ITEM.1.UNIT.PRICE(I)
1410      INPUT #1,ITEM.2.NUMBER(I)
1420      INPUT #1,ITEM.2.QTY(I)
1430      INPUT #1,ITEM.2.UNIT.PRICE(I)
1440      INPUT #1,ITEM.3.NUMBER(I)
1450      INPUT #1,ITEM.3.QTY(I)
1460      INPUT #1,ITEM.3.UNIT.PRICE(I)
1470      INPUT #1,ITEM.4.NUMBER(I)
1480      INPUT #1,ITEM.4.QTY(I)
1490      INPUT #1,ITEM.4.UNIT.PRICE(I)
1500      INPUT #1,AMOUNT.OF.INVOICE(I)
1510      INPUT #1,AMOUNT.LESS.THAN.30.DAYS(I)
1520      INPUT #1,AMOUNT.AT.30.DAYS(I)
1530      INPUT #1,AMOUNT.AT.60.DAYS(I)
```

Figure 6.36. (continued)

```
1540      INPUT #1,AMOUNT.AT.90.DAYS(I)
1550 NEXT I
1560 CLOSE #1
1570 RETURN
1580 REM *******************************
1590 REM * OPEN AND INPUT CUSTOMER FILE *
1600 REM *******************************
1610 PRINT:PRINT "LOADING THE CUSTOMER FILE"
1620 OPEN #1,.D2/CUSTOMER.DAT
1630 INPUT #1,CUSTOMER.FILE.SIZE     :REM OBTAIN THE RECORD COUNT
1640 FOR K = 1 TO CUSTOMER.FILE.SIZE
1650      INPUT #1,CUSTOMER.NAME$(K)
1660      INPUT #1,CUSTOMER.ADDR.1$(K)
1670      INPUT #1,CUSTOMER.ADDR.2$(K)
1680      INPUT #1,CUSTOMER.ADDR.3$(K)
1690      INPUT #1,CUSTOMER.ADDR.4$(K)
1700      INPUT #1,CUSTOMER.TERMS$(K)
1710 NEXT K
1720 CLOSE #1
1730 RETURN
1740 REM ************************************************************
1750 REM * ROUTINE USED MORE THAN ONCE TO DISPLAY THE CUSTOMER INFO *
1760 REM ************************************************************
1770 PRINT "CUSTOMER NAME:";TAB(25);CUSTOMER.NAME$(WHICH.CUST)
1780 PRINT "CUSTOMER ADDRESS:";TAB(25);CUSTOMER.ADDR.1$(WHICH.CUST)
1790 PRINT TAB(25);CUSTOMER.ADDR.2$(WHICH.CUST)
1800 PRINT TAB(25);CUSTOMER.ADDR.3$(WHICH.CUST)
1810 PRINT TAB(25);CUSTOMER.ADDR.4$(WHICH.CUST)
1820 RETURN
1830 REM **********************************************************
1840 REM * ROUTINE USED MORE THAN ONCE TO PRINT THE CUSTOMER INFO *
1850 REM **********************************************************
1860 OPEN #3,".PRINTER"
1870 OUTPUT #3
1880 PRINT "CUSTOMER NAME:";TAB(25);CUSTOMER.NAME$(WHICH.CUST)
1890 PRINT "CUSTOMER ADDRESS:";TAB(25);CUSTOMER.ADDR.1$(WHICH.CUST)
1900 PRINT TAB(25);CUSTOMER.ADDR.2$(WHICH.CUST)
1910 PRINT TAB(25);CUSTOMER.ADDR.3$(WHICH.CUST)
1920 PRINT TAB(25);CUSTOMER.ADDR.4$(WHICH.CUST)
1930 CLOSE #3
1940 RETURN
1950 REM *******************************
1960 REM * HEADING USED FOR THE DISPLAY *
1970 REM *******************************
1980 HOME
1990 X = ((80 - LEN(COMPANY.NAME$)) / 2)
2000 VPOS=2:HPOS=X
2010 PRINT COMPANY.NAME$
2020 FOR N = 1 TO 79:PRINT "-";:NEXT N:PRINT
2030 PRINT TAB(19);"ACCOUNTS RECEIVABLE PROCESSING PROGRAM"
2040 FOR N = 1 TO 79:PRINT "-";:NEXT N
2050 RETURN
```

Figure 6.36. (continued)

AGING

The employment of an accounts aging process is a recognition that time is money and that money tied up in receivables actually costs money. This program assigns the rate of 18 percent, or .015 per month on the unpaid balance.

There's an interesting thing about computers: their precision will drive you wacky. You'll find that out sometime when you try subtracting one number from another only to find peculiarly unexpected results. What you usually end up with is a number followed by several decimal points. If you pass that number through an editing mask (5&.2&), you'll find that the thousandths' place has been rounded since the final result permits display of only the two positions to the right of the decimal. Generally speaking, the number is rounded by 0.005. If a carry develops, it is reflected in the hundredth's position, and so on. What do you do, however, if you want the number to be rounded *in memory* rather than at display time? You merely add 0.005. You'll find that in this program.

A block diagram of the accounts aging process is shown in Figure 6.37. This program applies a consistent 1.5 percent interest to accounts that have been outstanding for more than 30 days. The basic theory is to apply the interest to the money in its age category rather than to reflect the new interest charge in current charges.

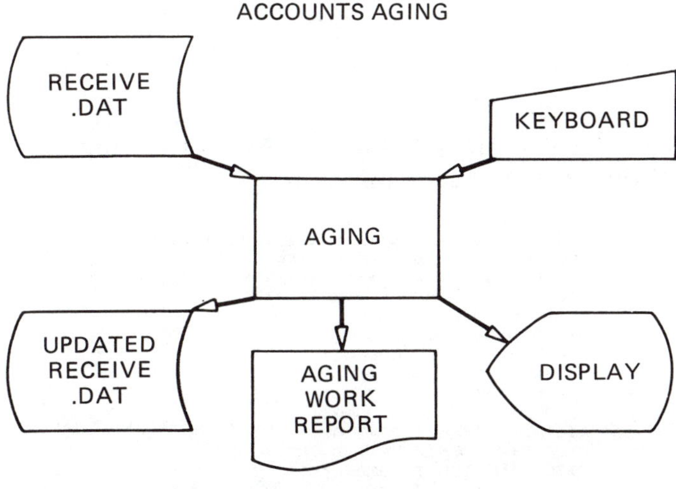

Figure 6.37.

The approach the program takes is to add the interest in place. If, for example, money has been owing for more than 90 days, then the interest is added to the more-than-90-day category. Afficionados of larger systems will dispute this approach, but its rationale is as follows: To begin with, since the interest figure on the statement is derived from adding *all* aging categories and then subtracting the amount of the original invoice, it doesn't matter where the interest is reflected insofar as the statement is concerned. Next, since payment posting is done from the oldest first, it seems better that the oldest money should reflect its entire worth. The approach is not difficult to change.

A work list of accounts being aged is presented in Figure 5.38. Because it is a work list, the numbers may look different. It can be modified to look prettier, if you wish, simply by printing the numbers with a PRINT USING "5&.2&".

```
                A G E   T H E   A C C O U N T S

ACCOUNT #:   1
BEFORE:   555.00          AFTER:   563.33          INTEREST:    8.33
----------------------------------------------------------------------
ACCOUNT #:   2
BEFORE:   814.79          AFTER:   827.01          INTEREST:   12.22
----------------------------------------------------------------------
ACCOUNT #:   3
BEFORE:   494.19          AFTER:   501.60          INTEREST:    7.41
----------------------------------------------------------------------

TOTAL INTEREST:   27.96
```

Figure 6.38.

Figure 6.39 shows the program AGING, which completes this discussion of the accounts receivable system.

```
10 REM ***********************************
20 REM * DIMENSION THE RECEIVABLES FILE. *
30 REM ***********************************
40 DIM CUSTOMER.NUMBER(100)
50 DIM DATE.OF.INVOICE$(100)
60 DIM DOCUMENT.NUMBER(100)
70 DIM ITEM.1.NUMBER(100)
80 DIM ITEM.1.QTY(100)
90 DIM ITEM.1.UNIT.PRICE(100)
100 DIM ITEM.2.NUMBER(100)
110 DIM ITEM.2.QTY(100)
120 DIM ITEM.2.UNIT.PRICE(100)
130 DIM ITEM.3.NUMBER(100)
140 DIM ITEM.3.QTY(100)
150 DIM ITEM.3.UNIT.PRICE(100)
160 DIM ITEM.4.NUMBER(100)
170 DIM ITEM.4.QTY(100)
180 DIM ITEM.4.UNIT.PRICE(100)
190 DIM AMOUNT.OF.INVOICE(100)
200 DIM AMOUNT.LESS.THAN.30.DAYS(100)
210 DIM AMOUNT.AT.30.DAYS(100)
220 DIM AMOUNT.AT.60.DAYS(100)
230 DIM AMOUNT.AT.90.DAYS(100)
```

Figure 6.39.

```
240 REM **********************************
250 REM * ROUTINE TO AGE THE RECEIVABLES *
260 REM **********************************
270 GOSUB 1030              :REM GET THE HEADING
280 PRINT TAB(22);"A G E   T H E   A C C O U N T S"
290 OPEN #3,".PRINTER"
300 OUTPUT #3
310 PRINT TAB(22);"A G E   T H E   A C C O U N T S"
320 PRINT:PRINT
330 CLOSE #3
340 GOSUB 730             :REM GET THE RECEIVABLES FILE
350 FOR J = 1 TO RECEIVE.FILE.SIZE
360     PRINT "ACCOUNT #: ";J
370     BEFORE.AMOUNT = 0
380     BEFORE.AMOUNT = BEFORE.AMOUNT + AMOUNT.LESS.THAN.30.DAYS(J)
390     BEFORE.AMOUNT = BEFORE.AMOUNT + AMOUNT.AT.30.DAYS(J)
400     BEFORE.AMOUNT = BEFORE.AMOUNT + AMOUNT.AT.60.DAYS(J)
410     BEFORE.AMOUNT = BEFORE.AMOUNT + AMOUNT.AT.90.DAYS(J)
420     BEFORE.AMOUNT = (INT((BEFORE.AMOUNT + .005) * 100) / 100)
430     AMOUNT.AT.90.DAYS(J) = AMOUNT.AT.90.DAYS(J) + AMOUNT.AT.60.DAYS(J)
440     AMOUNT.AT.90.DAYS(J) = ((AMOUNT.AT.90.DAYS(J)) * 1.015)
450     AMOUNT.AT.60.DAYS(J) = ((AMOUNT.AT.30.DAYS(J)) * 1.015)
460     AMOUNT.AT.30.DAYS(J) = ((AMOUNT.LESS.THAN.30.DAYS(J)) * 1.015)
470     AMOUNT.LESS.THAN.30.DAYS(J) = 0
480     AFTER.AMOUNT = 0
490     AFTER.AMOUNT = AFTER.AMOUNT + AMOUNT.LESS.THAN.30.DAYS(J)
500     AFTER.AMOUNT = AFTER.AMOUNT + AMOUNT.AT.30.DAYS(J)
510     AFTER.AMOUNT = AFTER.AMOUNT + AMOUNT.AT.60.DAYS(J)
520     AFTER.AMOUNT = AFTER.AMOUNT + AMOUNT.AT.90.DAYS(J)
530     AFTER.AMOUNT = (INT((AFTER.AMOUNT + .005) * 100) / 100)
540     PRINT "BEFORE: ";BEFORE.AMOUNT,"AFTER: ";AFTER.AMOUNT,"INTEREST:";
            (INT(((AFTER.AMOUNT - BEFORE.AMOUNT) + .005) * 100) / 100)
550     TOTAL.INTEREST = TOTAL.INTEREST + (AFTER.AMOUNT - BEFORE.AMOUNT)
560     FOR N = 1 TO 79:PRINT "-";:NEXT N
570     OPEN #3,".PRINTER"
580     OUTPUT #3
590     PRINT "ACCOUNT #: ";J
600     PRINT "BEFORE: ";BEFORE.AMOUNT,"AFTER: ";AFTER.AMOUNT,"INTEREST:";
            (INT(((AFTER.AMOUNT - BEFORE.AMOUNT) + .005) * 100) / 100)
610     FOR N = 1 TO 79:PRINT "-";:NEXT N
620     CLOSE #3
630 NEXT J
640 TOTAL.INTEREST = (INT((TOTAL.INTEREST + .005) * 100) / 100)
650 PRINT:PRINT "TOTAL INTEREST: ";TOTAL.INTEREST
660 OPEN #3,".PRINTER"
670 OUTPUT #3
680 PRINT:PRINT "TOTAL INTEREST: ";TOTAL.INTEREST
690 PRINT CHR$(12)
700 CLOSE #3
710 GOSUB 1140              :REM WRITE THE RECEIVABLES FILE
720 CHAIN .D2/RECIVBLE
730 REM ************************************
740 REM * OPEN AND INPUT RECEIVABLE FILE *
750 REM ************************************
760 PRINT:PRINT "LOADING THE RECEIVABLES FILE"
770 OPEN #1,.D2/RECEIVE.DAT
780 INPUT #1,RECEIVE.FILE.SIZE        :REM OBTAIN THE RECORD COUNT
790 FOR I = 1 TO RECEIVE.FILE.SIZE
800     INPUT #1,CUSTOMER.NUMBER(I)
810     INPUT #1,DATE.OF.INVOICE$(I)
820     INPUT #1,DOCUMENT.NUMBER(I)
830     INPUT #1,ITEM.1.NUMBER(I)
840     INPUT #1,ITEM.1.QTY(I)
850     INPUT #1,ITEM.1.UNIT.PRICE(I)
860     INPUT #1,ITEM.2.NUMBER(I)
870     INPUT #1,ITEM.2.QTY(I)
```

Figure 6.39. (continued)

```
880      INPUT #1,ITEM.2.UNIT.PRICE(I)
890      INPUT #1,ITEM.3.NUMBER(I)
900      INPUT #1,ITEM.3.QTY(I)
910      INPUT #1,ITEM.3.UNIT.PRICE(I)
920      INPUT #1,ITEM.4.NUMBER(I)
930      INPUT #1,ITEM.4.QTY(I)
940      INPUT #1,ITEM.4.UNIT.PRICE(I)
950      INPUT #1,AMOUNT.OF.INVOICE(I)
960      INPUT #1,AMOUNT.LESS.THAN.30.DAYS(I)
970      INPUT #1,AMOUNT.AT.30.DAYS(I)
980      INPUT #1,AMOUNT.AT.60.DAYS(I)
990      INPUT #1,AMOUNT.AT.90.DAYS(I)
1000 NEXT I
1010 CLOSE #1
1020 RETURN
1030 REM ********************************
1040 REM * HEADING USED FOR THE DISPLAY *
1050 REM ********************************
1060 HOME
1070 X = ((80 - LEN(COMPANY.NAME$)) / 2)
1080 VPOS=2:HPOS=X
1090 PRINT COMPANY.NAME$
1100 FOR N = 1 TO 79:PRINT "-";:NEXT N:PRINT
1110 PRINT TAB(19);"ACCOUNTS RECEIVABLE PROCESSING PROGRAM"
1120 FOR N = 1 TO 79:PRINT "-";:NEXT N
1130 RETURN
1140 REM **********************************
1150 REM * OPEN AND OUTPUT RECEIVABLE FILE *
1160 REM **********************************
1170 PRINT:PRINT "WRITING THE RECEIVABLES FILE"
1180 CREATE ".D2/RECEIVE.DAT",TEXT
1190 OPEN #1,.D2/RECEIVE.DAT
1200 PRINT #1,RECEIVE.FILE.SIZE       :REM PRODUCE THE RECORD COUNT
1210 FOR I = 1 TO RECEIVE.FILE.SIZE
1220      PRINT #1,CUSTOMER.NUMBER(I)
1230      PRINT #1,DATE.OF.INVOICE$(I)
1240      PRINT #1,DOCUMENT.NUMBER(I)
1250      PRINT #1,ITEM.1.NUMBER(I)
1260      PRINT #1,ITEM.1.QTY(I)
1270      PRINT #1,ITEM.1.UNIT.PRICE(I)
1280      PRINT #1,ITEM.2.NUMBER(I)
1290      PRINT #1,ITEM.2.QTY(I)
1300      PRINT #1,ITEM.2.UNIT.PRICE(I)
1310      PRINT #1,ITEM.3.NUMBER(I)
1320      PRINT #1,ITEM.3.QTY(I)
1330      PRINT #1,ITEM.3.UNIT.PRICE(I)
1340      PRINT #1,ITEM.4.NUMBER(I)
1350      PRINT #1,ITEM.4.QTY(I)
1360      PRINT #1,ITEM.4.UNIT.PRICE(I)
1370      PRINT #1,AMOUNT.OF.INVOICE(I)
1380      PRINT #1,AMOUNT.LESS.THAN.30.DAYS(I)
1390      PRINT #1,AMOUNT.AT.30.DAYS(I)
1400      PRINT #1,AMOUNT.AT.60.DAYS(I)
1410      PRINT #1,AMOUNT.AT.90.DAYS(I)
1420 NEXT I
1430 CLOSE #1
1440 RETURN
```

Figure 6.39. (continued)

PAYABLE

The next major element of the small business system is the Accounts Payable activity. As previously mentioned, this is not a true A/P activity, in that the purchases journal, what we call a checkbook, is not developed and maintained in the strictest sense of the concept. Also, the portion of the system that would produce checks is not installed, although it could be very easily within this system. Instead, recognizing that the owner of a small business controls his cash very carefully, the program offers the options shown in Figure 6.40.

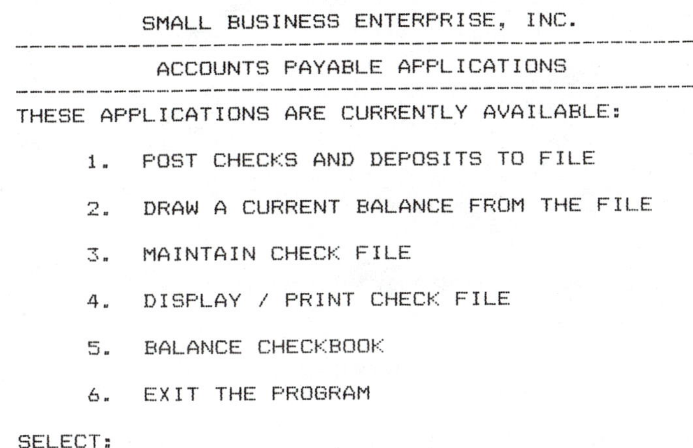

```
              SMALL BUSINESS ENTERPRISE, INC.
------------------------------------------------------------
               ACCOUNTS PAYABLE APPLICATIONS
------------------------------------------------------------
THESE APPLICATIONS ARE CURRENTLY AVAILABLE:

     1.   POST CHECKS AND DEPOSITS TO FILE

     2.   DRAW A CURRENT BALANCE FROM THE FILE

     3.   MAINTAIN CHECK FILE

     4.   DISPLAY / PRINT CHECK FILE

     5.   BALANCE CHECKBOOK

     6.   EXIT THE PROGRAM

SELECT:
```

Figure 6.40.

The first option is the posting of checks or deposits. As the system is designed, only checks and deposits find their way onto the file CHECK.DAT. Thus, the selection of the first menu option will produce the output shown in Figure 6.41.

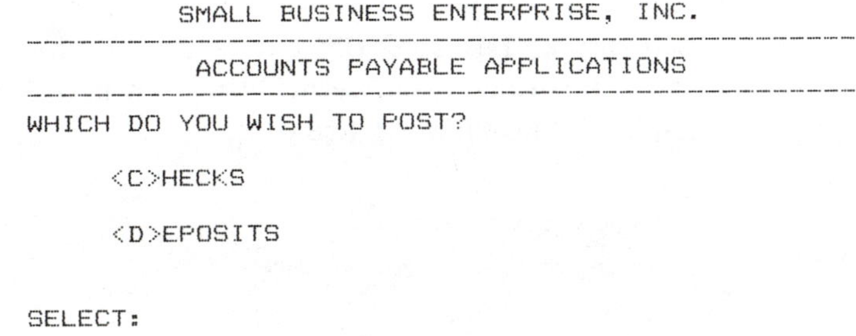

```
              SMALL BUSINESS ENTERPRISE, INC.
------------------------------------------------------------
               ACCOUNTS PAYABLE APPLICATIONS
------------------------------------------------------------
WHICH DO YOU WISH TO POST?

     <C>HECKS

     <D>EPOSITS


SELECT:
```

Figure 6.41.

For purposes of illustration, we'll walk through a deposit. Figure 6.42 indicates that the deposit selection has been made and that a deposit of $100 has been confirmed. The application is programed to allow for the entry of a specific date. Internally, the file is marked DEPOSIT, the date, and the amount.

```
            SMALL BUSINESS ENTERPRISE, INC.
--------------------------------------------------
             ACCOUNTS PAYABLE APPLICATIONS
--------------------------------------------------
WHICH DO YOU WISH TO POST?

     <C>HECKS

     <D>EPOSITS

SELECT:  DEPOSITS

ENTER AMOUNT OF DEPOSITS: $100

CORRECT (Y/N)? Y

ENTER DATE OF THE DEPOSIT:  05-21-1983

TERMINATE THE INPUT (Y/N)?
```

Figure 6.42.

The posting of checks works the same way. This application is *not* tied to the vendor file, primarily because it was felt that the small business should not be faced with having to put a vendor on the vendor file in order to be able to issue a check to that vendor. In larger systems, such an approach is mandatory. Since the small business *is* small, we have provided the proprietor with the capability of entering the name of the PAYEE individually.

The second option allows you to draw a balance on the basis of the deposits and checks in the file. On the assumption that you have entered all your deposits and posted the file with the checks you have written, this option should produce a figure that matches your checkbook. The display is shown in Figure 6.43.

```
            SMALL BUSINESS ENTERPRISE, INC.
--------------------------------------------------
             ACCOUNTS PAYABLE APPLICATIONS
--------------------------------------------------
CHECKBOOK CURRENT BALANCE ACCORDING TO THE FILE

READING THE CHECK FILE

CHECKBOOK BALANCE         $190.00

PRESS ANY KEY TO RETURN TO MENU
```

Figure 6.43.

In a larger system the auditors would go wild over the lack of an audit trail in the checkbook, but since the small business person will be keeping a check register anyway, the third option allows for the maintenance and modification of the check file. When you select option 3, you'll see Figure 6.44.

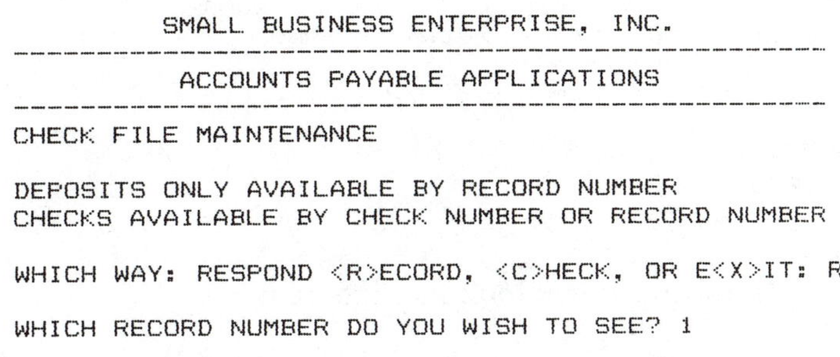

```
            SMALL BUSINESS ENTERPRISE, INC.
------------------------------------------------------
            ACCOUNTS PAYABLE APPLICATIONS
------------------------------------------------------
CHECK FILE MAINTENANCE

DEPOSITS ONLY AVAILABLE BY RECORD NUMBER
CHECKS AVAILABLE BY CHECK NUMBER OR RECORD NUMBER

WHICH WAY: RESPOND <R>ECORD, <C>HECK, OR E<X>IT: R

WHICH RECORD NUMBER DO YOU WISH TO SEE? 1
```

Figure 6.44.

During maintenance, you'll have the option to make changes either by record number or by check number. You must know the record number that contains the deposit if you wish to make changes, since deposits are not numbered. The relevant record number, if you do not know it, may be obtained with option 4, to be discussed subsequently.

If you do select by record number, you'll see the screen shown in Figure 6.45.

```
            SMALL BUSINESS ENTERPRISE, INC.
------------------------------------------------------
            ACCOUNTS PAYABLE APPLICATIONS
------------------------------------------------------
THIS IS THE REQUESTED RECORD:

RECORD NUMBER:                  1
DEPOSIT/CHECK NUMBER:         DEPOSIT
DATE:                         05-20-1983
AMOUNT:                           $100.00

YOU MAY: <D>ELETE THE ENTIRE RECORD
         <C>HANGE THE CONTENTS OF RECORD BY REENTRY
         <R>ETURN TO THIS SECTION'S MENU
SELECT:
```

Figure 6.45.

You can select a specific check for examination, as in Figure 6.46.

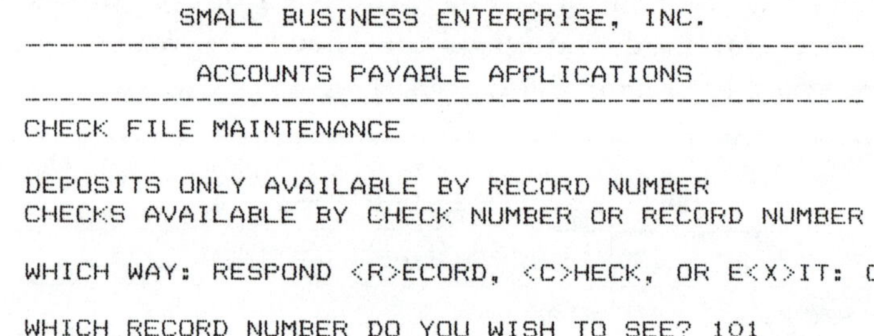

```
              SMALL BUSINESS ENTERPRISE, INC.
-----------------------------------------------------------
               ACCOUNTS PAYABLE APPLICATIONS
-----------------------------------------------------------
CHECK FILE MAINTENANCE

DEPOSITS ONLY AVAILABLE BY RECORD NUMBER
CHECKS AVAILABLE BY CHECK NUMBER OR RECORD NUMBER

WHICH WAY: RESPOND <R>ECORD, <C>HECK, OR E<X>IT: C

WHICH RECORD NUMBER DO YOU WISH TO SEE? 101
```

Figure 6.46.

The displayed check will look like Figure 6.47.

```
              SMALL BUSINESS ENTERPRISE, INC.
-----------------------------------------------------------
               ACCOUNTS PAYABLE APPLICATIONS
-----------------------------------------------------------
THIS IS THE REQUESTED RECORD:

RECORD NUMBER:                  2
DEPOSIT/CHECK NUMBER:          101
DATE:                          05-20-1983
AMOUNT:                            $10.00

YOU MAY: <D>ELETE THE ENTIRE RECORD
         <C>HANGE THE CONTENTS OF RECORD BY REENTRY
         <R>ETURN TO THIS SECTION'S MENU
SELECT:
```

Figure 6.47.

The fourth option will produce a display/printout of the file in record number sequence. See Figure 6.48. The program has purposely left off the name of the PAYEE because it was felt that manual records would be more than sufficient to provide the detail needed. It would not be difficult to modify the program to provide this data, as well, since it *is* already a part of the file.

The fifth and final option is the checkbook reconciliation. In this reconciliation, you must first post the checks that have been returned. You do so by check number until you have posted the last check, after which you press "X" and thus enter the reconciliation phase.

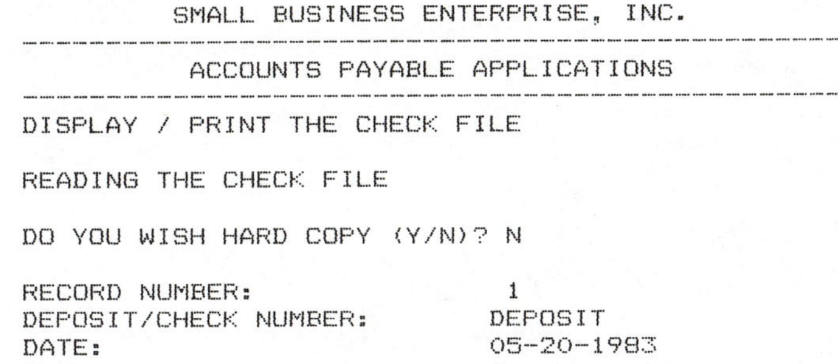

```
            SMALL BUSINESS ENTERPRISE, INC.
-------------------------------------------------------------
             ACCOUNTS PAYABLE APPLICATIONS
-------------------------------------------------------------
DISPLAY / PRINT THE CHECK FILE

READING THE CHECK FILE

DO YOU WISH HARD COPY (Y/N)? N

RECORD NUMBER:                  1
DEPOSIT/CHECK NUMBER:          DEPOSIT
DATE:                          05-20-1983
AMOUNT:                            $100.00
```

Figure 6.48.

You are now asked for any credit memoranda, any debit memoranda, and the service charges. If there is a record without a proper code, you will be notified that there is a type problem. This particular message is shown in Figure 6.49, as the fourth record in the file is a null record, one used for end-of-file after RETURNED checks have been compressed.

```
ENTER 'X' WHEN YOU HAVE COMPLETED

ENTER CHECK NUMBER: X

ENTER THE TOTAL AMOUNT OF CREDIT MEMO'S: 1.23

ENTER THE TOTAL AMOUNT OF DEBIT MEMO'S: 2.34

ENTER SERVICE CHARGES: 2.00

WRITING THE CHECK FILE

RECORD 4  HAS A TYPE PROBLEM

CHECKBOOK BALANCE IS:             $190.00
PLUS CREDIT MEMO'S:                  1.23
LESS DEBIT MEMO'S:                  -2.34
LESS SERVICE CHARGES:               -2.00
RECONCILIATION:                   $186.89

YOUR CHECKBOOK TOTAL SHOULD MATCH THIS FIGURE

PRESS ANY KEY TO RESUME
```

Figure 6.49.

The program PAYABLE is shown in Figure 6.50.

```
10 PRINT "FIRST TIME TO BUILD FILE (Y/N)? ";
20 GET Z$
30 DIMENSION.COUNT = 0
40 IF Z$ = "N" THEN 100
50 DIM CHECK.NUMBER$(1000)
60 DIM CHECK.PAYEE$(1000)
70 DIM CHECK.DATE$(1000)
80 DIM CHECK.AMOUNT(1000)
90 DIMENSION.COUNT = 1000
100 GOSUB 3990
110 PRINT
120 PRINT "THESE APPLICATIONS ARE CURRENTLY AVAILABLE:"
130 PRINT
140 PRINT TAB(15);"1.  POST CHECKS AND DEPOSITS TO FILE"
150 PRINT
160 PRINT TAB(15);"2.  DRAW A CURRENT BALANCE FROM THE FILE"
170 PRINT
180 PRINT TAB(15);"3.  MAINTAIN CHECK FILE"
190 PRINT
200 PRINT TAB(15);"4.  DISPLAY / PRINT CHECK FILE"
210 PRINT
220 PRINT TAB(15);"5.  BALANCE CHECKBOOK"
230 PRINT
240 PRINT TAB(15);"6.  EXIT THE PROGRAM"
250 PRINT
260 PRINT "SELECT: ";
270 GET Z$
280 IF Z$ = "1" THEN A = 1:
       PRINT "POST CHECKS AND DEPOSITS TO FILE":GOTO 360
290 IF Z$ = "2" THEN A = 2:
       PRINT "DRAW A CURRENT BALANCE":GOTO 360
300 IF Z$ = "3" THEN A = 3:
       PRINT "MAINTAIN CHECK FILE":GOTO 360
310 IF Z$ = "4" THEN A = 4:
       PRINT "DISPLAY / PRINT CHECK FILE":GOTO 360
320 IF Z$ = "5" THEN A = 5:
       PRINT "BALANCE CHECKBOOK":GOTO 360
330 IF Z$ = "6" THEN 3840
340 PRINT CHR$(7)
350 GOTO 100
360 GOSUB 4480
370 ON A GOSUB 390,1760,1970,2760,3100,3840
380 GOTO 100
390 REM *********************************************
400 REM * ROUTINE TO DEVELOP A FILE OF CHECKS WRITTEN *
410 REM *********************************************
420 GOSUB 3990
430 PRINT
440 PRINT "IS THIS THE FIRST TIME THE FILE HAS BEEN BUILT (Y/N)? ";
450 GET Z$
460 PRINT Z$
470 IF Z$ < > "Y" THEN 940
480 REM ******************
490 REM * FIRST BUILDING *
500 REM ******************
510 FOR I = 1 TO 1000
520     GOSUB 3990
530     PRINT:PRINT "WHICH DO YOU WISH TO POST?":PRINT
540     PRINT TAB(15);"<C>HECKS":PRINT
550     PRINT TAB(15);"<D>EPOSITS":PRINT
560     PRINT "SELECT: ";
570     GET Z$
580     PRINT Z$;
590     IF Z$ = "C" THEN PRINT "HECKS":GOSUB 4480:GOTO 730
600     IF Z$ = "D" THEN PRINT "EPOSITS"
```

Figure 6.50.

```
610       IF Z$ < > "D" THEN PRINT CHR$(7):GOTO 520
620       GOSUB 1640
630       IF SUB.ERR$ = "YES" THEN SUB.ERR$ = "NO":GOTO 520
640       IF Z$ < > "Y" THEN 520
650       PRINT:PRINT "IF TODAY'S DATE, JUST PRESS ENTER KEY":PRINT
660       INPUT "ENTER DATE OF THE DEPOSIT: ";DEPOSIT.DATE$
670       IF DEPOSIT.DATE$ = "" THEN DEPOSIT.DATE$ = DATE$
680       PRINT "DATE USED: ";DEPOSIT.DATE$
690       GOSUB 4480
700       CHECK.DATE$(I) = DEPOSIT.DATE$
710       GOTO 850
720 REM ******************
730       GOSUB 1310                    :REM OBTAIN THE CHECK NUMBER
740       CHECK.FILE.SIZE = I
750       TEMP.CHECK.NUMBER$ = "C" + CHECK.NUMBER.ENTERED$
760       FOR J = 1 TO CHECK.FILE.SIZE
770           IF TEMP.CHECK.NUMBER$ = CHECK.NUMBER$(J) THEN PRINT
                 "THAT CHECK NUMBER IS ALREADY IN USE":GOSUB 4480:
                 GOTO 730
780           NEXT J
790       GOSUB 1430            :REM OBTAIN THE PAYEE, DATE, AND AMOUNT
800       IF SUB.ERR$ = "YES" THEN SUB.ERR$ = "NO":GOTO 520
810       CHECK.NUMBER$(I) = "C" + CHECK.NUMBER.ENTERED$
820       CHECK.PAYEE$(I) = PAYEE.ENTERED$
830       CHECK.DATE$(I) = DATE.ENTERED$
840       CHECK.AMOUNT(I) = AMOUNT.ENTERED
850       PRINT:PRINT "TERMINATE THE INPUT (Y/N)? ";
860       GET Z$
870       PRINT Z$
880       IF Z$ = "Y" THEN CHECK.FILE.SIZE = I:GOTO 910
890       NEXT I
900 CHECK.FILE.SIZE = I - 1
910 GOSUB 4330                        :REM WRITE THE CHECK FILE
920 RETURN
930 REM ******************
940 GOSUB 4100                        :REM READ THE CHECK FILE
950 GOSUB 3990
960 PRINT:PRINT "WHICH DO YOU WISH TO POST?":PRINT
970 PRINT TAB(15);"<C>HECKS":PRINT
980 PRINT TAB(15);"<D>EPOSITS":PRINT
990 PRINT "SELECT: ";
1000 GET Z$
1010 PRINT Z$;
1020 IF Z$ = "C" THEN PRINT "HECKS":GOSUB 4480:GOTO 1150
1030 IF Z$ = "D" THEN PRINT "EPOSITS"
1040 IF Z$ < > "D" THEN PRINT CHR$(7):GOTO 950
1050      GOSUB 1640
1060      IF SUB.ERR$ = "YES" THEN SUB.ERR$ = "NO":GOTO 950
1070      IF Z$ < > "Y" THEN 950
1080      PRINT:PRINT "IF TODAY'S DATE, JUST PRESS ENTER KEY":PRINT
1090      INPUT "ENTER DATE OF THE DEPOSIT: ";DEPOSIT.DATE$
1100      IF DEPOSIT.DATE$ = "" THEN DEPOSIT.DATE$ = DATE$
1110      PRINT "DATE USED: ";DEPOSIT.DATE$
1120      GOSUB 4480
1130      CHECK.DATE$(I) = DEPOSIT.DATE$
1140      GOTO 1250
1150 GOSUB 1310                        :REM OBTAIN THE CHECK NUMBER
1160 TEMP.CHECK.NUMBER$ = "C" + CHECK.NUMBER.ENTERED$
1170 FOR I = 1 TO CHECK.FILE.SIZE
1180      IF TEMP.CHECK.NUMBER$ = CHECK.NUMBER$(J) THEN PRINT
              "THAT CHECK NUMBER IS ALREADY IN USE":GOSUB 4480:
               GOTO 950
1190      NEXT I
1200 PRINT
1210 PRINT "THE CHECK CAN BE ENTERED"
```

Figure 6.50. (continued)

```
1220 CHECK.FILE.SIZE = I
1230 GOSUB 1430                    :REM OBTAIN THE PAYEE, DATE, AND AMOUNT
1240 IF SUB.ERR$ = "YES" THEN SUB.ERR$ = "NO":GOTO 950
1250 PRINT:PRINT "TERMINATE THE INPUT (Y/N)? ";
1260 GET Z$
1270 PRINT Z$
1280 IF Z$ = "Y" THEN CHECK.FILE.SIZE = I:GOSUB 4330:GOTO 1300
1290 GOTO 950
1300 RETURN
1310 REM *******************
1320 REM * GET CHECK NUMBER *
1330 REM *******************
1340 GOSUB 3990
1350 PRINT
1360 INPUT "ENTER THE CHECK NUMBER: ",CHECK.NUMBER.ENTERED$
1370 PRINT
1380 PRINT "CORRECT (Y/N)? ";
1390 GET Z$
1400 PRINT Z$
1410 IF Z$ < > "Y" THEN SUB.ERR$ = "YES"
1420 RETURN
1430 REM ******************************
1440 REM * GET PAYEE, DATE, AND AMOUNT *
1450 REM ******************************
1460 PRINT
1470 INPUT "ENTER PAYEE: ";PAYEE.ENTERED$
1480 PRINT
1490 PRINT "FOR TODAY'S DATE SIMPLY PRESS ENTER KEY"
1500 PRINT
1510 INPUT "ENTER DATE:  ";DATE.ENTERED$
1520 IF DATE.ENTERED$ = "" THEN DATE.ENTERED$ = DATE$
1530 PRINT "DATE USED: ";DATE.ENTERED$
1540 PRINT
1550 INPUT "ENTER AMOUNT: $",AMOUNT.ENTERED
1560 PRINT
1570 PRINT "CORRECT (Y/N)? ";
1580 GET Z$
1590 PRINT Z$
1600 IF Z$ = "Y" THEN 1630
1610 PRINT CHR$(7)
1620 SUB.ERR$ = "YES"
1630 RETURN
1640 REM ***************************
1650 REM * GET DEPOSIT INFORMATION *
1660 REM ***************************
1670 PRINT:INPUT "ENTER AMOUNT OF DEPOSIT: $",AMOUNT.OF.DEPOSIT
1680 PRINT:PRINT "CORRECT (Y/N)? ";
1690 GET Z$
1700 PRINT Z$
1710 IF Z$ < > "Y" THEN SUB.ERR$ = "YES":GOTO 1750
1720 CHECK.NUMBER$(I) = "D"
1730 CHECK.PAYEE$(I) = ""
1740 CHECK.AMOUNT(I) = AMOUNT.OF.DEPOSIT
1750 RETURN
1760 REM ***********************************************************
1770 REM * ROUTINE TO CALCULATE THE CURRENT BALANCE OF THE CHECKBOOK *
1780 REM ***********************************************************
1790 GOSUB 3990
1800 PRINT:PRINT "CHECKBOOK CURRENT BALANCE ACCORDING TO THE FILE"
1810 GOSUB 4100          :REM READ THE CHECK FILE
1820 CHECKS = 0:DEPOSITS = 0
1830 FOR I = 1 TO CHECK.FILE.SIZE
1840      IF LEFT$(CHECK.NUMBER$(I),1) = "C" THEN 1930
1850      IF LEFT$(CHECK.NUMBER$(I),1) = "D" THEN 1950
1860      PRINT:PRINT "RECORD";I;" HAS A TYPE PROBLEM"
```

Figure 6.50. (continued)

```
1870      NEXT I
1880 PRINT:PRINT "CHECKBOOK BALANCE IS: ";
1890 PRINT USING "$5&.2&";(DEPOSITS - CHECKS)
1900 PRINT:PRINT "PRESS ANY KEY TO RETURN TO MENU"
1910 GET Z$
1920 RETURN
1930 CHECKS = CHECKS + CHECK.AMOUNT(I)
1940 GOTO 1870
1950 DEPOSITS = DEPOSITS + CHECK.AMOUNT(I)
1960 GOTO 1870
1970 REM **************************************
1980 REM * ROUTINE TO MAINTAIN THE CHECK FILE *
1990 REM **************************************
2000 GOSUB 4100          :REM READ THE CHECK FILE
2010 GOSUB 3990
2020 PRINT:PRINT "CHECK FILE MAINTENANCE"
2030 PRINT:PRINT "DEPOSITS ARE ONLY AVAILABLE BY RECORD NUMBER"
2040 PRINT "CHECKS ARE AVAILABLE BY EITHER CHECK NUMBER OF RECORD NUMBER"
2050 PRINT:PRINT "WHICH WAY: RESPOND <R>ECORD, <C>HECK NUMBER, OR E<X>IT: ";
2060 GET Z$
2070 PRINT Z$
2080 IF Z$ = "X" THEN 2640
2090 IF Z$ = "C" THEN 2130
2100 IF Z$ < > "R" THEN 2010
2110 PRINT:PRINT:INPUT "WHICH RECORD NUMBER DO YOU WISH TO SEE? ",I
2120 GOTO 2220
2130 PRINT:PRINT:INPUT "WHICH CHECK NUMBER DO YOU WISH TO SEE? ",WHICH.CHECK$
2140 WHICH.CHECK$ = "C" + WHICH.CHECK$
2150 FOR I = 1 TO CHECK.FILE.SIZE
2160      IF CHECK.NUMBER$(I) = WHICH.CHECK$ THEN 2220
2170      NEXT I
2180 PRINT:PRINT "THE REQUESTED CHECK IS NOT IN THE FILE"
2190 GOSUB 4480
2200 RETURN
2210 REM *******************
2220 GOSUB 3990
2230 PRINT:PRINT "THIS IS THE REQUESTED RECORD:"
2240 PRINT:PRINT "RECORD NUMBER: ";TAB(30);I
2250 PRINT "DEPOSIT/CHECK NUMBER:";TAB(30);
2260 IF CHECK.NUMBER$(I) = "DELETED" THEN PRINT "DELETED":GOTO 2290
2270 IF LEFT$(CHECK.NUMBER$(I),1) = "D" THEN PRINT "DEPOSIT"
2280 IF LEFT$(CHECK.NUMBER$(I),1) = "C" THEN PRINT
     RIGHT$(CHECK.NUMBER$(I),(LEN(CHECK.NUMBER$(I)) - 1))
2290 PRINT "DATE: ";TAB(30);CHECK.DATE$(I)
2300 PRINT "AMOUNT:";TAB(30);
2310 PRINT USING "$5&.2&";CHECK.AMOUNT(I)
2320 PRINT:PRINT "YOU MAY:";TAB(20);"<D>ELETE THE ENTIRE RECORD"
2330 PRINT TAB(20);"<C>HANGE THE CONTENTS OF THE RECORD VIA RE-ENTRY"
2340 PRINT TAB(20);"<R>ETURN TO THIS SECTION'S MENU"
2350 PRINT"SELECT: ";
2360 GET Z$
2370 IF Z$ = "R" THEN 2010
2380 IF Z$ = "D" THEN PRINT "DELETE":GOSUB 4480:GOTO 2580
2390 IF Z$ < > "C" THEN 2010
2400 PRINT "CHANGE"
2410 IF LEFT$(CHECK.NUMBER$(I),1) = "C" THEN 2490
2420 GOSUB 1640
2430 IF SUB.ERR$ < > "YES" THEN 2010
2440 SUB.ERR$ = "NO"
2450 PRINT CHR$(7):PRINT "RE-ENTER"
2460 GOSUB 4480
2470 GOTO 2010
2480 REM *******************
2490 GOSUB 1310
2500 GOSUB 1430
```

Figure 6.50. (continued)

```
2510 IF SUB.ERR$ = "YES" THEN SUB.ERR$ = "NO":GOTO 2010
2520 CHECK.NUMBER$(I) = CHECK.NUMBER.ENTERED$
2530 CHECK.PAYEE$(I) = PAYEE.ENTERED$
2540 CHECK.DATE$(I) = DATE.ENTERED$
2550 CHECK.AMOUNT(I) = AMOUNT.ENTERED
2560 GOTO 2010
2570 REM ******************
2580 CHECK.NUMBER$(I) = "DELETED"
2590 CHECK.PAYEE$(I) = ""
2600 CHECK.DATE$(I) = ""
2610 CHECK.AMOUNT(I) = 0
2620 GOTO 2010
2630 REM ******************
2640 I = 1
2650 FOR J = 1 TO CHECK.FILE.SIZE
2660      IF CHECK.NUMBER$(J) = "DELETED" THEN 2720
2670      CHECK.NUMBER$(I) = CHECK.NUMBER$(J)
2680      CHECK.PAYEE$(I) = CHECK.PAYEE$(J)
2690      CHECK.DATE$(I) = CHECK.DATE$(J)
2700      CHECK.AMOUNT(I) = CHECK.AMOUNT(J)
2710      I = I + 1
2720      NEXT J
2730 CHECK.FILE.SIZE = I - 1
2740 GOSUB 4330                    :REM WRITE BACK THE COMPRESSED FILE
2750 RETURN
2760 REM ****************************************
2770 REM * ROUTINE TO DISPLAY / PRINT THE CHECK FILE *
2780 REM ****************************************
2790 GOSUB 3990
2800 PRINT:PRINT "DISPLAY / PRINT THE CHECK FILE"
2810 GOSUB 4100          :REM READ THE CHECK FILE
2820 PRINT:PRINT "DO YOU WISH HARD COPY (Y/N)? ";
2830 GET Z$
2840 PRINT Z$
2850 IF Z$ = "Y" THEN HARDCOPY$ = "YES":GOTO 2870
2860 HARDCOPY$ = "NO"
2870 FOR I = 1 TO CHECK.FILE.SIZE
2880      PRINT:PRINT "RECORD NUMBER: ";TAB(30);I
2890      PRINT "DEPOSIT/CHECK NUMBER";TAB(30);
2900      IF LEFT$(CHECK.NUMBER$(I),1) = "D" THEN PRINT "DEPOSIT"
2910      IF LEFT$(CHECK.NUMBER$(I),1) = "C" THEN PRINT
              RIGHT$(CHECK.NUMBER$(I),(LEN(CHECK.NUMBER$(I)) - 1))
2920      PRINT "DATE: ";TAB(30);CHECK.DATE$(I)
2930      PRINT "DEPOSIT/CHECK AMOUNT:";TAB(30)
2940      PRINT USING "$5&.2&";CHECK.AMOUNT(I)
2950      IF HARDCOPY$ = "YES" THEN 3010
2960      GOSUB 4480
2970      NEXT I
2980 RETURN
2990      OPEN #3,".PRINTER"
3000      OUTPUT #3
3010      PRINT:PRINT "RECORD NUMBER: ";TAB(30);I
3020      PRINT "DEPOSIT/CHECK NUMBER";TAB(30);
3030      IF LEFT$(CHECK.NUMBER$(I),1) = "D" THEN PRINT "DEPOSIT"
3040      IF LEFT$(CHECK.NUMBER$(I),1) = "C" THEN PRINT
              RIGHT$(CHECK.NUMBER$(I),(LEN(CHECK.NUMBER$(I)) - 1))
3050      PRINT "DATE: ";TAB(30);CHECK.DATE$(I)
3060      PRINT "DEPOSIT/CHECK AMOUNT:";TAB(30)
3070      PRINT USING "$5&.2&";CHECK.AMOUNT(I)
3080      CLOSE #3
3090      GOTO 2970
3100 REM ************************************
3110 REM * ROUTINE TO BALANCE THE CHECKBOOK *
3120 REM ************************************
3130 GOSUB 3990
```

Figure 6.50. (continued)

```
3140 PRINT:PRINT "HAVE YOU ENTERED ALL CHECKS WRITTEN AND DEPOSITS (Y/N)? ";
3150 GET Z$
3160 PRINT Z$
3170 IF Z$ < > "Y" THEN PRINT "THAT MUST BE DONE FIRST":GOSUB 4480:RETURN
3180 GOSUB 3990
3190 GOSUB 4100                    :REM READ THE CHECK FILE
3200 PRINT:PRINT TAB(15);"C H E C K B O O K   R E C O N C I L I A T I O N"
3210 PRINT:PRINT "ENTER THE CHECKS YOU GOT BACK WITH YOUR STATEMENT"
3220 PRINT "ENTER 'X' WHEN YOU HAVE COMPLETED"
3230 PRINT:INPUT "ENTER CHECK NUMBER: ",RETURNED.CHECK.NUMBER$
3240 IF RETURNED.CHECK.NUMBER$ = "X" THEN 3370
3250 RETURNED.CHECK.NUMBER$ = "C" + RETURNED.CHECK.NUMBER$
3260 FOR I = 1 TO CHECK.FILE.SIZE
3270      IF RETURNED.CHECK.NUMBER$ = CHECK.NUMBER$(I) THEN 3330
3280      NEXT I
3290 PRINT "THAT CHECK IS NOT IN THE FILE - SET IT ASIDE"
3300 PRINT "IT MUST BE ENTERED AND THE RECONCILIATION REPEATED - CONTINUE";
3310 PRINT "TO POST CHECKS"
3320 GOTO 3210
3330 CHECK.NUMBER$(I) = "RETURNED " + CHECK.NUMBER$(I)
3340 PRINT "CHECK FOUND AND REMOVED"
3350 GOTO 3210
3360 REM *******************
3370 I = 1
3380 FOR J = 1 TO CHECK.FILE.SIZE
3390      IF CHECK.NUMBER$(J) = "DELETE" THEN 3460
3400      IF LEFT$(CHECK.NUMBER$(J),8) = "RETURNED" THEN 3460
3410      CHECK.NUMBER$(I) = CHECK.NUMBER$(J)
3420      CHECK.PAYEE$(I) = CHECK.PAYEE$(J)
3430      CHECK.DATE$(I) = CHECK.DATE$(J)
3440      CHECK.AMOUNT(I) = CHECK.AMOUNT(J)
3450      I = I + 1
3460      NEXT J
3470 CHECK.FILE.SIZE = I
3480 CHECKS = 0:DEPOSITS = 0
3490 PRINT:INPUT "ENTER THE TOTAL AMOUNT OF ANY CREDIT MEMO'S: ",CREDIT.MEMO
3500 PRINT:INPUT "ENTER THE TOTAL AMOUNT OF ANY DEBIT MEMO'S: ",DEBIT.MEMO
3510 PRINT:INPUT "ENTER SERVICE CHARGES: ",SERVICE.CHARGE
3520 GOSUB 4330          :REM WRITE THE CHECK FILE
3530 FOR I = 1 TO CHECK.FILE.SIZE
3540      IF LEFT$(CHECK.NUMBER$(I),1) = "C" THEN 3610
3550      IF LEFT$(CHECK.NUMBER$(I),1) = "D" THEN 3630
3560      PRINT:PRINT "RECORD";I;" HAS A TYPE PROBLEM"
3570      NEXT I
3580 PRINT:PRINT "CHECKBOOK BALANCE IS: ";TAB(30);
3590 PRINT USING "$5&.2&";(DEPOSITS - CHECKS)
3600 GOTO 3650
3610 CHECKS = CHECKS + CHECK.AMOUNT(I)
3620 GOTO 3570
3630 DEPOSITS = DEPOSITS + CHECK.AMOUNT(I)
3640 GOTO 3570
3650 PRINT "PLUS CREDIT MEMO'S:";TAB(32);
3660 PRINT USING "5&.2&";CREDIT.MEMO
3670 DEBIT.MEMO = (DEBIT.MEMO * -1)
3680 PRINT "LESS DEBIT MEMO'S:";TAB(32);
3690 PRINT USING "5&.2&";DEBIT.MEMO
3700 SERVICE.CHARGE = (SERVICE.CHARGE * -1)
3710 PRINT "LESS SERVICE CHARGES:";TAB(32);
3720 PRINT USING "5&.2&";SERVICE.CHARGE
3730 PRINT "RECONCILIATION:";TAB(30);
3740 RECONCILIATION = 0
3750 RECONCILIATION = RECONCILIATION + (DEPOSITS - CHECKS)
3760 RECONCILIATION = RECONCILIATION + CREDIT.MEMO
3770 RECONCILIATION = RECONCILIATION + DEBIT.MEMO
3780 RECONCILIATION = RECONCILIATION + SERVICE.CHARGE
```

Figure 6.50. (continued)

```
3790 PRINT USING "$5&.2&";RECONCILIATION
3800 PRINT:PRINT "YOUR CHECKBOOK TOTAL SHOULD MATCH THIS FIGURE"
3810 PRINT:PRINT "PRESS ANY KEY TO RESUME"
3820 GET Z$
3830 RETURN
3840 REM ***********************
3850 REM * PROGRAM TERMINATION *
3860 REM ***********************
3870 PRINT "DO YOU WISH TO REPEAT THE PROGRAM (Y/N)? ";
3880 GET Z$
3890 PRINT Z$
3900 IF Z$ < > "Y" THEN 3980
3910 FOR N = 1 TO DIMENSION.COUNT
3920      CHECK.NUMBER$(N) = ""
3930      CHECK.PAYEE$(N) = ""
3940      CHECK.DATE$(N) = ""
3950      CHECK.AMOUNT(N) = 0
3960      NEXT N
3970 GOTO 100
3980 CHAIN .D2/BUSINESS
3990 REM *******************************
4000 REM * HEADING USED FOR THE DISPLAY *
4010 REM *******************************
4020 HOME
4030 X = ((80 - LEN(COMPANY.NAME$)) / 2)
4040 VPOS=2:HPOS=X
4050 PRINT COMPANY.NAME$
4060 FOR N = 1 TO 79:PRINT "-";:NEXT N:PRINT
4070 PRINT TAB(25);"ACCOUNTS PAYABLE APPLICATIONS"
4080 FOR N = 1 TO 79:PRINT "-";:NEXT N
4090 RETURN
4100 REM ***************************
4110 REM * OPEN AND INPUT CHECK FILE *
4120 REM ***************************
4130 OPEN #1,.D2/CHECK.DAT
4140 PRINT:PRINT "READING THE CHECK FILE"
4150 INPUT #1,CHECK.FILE.SIZE      :REM OBTAIN THE RECORD COUNT
4160 REM ********************************************
4170 REM * DIMENSIONING ESTABLISHED ON THE FIRST RECORD *
4180 REM ********************************************
4190 IF DIMENSION.COUNT = 1000 THEN PRINT CHR$(7):END
4200 DIMENSION.COUNT = CHECK.FILE.SIZE + 1000
4210 DIM CHECK.NUMBER$(DIMENSION.COUNT)
4220 DIM CHECK.PAYEE$(DIMENSION.COUNT)
4230 DIM CHECK.DATE$(DIMENSION.COUNT)
4240 DIM CHECK.AMOUNT(DIMENSION.COUNT)
4250 FOR I = 1 TO CHECK.FILE.SIZE
4260      INPUT #1,CHECK.NUMBER$(I)
4270      INPUT #1,CHECK.PAYEE$(I)
4280      INPUT #1,CHECK.DATE$(I)
4290      INPUT #1,CHECK.AMOUNT(I)
4300      NEXT I
4310 CLOSE #1
4320 RETURN
4330 REM ****************************
4340 REM * OPEN AND OUTPUT CHECK FILE *
4350 REM ****************************
4360 CREATE ".D2/CHECK.DAT",TEXT
4370 OPEN #1,.D2/CHECK.DAT
4380 PRINT:PRINT "WRITING THE CHECK FILE"
4390 PRINT #1,CHECK.FILE.SIZE      :REM PRODUCE THE RECORD COUNT
4400 FOR I = 1 TO CHECK.FILE.SIZE
4410      PRINT #1,CHECK.NUMBER$(I)
4420      PRINT #1,CHECK.PAYEE$(I)
4430      PRINT #1,CHECK.DATE$(I)
```

Figure 6.50. (continued)

```
4440        PRINT #1,CHECK.AMOUNT(I)
4450        NEXT I
4460 CLOSE #1
4470 RETURN
4480 REM **************
4490 REM * TIMER LOOP *
4500 REM **************
4510 FOR Z = 1 TO 1500:NEXT Z
4520 RETURN
```

Figure 6.50. (continued)

INCOME

Recall that you had loaded figures (VALUE) for each income and each expense account established on the Chart of Accounts. Later, the receivables application ensured the existence of a Cash Account and an Interest Expense Account. This particular income statement does not happen to reflect the interest expense, since it was drawn before the interest was posted, and the numbers have no specific relation to the figures that had gone before. But suffice it to say that the data identified as INCOME and EXPENSE is summarized as in Figure 6.51.

```
              SMALL BUSINESS ENTERPRISE, INC.
                     INCOME STATEMENT
                 FOR PERIOD: MAY, 1983
---------------------------------------------------------------
INCOME
     SALES INCOME              30,000.00
     RENTAL INCOME                473.00
     ROYALTY INCOME            20,000.00
                              -----------

TOTAL INCOME                                        50,473.00

EXPENSE
     RENT EXPENSE                 600.00
     TRAVEL EXPENSE               225.00
     TELEPHONE EXPENSE             75.00
                              -----------

TOTAL EXPENSE                                          935.47
                                                  -----------
NET INCOME <LOSS>                                  $49,537.53
                                                  ===========
```

Figure 6.51.

A block diagram of the preparation of the income statement is shown in Figure 6.52. This program works with the Chart of Accounts (CHART.DAT) and with the Account File for the period for which this income statement is to be drawn. The small business system is designed to deal with periods individually. If the system has to deal with an aggregate number of individual periods, it will be necessary to modify the program so that it can receive several independent inputs.

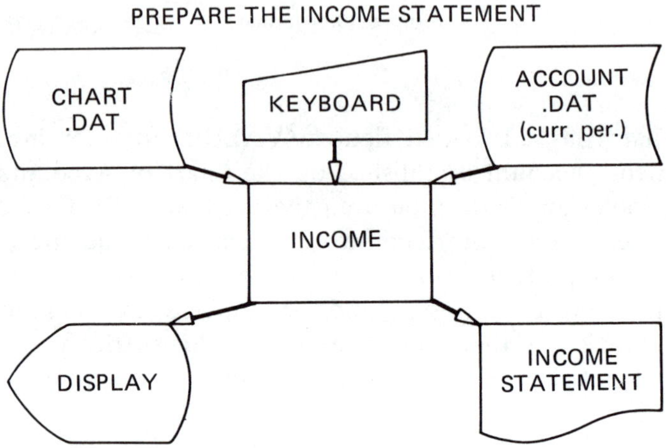

PREPARE THE INCOME STATEMENT

Figure 6.52.

As you look at the program, you'll see that only those accounts whose codes are I or E are extracted from the selected account file. It's important to note that the program is structured to accept the Chart of Accounts (CHART.DAT) plus *one* account file, whose name you will specify. Note also that the file counts for the two files are matched and that processing is halted if they do not match. Thus it becomes very important to ensure that the number of figures on the account file matches the number of accounts on the Chart file – and that means that you must set your accounts up properly in the first place – or you must be prepared to reload them when the size of the file changes.

Now, if it is your desire to consolidate data from several periods, you must incorporate the routines to do so. It would be necessary to incorporate the instructions for reading the specified number of files, beginning with INPUT#2. It should be remembered that you can reuse the buffer if you will CLOSE it before using it again. Once you have begun the file load, it's a simple matter to go beyond the value of I (the index variable). If you do *that,* however, you must make certain that the arrays are DIMensioned in a size large enough to accommodate everything to be entered.

The program INCOME is given in Figure 6.53.

```
10 HOME
20 GOSUB 950
30 REM ***************************************************************
40 REM * T$ HOLDS THE ACCOUNT TYPE;  N$ HOLDS THE ACCOUNT NAME; *
50 REM * A HAS THE BALANCE OF THE ACCOUNTS .  T1$ WILL HOLD     *
60 REM * IDENTIFIERS FOR INCOME AND EXPENSES.                    *
70 REM ***************************************************************
80 DIM T$(25),N$(25),A(25),T1$(2)
90 T1$(1) = "INCOME"
100 T1$(2) = "EXPENSE"
110 FILE.1$ = .D2/CHART.DAT
120 PRINT
130 INPUT "ENTER THE NAME OF THE ACCOUNT FILE (I'LL ADD .DAT): ",FILE.2$
140 FILE.2$ = ".D2/" + FILE.2$ + ".DAT"
150 GOSUB 230            :REM OPEN AND READ THE FILES
160 GOSUB 400            :REM PREPARE THE STATEMENT
170 REM **********************
180 REM * PROGRAM TERMINATION *
190 REM **********************
200 CLOSE #1
210 CLOSE #2
220 CHAIN .D2/BUSINESS
230 REM **************************************************************
240 REM * OPEN AND READ (CHARTS AND THE SELECTED ACCOUNT FILE) *
250 REM **************************************************************
260 OPEN #1,FILE.1$
270 OPEN #2,FILE.2$
280 INPUT#1,FILE.1.COUNT
290 INPUT#2,FILE.2.COUNT
300 IF FILE.1.COUNT = FILE.2.COUNT THEN 350
310 PRINT "THE FILES DO NOT MATCH:"
320 PRINT TAB(5);FILE.1$;" RECORD COUNT IS: ";FILE.1.COUNT
330 PRINT TAB(5);FILE.2$;" RECORD COUNT IS: ";FILE.2.COUNT
340 GOTO 170
350 FOR I = 1 TO FILE.1.COUNT
360      INPUT#1,T$(I),N$(I)
370      INPUT#2,A(I)
380      NEXT I
390 RETURN
400 REM ********************************
410 REM * PREPARE THE INCOME STATEMENT *
420 REM ********************************
430 REM * REPORT HEADING *
440 REM ******************
450 INPUT "ENTER THE REPORT PERIOD: ",REPORT.PERIOD$
460 PRINT
470 PRINT "POSITION THE PAPER AND THEN PRESS ANY KEY"
480 GET Z$
490 X = ((80 - LEN(COMPANY.NAME$)) / 2)
500 OPEN #3,".PRINTER"
510 OUTPUT #3
520 PRINT TAB(X);COMPANY.NAME$
530 INCOME.STATEMENT$ = "INCOME STATEMENT"
540 X = ((80 - LEN(INCOME.STATEMENT$)) / 2)
550 PRINT TAB(X);INCOME.STATEMENT$
560 REPORT.PERIOD$ = "FOR PERIOD: " + REPORT.PERIOD$
```

Figure 6.53.

```
570 X = ((80 - LEN(REPORT.PERIOD$)) / 2)
580 PRINT TAB(X);REPORT.PERIOD$
590 FOR N = 1 TO 79:PRINT "-";:NEXT N:PRINT
600 PRINT:PRINT
610 REM ********************************
620 FOR I = 1 TO FILE.1.COUNT
630     IF T$(I) = "I" THEN 660
640     NEXT I
650 GOTO 200
660 SO.FAR = I
670 J = 1
680 PRINT TAB(5);T1$(J)
690 FOR I = SO.FAR TO FILE.1.COUNT
700     IF (T$(I) = "E") AND (J = 1) THEN 750
710     PRINT TAB(10);N$(I);TAB(40);
720     PRINT USING "5&.2&";A(I)
730     CATEGORY.TOTAL = CATEGORY.TOTAL + A(I)
740     NEXT I
750 PRINT TAB(36);"-------------"
760 PRINT TAB(5);"TOTAL ";T1$(J);TAB(59);
770 PRINT USING "5&.2&";CATEGORY.TOTAL
780 PRINT
790 IF J = 1 THEN NET.INCOME = NET.INCOME + CATEGORY.TOTAL
800 IF J = 2 THEN NET.INCOME = NET.INCOME - CATEGORY.TOTAL
810 J = J + 1
820 CATEGORY.TOTAL = 0
830 SO.FAR = I
840 IF J < = 2 THEN 680
850 PRINT TAB(55);"-------------"
860 IF NET.INCOME > 0 THEN PRINT TAB(5);
        "NET INCOME <LOSS>";TAB(57);
870 IF NET.INCOME > 0 THEN PRINT USING "$5&.2&";NET.INCOME
880 IF NET.INCOME < 0 THEN PRINT TAB(5);
        "NET INCOME <LOSS>";TAB(61);"<";
890 IF NET.INCOME < 0 THEN PRINT USING "$5&.2&";NET.INCOME;">"
900 IF NET.INCOME = 0 THEN PRINT TAB(5);
        "NET INCOME <LOSS>;TAB(61);"- 0 -"
910 PRINT TAB(55);"============="
920 PRINT CHR$(12)
930 CLOSE #3
940 RETURN
950 REM ********************************
960 REM * HEADING USED FOR THE DISPLAY *
970 REM ********************************
980 HOME
990 X = ((80 - LEN(COMPANY.NAME$)) / 2)
1000 VPOS=2:HPOS=X
1010 PRINT COMPANY.NAME$
1020 FOR N = 1 TO 79:PRINT "-";:NEXT N:PRINT
1030 PRINT TAB(26);"INCOME STATEMENT PREPARATION"
1040 FOR N = 1 TO 79:PRINT "-";:NEXT N
1050 RETURN
```

Figure 6.53. (continued)

BALANCE

Like the Income Statement, the Balance Sheet program surveys the Chart of Accounts and account period files, extracting the data necessary for the report. Many of the very same remarks made about the Income Statement apply here, especially as they relate to the handling of multiple files.

The Balance Sheet is as shown in Figure 6.54.

```
                    SMALL BUSINESS ENTERPRISE, INC.
                             BALANCE SHEET
                         AS OF: MAY 31, 1983
-------------------------------------------------------------------------
                                ASSETS

ASSETS
     CASH                                      101.23
     ACCOUNTS RECEIVABLE                     1,000.47
     EQUIPMENT                                 200.00
     PREPAID INSURANCE                         400.00
     ROLLING STOCK                           4,000.00
                                            -----------
TOTAL ASSETS                                                  5,701.70

                      LIABILITIES AND CAPITAL

LIABILITIES
     ACCOUNTS PAYABLE                          637.34
     NOTES PAYABLE                           1,245.78
                                            -----------
TOTAL LIABILITIES                                             1,883.12
                                                             ----------
CAPITAL
     NET INCOME/LOSS(-)                      3,608.70
     SBE DRAW                                  209.88
                                            -----------
TOTAL CAPITAL                                                 3,818.58
                                                             ----------

TOTAL LIABILITIES AND CAPITAL                                 7,701.70
                                                             ==========
```

Figure 6.54.

A block diagram for the preparation of the Balance Sheet is shown in Figure 6.55. This program works with the Chart of Accounts (CHART.DAT) and with the Account File for the period for which the Balance Sheet is to be drawn. The small business system is designed to deal with the periods individually. If the system has to deal with an aggregate number of individual periods, it will be necessary to modify the program so that it can receive several independent inputs.

It should be mentioned that no tie was designed to effect a transition from the Income Statement to the Balance Sheet, even though the net income or loss is a required input. That procedure could be done easily enough by writing a one-record file in the Income Statement program and reading it in the present application. Because it would mean yet another file, however, and so small a file at that, it

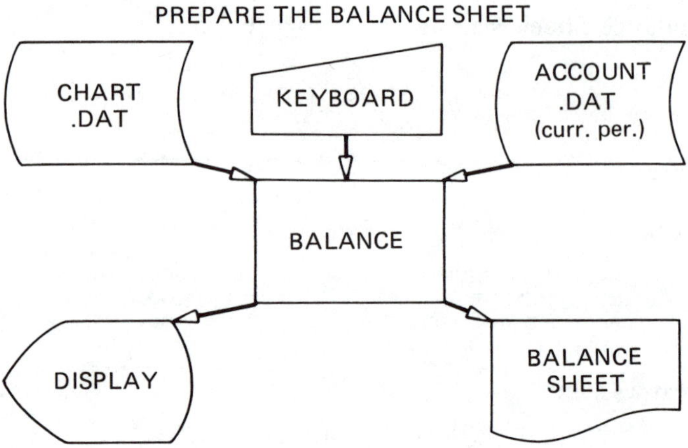

Figure 6.55.

was felt that the single number required to satisfy the inquiry could just as easily be given from the keyboard. Otherwise, the approach to producing a Balance Sheet is precisely the same as that used for the Income Statement.

Figure 6.56 shows the program BALANCE.

```
10 HOME
20 GOSUB 1080
30 REM ***************************************************************
40 REM * T$ HOLDS THE ACCOUNT TYPE;  N$ HOLDS THE ACCOUNT NAME;   *
50 REM * A HAS THE BALANCE OF THE ACCOUNTS .  T1$ WILL HOLD        *
60 REM * IDENTIFIERS FOR BALANCE SHEET HEADINGS.                   *
70 REM ***************************************************************
80 DIM T$(25),N$(25),A(25),T1$(3)
90 T1$(1) = "ASSETS"
100 T1$(2) = "LIABILITIES"
110 T1$(3) = "CAPITAL"
120 FILE.1$ = ".D2/CHART.DAT"
130 PRINT
140 INPUT "ENTER THE NAME OF THE ACCOUNT FILE (I'LL ADD .DAT): ",FILE.2$
150 FILE.2$ = ".D2/" + FILE.2$ + ".DAT"
160 PRINT
170 INPUT "ENTER THE NET INCOME OR LOSS (-) FOR THE PERIOD: ",NET.INCOME
180 GOSUB 260           :REM OPEN AND READ THE FILES
190 GOSUB 430           :REM PREPARE THE STATEMENT
200 REM ***********************
210 REM * PROGRAM TERMINATION *
220 REM ***********************
230 CLOSE #1
240 CLOSE #2
```

Figure 6.56.

```
250 CHAIN O#/BUSINESS
260 REM ***********************************************************
270 REM * OPEN AND READ (CHARTS AND THE SELECTED ACCOUNT FILE) *
280 REM ***********************************************************
290 OPEN #1,FILE.1$
300 OPEN #2,FILE.2$
310 INPUT#1,FILE.1.COUNT
320 INPUT#2,FILE.2.COUNT
330 IF FILE.1.COUNT = FILE.2.COUNT THEN 380
340 PRINT "THE FILES DO NOT MATCH:"
350 PRINT TAB(5);FILE.1$;" RECORD COUNT IS: ";FILE.1.COUNT
360 PRINT TAB(5);FILE.2$;" RECORD COUNT IS: ";FILE.2.COUNT
370 GOTO 200
380 FOR I = 1 TO FILE.1.COUNT
390      INPUT#1,T$(I),N$(I)
400      INPUT#2,A(I)
410      NEXT I
420 RETURN
430 REM *****************************
440 REM * PREPARE THE BALANCE SHEET *
450 REM *****************************
460 REM * REPORT HEADING *
470 REM ******************
480 PRINT:INPUT "ENTER THE REPORT DATE: ",REPORT.DATE$
490 PRINT
500 PRINT "POSITION THE PAPER AND THEN PRESS ANY KEY"
510 GET Z$
520 X = ((80 - LEN(COMPANY.NAME$)) / 2)
530 OPEN #3,".PRINTER"
540 OUTPUT #3
550 PRINT TAB(X);COMPANY.NAME$
560 BALANCE.SHEET$ = "BALANCE.SHEET"
570 X = ((80 - LEN(BALANCE.SHEET$)) / 2)
580 PRINT TAB(X);BALANCE.SHEET$
590 REPORT.DATE$ = "AS OF: " + REPORT.DATE$
600 X = ((80 - LEN(REPORT.DATE$)) / 2)
610 PRINT TAB(X);REPORT.DATE$
620 FOR N = 1 TO 79:PRINT "-";:NEXT N:PRINT
630 PRINT:PRINT
640 REM *********************************
650 T = 50
660 SO.FAR = 1
670 T$(0) = T$(1)
680 FOR J = 1 TO 3
690      IF J = 1 THEN X = ((80 - LEN(T1$(1))) / 2)
700      IF J = 1 THEN PRINT TAB(X);T1$(1)
710      IF J < > 2 THEN 770
720      T = 40
730      L.AND.C$ = "LIABILITIES AND CAPITAL"
740      X = ((80 - LEN(L.AND.C$)) / 2)
750      PRINT TAB(X);L.AND.C$
760      LIABILITIES.AND.CAPITAL = 0
770      PRINT
780      PRINT TAB(5);T1$(J)
790      IF J < > 3 THEN 830
800      PRINT TAB(10);"NET INCOME/LOSS(-)";TAB(T);
810      PRINT USING "5&.2&";NET.INCOME
820      CATEGORY.TOTAL = CATEGORY.TOTAL + NET.INCOME
830      FOR I = SO.FAR TO FILE.1.COUNT
840           IF T$(I) < > T$(0) THEN 910
850           SUB.ITEM = A(I)
860           PRINT TAB(10);N$(I);TAB(40);
870           PRINT USING "5&.2&";SUB.ITEM
880           CATEGORY.TOTAL = CATEGORY.TOTAL + SUB.ITEM
890           SUB.ITEM = 0
```

Figure 6.56. (continued)

```
900         NEXT I
910      PRINT TAB(35);"----------------"
920      PRINT TAB(5);"TOTAL ";T1$(J);TAB(55);
930      PRINT USING "5&.2&";CATEGORY.TOTAL
940      IF J = 1 THEN PRINT TAB(53);"==============="
950      SO.FAR = I
960      PRINT
970      LIABILITIES.AND.CAPITAL = LIABILITIES.AND.CAPITAL + CATEGORY.TOTAL
980      CATEGORY.TOTAL = 0
990      T$(0) = T$(I)
1000     NEXT J
1010 PRINT TAB(53);"---------------"
1020 PRINT TAB(5);"TOTAL LIABILITIES AND CAPITAL";TAB(55);
1030 PRINT USING "5&.2&";LIABILITIES.AND.CAPITAL
1040 PRINT TAB(53);"==============="
1050 PRINT CHR$(12)
1060 CLOSE #3
1070 RETURN
1080 REM ********************************
1090 REM * HEADING USED FOR THE DISPLAY *
1100 REM ********************************
1110 HOME
1120 X = ((80 - LEN(COMPANY.NAME$)) / 2)
1130 VPOS=2:HPOS=X
1140 PRINT COMPANY.NAME$
1150 FOR N = 1 TO 79:PRINT "-";:NEXT N:PRINT
1160 PRINT TAB(28);"BALANCE SHEET PREPARATION"
1170 FOR N = 1 TO 79:PRINT "-";:NEXT N
1180 RETURN
```

Figure 6.56. (continued)

That's it for the small business system. The system, remember, is broken into a number of small pieces, the largest of which is the Accounts Receivable subsystem.

There is one thing you must learn about business applications. No matter how well tested they are, some combination of things will eventually occur and cause problems. Even the slightest change can cause unpredictable output. After the development of these applications, they were tested as time would permit. Conversion of programs to the Apple III has been done as carefully as possible. Despite this, errors may have been made, errors which it will fall to you to correct. No warrantee, expressed or implied, is made. Some of the displays were changed to tailor the text for printing and may appear slightly different on the display.

Most of what has been presented here is the development of the author. Some is adapted from other products and dovetailed and explained to give you the best possible product within the confines of a book.

We'll accept all suggestions for inclusion. If you find an error we haven't found, we'd appreciate knowing about it.

Postscript

It has been said that a teacher ought to be one of his own best pupils. As a teacher by book, I became one of my own pupils while developing manuscript for this series.

Earlier in the book we discussed the concept of an in-memory sort, concentrating upon a type of sort known as a "Bubble Sort." Among all the available sorts, the bubble sort is most easily explained. It can be clearly diagramed and can be programed in any language with a minimum of effort. Further, for systems without extensive input/output media, it has been most simply executed by the programer himself. As mentioned in that chapter, the bubble sort tends to be slow.

I've been teaching the bubble sort for years – in the classroom and in print. And I've used the bubble sort in programs. But in both cases, it was always for a small number of elements where the amount of time it took was relatively insignificant. If longer files of data were involved, I merely invoked a sort utility, and on the larger machines, that's easy to do, particularly when you're talking about having 50 million bytes of disk storage with which to work.

Years ago, when it became necessary to index the second edition of the *CDP Review Manual,* the effort was staggering, requiring extensive hand writing upon little cards and subsequent sorting, and then typing of the cards into a form which could be worked with by the publisher. This time I had a computer – no way was I going to do the same thing when it came time for the third edition to be indexed. So I devised a system of data capture, maintenance, presentation, and organization which would take away all that drudgery. The sort module was duly written as an in-memory bubble sort. I extracted the letter "A" from my data disks and was off and running to sort them for printing. *Fifty-three hours later,* the sort was complete – and then something happened and I couldn't get the sorted file written back to disk in the new sequence. I lost everything. The sort was begun at 5 p.m. one night and two days and five hours later, it completed. By itself, that wouldn't be astounding – until you know the size of the file: 507 records, to be sorted on two fields. That time was a bit much.

Some digging brought up a technique for in-memory sorting known as the *Shell-Metzner Sort,* reputed to be a bit faster. I guess so! The sort which had taken fifty-three hours to complete via the bubble route took one hour, 20 minutes with the Shell Sort. Obviously, you needed to be told about such a difference.

I learned a few things about BASIC in the process. Even with 128K on the Apple III, sooner or later the space will be taken up with unused variables. I should have known that. What was news was that the variables were not directly reused. Thus, my 32-byte record occupied 96 bytes with each iteration involving an exchange. Thus, 96 bytes, and then 192, then 288, 384, and so on, *without releasing the unused space.* The space was posted as being unused, but the available memory decreased in leaps and bounds, especially when things were significantly out of order. Any sort will take an amount of time based on the condition of the initial file. A file already in sequence will require only passing time. The most extreme is a file which is completely reversed. Anything in the middle involves a shorter amount of time, naturally – but the more out of sequence the file is, the more exchanges would be made, the quicker the memory would be utilized, until there simply wasn't any more memory available. At that time the whole process would come to a screeching halt while BASIC cleaned up its memory. With 128K or 256K the Apple III has less of a problem in that regard than other machines. When the unused memory was cleaned up, the sort would take off again.

Using this logic, the smaller the input file was, the more memory would be available before the cleanup process would be required. I learned to sort small amounts of data, where possible, and while the cleanup process took longer, there were fewer of them. We tend to think of a computer as magic and that it can do things quickly. But a file of 274 records still took 29 minutes to load and sort. When the instructions were included to show available memory, then the understanding was clearer. Though it took time to display moving data on the screen, and though the sort would certainly work faster if that had not been done, I chose to see some of the data while it was moving – simply as reassurance. The concept of the bubble sort was kept. The first item of the pair was moved to a work area. The second was moved into the position of the first. And the item in the work area was moved into the position of the second. This could have been shortened somewhat (and the time speeded and lower memory consumption maintained, as well) by using the SWAP instruction. It was felt that this manner would provide the easiest vehicle to explain.

Here is a "barebones" Shell-Metzner Sort. See Figure PS.1. The general concept is that the file is not examined in contiguous pairs, as is the case with the bubble sort, but rather in terms of halves of the file.

```
100 REM ****************************
110 REM * THE ARRAY MUST BE LOADED *
120 REM * FROM DISK OR KEYBOARD TO *
130 REM * PREPARE FOR THIS ROUTINE *
140 REM ****************************
150 M = LAST
160 M = INT(M/2)
170 IF M = 0 THEN 430
180 J = 1
190 K = LAST - M
200 I = J
210 L = I + M
220 IF A$(I) < = A$(L) THEN 360
230 PRINT
240 PRINT I,L,M,K
250 REM ****************************
260 REM * T$ IS A TEMPORARY HOLD   *
270 REM * AREA.  OTHER VARIABLES   *
280 REM * ARE EXPLAINED IN TEXT.   *
290 REM ****************************
300 T$ = A$(I)
310 A$(I) = A$(L)
320 A$(L) = T$
330 I = I - M
340 IF I < 1 THEN 360
350 GOTO 210
360 J = J + 1
370 IF J > K THEN 160
380 GOTO 200
390 REM ****************************
400 REM * THE ARRAY IS NOW SORTED  *
410 REM * AND IS READY TO BE USED. *
420 REM ****************************
430 REM INSTRUCTIONS BEGIN HERE
```

Figure PS.1.

The file is split in two and those things which belong in the first (left) half are exchanged with those that belong in the second (right) half. Then each half is split into quarters, with the same process taking place within each half. And then into eighths, etc. The work space continues to diminish until everything is in its proper sequence. The example assumes that you have already read from your disk file and stored the data in the array A$. The process begins where that has occurred and the variable LAST is the count of records. Variable M is used to develop the midpoint. Variable I is what we'll call the left-pair, left-side marker. Variable J is the left-pair, right-side marker. Variable K is the right-pair, left-side marker. And Variable L is the right-pair, right-side marker. If you can think of the left side as being the first half of the array to be sorted and the right side as being the second half of the array to be sorted, then you should be able to figure it out.

Then try SWAP of A$(I) with A$(L) in place of statements 300 to 320.

It works, though it's not easily understood. One hour, twenty minutes versus 53 hours shows an improvement of almost 4000 percent. It seemed worthwhile to add this Postscript.

Kenniston W. Lord, Jr.

Appendix

In this appendix are summarized the elements of Business BASIC. The majority of them have been dealt with in this book. Some were not applicable to the book, dealing with color or with analog devices, such as game paddles. Some are mathematical functions which had no place in a book designed for business application, but which are, nonetheless, a part of the language. All are presented here as a quick reference.

COMMANDS

CATALOG	Lists a disk directory.
CHAIN	Executes a program from disk, leaving variables intact.
CLEAR	Clears a program's variables.
CONT	Continues an interrupted program.
CREATE	Creates a new file of directory on disk.
DEL	Deletes a range of BASIC program statements.
DELETE	Deletes a file from disk.
HOME	Clears current text window and places cursor in the upper left-hand corner.
INVERSE	Sets text output to inverse video characters.

LIST	Lists the BASIC program on the display.
LOAD	Loads a BASIC program from diskette.
LOCK	Sets protection on a disk file.
NEW	Clears memory of any programs or variables.
NORMAL	Sets text output to normal characters.
NOTRACE	Turns off the TRACE option.
UNLOCK	Removes the protection from a disk file.
RENAME	Changes the name of a disk file.
RUN	Loads and runs program from disk; runs program in memory.
SAVE	Saves the program currently in memory to a disk file.
TEXT	Sets the screen to text mode with full screen window.
TRACE	Turns on the trace option.

STATEMENTS

CLOSE	Closes all open files.
CLOSE #	Closes a specific file.
DATA	Defines internal constants: DATA statements.
DEFD FN	User-defined function specification.

DIM	Dimension an array.
END	Ends the program, returns to BASIC ready prompt.
FOR ... NEXT	Controlled loop.
GET	Reads a single character from the keyboard.
GOSUB	Performs a subroutine.
GOTO	Changes direction unconditionally.
IF ... GOTO ... ELSE	IF statement with two option directive.
IF ... THEN ... ELSE	Ditto.
IMAGE	Defines a printing mask for a PRINT USING statement.
INPUT	Reads data entered from the keyboard.
INPUT #	Reads data entered from a disk file.
INVOKE	Loads an external file module of assembly programs.
ON EOF #	Establishes an end-of-file trap and directive.
OFF EOF #	Removes the end-of-file trap.
ON ERR	Establishes error trapping.
OFF ERR	Removes error trapping.
ON KBD	Establishes keyboard interrupt handling.

OFF KBD	Removes keyboard interrupt handling.
ON GOSUB	Computed subroutine linkage statement.
ON GOTO	Computed unconditional branch statement.
OPEN # ... AS	Opens a file as INPUT, OUTPUT, or EXTENSION.
OUTPUT #	Sends output intended for the display screen to another file.
PERFORM	Executes a previously invoked assembler language program.
POP	Removes one level of subroutine nesting.
PRINT	Prints to the current output device (normally the display screen) or file designated in a previous OPEN and OUTPUT statement.
PRINT USING	Prints using the format contained thereafter or in an associated IMAGE statement.
PRINT #	Prints to a particular output device or file.
PRINT # USING	Prints to a particular file or device using a given format.
READ	Reads information from DATA statements.
READ #	Reads information from a randomly organized data file.
REM	Remark statement.

RESTORE	Resets read pointer to start of DATA statements.
RESUME	Returns from ON ERR statement.
RETURN	Returns from subroutine, ON EOF, or ON KBD routine.
SCALE	Adjusts the decimal point position in a PRINT USING statement.
SPC	Output numbers of blank characters in PRINT statements.
STOP	Stops the program execution.
SWAP	Swaps the values of two given variables.
TAB	Used in PRINT statements to position the cursor to a particular column.
WINDOW	Establishes window size and position for text and scroll.
WRITE #	Writes information to a randomly organized data file.

FUNCTIONS

ABS	Returns the absolute value of a variable.
ASC	Converts an ASCII character to its numeric value.
ATAN	Returns the arctangent.
BUTTON	Returns the state of the paddle-button.
CHR$	Converts numbers to equivalent ASCII characters.

CONV	Returns real number value.
CONV$	Returns string value.
CONV&	Returns long-integer value.
CONV%	Returns integer value.
COS	Returns the cosine.
EXFN	Executes an invoked external function which returns a real number.
EXFN%	Executes an invoked external function which returns an integer.
EXP	Exponent to the base.
HEX$	Returns a string containing a hexadecimal value.
INSTR	Searches a string for the presence of a substring and returns its location.
INT	Returns the integer of the number.
LEFT$	Returns a substring beginning with the first (leftmost) character.
LEN	Returns the length of a string.
LOG	Returns the natural logarithm of a number.
MID$	Extracts a substring of a defined length commencing with a defined position from a larger string.
PDL	Returns a game paddle position.
REC	Returns the current file record number.

RIGHT$	Takes the substring ending with the last (rightmost) character.
RND	Returns a random number less than 1.
SGN	Returns the sign of an argument.
SIN	Returns the sine of a number.
SQR	Returns the square root of a number.
STR$	Converts a number to a string variable.
SUB$	Inserts a substring into a given string.
TAN	Returns the tangent of a number.
TEN	Converts the last four characters of a string from hexadecimal to decimal.
TYP	Returns the data type of a file record.
VAL	Converts a string to a numeric value.

RESERVED WORDS

EOF	Contains the reference number of the file causing an end-of-file error.
ERR	Contains the error type code of the most recent error.
FRE	Contains the amount of remaining bytes of memory.
HPOS	Positions the cursor along the X axis.
INDENT	The spaces to indent FOR ... NEXT loops.

KBD	Contains the ASCII character of the last key pressed.
OUTREC	Determines the maximum line length for the LIST command.
PREFIX$	Sets or holds the SOS pathname prefix.
VPOS	Contains the Y axis position.

GRAPHIC PROCEDURES

DOTAT	Plot a single dot at a specified position.
DOTREL	Plots a dot relative to the current position.
DRAWIMAGE	Draws a rectangular bit-map image at the current position.
FILLCOLOR	Sets the background color.
FILLPORT	Fills the current VIEWPORT with the FILLCOLOR.
GLOAD	Loads and displays a graphics (FOTO) file from disk.
GRAFIXMODE	Specifies the graphics mode and the chosen buffer.
GRAFIXON	Switches the display to the current graphics mode and the selected buffer.
GSAVE	Saves the current graphics to a file (FOTO) on disk.
INITGRAFIX	Sets full-screen VIEWPORT, locates the cursor at the upper left corner and sets normal color and transfer tables.

LINEREL	Draws a line relative to the current position.
LINETO	Draws a line from the current position to a specified absolute position.
MOVEREL	Positions the cursor relative to the current position.
MOVETO	Positions the cursor at an absolute location.
NEWFONT	Used to specify a new graphics character font.
PENCOLOR	Sets the current PLOT and DRAW color.
RELEASE	Frees the highest graphics buffer memory.
SETCTAB	Sets a color-table entry.
SYSFONT	Causes normal system character set to be used as the graphics character font.
VIEWPORT	Defines the graphics-drawing window size and position.
XFEROPTION	Defines the logical operation that places dots on the screen.
XLOC	Returns the graphics cursor X position.
XYCOLOR	Returns the color of the dot on the screen at the current position.
YLOC	Returns the graphics cursor Y position.

Index